P9-DFA-781

10118

CHARLIE COMPANY'S
JOURNEY HOME

OSPREY
PUBLISHING

CHARLIE COMPANY'S JOURNEY HOME

The Boys of '67 and the War They Left Behind

ANDREW WIEST

OSPREY PUBLISHING
Bloomsbury Publishing Plc
PO Box 883, Oxford, OX1 9PL, UK
1385 Broadway, 5th Floor, New York, NY 10018, USA
E-mail: info@ospreypublishing.com
www.ospreypublishing.com

OSPREY is a trademark of Osprey Publishing Ltd

First published in Great Britain in 2018

ISBN: HB 9781472827494; PB 9781472827463; eBook 9781472827487;
ePDF 9781472827470; XML 9781472827456

18 19 20 21 22 10 9 8 7 6 5 4 3 2 1

Index by Sharon Redmayne
Originated by PDQ Digital Media Solutions, Bungay, UK
Printed in the US by Berryville Graphics, Inc

Cover image: Photograph © Mark Owen / Trevillion Images

Osprey Publishing supports the Woodland Trust, the UK's leading woodland conservation charity. Between 2014 and 2018 our donations are being spent on their Centenary Woods project in the UK.

To find out more about our authors and books visit **www.ospreypublishing.com**. Here you will find extracts, author interviews, details of forthcoming events and the option to sign up for our newsletter.

CONTENTS

PROLOGUE

It was like a scene from a movie, but it was all too real. Noemi Sauceda stood transfixed, as the sights and sounds of her home slipped into background obscurity. The soft whir of the ceiling fan as it struggled against the Texas heat; the ubiquitous pictures mounted on the wall with infinite care that chronicled married life – images of the important moments in the lives of her children Jose, Omar, and Belinda. Elementary school graduation. Vacations. But the familiar sights were momentarily forgotten in a moment of blinding, transfixing terror.

Noemi had seen handguns before. In Texas, guns, from handguns to heirloom hunting rifles, were everywhere. But she had never seen the barrel of a gun look so big; so big that it seemed to swallow the entire room. That barrel seemed to melt her very soul. The gun was a pistol, she didn't know the brand or make, and it was held in the hand of her husband Jose. The sweat from a hard day of work played around Jose's features as his brow furrowed in a deep, black anger mixed with a look of confusion. The hand clutching the gun shook and trembled. She absently wondered if shaking so badly could cause the gun to fire, ending her life. Maybe Jose was talking, perhaps even yelling. But whatever words passed his lips were ignored, meaningless – sucked into the void created by the cold blue steel of the pistol barrel.

Living along the Mexican border, the residents of Mercedes, Texas were familiar with and wary of violence. As a police officer, Vietnam veteran Jose Sauceda was something of a connoisseur of physical threat; he had it down to a science. Coyotes – smugglers of people, with their desperate human cargo often tightly packed in the sweltering heat of a van or the nearly airless trailer of an 18-wheeler – usually preferred to ditch their freight at the first sign of danger. Flight – abandoning their hapless "customers" as a diversion, leaving the American cops to clean up the human mess – let the Coyotes live to smuggle another day. Drug smugglers were another matter. There were those smugglers, maybe high on their own product, who ditched and ran. But to others – the smuggling professionals – their shipment was worth more than their lives. Those smugglers were dangerous. Deadly dangerous. Sauceda knew the risks and was good at his job. But the stress was palpable. On this particular summer evening the stress had been too much. There must have been a proximal breaking point. A word out of place – the onset of an argument. Perhaps the worn and rehearsed arguments that become commonplace in a marriage that has endured the decades. The causation, though, would be forever lost in the event itself. Jose had drawn his weapon and had it trained on his own wife.

Noemi had lived a guarded childhood. Her father Luiz drove an 18-wheeler delivering Jax Beer across southern Texas, while her mother Viola worked for the local water department and did her best to raise their three children. Even though she was the eldest, Noemi had always felt a bit left out. As an asthmatic she remembered sitting in the window watching wistfully as the other children played and romped through the neighborhood. But everything had changed when she was 15 – everything changed the day that she met Jose Sauceda. Noemi had long known that there was no such thing as fairy tales, but it had been love at first sight. She knew that he was the one pretty much from the first moment he strolled into her field of vision. As a migrant worker Jose had a strong build, wiry but with just enough muscle to draw her eyes for a second, lingering look. Jet-black hair that hung down near his eyes framed his face perfectly – a face that was almost always smiling. It was one of those honest smiles, the smile of a true friend. It was that smile, the ready humor, the constant willingness to help that had won Noemi over in the end. Jose Sauceda was a good person – the kind of person you can trust with your life. The kind of person you want to marry.

That same person now stood in front of Noemi with a pistol. The ready smile had been replaced by something that looked more like a grimace of pain. His nightmares had begun soon after he had returned from Vietnam – the kind of nightmares where he yelled and punched in his sleep. More like night terrors. Sometimes he dropped to the floor at loud noises. Noemi never asked him about the war, though, and he never offered information. The experience of war, whatever that was, was a part of his past, not of his present. The present meant the hard work of raising a family and holding down jobs. Once, though, things had gotten so bad that Jose had gone to the Veterans Administration seeking some kind of help. But they had told him that he was fine. No help was needed. But here he stood, with the nightmares of sleep having overtaken his waking mind. Here he stood with a gun pointed at her. That smiling teenager was gone. The jokes and good humor had fallen silent, stilled by the demons that haunted Jose's memories. Even as her thoughts focused on that barrel and how to remain alive, Noemi couldn't help but wonder what kind of bloody past had reached into the present to transform her husband so fully and so frighteningly.

Jose had never talked about Vietnam. It had always been there, and Noemi knew that the war had been a powerful and transformative experience. But she never knew why. Jose had guarded her from Vietnam and what had happened there. He had built a wall between his memories and his family – a wall that he hoped would keep his family protected from what he had seen and done. There had been good times in Vietnam, good times of camaraderie and the boozy fellowship shared with young men at war, especially with his best friends Forrest Ramos and Jim Cusanelli. But those good times were nowhere to be found on this night.

His eyes weren't quite focused, more as if he was looking through Noemi instead of at her. Jose's consciousness didn't stop to make specific note of the visions that flickered through his mind, to grab at the memories of Vietnam that flowed past in a torrent. Amid the mental frenzy, the tropical sun bore down on a forlorn rice paddy in the Mekong Delta. It was 1967 and the small-unit war was slowly ripping Charlie Company to pieces, one day, one sniper, one booby trap at a time. Suddenly fire erupted from seemingly everywhere at once. Jose's 3rd Platoon of Charlie Company, 4th Battalion of the 47th Infantry, was caught in an L-shaped ambush. Machine guns and small arms roared their greeting as Charlie Company faced its first test of battle. Jose dove face first into a small canal, the type used to irrigate the rice paddies, crashing down near his friend Jim Cusanelli. It was a symphony of fear, adrenaline, and activity. The world had shrunk down to just two men, Jose and Jim. What was going on 20 feet away might as well have been happening on Mars. Their attention was fixed to their front, to the incoming fire, to the Viet Cong they could see in nearby bunkers. Their attention was fixed on survival. The war and the world had narrowed to a stark focus on the few square feet that mattered in what was a moment of life or death.

Suddenly a Viet Cong soldier stood up. Actually stood up – a suicidal action in a battle where bullets buzzed by from all directions. The movement barely had time to register in Jose's consciousness. His focus narrowed to a single point. Even the harsh sounds of battle seemed to still. The Viet Cong had a Rocket Propelled Grenade launcher aimed directly at him. In a burst of fire the rocket grenade left the tube and sped toward him. It seemed like time had stopped. How could something so fast move so slowly? The grenade split the air between Jose and Jim Cusanelli and impacted the side of the canal just a foot or two away. He was dead; life was over. Did his eyes close waiting for the roar of the warhead's detonation? Did he stare at the hole in the bank of the canal to see the flash that preceded the white heat of the explosion that ended his life? It all happened too quickly for accurate memory creation. But the warhead didn't explode – perhaps because the bank of the canal was a soupy, muddy mess. He and Jim were alive, a fleeting moment of transcendent joy that he couldn't even pause to register. The desperate fighting continued, and Jose remained in mortal danger.

Jose looked up from his moment of life-altering good fortune just in time to see his platoon mate James "Smitty" Smith get hit by a machine-gun bullet. It was the first time he had ever seen a bullet slap through the flesh of a human being. And it did slap through the flesh, making a sickening sound unlike any that Jose had ever heard. Smitty was down, and the bullets were still flying everywhere. Jose wasn't a hero. He was just a young man who had happened to be drafted. It was only by outlandish happenstance that he was here with these men on this field on this day. But he knew what he had to do without it ever truly permeating his consciousness. Jose left the cover of the little, muddy canal that had already saved his life and crawled out onto the battlefield to help his buddy. As bullets ripped and popped through the high rice and kicked up puffs of dirt around his feet, Jose moved forward and helped to pull Smitty to safety. His mind didn't have time to make note of the incredible danger of what had just happened – the battle lingered on and was no less deadly for several hours until US artillery and airpower forced the Viet Cong to flee. Then it was the Americans' turn. Hundreds of Viet Cong were jumping up from their fighting positions and running in all directions. Jose and the rest of Charlie Company poured fire into them, littering the ground with 150 corpses. The human refuse of a defeated foe. Having cheated death twice that day, Jose had become a killer.

Just over a month later Charlie Company faced its sternest ever test, engaging a powerful enemy force in a day-long battle. Charlie Company had ten men killed on June 19, 1967, along with 40 badly wounded, while killing 250 Viet Cong. While the enormity of the day's tragedy was not lost on Jose, for him the memory of June 19 will always be intensely personal. In the opening burst of fire Forrest Ramos had been wounded. Sharing a language and a common Hispanic heritage, Forrest and Jose had been especially close. The injury was perfect. A clean penetration of the right arm, shattering the elbow. Forrest Ramos had a "million-dollar wound"; the kind that was bad enough to get you sent home, but not bad enough to disable or disfigure you forever. The war had deepened, matured and had taken so many members of Charlie Company – had taken so many of Jose's friends. But Forrest had survived, and was only a helicopter ride and a hospital stay from being home with his family.

Spraying water in all directions a dustoff helicopter thundered in – rotor blades still blasting at full speed. The landing zone, though, was incredibly hot, with fire coming in from all directions. Facing such great risk, the chopper was all business, landing, the wounded being tossed on, and taking off in seconds. Forrest was on that chopper, wearing a beaming smile. He waved goodbye to his friends. Vietnam was over for him, and Jose was happy. His friend had made it.

After rising to nearly 60 feet, the chopper suddenly lurched as it was struck by machine-gun fire. For an agonizing moment or two it spun wildly in the air. The pilot somehow managed to regain control and the machine lurched forward. Then the impact of more machine-gun bullets. The chopper rose and stood on its tail – something that helicopters can't do, but this one did. The stricken craft then rolled over on its side, and Forrest Ramos came tumbling out. He dropped to the rice paddy below and the helicopter crashed down onto him. Jose and others from 3rd Platoon rushed to the scene. They were oblivious to the heavy incoming fire and the risk posed by the smoldering chopper, which could explode in a ball of flame at any moment. They could see Forrest. The skid of the chopper had forced him down in the deep mud. Whether he was alive or dead, nobody knew. Some tried to dig, others to lift the massive chopper. But Jose Sauceda and his brothers-in-arms of the 3rd Platoon couldn't do anything to help. Forrest Ramos was dead.

Two days later, in a war that had transformed into a fog of mental anguish, Jose gathered up Forrest's belongings to send home to his grieving parents. He also wrote them a letter telling them how dear Forrest had been to him, how he would cherish his memory, and how he would work the rest of his life to make himself a better person to honor the loss of his friend.

Even with all of that, the events of the day and the battles really didn't register yet – the war went on. Survival went on. Killing went on. It was only when Jose got home, when he reached the safety of his family, that he had time to deal with the memories – the haunting memories of friends lost, of a life altered, and of men killed. Of all of the memories, it was the loss of Forrest Ramos that weighed Jose down almost physically. In his nightmares he could see his friend smiling and waving from the departing chopper. Then the sickening thud of the bullets impacting metal. The sight of the helicopter rising to stand on its tail. The dreams were so real; just like being back there in Vietnam. His sleeping mind recreated everything in agonizing detail, even the sound. Who knew that engines straining beyond their breaking point and the scream of tearing metal could have combined to make such an unearthly wail? Then the hopelessness of not being able to rescue Forrest from underneath the crushing skid. The memories were Jose's burden, a burden he could not share with his family. They were the events that had changed his life.

Was it the moment of death in the rocket grenade impact, the killing of the Viet Cong, Forrest falling, or some unholy combination that played on a loop of pain in Jose's mind that night as he stood there clutching his pistol and staring into the distance beyond Noemi?

Mercifully the couple's three small children were in the next room and did not witness the evening's events. But the youngest was crying. The sound cut through Noemi's mental haze like a scalpel, snapping her back to true awareness. She wanted to leave, needed to leave. But Jose stood between her and the door, blocking any thoughts of flight. And her children needed her; the crying only reinforced that. She just stood there frozen, eyes locked on the blue steel of the gun barrel. Even if she could get words out, what would she say? Jose, her beloved Jose, wasn't there. The smile, the joy, the wonderful father – they simply weren't there. This Jose was lost; lost in a past that she didn't know and couldn't guess. She could only wait for the real Jose to return, for the past to lose its grip over Jose's present.

Like the severing of a taut wire, a knock at the door snapped the tension with a startling abruptness. The smells, heat, and fear of Vietnam receded back into the dark corners of Jose's subconscious and lost their power over his immediate actions. The gun disappeared like it had never been there. One of Noemi's brothers had come to visit. To this day she cannot recall which brother it was, but his appearance had reset the evening to a semblance of normalcy. The real Jose was back, sporting a smile and offering her brother a hearty welcome. Noemi had to blink and shake her head a few times to clear her thoughts because the change was so dramatic. Like walking out of a darkened room and into the light, it took a few minutes to adjust. In the back of her mind it also registered that the baby had even stopped crying.

Noemi loved Jose. She was no longer the infatuated 15-year-old who had fallen for Jose's ready smile. The love was more mature and had been tested by the buffeting winds of a long marriage. Jose loved her and was fiercely devoted to their children. He was both a good man and a good father. In the coming weeks, months, and years the couple would reaffirm their devotion and come better to understand the events of that most difficult night of their marriage. It was in coming to grips with that terrible night, with the image of her own husband pointing a gun to her head, that Noemi Sauceda reached something of an epiphany.

The Vietnam War – a war that she had never served in or been to – was the single most important event of her life.

PREFACE

In some ways this work follows on from my book *The Boys of '67: Charlie Company's War in Vietnam*. In others, though, this work – from its impetus, to its characters, to its conclusion, is entirely separate and new. *The Boys of '67* told the story of a unique combat company and its wartime experiences in Vietnam – it was a book of camaraderie, battle, postwar readjustment, and humanity. As I struggled to weave the written tapestry of a combat company at war, though, something was always tugging at my writing consciousness, like an insistent background voice that is always there but you somehow succeed in ignoring its pleas. In my rush to focus on the lives of the men of Charlie Company at war, I missed what gave those lives meaning – their wives and families. The men of Charlie Company didn't fight for themselves; they fought for something greater. They didn't survive just for themselves; they survived for their loves and futures as husbands and fathers. As the men of Charlie Company boarded the troopship for Vietnam they simultaneously looked toward an unsure future and back toward the relationships that would define that future. War loomed, but the Boys of '67 remained forever connected to the world they left behind – their loved ones, their lives, and their hope. After a year of death, camaraderie, and adrenaline, the Boys of '67 dared to hope that they could return to the shards of their lives and leave the war behind as they boldly strode into their futures. Such hopes, though, were in vain. The war left behind stubbornly refused to be relegated to the past. In many guises and forms Vietnam would remain with them always. War would become a part of their lives, and those of their families, forever.

INTRODUCTION

So many wives and families were left behind for war. Between 30 and 40 percent of soldiers who saw service in the Vietnam War were married, with just under 20 percent having had children. With roughly 3 million serving in theater during the conflict, this ratio means that there were over 1 million wives and more than 600,000 children on the home front who awaited the return of a husband or father from war. Narrating the collective story of over a million women is, of course, impossible. The question was, how best should I attack this daunting topic even to reveal the barest tip of this historical iceberg? Facing this dilemma I chose a narrow focus to allow for the fullest recounting of war's complex interplay with family and married life. In writing *The Boys of '67* I became about as close to the story of a single infantry company as an outsider can ever hope to get. Nearly 100 original oral interviews,* combined with a wealth

---

* Oral histories are central to this study and are sometimes quoted directly. Oral history, in its raw form, does not always make for riveting reading. Interviews are often somewhat conversational in nature, full of asides and bantering between interviewer and interviewee. When directly quoted the oral histories are edited enough to make them readable. The questions from the interviewers are all edited out, while others might be incorporated into the transcript when needed to help the answer make sense. Things not germane to the story at hand, stammers, asides, and interruptions are all edited out. Some colloquialisms, when not central to the story, are cleaned up. Quotes from oral histories will not include ellipses to indicate omissions – or the entire manuscript would be littered with endless dots. In the end, the author had to strike a balance between

of corresponding documents from personal collections and the National Archives, allowed me to recreate the lives and times of Charlie Company, 4th of the 47th Infantry with a depth and level of completeness never before achieved. Given that base of historical understanding, I decided to approach the subject of combat wives through the same focus. For this project I undertook extensive additional interviews with the 24 Charlie Company wives who were married at the time their husbands went off to war.* I was also entrusted with eight major letter collections, which allowed an unprecedented look at how the lives of these new families unfolded while the soldier was away in Vietnam.

Going with what I knew best had the advantage of familiarity and depth, but choosing this group also had its limitations. Charlie Company was almost entirely made up of draftees, and served in 1967 at the high point of the war and at a time before the war reached its peak of contention on the home front. The experiences of this sample group cannot pretend authoritatively to speak regarding women in 1965 or 1972 when the wartime experience was very different indeed. Charlie Company was a combat unit in the Mekong Delta, so this sample group cannot pretend to represent the experiences of non-combatant soldiers, or speak for the experience of Marines, or pilots, or advisors. The Vietnam War was unparalleled in its individuality of experience in both time and place. As a result, no study of limited size can truly pretend to represent the whole. Combat, though, has commonalities both great and small. For Marines along the Demilitarized Zone (DMZ) in 1967 and grunts in the Cambodian Incursion of 1970, fear, adrenalized courage,

---

readability and transcript accuracy. The editing attempted to adhere as closely as possible to the original transcript, with its original meaning maintained intact at all costs.

* There is an entire separate book that could be written on the stories of wives who married Vietnam veteran husbands. But theirs is a very different history than that of women who were married before their husbands went off to war. One further clarification. There are two couples included in this book – the Rademachers and the Hoppers – that technically were not married before the husbands went off to war. However, both were engaged and acted as a coherent couples even while their husbands were away overseas. They married as soon as they could after their husbands' return; so I included their stories in this work.

death, wounding, boredom, loss, and camaraderie were all the same. For marriages experienced at long distance in war, loneliness, anxiety, fear, longing, and change were points of commonality. These things are eternal concerns of young marriages at war. Any sample group can speak to them, and this particular sample group allows for the fullest yet investigation of their workings and indelible impacts.

Charlie Company itself was very representative of the heterogeneous nation of the time. A total of 36 percent of the unit's draftees hailed from the American west, with 26 percent of the company coming from California alone, especially the Los Angeles area. Another 31 percent of Charlie Company came from the Midwest, with draftees from Cleveland accounting for 10 percent of the unit's strength. Draftees from the south comprised 30 percent of Charlie's total, with a final concentration of 17 percent of the unit's men hailing from Texas and Louisiana.

Only 2 percent of the men of Charlie Company claimed a privileged or upper-class background, while 31 percent were members of the middle class – sons of businessmen, professionals, and skilled workers. A total of 24 percent of the unit identified as lower middle class, while 42 percent came from poor families. The racial makeup of Charlie Company closely mirrored that of the American military of the 1960s – 68 percent of the unit was white, 15 percent black, and 13 percent Hispanic. Approximately 23 percent of the members of Charlie Company hailed from urban environments; another 42 percent of the draftees came from the country's societal "middle ground" of the suburbs and mid-size towns. A final 34 percent of the unit's members lived in rural areas, on independent farms or tiny villages.

Since relatively so few of the Charlie Company originals were married, only 29 that I have been able to discover, the sample group of wives is by definition more constricted and haphazard. The group is quite varied in terms of military rank, numbering the wives of the battalion chaplain, the company commander, a platoon leader, and the company first sergeant, with the remainder being enlisted men including a medic. As did their warrior husbands, Charlie Company wives hailed from a diverse set of backgrounds, with hopes, dreams, and experiences that varied widely and that were often greatly influenced by their place of origin and upbringing.

My sample group, then, is defined by its very lack of definition. It is a group that on one hand is idiosyncratic but on the other is deep and quite multifaceted. While its limitations mean that it serves only to begin to tell the story of how combat wives experienced war and its aftermath, its strengths allow it to tell a story unlike any other. This is a story of how real lives and dreams were altered by love, happenstance, and brutality. This is a story of how real young women in a transformative age had their lives forever altered by a war that they did not fight, but yet they did fight. Theirs is a story of silent bravery, desperate despair, bitter defeat, and triumphant victory. Wars greatly impact the lives of the families of the soldiers who fight them. For as long as there have been soldiers there have been supporting wives and grieving widows. For as long as there have been veterans there have been wives and family members who struggled to understand, struggled to cope – with some marriages persevering and others imploding.

———— † ————

From the very beginning of their interviews, every one of these women asked why I was interviewing them. They weren't the makers of history; that was a distinction reserved for their husbands. Their stories wouldn't be important; couldn't be important. Why would anyone want to hear their stories? After their perplexity at being interviewed in the first place, all of the women assured me that their interview would be a short one. After all they were just regular gals who hadn't done anything other than live their lives the best that they knew how. These women were sure that their experiences did not amount to a hill of beans in the greater scheme of things.

But many of their husbands came back from war changed – changes that had deep impacts on their wives and families; changes that resulted in profound alterations of what these women sought from life and expected of their futures. It took decades before Americans began to grapple with the psychological fallout of the Vietnam War. After such a slow start, though, the subject of PTSD was finally fully broached, rightfully focusing governmental, community, and religious efforts on mitigating the experiences of our long-forgotten fighting men. The situation was far from perfect, but from the dedication of the Vietnam Memorial, to Veterans Administration (VA) counseling groups, to Veterans of Foreign Wars (VFW) halls American Vietnam veterans began to form communities and work to overcome years of national neglect. There was nothing, though, for the wives and families. Although they rarely put their feelings into direct words, it was plain that these women were still alone. When their husbands had returned the wives in many ways were marooned amid a sea of family, acquaintances, and friends who did not share or understand their experiences. Oftentimes they were even alone in their own home, personally reeling from their own Vietnam experience but with a husband who was silent about that experience in an effort to protect them from it. While history would eventually redeem their husbands, the contributions and difficulties of the wives remained unnoticed, leaving them solitary figures in a crowded world.

When I spoke to these women, they had been alone for so long and their experiences had been invisible for so long, that they were sure that they didn't have a story to tell. They were sure that nobody was interested in them. The singular loneliness of a combat wife is nothing new. There have always been women who have struggled to come to grips with war and its impact on the love of their life. There are women who deal with these same life-changing events today as their husbands endure multiple deployments to Iraq or Afghanistan. They, too, are alone in a sea of friends. They live with husbands who try to protect them from the truth. *Charlie Company's Journey Home* is a chance for women like them to be heard. It is a chance for them to know that they aren't alone.

Charlie Company's Journey Home is for Jeannie Hartman, and all those like her whose voices need to be heard:

[After her husband Ernie came home from Vietnam] mostly I just prayed a lot. There wasn't a whole lot I could do. He would not mention it [Vietnam]. He would not talk about it whatsoever to me or to anyone. He held it inside for years. Several nightmares were just terrible for him. He would either punch me or pick me up, not realizing it, thinking he was in Vietnam. Before the war he wasn't an alcoholic, and he wasn't violent. He had a wonderful, wonderful sense of humor, just a wonderful all around guy.

Ernie quit believing in God when he was in Vietnam. He does not believe in God, so that has become very difficult for me. I used to go to church every week, and I quit going to church because every time I went to church, he went to a club and drank.

He finally started talking to some counselors about Vietnam, and they had told him he needed to be talking to me. And he told them he didn't want to talk to me because it was such a bad time in his life he didn't think that I needed to know it or worry about it. He didn't want to drag me into it. And I kept telling him he really needed to confide in me because I was married to him and stuck by him all this time that I needed to know something.

I have had a lot of people ask me why I haven't left him. And I guess, when we got married it was like, you get married, you're on your own. Don't come running back home, although, I know they would have taken me. And I really do love him, and he's a wonderful person. And when he isn't like this, he is wonderful. And I keep trying to remember that. I keep trying to remember, he is a good person. And he can be a wonderful husband.

Sometimes, I'm not sure how to stay sane. Right now Ernie is terrible. It's awful. He's probably worse than I have seen him, depression-wise. And I asked for some counseling, but my insurance won't pay it. So, I have nobody to talk to, no one. My mother had a stroke four years ago, so I don't have her to talk to anymore. And I can't afford to pay for counseling. So, I don't really have anyone to vent to, so I do a lot of praying.

CHAPTER 1

THE WOMEN OF CHARLIE COMPANY

I was the middle child. I heard on the radio the other day that your middle child is typically obnoxious and is the one that gives you a lot of trouble because they want attention. But I wanted to get attention in a completely different way; I wanted to be perfect. So I did everything to please my parents. Initially when I was in high school I wanted the typical vision of a 16-year-old at that time – to get married, have kids, and live with a white picket fence. That's a typical thing that 16-year-olds in my day thought. But as time goes on you realize that the world is not perfect like that and if you want to excel you have to take it upon yourself to do a heck of a lot more. You have to get an education. But I got married pretty young, so my life took a different turn. Everybody has a different triggering point, and there was a triggering point for me where my whole philosophy changed in life.

Iris Sclimenti

My parents died early in life, my mom at 49 and my dad at 52. We lived in middle-class America. My mother only went to school to the age of 16 when she married my father during World War II. My father was raised in a Catholic orphanage. I was closest to my father. When she was seven and I was five my sister and I both got sick at the same time with German measles. She got encephalitis from a high fever, but my fever broke. From that point on my sister has required 24/7 care. My mom was an alcoholic and my dad drank beer all the time. Maybe my sister's sickness and disability pushed them over the edge. Mom had my sister when she was only 18, which meant she was a pretty young mom to have so many dramatic things to deal with. They never pushed me toward college or to do anything. Any pushing I did on my own. I had to grow up early. Vietnam forced a lot of young people to grow up early.

Susan Reed

America's "Greatest Generation" returned home from World War II and quickly settled down to the business of creating a bright future, resulting in the "Baby Boom." There were 2.9 million births recorded in the United States in 1945, which increased by nearly 20 percent to 3.4 million births in 1946. Births continued to rise through the remainder of the decade and into the 1950s, peaking at 4.3 million births in 1957. Most historians place the end of the baby boom in 1964, by which time there were more than 76 million boomers, accounting for more than 37 percent of the nation's total population – the largest demographic bubble ever in American history. With their parents determined to give them a better life in an America that had reached the pinnacle of its mighty power, boomers grew up in an age of unprecedented wealth and personal agency. Boomers were sure that they mattered, that their lives counted, that they could change the world. Although the age range of the women interviewed as part of this study varies, most of them graduated high school around 1965 or 1966, representing the heart of the baby boom. These were the very women that *Time* magazine had in mind in 1966 when it declared its "Man of the Year" to be all those in America who were 25 and under.

As the greatest generation got down to the business of having and raising families, a smallish piece of government legislation pushed the US into an unmatched period of unexpected societal transformation that would come to define baby boomers. Officially known as the Servicemen's Readjustment Act of 1944, the main purpose of the GI Bill was to ease the process of societal reintegration for the boomers' war veteran parents. America's servicemen and women had done what the nation had asked of them in its darkest military days; the least the nation could do in return was to give them a monetary welcome home. Billions of dollars were made available to veterans for unemployment benefits, for educational purposes, and for home loans. Flush with government cash, veterans flocked to universities, colleges, and technical schools across the country, where they received education and training that allowed them to take their place as newly minted members of an increasingly consumer-crazy middle class.

Well-paying jobs and rock bottom consumer costs, coupled with the freedom of automobile ownership, placed a huge crunch on the housing market. The new parents and their boomer children wanted to move out of dad's house on the farm; out of their tiny apartments in the cities. There were loans aplenty but few homes to buy. Sensing a payday, builders William and Alfred Levitt bought up land on Long Island and began to build inexpensive cookie cutter homes in what became the first modern suburb. In their first prefabricated "Levittown" that included everything from swimming pools to churches, the Levitts eventually built 17,000 homes that housed nearly 80,000 people. Demand for the new homes was through the roof, with the price of a two-story unit listed at $7,900. With the average salary for local families running at $3,000 per year, the down payment of $90 and the monthly payment of $58 to live in a Levittown home was eminently attractive.

Builders and entrepreneurs across the nation seized upon the Levitt's formula as a path to riches, and suburbs exploded across the American countryside from Chicago, to Kansas City, to Los Angeles. The GI Bill alone allowed 5 million veterans to buy homes at a cost of over $14 billion, and soon good jobs, low costs, and guaranteed financing had changed the living patterns of an entire nation. In the two decades following World War II the number of people living in suburbs nearly doubled, and by 1960 one-third of the American population was living the suburban life.

———— † ————

I loved the music of the 50s; Elvis and Doo Wop especially. My parents were real active in the church, and the Southern Baptists were firm believers in no dancing. Bob [her boyfriend and later husband] wasn't raised that way; Bob was in the Methodist Church. At the Friday night dances down at the rec center he was the one dancing. I probably could have gone; I don't think that my parents would have refused to let me go. But they wouldn't have wanted me to dance. My friends were friends from church, and they didn't go either, so we went other places than dances. The only dance I ever went to was when Bob invited me to the senior prom. We went, but I didn't dance. In college I learned to slow dance and do the twist, but I never really learned much. Bob was the dancer, not me. I wish I really had learned to dance. My granddaughter is 16 and she is out there with them like all the other kids.

Kaye French

Ensconced in their gleaming suburban enclaves and wielding a wealth never before seen by the youth of any generation, boomers and their new world drove seismic cultural shifts and were immersed in and affected by those shifts. From leafy cul-de-sacs to mean inner city streets, the cultural changes of the baby boom were everywhere to be seen, quite literally landing in the family living room through the new medium of television. In 1947, with the lifting of wartime restrictions in the United States, the first batch of 175,000 mass-produced 7-inch black and white TV sets sold out in record time. By 1962 90 percent of the population owned a TV. Along with the increase of TV ownership came a corresponding explosion of programming, much of which was aimed specifically at the boomer market. Smash hits like *I Love Lucy*, *Make Room for Daddy*, and *Leave it to Beaver* depicted a happy country, the one boomers were convinced they lived in, ruled by laughter and home-spun truth doled out in 30-minute dollops.

Henry Ford had once dreamed that very nearly every American would be able to own a car, and his dream was realized during the baby boom. Facing wartime restrictions there had been only 25 million automobiles on the road in 1945, many of which predated the war. By 1958 there were 67 million cars on the road. Sprouting fins and chrome, and boasting V-8 power, cars from Chryslers to Corvettes became a ubiquitous part of youth culture, as did hot rodding and cruising.

All of the technology and entitlement made for an era of boundless optimism for those on the good side of boomer history. The future was theirs, and they were determined to seize it through education. In 1940 the average US student completed just over eight years of school, a number that rose to nearly 11 years of school in 1960. Perhaps of even greater significance is that the number of college students in the United States more than doubled between 1940 and 1960 to 3.6 million. While the overall statistics seem small by modern standards, with just over 11 percent of adult men and nearly 7 percent of adult women having achieved four-year collegiate degrees overall, the gains were still great. College was a real social possibility for men and women alike, opening a brighter future than ever before for an exceptionally educated baby boomer generation.

———— † ————

Mom had gone to Mrs. Hickey's Business School in Saint Louis. Dad was a farm boy who had gone to fight in World War II. Mom's view of success for her was an intact family, even if the outside world just thought that is what it was, that is what was important to her. They knew that I was going to go to college to become a teacher. They were all about it. Came time for school to start and [her boyfriend] Steve came home [from training at Fort Riley], and we talked about getting married and I told mom that I wasn't going to go to college. I was a pretty willful child. I sometimes wonder what would have happened if mom would have said, "You are too going, young lady! You can still marry him in a year when he comes home, but you are at least going and get your first year out of the way." I never did know if mom was disappointed for me because I didn't get the year of college I could have had, or if she was disappointed because she had wanted to be able to say that all of her kids went to college.

Jennifer Hopper

As the baby boom era dawned, the mass culture still made it quite clear what a woman should do with her life. She should get married, settle down, and have a family. From television shows like *Bewitched* and *Leave it to Beaver* to magazines like *Vogue* and *Good Housekeeping*, the largely male-dominated world of the mass media portrayed the ideal woman as one who was distinctly second to a successful husband who acted both as breadwinner and as the leader of the home. Upon the husband's return from a hard day at work, dinner would be waiting on the table. The children would be nearby, but rarely ever loudly so, taking in their newly luxurious world by watching television, riding bikes, or playing in their suburban yard. The wife would have spent her day industriously cooking in her well-appointed kitchen or doing laundry in a thoroughly modern washer and dryer. Ever the slave to fashion, the homemaker would always be portrayed as well dressed, sporting full makeup, a necklace of pearls, and wearing high heels even while vacuuming around the house.

From the *Honeymooners* to the *Dick Van Dyke Show*, from *Seventeen* to *Ladies Home Journal*, the world as portrayed to boomer women was the world of the women of *Charlie Company's Journey Home*. Although more educational and societal doors were opening to them, there remained a societal tension for the women of Charlie Company as they considered their paths to their personal futures. Theirs was still a world where the public image was of women who married young, stayed at home, and raised families. Theirs was still a world where it was expected that the home was theirs and much of the remainder of life fell to their husbands. Theirs was still a world in which the *American Journal of Psychiatry* found that American women devoted 39 percent of their time to doing household chores in an average week.[1] But theirs was also a world in which stereotypes about women and their place in society were beginning to crumble.

— † —

I met Tom at a football game when I was 14½; he was a junior when I was a freshman. We would go to the A & W, or the bowling alley and hear what the other kids were doing and what was going on. In the middle of my freshman year Tom bought me a necklace that had a heart that said "Tom" on it and asked me to go steady. That was 54 years ago, and I still have that. When I was a junior at 17 he got me an engagement ring and we had an engagement party. And I knew that after graduation I was going to marry him. I couldn't imagine life without him. My parents were okay with that as long as I stayed in school, and that was never a question. Back then if you weren't married or going with someone by the time you were 20 something was wrong with you. It was just a whole different culture. You were young; you got married. It's the way it was. Whether it was right or wrong it is just the way it was in our town. My parents just wanted to make sure that I graduated, and it was fine.

Vivian Conroy

While still popular paradigms, female television stars like June Cleaver, Aunt Bee, and Donna Reed had fallen out of touch with societal reality, and their portrayals of the perfect woman no longer represented the real woman. By 1960 40 percent of all women over the age of 16 held a job, doubling women's representation in the American workforce since 1940. The proportion of wives who worked had doubled from 15 percent in 1940 to 30 percent in 1960. Numbers were even greater in the African-American community, with 57 percent of black women already working outside of the home as early as 1950. Boomer women had better educations than any generation ever before, with the women's high school completion rate rising from 56 percent in 1947 to over 70 percent in the late 1960s. More and more women also decided to continue their education in college, with the proportion of women aged 18–19 attending college exploding from 12 percent in 1947 to 35 percent in 1970, the heart of the boomer years.

My mom was divorced and raised us on her own cleaning for people. We went to bed hungry many times. We were raised to want something better, and I wanted to become a schoolteacher. I was raised in the Nazarene Church. Back then they didn't believe in television or short sleeves or anything like that. My sister had gone to Lindsay Wilson College and had got married in her sophomore year, so my mother said that I wasn't going to go over there. She was afraid I would get married. She said that I was going to Nashville where my brother went to Trevecca Nazarene College. And I said, "I'm not going down there and have to have long sleeves on and everything. Mom, I just won't go." She said, "Well you're going," and I said, "We'd better think about this." Because I wanted to go to Lindsay Wilson because it was close to home [and as a Methodist school it wasn't as religiously strict]. She finally bowed down and let me go to Lindsay Wilson and I didn't get married, so she was excited.

Norma Crockett

———— † ————

There were many, though, who fell through the myriad cracks of the dominant boomer culture, and for whom America's rush into a future that was full of fast cars and television sets was only a distant and seemingly impossible dream. In 1959 over 39 million Americans lived in poverty, with African Americans and Hispanics three times more likely to live in poverty than white Americans.[2] Poor African-American and Hispanic women didn't often see themselves on boomer television, didn't have marketing campaigns aimed at them in fashion magazines, and didn't have many of the same generational opportunities. For these women, and their many white rural contemporaries, life remained limited and full of the hard labor of basic survival. The wave of boomer modernity would be slower to reach them, and often only crashed ashore when their husbands joined the military, an event that threw these women into a broader, and often foreign, culture.

> We lived in Johnson City, Texas, where my dad worked on the Johnson Ranch. We didn't have any money. He died at a very young age, when I was 11. My mom worked cleaning houses. I got my first job on the graveyard shift waiting tables when I was 12 and dropped out of school when I was 15 and got married when I was 16. Back in those days people were just trying to survive. There was no education really; that wasn't the priority in the family. The priority was surviving; going to work and just getting by. My dream was just to have a better life.

> *Aurora Salazar*

———— † ————

The women of Charlie Company lived through times of tumult and are part of a groundbreaking generation. For some, boomer dreams were societally unavailable, but many of the women were the first in their families to grow up in the suburbs; they watched television voraciously; they idolized the Beach Boys and the Beatles. They double dated at the local drive-in and cruised the streets with their best guy. They had bouffant hairdos, held in place by a cloud of aerosol spray. Once they were grown they had to balance the ideas of work, marriage, and children in a time when America's culture gave a very specific set of rules and answers to questions about their personal futures. And they had to strike a balance on these issues in a time of war and amidst the great emotional uncertainty of potentially losing a husband to combat. As the shockwave that was the 1960s expanded and engulfed society, what was its graduated impact on the lives of ordinary women? And what of the women who were shut out of the boomer dream? Did the women of Charlie Company notice the changes that history normally ascribes to their generation? Did they make conscious choices of modernity? Did they yearn for a past they really didn't know or understand? Were they victims of the past, agents of the future, or perhaps neither? Instead of projecting history into their lives, *Charlie Company's Journey Home* allows these women of the baby boom their own agency; it allows them to tell their stories. Stories of a generation that came to define an American century.

————— † —————

Jacqueline Bradfield

Jacqueline Boyd was born on December 11, 1949, to Betty and Roman Boyd. Roman's mom, Vaselee, had moved her family of three boys north from Tennessee to Cleveland looking for a better life in a place where she hoped that segregation and Jim Crow did not exist. There were no abstract dreams about the place of baby boomers in society or vain hopes of moving to the tree-lined streets of America's new suburbs. Vaselee simply wanted her children to have a better chance to succeed in life than she had in a south that still separated black and white, so they moved north of the Mason Dixon, and she sent her sons to a Catholic school where they could get teaching, God, and discipline. Things, though, didn't work out quite as Vaselee had planned. When he was about ready to graduate from high school her oldest son, Roman, announced that his girlfriend Betty was pregnant. Vaselee was as angry as any one woman could be. Roman's chances for a better life might have just evaporated. But, after some reflection, she knew that her son had to own up to his mistake and to his future, and she convinced him that he and Betty needed to get married.

Almost as quickly as the marriage happened it began to fall apart. Having Jacqueline didn't help matters; it only served to push Betty and Roman further away from each other. Soon Roman had moved out, and, though still married, both he and Betty had begun to see other people. At age two-and-a-half Jacqueline was spending the day with her dad, which wasn't unusual. But at the end of the day Roman took her to Vaselee's house and not back to mom's, which was unusual. As it turned out, Betty had been trying to break up with a new boyfriend. When he received the news, the new boyfriend had flown into a fit of rage, picking up a nearby pair of scissors and stabbing Betty so many times that the coroner nearly lost count. A few days later Jacqueline attended her mom's funeral. She wasn't tall enough to see into the casket, so her dad picked her up to look; to say goodbye. That moment is the first clear memory of Jacqueline's life.

Roman, who everyone thought was quite handsome, was now single. He had a good job, and supplemented his wages by hustling pool at night. With money in his wallet and women at his beck and call, Roman didn't have time to play father. So he took Jacqueline to live with his mom Vaselee and his two younger brothers. Jacqueline was heartbroken; she didn't want to live with grandma. She wanted her dad.

Grandma was young, only in her 40s, and was a beauty. She had only ever raised boys, three rough and tough boys, and was very nearly through raising them. She wasn't used to having a little girl around, and she plainly resented having to start parenting all over again. Vaselee was strict with Jacqueline, keeping her clean and making sure that she went to school. Jacqueline learned discipline, not to talk back and to do what she was told. She learned how to cook and clean, being put in charge of many of the chores in the family apartment. But Vaselee was distant, and seemingly didn't know how to love Jacqueline or didn't care to. Grandma did her job, but didn't give Jacqueline what she needed most: someone who cared.

Jacqueline also lived with two of her uncles, Vaselee's youngest sons, who effectively functioned as much older brothers given the family's situation. From the moment of her arrival, her uncles took a dislike to Jacqueline. They had to give up space to her, both bedroom and bathroom space. And they deeply resented the time that Vaselee spent with Jacqueline – time that they thought should be theirs by right. Both uncles took their frustrations out on Jacqueline with beatings. The elder uncle didn't beat her often, really only when she didn't listen to him. Her younger uncle would hit her and threaten her on a much more regular basis, but took care to hide it from Vaselee. When Jacqueline would cry and ask why her uncle was beating her he would say, "Your dad used to beat us. Now we get to beat you."

The nearly constant turmoil in her life weighed heavily on Jacqueline: she had no base; she had no family; she had no one who cared. What input she received was all negative. She was the problem, and everyone let her know it. It left her with no self-worth. If no one else believed in her, how could she believe in herself? While other kids in school were going out for the cheer squad or trying to get an allowance to go to the movies with friends, Jacqueline was shutting down and turning inward. While other girls were torn between dreams of marriages and families on one hand or of college and a career on the other, Jacqueline was incapable of envisioning a future for herself. To have dreams someone has to value you first, and no one did.

Cowed by life, Jacqueline didn't know who she was or how to make things better. But at least she didn't have it as bad as a neighbor lady in the apartments who was essentially a shut-in. She liked visiting with the lady from time to time; it broke the monotony of her life and let her feel something. A steady stream of women came to visit her neighbor: women who seemed different somehow. They were always so well dressed and well mannered. They were there to help their friend cope, which was something new to Jacqueline. One day both Jacqueline and the well-dressed women visited the poorly neighbor lady at the same time, and one of the well-dressed women asked Jacqueline to church. With nothing better to do, Jacqueline accepted the offer. Grandma Vaselee had taken her to church many times, but this experience was different. The congregation and pastor were so accepting, and the well-dressed women treated her like she actually mattered. Jacqueline went to church with the well-dressed women, sanctified women, as often as she could – spending entire afternoons and evenings at the church. Sometimes she even spent the night.

One song at church quickly became her favorite. "This little light of mine, I'm gonna let it shine." I won't hide it under a bushel. I won't let Satan blow it out. I'm gonna let it shine until Jesus comes. It meant that she, Jacqueline – even Jacqueline – had a light, an eternal light that life could not extinguish. That song spoke to her and rekindled a sense of self-worth that she had long forgotten. Singing gave way to Bible study, where she encountered John 3:26, "For God so loved the world, that He gave His only begotten Son, that whosoever believeth in Him should not perish, but have eternal life." For someone so thoroughly lost as Jacqueline the words carried immeasurable depth. And the word that stood out was "eternal." She was eternal and worthy of friendship and of God's love. It also meant that God was eternal. Everyone else in her life who had mattered had left her, but God was eternal. He wouldn't die. He wouldn't leave. It was comforting, but it was also frightening.

Jacqueline met John Bradfield when she was 12 and he was 16. They lived near each other and attended the same school, so he was easy to notice. He was handsome, and always so well dressed and mannered. Steeped in responsibility, John always stood apart from the other boys his age – while they were playing ball and getting in trouble, he was working and helping out his family. He was a rock of stability. John Bradfield was exactly what Jacqueline needed – a father who would hug her and make her feel like she had value; like she had a future. With John, Jacqueline found contentment for the first time in her life. John's mother Varema, though, was another matter entirely. She didn't approve of Jacqueline being around, and made her objections plain for everyone to hear. Who was this little girl hanging around with her son anyhow? After it became clear that, try as she might, she would not be able to split John and Jacqueline apart, Varema relented and allowed Jacqueline to visit, as long as she was there to chaperone. For her part grandma Vaselee accepted the relationship from the beginning but told Jacqueline that she had better not come home pregnant from one of her visits to Bradfield's house.

————— † —————

Becky Lind

Becky was born the second child of Clyde and Nawdean Barth on a bitterly cold day in December 1943, and her childhood in Nebraska was something of a throwback to a more traditional rural time in America. The Barths' farmhouse did not yet have electricity, hot water, or indoor plumbing, and Becky's parents rose with the sun and worked the land like their family had for generations. With dad working the farm and mom tending house and working the garden, money was scarce. At a very early age all of the children, eventually including Gay, Becky, Russell, and Lewis, were put to work helping with canning and preserving food and tending to the chickens. Flour and feed were purchased in 50-pound muslin bags, which were then converted into home-made clothing for the youngsters. As a treat, the kids all received one store-bought outfit of clothes every Christmas. The children were given one new pair of shoes every year, usually just before the beginning of school in the fall. By summer, though, growing feet and the wear and tear of country living had worked their magic, and the children had to cut the toes out of their shoes for them to fit at all.

In 1952 farming was still very much on the upswing, and the Barths moved into the very lap of luxury – a two-story house with cold running water for both the sink and the bathtub. There was electricity and even a rotary phone, although it was on a party line, which took some getting used to. The house had a central heater in the basement that functioned by burning the corn cobs that were ubiquitous on the farm. Gay and Becky shared an upstairs room. Uninsulated, and with only one heating duct in the center of the room, it was far from perfect, especially in the winter when the snow would blow in through the windows. But the girls put blankets over the windows to keep out the snow, and also to keep their parents from seeing that they often had their lights on to read well past their bed times.

The house had an outside toilet, but at least it was a two-seater. There was a small hole for the kids and a big one for the grown-ups.

There was also a cover that kept the odor in that had a nail sticking out of it so that you could raise it up and down when you needed. Toilet paper was non-existent. Instead, perched nearby was a Sears catalogue or a phone book. On the worst occasions of all, there were no catalogues or phone books and you had to rely on the final, and unfailing option; corn cobs. During the winter, the cover from the privy doubled as a sled, with Becky and the other Barth children using the lone nail as a kind of steering device. They all knew that upon pain of punishment they had better put the privy seat cover back in place once the fun was over.

Life changed for the Barths as Becky made ready to enter high school with her dad taking a job on a dairy farm. The move meant that Becky no longer went to a one-room schoolhouse, but to a school with separate grades and even indoor bathrooms. As was standard for farm children at the time, Becky worked hard to help out at home, baling hay and milking 32–35 cows twice a day every day. During her freshman year in high school Becky took an additional job as a substitute janitor for extra money. Since she was too young to work at such a job, they paid her in cash. Through it all, Becky remained intensely devoted to her own schoolwork and chores. Her parents were determined that Becky and her siblings would have a better lot in life and broader horizons. From her earliest days, even though she was only a girl from the country, Becky always knew that she was going to college to train to be a teacher.

It was in her new part-time job as a waitress in a local restaurant to help raise money for college that Becky first met Herb Lind. He and his family had come in for a very early breakfast one morning, and she rushed her clearing of two nearby tables to make sure that she was the one who got to wait on that cute boy. Unfortunately Becky's rush caused her to catch a cup handle on a nearby beer tap, and her entire double armload of dirty dishes came crashing down. Mortified, Becky went and hid in the kitchen, sure that she would never see that cute boy again. As luck would have it, though, he had noticed Becky and called to make a date to go out and get a coke – something Becky had never done. Her family had not been able to afford drinks from bottles, so she didn't quite know what to do. That Herb was from a more well-off family quickly became clear. He didn't seem to think twice about driving 20 miles to a restaurant, a huge expense with gas at 23 cents a gallon. But they had a great time in one another's company, and soon they were officially a couple. A pending separation, though, left their future decidedly murky. Herb was enrolled at Nebraska Wesleyan while Becky embarked on her dream and began to take classes at the University of Nebraska Agricultural Campus.

—————— † ——————

Aurora Salazar

Aurora was the sixth child of Paul and Otillia Gonzales, and was born in Nebraska while her father was there working as a farm laborer. Soon, though, the family moved to Johnson City, Texas, where farm jobs were plentiful and where there was a larger Hispanic community to make them feel more at home. Paul went to work as a ranch hand, often finding employment on the expansive Lyndon Baines Johnson ranch. Otillia worked at very nearly every job that she could find, but mainly as a maid in the homes of the local elite, including LBJ's mother Rebekah.

As a tiny town of fewer than 1,000 people, Johnson City didn't have much in the way of economic opportunity or diversity. In Aurora's tiny class at school there were no blacks at all, and only three other Hispanic students, and she was laughed at for only bringing a bag of tacos to school for lunch. Both Paul and Otillia had dropped out of school early to help their families get by, and education was not high on their list of priorities for their children. There were no Christmas presents or birthday presents. Paul and Otillia's horizons were very limited, and their vision of the future was harshly restricted by the bitter realities of life. The world had not allowed them to go anywhere, and it was better that their children learn that lesson early in life instead of wasting time dreaming.

After a lengthy sickness Paul passed away when Aurora was 11 years old, and the family fell off of the deep end of the financial spectrum, often having to wonder where the next meal was coming from. Aurora's oldest brother dropped out of school immediately and became a mechanic, while another quit to work as a plumber. The whole town seemed to get together to help them get by, but, despite the good intentions, the crushing poverty remained. Whether it was through grief for a husband lost, or a fear of the future, Otillia very quickly remarried after Paul's death. Aurora's new stepfather promised that he was there to help raise the children and to help lift the family out of its financial turmoil. But soon Otillia was pregnant again, and she chose to leave her children behind. Four of the children were still living at home – two older sisters aged 18 and 13, an older brother aged 16, and Aurora aged 12. Otillia left them a place to live, but left them all the same. As far as she was concerned Paul's children were grown up enough to make it in the world on their own.

Although she was too young to work legally, Aurora took her first job at age 12 working the graveyard shift at a local 24-hour restaurant. The pay wasn't good, and the hours were miserable. On most days Aurora spent a whole day at school, followed by far too little time to get her homework done, and then it was off to the late night shift waitressing and washing dishes; a shift that would sometimes last until 3am. Her schoolwork suffered due to her nearly constant lack of sleep, and there was no time for a true adolescence, but Aurora Gonzales had no choice. She wasn't yet a teenager, but it was time to be a grown-up. However, Aurora's difficult life had an odd upside. When I asked her if she perceived any limits on her life growing up as a woman Aurora was incredulous. She didn't even know what limits were. There were no limits to a woman's ability to do hard work. There were no gender limits to her dreams. For Aurora there was an equality of suffering when your dreams are ones of survival, of simply having a better life and knowing that you will be fed. No man or woman, no limits of gender or ethnicity, were going to stand between Aurora and a better future.

When she turned 15 Aurora decided that she had to shift over to work full time, and dropped out of school. Now that she no longer had classes to take and had a bit of free time during the day she spent more time with her oldest brother in nearby Austin, where her favorite haunt was 6th Street. It was a tough part of town, a ghetto of run-down housing and sketchy businesses; no place for a 15-year-old. She could have met any number of bad folks on 6th Street, but instead she met Jimmie Salazar. At 18 years of age he was a good deal older than Aurora, but so were most of the guys she met. He was handsome with his dark eyes and wavy hair. But most importantly he was nice. He was respectful, thoughtful, and seemed to have room for Aurora in a future that was considerably wider than her own. He had dreams of moving off to a big city and making something of himself by getting a job at the post office; dreams that were beguiling to a 15-year-old with so little hope.

Jimmie had completed high school and was working for a company that assembled boats. It was decent, hard work, and he was able to set aside some money toward his future. When Jimmie and Aurora started dating, his parents were a bit shocked by her young age, but were impressed by her deep maturity. The young couple liked to go paddle boating and to the movies, but mainly they just spent time at the Salazar home watching television, listening to music, and enjoying each other's company. For Aurora it was fun to see a real family in action. There were seven Salazar children and two very involved parents – real, caring parents. Aurora still had a relationship with her mom, but it was nothing like this. Richard and Ramona welcomed Aurora into their home and treated her as one of their own, giving Aurora the first real family that she could remember. They gave her love; they gave her morals. They didn't leave her. Finally Aurora felt wanted.

———— † ————

Mary Ann Maibach

Born in 1941 to Ernest and Louise Graf, Mary Ann was the first of what would eventually be eight siblings, although Jane, the youngest of her sisters, died only four hours after she was born. Ernest raised and sold vegetables on a 14-acre farm on the outskirts of Akron, Ohio, supplementing his meager income by driving fuel trucks in the winter. Onions and lettuce were the farm's staples, and Ernest would get up well before dawn to tend the fields, ready the crops for sale, and make deliveries to customers all over Akron. On days when he would take crops to the market, Ernest would get up before 3am, often taking one of his children with him and treating them to cocoa and hot rolls after the day's labor.

Louise had been a maid before her marriage to Ernest, but gave up employment to be a full-time wife and mother. She had a very busy life taking care of the burgeoning family, but also helped out on the farm especially in the preparation of the vegetables for sale. As the children aged they were all expected to pitch in with the housework and in tending the farm, and it fell to Mary Ann, as the eldest, to take charge of much of the house and to keep her boisterous, ornery younger brothers in line and out of their parents' hair. The Grafs were poor, wearing hand-me-down clothes and with nothing in the way of luxuries. But they were always well fed, loved, and looked after.

The Graf family were members of the Apostolic Christian Church, in which Ernest served as a minister and sometimes also traveled to preach to other congregations. The church has a long history of non-resistance and a strong Mennonite background. Church membership for Mary Ann meant a very "traditional" upbringing as part of an expansive and nurturing community, with daily Bible readings and prayers. Long, tastefully done hair was expected of Mary Ann, with makeup and most jewelry being out of bounds. There were, of course, both boys and girls among the youth of the church, but they did not interact in a one-on-one basis with members of the opposite sex. Dating was not an option. Mary Ann wanted love, a marriage, and a family; but she wanted it to be within the confines of her religious beliefs. However her youth grouping at her church was a small one, often fewer than 20 people. With such limited options Mary Ann slowly became content knowing that love and marriage might not be in her future plans.

There was another calling in Mary Ann's life, however. At age 11 Mary Ann had fallen quite ill and had had to be rushed to the hospital for an appendectomy. The doctors impressed her with their skill and professionalism, but it was the nurses that she admired the most. They were always there, just like her mother was at home. They were so smart and talented. Mary Ann knew from that moment on that she wanted to study to become a Registered Nurse. The Apostolic Christian Church has a strong history of women working outside of the home, and an even stronger history of service in the medical profession. When Ernest and Louise learned of Mary Ann's dreams they were fully supportive.

Having worked in the school cafeteria, as a baby sitter, and at the local library to help save money for her education, after high school graduation Mary Ann had the $300 necessary to attend the Akron City Hospital Idabelle Firestone School of Nursing. Everyone needed nurses at the time, and Mary Ann had no problem finding a job immediately upon graduation. Her real passion for nursing was obvious to anyone who saw her in action, and promotions came at a rapid rate, so that she rose to the position of head nurse in record time. Mary Ann's life was good, and her future was bright. She still harbored hope for love and marriage, but down deep Mary Ann believed that she would wind up living her life alone.

———— † ————

Judy Lilley

Born the middle of seven girls to Doc and June Wittman, Judy was raised on a company farm. Her father hired workers for a main farm of the DiGiorgio Corporation, which controlled much of the fruit production of central California. Like many of the employees the Wittmans lived in a small corporate-owned and operated town, and the children attended a corporate-run school with 25 students in each graduating class. Next door to the corporate town was a less affluent camp for the Hispanic farm workers, meaning that Judy grew up in a very ethnically and class mixed environment, but one where employment level greatly affected the standard of living.

At a young age Judy learned that everyone had to do their share to make the house run smoothly and to make ends meet. She started with ironing and less demanding chores, but before long she found herself in charge of her younger sisters' upbringing. And there were farm chores when needed as well. With her parents busy working around the farm, and with her three older sisters moving out to start lives of their own, Judy had to grow up early. The family didn't have much money, but that never really seemed to matter. There was lots of love, never any spankings, and an understanding that college and a further education were part of her expectations.

When she graduated from the 8th grade, Judy's parents made a momentous decision. They were going to pick up stakes and move the family to Boron, California. It was a sleepy little town, but one of Judy's sisters lived there and was convinced that the area was about to take off. Doc and June opened a soda fountain together, very much a family business, that they hoped would seize upon the culture of the time and become a place where kids and adults alike came to eat and socialize. It was a wonderful time for Judy. Her family was better off than ever. She really liked the small local high school where she was an exceptional athlete, winning medal after medal in the school's fitness challenge. The school didn't have many team sports for girls, which seemed wrong to Judy. So she decided that she was going to do something about it. She couldn't change her own school, so she decided that she was going to go to college to learn to teach physical education. Then she could help to bring girls' sports to other schools to make sure that the next generation of girls had the opportunities that she lacked.

At the end of her junior year in high school, Judy's father died of a sudden heart attack; he was only 52. He was still supposed to be there, guiding the family to its future. But life did continue, and it had to change. The soda fountain dreams were no more, and the family moved back to the Bakersfield area. There wasn't much life insurance, and June knew that she couldn't even afford to feed everyone, let alone send all of her children to college, even though she worked as a hospital aide. So June decided to get a better job.

One of her sisters operated a beauty school and offered to take June in first as a student and then as an employee. The pay wasn't great, but it was better than the meager hospital salary; at least the family would be fed. It was tough on Judy, losing her father, but it was even tougher watching her mother take it all so hard; mom's world had darkened almost instantly, replacing hope for the future with a kind of ache that constantly showed on her face and in her demeanor.

Still, while life got more difficult, Judy always had her sisters, especially Cheryn, who, at only 11 months her junior, was almost like her twin. One Saturday Judy was at school when she got the news that Cheryn had been involved in a horrible car accident. By the time that Judy reached the hospital to see her sister it was too late. Her mom walked up, hugged her, and said, "There is nothing we can do for Cheryn." Family and friends gathered from all around to bury Cheryn just a few days short of her 17th birthday. It was the great crisis of Judy's young life. Losing her father less than a year before had hurt, terribly. But losing Cheryn was like losing a part of herself. Only in retrospect did Judy realize that it had to have been even more difficult for her mom. What must it be like to lose a husband and a daughter in such a short space of time? Grief for one had not even run its course before the other was taken. June Wittman had to be broken. Had to be. But she still had three children at home; three children in school. June Wittman couldn't afford to be broken. If she failed, then her family would surely fail, and June Wittman refused to let that happen. She stayed in school. Got her job. Cared for her family. Planned the funeral, and kept her family together. At that point June Wittman went from being Judy's mom to being her idol.

Any dreams of what boomer women could and should be were forgotten. Dreams of college and a future of leading girls to new opportunities in sports were just that. Dreams. Judy knew that she had to do something, anything, to help her family. So she enrolled in beauty school right alongside her mother. She threw herself into her new life with determination, going to beauty school on nights and weekends along with her normal high school studies. When

Judy graduated in 1965 she also graduated from beauty school and was ready to work full time. She was ready to become a tough woman like her mom.

—————— † ——————

Esther Windmiller

As the senior member of the Charlie Company wives, Esther Windmiller's experience was different in part because of her marriage's relative maturity when it was impacted by war. Esther came from a lower-middle-class background, with her father, Kenneth Avery, working sometimes for the Work Projects Administration and then employed at a machine shop and her mother, Lydia, sometimes teaching school but mainly working as a homemaker. The family, which included a total of five children, lived in Wellington, Ohio, a rural area just about an hour out of Cleveland. Her father worked hard, and provided as best he could at his pay rate of 50 cents an hour, but it was Esther's mother Lydia who had the greatest impact on her young life. While dad had dropped out of school in the 8th grade, Lydia had completed high school and had even attended three years of college at Kent State University. Lydia was in the town's literary club and told anyone who listened that, once her children were grown, she was going back to college to complete her degree and become a school teacher. Maybe life was different for other girls of her era, but for Esther Avery education, college, and a career were a family inheritance.

Lydia had been raised strictly Mennonite by parents who had fled Germany to avoid religious persecution. Both she and Kenneth made certain that their children were raised in accordance with their deep Christian faith, attending a local Baptist church. The fundamental quality of the church was a little socially limiting; Esther couldn't dance or drink. The church even frowned on going to the movies, and loved to pass judgment on girls who did so. Her father, though, had always had something of a rebellious streak, loving to press the rules with which he didn't agree. So he snuck away with his daughter to a nearby town where they wouldn't be recognized and took her to see the movie *Cinderella*. It all seemed so daring!

Maybe Esther inherited some of her father's rebellious streak, because, while all of the other girls her age wanted to get married and get down to farming and raising a family, Esther wanted to be a nurse. Fully supported by her parents, Esther went to Wheaton College outside Chicago, a place where her devout faith and her dreams could mix. Going to college in Chicago. It all seemed like such a grand idea until she got there. Esther was so homesick so quickly that she called her mom collect nearly every night, crying. But Lydia told her that she just needed to persevere and study hard. So that is what Esther did. The boomer culture of the 1950s was everywhere in Chicago, from Little Richard to James Dean in *Rebel Without a Cause*. But for Esther it was her studies and her dream that mattered.

In 1954, during her last semester at Wheaton, she met him at a friend's wedding. Bernie Windmiller – tall, dark, and handsome. For Esther it was love at first sight, just like you see in the movies. Bernie was dapper, smart, and kind. He was from a similar religious background and wanted to join the ministry. But his religious nature seemed more tolerant and less judgmental. He had achieved the faith – a profound faith that lets others be themselves – to which Esther aspired. It didn't take long before he popped the question while the couple sat on the front porch swing at her parents' home. But before arrangements could be made for the wedding, Bernie was drafted.

After Bernie's return from his first deployment to Korea the couple married, and Bernie enrolled at a Mennonite college in Bluffton, Ohio. Esther went to work at a nearby hospital to pay the bills while Bernie studied. The couple lived in a tiny trailer on campus, and Bernie helped out by serving as choir and youth director at a local church located in the middle of a corn field. Life got even more complex and wonderful for the young couple with the birth of their first child, Beth, on January 14, 1958. After graduation Bernie was accepted at Fuller Theological Seminary in Pasadena, California. Hitching up their trailer, the little family drove west to start the new chapter in their lives.

Esther gave up her nursing career to become a full-time mom. It wasn't what she had dreamed, but it was what she wanted. Lives change, and being the best mom, homemaker, and wife she could be meant the world to Esther. Times were difficult. Bernie got some work as a youth minister, but spent most of his time studying. Sometimes there just wasn't any money – none at all. Esther prayed a lot during those years; prayed for the ability to feed her growing family. Whether it was prayers answered, or the kindness of local congregants, or both, grocery bags of food would sometimes turn up on the Windmillers' front stoop – always just in the nick of time.

After three years of study, and the arrival of three more children, finally the big day came. Bernie was ordained and began his ministry at a small Evangelical Covenant church in south Chicago. Pay remained low, though, which meant that the growing family still had to scrimp and save to get by. And Esther couldn't shake the idea that living as the pastor's family meant living in a uniquely uncomfortable fishbowl with everyone constantly watching and judging. But this was the future that the Windmillers had been searching for. Then a call came in from the Evangelical Christian Church; there was a need for chaplains in Vietnam. Accepting this calling would mean going to war, and chaplains were not immune to bullets. Somehow, though, it just seemed so right. Who needs God's presence more than men at war? Esther packed up the family once again, this time to take them to Fort Riley, Kansas, so Bernie could join the 9th Infantry Division.

Chapter 2

MARRIAGE AND TRAINING

Gene was home on a two-week leave, so we ran down and got our marriage license, and we bought our rings at Fedco Department Store. Two wedding bands. They were $60 for mine and $70 for his. I didn't care. I just wanted to marry him. He was the love of my life. If he would have given me a cigar band I would have taken it. We got married on November 19, 1966. I knew all along that these boys were being groomed for Vietnam. That was the whole purpose of the mass draft. That was even in the news; everybody knew that was what was happening. I knew that they were going, but I didn't know exactly when. I thought that he still had more training to do and that we might have six months or so to enjoy married life. He and his mom had asked the minister not to mention this because the bride to be doesn't know that he is going to Vietnam very quickly. But the preacher when he was performing our vows said, "Please everybody say a prayer for this young couple because Gene will be going to Vietnam on January 1st." I'm standing there sweating bullets, and all of a sudden my Bible started to slip out of my hand, and I looked at him and my eyes swelled up with tears. I didn't know what to do there in front of a church full of people. So I thought, "Well, I'm going to have to make the best of this." He was very sad and apologetic that I found out that way. He was planning on telling me on the honeymoon.

Deana Harvey

I was at Bill's house when he got his draft notice. His mom was so upset. It was all upsetting. None of these guys really wanted to go off to this war. They didn't know why they were being sent there. There was never any doubt as to the seriousness of this war. I knew that he might not come home. We thought if we were only going to have a short time together we might as well be married to each other. We were young, and we really loved each other. That is the only thing that stood out in our minds. And I knew in my heart that I wanted to support him 100 percent. And I felt if I could give him all of my support that would maybe make him want to take care of himself even more. I'd heard stories of guys if they didn't have a wife or a very serious girlfriend that they just maybe took too many risks. He would always know that he had the support back home of his wife. We arranged the wedding quickly. It was in a church, and I had a white dress that I borrowed from a girlfriend. We had the wedding reception in my grandparents' restaurant. In our pictures we look so young; like children. But it was a very serious time.

Susan Reed

1965 was a bumper crop year for marriages. The 1.8 million weddings performed during the year were a near-record spike, only surpassed by the anomaly of the peak of post-World War II weddings seen in 1948 and 1949. Most of the new brides, some 80 percent, opted for traditional religious marriages in churches. With their veils and fitted dresses, the brides marched down the aisles to join the vast majority of American women in an institution that was so ubiquitous that really nobody noticed truly how ubiquitous it was – 74 percent of the women over the age of 15 in the United States were married. The number was closer to 80 percent for males over the age of 15. Not only was marriage an unquestioned cornerstone of boomer life, marriages were taking place at an earlier age than ever in US history. Boomers' parents, in 1940, married early, at an average age of 24.3 for males and 21.5 for females. Boomers' children, in 1980, married relatively later at an average age of 24.7 for males and 22 for females. Boomers' grandchildren, in 2005, waited longer than ever to wed at an average age of 27.1 for males and 25.3 for females. Boomers, though, in 1965 broke the proverbial mold, marrying at an average age of 22.8 for males and 20.6 for females. In 1965 boomer women flooded the altars at a younger age and in greater numbers than ever before or since. The numbers don't lie. Even though access to a college education or a career was on the societal rise, for most women in 1965 marriage was the first priority.[3]

———— † ————

The women of *Charlie Company's Journey Home* represent a tiny fraction of the institution that was boomer marriage. The limited sample size, though, allows for an in-depth investigation of what marriage meant. Our story includes 22 women who were married at the time their husband went to war in 1967 as a part of Charlie Company.*

The women of Charlie Company married young – 15 getting married as teenagers, and seven walking down the aisle in their 20s. The youngest Charlie Company bride married at 16, the largest single number of brides included seven who married at age 18, and the oldest Charlie Company bride was a mere 25.

While the Charlie Company marriages can certainly be seen in the light of marriage statistics of the time, there is one thing that set them apart dramatically. War. From when they started to how they progressed and ended, Charlie Company marriages were and are inexorably linked to the violence of combat. Vietnam stood as a chasm in each marriage – a vast personal gulf of time, distance,

---

*   Again with the exception of the Hoppers and Rademachers, who were married just after their husbands' return from Vietnam but are included in this study.

experience, and emotion that not only separated man and wife but also set these combat marriages apart from all others of their time. Only seven of the Charlie Company couples were married for a year or more before the husband left for war, with one marriage having endured for 11 years and another seven, while five had lasted for only a single year before the husband waved goodbye from the troop train. Two of these couples, the Windmillers and the Crocketts, had had a chance to experience much of the fullness of married life. Five, though, arguably remained in that earliest segment of marriage when couples are still trying to sort out their personal spaces in a union of souls and lives.

Thirteen of the Charlie Company couples married only *after* the husband had been drafted, with one marrying after the soldier's combat tour had already begun. Six of these marriages took place during the husband's final leave from training and had lasted less than a month before his departure for Vietnam. For these marriages, roughly 60 percent of the marriages in Charlie Company, the couples in many ways weren't even really married. They had never really had a chance to live together; even if the wife followed her husband to Fort Riley he was so busy with training that the marriages didn't have any real time to grow and blossom. These women had the incredibly difficult and lonely task of learning what it was to be married while the husband was an ocean away serving in a combat environment they would never understand. Coming to understand what marriage really means can be both rewarding and intensely frustrating. Most of the Charlie Company wives would have to undertake that transformational marriage learning period alone, with only distant letters to guide them.

Most of the women of Charlie Company saw marriage and raising a family going hand in glove. Five Charlie Company wives had children before their husband went to war. One family, the Windmillers, who had been married for 11 years, had four children, with the eldest being ten when the husband left for Vietnam. The Crocketts, who had been married for seven years, had a five-year-old. The remaining children were still in diapers, with two being newborns, when their fathers shipped out. There were also six children born to Charlie Company wives *after* their husbands had gone to war. Two gave birth as their husbands were on the troopship to Vietnam and the last wife had her baby in September, almost exactly nine months after her husband had departed.

That Charlie Company marriages came in all shapes and sizes makes this study especially rich and varied. On one level there were marriages that had transformed into a comfort level of practical love – a love that had matured over time; a love that was less explosive and more stable. These marriages were full and rich before their husbands went to war, allowing the spouses to come to terms with their places in their married worlds and to become comfortable with the idea of raising children. The Charlie Company wives in these marriages lost a trusted helpmeet when their husband shipped out, leaving them to captain the family – forcing them to adopt the roles of both father and mother in a world that had suddenly become much more lonely. On another level there were still the marriages that were in the throes of passionate love – a love that had yet to mature and remained full of a strident urgency. Wives in these young marriages, some less than a month old, didn't even know how to live with their husband yet; was he a slob? What kind of food did he like? Did he mind if she had a job? Although married, these women would have to wait for a year to find out what marriage, its beautiful moments and its hard knocks, was really like. A number of these wives lived through a similar state of wedded uncertainty while also pregnant; having children while the child's father was stranded an ocean away.

On the surface many Charlie Company marriages seemed so different – some were mature and full, while others had only begun to blossom. Amidst these marriages that seemed so different, marriages and families old and new, there was one thing that was constant. These women of Charlie Company had not only married men. They had also married Vietnam.

We really didn't get engaged, because I got pregnant. I was three months pregnant when we got married. We were married August 1, 1966. We had a big wedding at the church and then a big dance. It was pretty nice. My parents were okay with the idea of me getting married until they found out I was pregnant. Then my mother got very upset. At that time you couldn't go to school if you were pregnant, so I dropped out. I was almost a senior. I had to grow up in a big hurry. I didn't know how to cook or do laundry or anything like that. And I had a baby on the way, so I really had to grow up fast. After our wedding I had to go and live with my parents, because he had to go to Vietnam. Jose getting his draft notice was so scary. It meant that he had to leave and I would be at home pregnant. I was so young and so naïve that when he left for training and Vietnam I didn't ask any questions. I was just so young. It was crazy. He left for training and before I knew it he was in Vietnam.

Noemi Sauceda

In my first week at a new high school my brother took me around to introduce me to everybody, all the big people. And John was extremely popular; he was probably the most popular guy in school. I fell for him almost immediately, because he was funny. He could really make you feel good. He was just fun to be around. He was also a fabulous dancer; everybody wanted to dance with him. Pretty soon everybody knew that we were a couple. I was set to graduate in June 1966, and John was drafted in March. I think that he was scared, but he said, "It is what it is. I have to do this." I knew what getting drafted meant, and I was scared to death. But I was also very positive. In my mind I knew that he would come home. I always knew that he would come home, and we would start our life. We were both really young.

John was going to be sent out to Vietnam after Christmas, and my parents didn't know it, but I went to visit him in Fort Riley. I stayed about a week. He had a friend who had an apartment and let us sleep in the living room. It was an adventure. About two months later I found out I was pregnant. When I had it confirmed I was panicky. I was so concerned about my parents. When I told them, they were the sweetest people in the whole world. At the end of March they were able to bring John home from Vietnam for three weeks to marry me. We got married in Las Vegas. He was happy, but scared that he might not be there to be able to take care of his child.

Iris Sclimenti

———— † ————

As wives and girlfriends fretted, husbands and boyfriends went to train for war, beginning a discrete set of experiences that would change the men forever. Experiences that have to be understood to see their true impact and reflection in the lives of their wives and families. In May of 1967 buses disgorged their complements of newly minted soldiers onto the parade grounds of Fort Riley, Kansas, to become part of the newly reactivated 9th Infantry Division. In military terms, Charlie Company, as part of the 9th Division, was something of an anomaly. Raised through the draft, the men of Charlie Company would train together and then go to Vietnam for their year-long combat tour together, serving in the perilous Viet Cong homeland of the Mekong Delta. In unit terms this arrangement was nearly unique in the Vietnam War. Instead of being trained as individual replacements for an existing unit, as was the norm in the Vietnam War, Charlie Company trained together for nearly eight months – working from basic training through advanced unit training as a group. Unlike so many of their Vietnam War combat brethren, Charlie Company soldiers had become brothers through the rigors of training before they went to war. The white heat of combat, and the loss of so many of their brothers to ghastly wounds, only drew the men closer during their year in Vietnam. But in personal terms none of that mattered as those bus doors swung open. City slickers from Cleveland, surfers from California, and farm boys from the Midwest stepped down to the pavement. Meeting them was Sergeant Lynn Crockett, who was yelling and screaming to beat the band. Curse words flew with the artistry demonstrated only by a true master. Pushups; marching; obeying – all of the rigors of training began on that day:

> All these young civilians getting off of that bus. I had to start to make them into a unit. There were some tough cases, a few objectors. But I had to start that long road of converting a civilian into a soldier. If they didn't have discipline, I knew that Vietnam was going to be a difficult experience. I had to train them to accept commands without question; it is the only way to survive in combat, and they were headed to combat. I took my job very seriously; I wanted to keep them alive. My wife Norma and son Gregory were there with me at Fort Riley. She knew that the unit was being trained to go to Vietnam, and she wasn't all that happy about it. I had some surgery done in November of 1966, which could have kept me from going to Vietnam for several months. But I didn't want to go to war as some replacement; I wanted to go with my unit. So I asked the doctor if I could go, and he told me yes. Norma wasn't happy, but it was something I had to do.

> *Lynn Crockett*

In the next few days the trainees met such luminaries as Captain Lind and Lieutenant Benedick. Chaplain Windmiller? He was so high up the chain of command that you had to stand on a stepladder to see him. The trainees lived in a three-story barracks atop Custer Hill, to which they were confined for much of their early training. The officers and non-commissioned officers had it a bit better, often living in tiny quarters off base – but all of their schedules were rigorous almost beyond imagining. Up before dawn; classes and strenuous activity, ranging from the dreaded bayonet course to low crawling through the mud, all day; a return to barracks or home with only enough time to get enough sleep to bear it all again the next day. These men were going to war together – officer, non-commissioned officer, and enlisted man alike. They knew that their lives depended on their training and the training of the man next to them.

There was no place in the world in the 1960s more masculine than military training. Individuality had to be lessened, necessitating exhaustion, yelling, punishments, forced marches, and pure sweat. Aggression had to be harnessed. The men had to be hardened and sharpened to the point of becoming killers; that was, after all, going to be their job. And those who didn't become killers could very easily wind up dead. Training had its technical side, of course, ranging from artillery spotting, to dead reckoning marches, to the care and accurate use of weaponry. But training also involved men pushing other men to the limit of their abilities, both physical and mental, to ensure survival under the most difficult of circumstances in the bloody, small unit war that was Vietnam.

Marriages and wives had to be relegated to a tiny corner of the world of military training. For the enlisted men there was no question – they were there to do what they were told, and wives were most certainly not a part of the equation of basic training. It was only later that some of the men were allowed to find off-base housing so that their wives could come and join them. For most "off-base housing" meant finding a cramped apartment or perhaps sharing a beat-up rental home with another couple or even two. Housing in the area was always at a premium, with trainees and trainers coming and going at a rapid clip. So the enlisted men put up with whatever they could get. After the first two months of training, sometimes the enlisted men were allowed to go home in the evenings to be with their wives. On other occasions they were confined to base. Usually weekends were free during the latter stages of training, but the men were so exhausted that they often spent a good bit of the weekend catching up on sleep. Since their time at Fort Riley was relatively short, most couples didn't see the need to buy much in the way of furniture or amenities. Life was difficult for the men, but it was no less so for their wives. For the enlisted wives these were the opening days of their marriages. These were the days of passionate love, and the days of discovery. These were the days of forging a new life. But these wives found themselves marginalized in their own marriages. The husbands meant well, but their time was dominated by matters of life and death. By nature and design their husbands were distant and distracted in a time when marriages were supposed to be taking root.

> Getting off of that bus; I will never forget how big Sergeant Crockett looked or how scared I was. After Basic Training, Don Peterson, Don Deedrick, and I pooled our money so our wives could come out to Fort Riley to be with us. I really didn't know what I was in for, but was pretty sure I was headed to war. My wife Karen didn't like the situation much, but there was nothing we could do about it. Training was even harder than I had heard. We all lived in a huge old house, and us guys were only there on the weekends, often only on Sunday. The wives were together all of the time and became good friends. Don Peterson was so happy and crazy about his wife; he would protect her from anything that would ever happen. He was so proud that he was married, and so proud that he was going to be a father soon. My mother and my wife didn't say much about it when we left for Vietnam; they were just kind of quiet. It was my dad who was the most frightened for me. He just couldn't let it go.

> *Steve Huntsman*

Perhaps most difficult for the wives, though, was the loneliness. The trainees were busy making some of the closest relationships of their lives, forging lasting and deep bonds with a support group of military brothers that remains intact until this very day. Their young wives, though, had no such support group. Maybe some had roommates, and friendships were certainly born and maintained. But most of the wives felt that they were on their own. Many of the wives had until recently been living in a room at their parents' home. Living as a married couple; making a first home – those are difficult transitions in the best of circumstances. And life at Fort Riley was not the best of circumstances. There was no mom close by to help. No longtime friends to whom wives could turn for support. They were on their own, making their way alongside husbands who were preparing to go to war. But these stories, tales of marriages begun in competition with military training, are in the Charlie Company minority. Of the 17 wives of trainees, only six were able to follow their husbands to Fort Riley to set up house. For the other enlisted wives the story of their marriages was really yet to begin. Those who were unable to follow their husband to the wilds of Kansas, whether because of a lack of money or because they were still in school, found themselves married in name only. Their husbands were letters, or rare phone calls. Sometimes their husbands were short visits – visits during which time alone was at a premium. The wives had to share their soldier boy with everyone from parents, to cousins, to friends. By and large, these distant wives still lived at home, most with their own parents and a few with their new in-laws. For them, learning who their husbands were and what married life was like would have to wait until their husband's duty to the nation was complete.

All of the wives of Charlie Company officers and non-commissioned officers were able to join their husbands for most of Charlie Company's training. As military wives, these women were used to moving, having to pick up stakes on a regular basis to relocate lives and schools. Being expected, though, was quite far from making it easy. Accommodations were sparse, ranging from small apartments to dilapidated trailers. The lives of their husbands were no less demanding than those of the enlisted men. Their husbands had to leave earlier, stay later, arrange for the training, and adjudicate the training – they were the ones tasked with transforming civilians into solders capable of survival in the crucible of war. They were gone constantly. When they were home they were often out of the house before 4am and back only in the late evening with just enough time to eat and sleep before the alarm rang once again. They were present, and they tried desperately to be husbands and fathers, but in many ways they could be neither. The families existed in a kind of limbo. The husbands were not gone to war yet, but they were most certainly gone. In marriages that had developed into true team efforts, all of the chores of life now fell to the wives. From getting children to school, taking care of illnesses, changing diapers on one child while solving a dispute between others, to keeping house, to getting dinner ready, to making sure that the husband knew that he was loved – the lives of these Charlie Company wives altered dramatically. They were married; they had husbands; but they were alone.

As some marriages sputtered to life and others abruptly shifted gears, they did so against the backdrop of a gathering darkness. Most of the young families didn't talk about it much at all, perhaps hoping that if they didn't stare at the future too closely it might somehow pass them by. On other occasions the future demanded attention; after all there were life insurance forms that needed filling out and there were burial wishes to be registered. Over each of the Charlie Company marriages Vietnam loomed, like a line of distant storm clouds bearing down on young lives. Each Charlie Company wife dealt with the uncertainty of war in her own way. Some turned to a deeper faith, others cried silently into pillows after their husbands went to training, and others retained the faith of youth that, while death might come for others, it would not come for their husbands. Their husbands would come back to them – after all, their lives were just starting.

———— † ————

We drove across the country in a purple 1955 Chevy. I was 18 and had never been out of town, and now I am driving to Kansas to be with Tom. I didn't think we were ever going to get there. I felt like I was going to Alaska. I had never been away from my mom. I wondered how I would be able to go on for three or four months without my mom close by. We were so young, and it was overwhelming. We'd never been in places where they had cockroaches. You would turn on the lights and those things ran all over. Three of us couples rented a house. A couple from Illinois lived upstairs, and we and Sue and Bill Reed rented rooms downstairs. The guys were gone on maneuvers a lot, but spent the evenings at home. We three girls spent time together, window shopping and making dinners. When the guys were able to come home we always had a nice dinner for them. It was fun. My first experiment at homemaking. But it was awkward too, living with people you really didn't know. When I talked with Tom about Vietnam it was always about when he was going to get home, about how we would get a house and start a family. It was always when I get home, not if I get home. After training we drove home in Tom's 58 Chevy. We stayed at my parents' house. We didn't have a lot of time. I remember taking him to the airport. It was so sad. I drove him to the airport myself, and it was hard to drive because I was crying so hard. It was hard. It was hard.

Vivian Conroy

We had it all planned to get married in August. But then his draft notice changed everything. We knew that he would be leaving, and that Vietnam was going on full blast. His training meant that he wasn't able to come home for an August wedding. I panicked. All the arrangements – bridesmaids' dresses, caterers. But he came home earlier, and that was fine. My mom and I sat down and crossed through the date on the engraved invitations and changed it from August 4 to July 29. We got married, and on the very next morning drove to Kansas. I'm 20 and I'd never lived away from home, and here I am on the road, a new wife, and we are headed to Fort Riley without knowing what to expect. We were worried about where I was going to live. Then it dawned on me that I would be all alone since he would be out in the field most of the time. We found a place for me to live; a little bitty basement apartment – all one room. That first night that I had to take him to the post I was just exhausted and cried myself to sleep. It was a big growing up experience for me. I got to meet some of the other wives who were in the same boat I was, especially June Layman and Sandy Ferro. June and I didn't want to be alone so much, so we went out looking for a job, but as soon as they found out that we had a husband in the military they wouldn't touch us. They knew that they were all shipping out. We knew that they were going to Vietnam, but as young as we were, as dumb as we were, and as in love as we were it didn't matter. I really thought that he would be coming home. But I also thought that I really wanted to have a baby in case it doesn't work out and he doesn't come home. We went home on his two-week leave before Christmas, then he left for Vietnam. It was while he was on the troop carrier that I decided that I had better go to the doctor. I'm pretty sure I'm pregnant. Sure enough I am. Very mixed emotions. I was tickled to death because that's what we wanted, but on the other hand I was going to have the baby without him here. He's in Vietnam. I went home and burst into tears and told my mom that I was pregnant.

Kaye French

Jack was the executive officer of a basic training company in Fort Leonard Wood when we had our first house, shortly after having Jack Junior. I found out that he was going to Vietnam from one of our neighbors. I was pushing Jackie in the stroller and one of the neighbors said, "What do you think about the guys going to Vietnam?" I said, "What?" And she said, "They volunteered to go!" So I turned around and went home and told Jack "What do you mean you're going to Vietnam?" He said, "Well, I was going to tell you. I just hadn't figured out a way to do it yet." When we went to Fort Riley it was a very good time. He was very involved in his training, and I spent much of my time with Jackie, reading and working on crafts and being a mom. I did the wifely thing. It was peaceful; we were a family and we were together. Jack would come home from training and sit in his shorts and read the paper, and Jack Junior would read it with him on the sofa. We only had a sofa, the rest was army furniture. When training ended he took me home to live with my parents. I was just totally naïve. I didn't have a grown-up perspective of what war was. It was what he wanted to do; it was his job. I wasn't real happy because he would be leaving his nine-month-old child. I hoped that Jack Junior would remember him when he came back. I didn't think about the bad things. I dreaded the loneliness, but didn't fear for his life. Once he had been helping his dad shingle the roof and was hopping around on one leg with a big 50-pound bag of shingles over his shoulder. I asked him what he was doing, and he said that he was practicing in case he ever lost a leg. That said who he was. I believed that he was invincible. He was bigger than life. I couldn't conceive of anything happening to him.

Nancy Benedick

———— † ————

Jacqueline Bradfield

After four years Jacqueline's relationship with John Bradfield had blossomed into fully fledged romantic love. John was a hard worker, determined to make a better life for himself out of sheer willpower. He dreamed of marriage and maybe owning a business in California, where things were supposed to be so much better than in Cleveland. In high school his good grades had resulted in him receiving permission to take the afternoons off so that he could work shifts at a department store as a kind of paid apprenticeship. He also worked weekends as a caddy at a local golf course. All the while his relationship with Jacqueline became more and more serious. The couple had not talked marriage yet, because she still had so many years of school left to go. After his graduation in June of 1965 John went to work for a tool manufacturing company. His pay was good. Jacqueline was progressing through school, and the future for the young couple seemed bright. John's choice of work over college, though, had left him open to the draft, and a greetings letter arrived from Uncle Sam in due course in the spring of 1966.

John Bradfield left for Fort Riley and training as part of Charlie Company in May of 1966, the same time that the couple discovered that Jacqueline was pregnant. The news hit Jacqueline like a thunderclap. She was in the 10th grade, and she was pregnant. Even worse, she knew that both her grandmother Vaselee and John's mother Varema were going to be furious. John tried to get ahead of the situation and told Jacqueline that he would be home in eight weeks from basic training and they would get married. He wasn't overjoyed, and he wasn't mad. He just took the news of her pregnancy in stride. She was going to be his wife, this was going to be his family, and he was going to work hard to make things right by everyone. But matters were far from simple. Vaselee and Jacqueline's father Roman were enraged by the news of Jacqueline's pregnancy. If anything John's mother, Varema, was even more upset, and she took her anger out on young Jacqueline. Varema told her son that he was too young to get married, that the whole thing was a mistake. But John dug in his heels. He was going to get married. He was going to give his child his name. He had never really had a father, and he was determined that the same would not happen to his child. It was John who took the lead in tamping down the raging family fires. In her young life Jacqueline had always felt alone, shut out by a family that couldn't show love. But with her pregnancy, she was more alone than ever. And the one man who had been there for her was gone in Fort Riley. It seemed like her whole world was falling apart.

In August of 1966 John came home for a short leave after basic training determined to marry Jacqueline. Vaselee and Roman remained angry, but they had seen the writing on the wall. Jacqueline had to get married, and, since she was under age, she needed their permission. Reluctantly Vaselee and Roman signed the papers. Varema, though, was another matter entirely. She remained violently opposed to the marriage, and John's strong sense of family duty forbade him from getting married without his mother's blessing. Before he knew it his short leave was over, and he had to leave to return to Fort Riley with the matter unresolved. So Jacqueline had to wave goodbye to John for a second time as he left for Advanced Individual Training – further along in her pregnancy, but no closer to marriage.

But family troubles, no matter how important, were not the center of John Bradfield's world. He was preparing to go to war. He knew that training was going to be taxing in the extreme, and that it was being done for their own good to weed out those who were not capable of standing and fighting in the face of combat:

When we got off that bus I was wondering, "Why are all of these guys hollering at the tops of their voices?" I figured that if they really wanted me to do something they would come and tell me instead of screaming as loud as they can. Some guys were crying, and others were having to do pushups from the minute that they got off of the bus. I just started smiling; glad that it wasn't me. Some sergeant saw me grin, though, and yelled, "Drop and give me 50!" I jumped down to the ground and pounded them pushups out fast and got back to my feet and looked at that sergeant. He said, "You are a smart one, huh? Get down and give me 50 more!" Those guys didn't tolerate any disrespect. They had a job to do to keep us alive. Maybe it was low crawling through the mud or working with an M14 – we did it all. My buddy Tim Fischer and I talked about how we could die in Vietnam. We weren't just training; we were training for war. We couldn't have any fear.

John Bradfield

John returned from training in December 1967 one last time before shipping out to Vietnam. Well aware that he was headed for war, he was determined to get married, regardless of any objections. Vaselee and Roman made their continued displeasure known, but went down to the courthouse and got the permission papers signed once again. John dealt with his mother. Jacqueline never knew what he said to her, but it finally worked. On December 21, 1966, John and Jacqueline wed at the courthouse in front of the local Justice of the Peace. Nobody came to attend the rushed service. Given all of the family strife, it somehow seemed fitting that it was just the two of them, alone. There was no wedding reception; no dance. The couple went to Vaselee's house where Jacqueline had already gotten a crib and other baby furniture ready. She had been forced to drop out of school, but was still holding down a job. Jacqueline knew that her near future was going to be difficult. Maybe other Charlie Company wives could be worried about Vietnam looming in their lives. Maybe other women in the country could be worried about their place in a changing society. But Jacqueline Bradfield had to worry about the here and now. She had to be worried about her baby.

——— † ———

Becky Lind

Having grown up on farms using a privy cover as a sled, college life was exciting and new for Becky Barth. She lived in Love Memorial Hall, a cooperative dorm where the 48 resident girls did all of the hall cleaning, shopping, meal preparation, and cleaning in two-week shifts. Her new boyfriend Herb Lind would drop by from his own college as often as he could, and he took Becky to the Love Hall spring formal. Everything was going well, and Becky's future was in sight. But Herb held down a part-time job in 1961 in an effort to help pay for his own college; a part-time job that limited the number of credit hours he was able to take at Nebraska Wesleyan, making him eligible for the draft. His draft notice arrived in the fall of 1961, but was deferred once Herb agreed to volunteer for service after his graduation. And just as things were looking so bright for Becky, Herb had to report for military duty.

After training and his first posting after Officer Candidate School, Herb came home, and the couple married on December 19, 1965. The Linds settled down into a small apartment in Saint Louis, near to Herb's next duty station. Becky busied herself with learning bridge and discerning what it meant to be an officer's wife, but she also wanted a job, which she found substitute-teaching in local schools.

In August of 1966 Herb's orders changed – he was called to duty at Fort Riley, Kansas, to help train a unit to go to Vietnam. But, with the quick formation of the 9th Infantry Division, there were no places for rent in the nearby towns of Manhattan or Junction City, so Becky took to visiting the offices of the local newspapers every morning at opening time. As soon as the papers came off of the presses, she and other military wives would look for housing advertisements and then race to be the first one to get to the listed address. One listing was for a trailer that wasn't even set up yet, but the Linds took it, offering to help hook it up and skirt it themselves.

The life of an officer's wife was anything but glamorous. Herb left for training at 5am and would not get back home until between 8 and 11 at night. Becky spent her days whipping the sorry trailer, and its even sorrier furniture, into some kind of livable shape. There wasn't enough water pressure for showers, so Becky always tried to have a bath ready for Herb when he came home – a bath that took hours to prepare because the water heater was so old and rickety. Often when Herb got home all he had the energy to do was gulp down some dinner, take his bath, and go to sleep. There was only one small kerosene furnace in the trailer, and it was a long way from the bedroom; so every night seemed to be cold. And, as it turned out, Herb had a bad habit of hogging the covers, leaving Becky's feet uncovered and icy. Only once did she try to warm those feet on Herb. As soon as they touched him, he jumped up, shouting "What the hell??" After that experiment Becky simply took to wearing a couple of pairs of Herb's military issue wool socks to bed. Throughout the trials and tribulations of both early married life and a new service life, Herb knew that Becky's support was crucial:

> Since it was known that we were headed to Vietnam we weren't even authorized family quarters in Fort Riley, so Becky and I lived in a trailer park. We only had one car, so she was either stranded or had to take me into work at the crack of dawn. It wasn't very luxurious, and it was tough on the wives, but we had a lot of fun. Even though it was supposed to be classified, it was no secret that we were off to Vietnam. Becky was very supportive of me, my career, and of my going to Vietnam. I was busy with the men so often; and her support meant the world to me.

> *Herb Lind*

In December Herb decided that it was high time to do something special. Training was still going full blast, and was more urgent than ever with deployment to Vietnam looming in less than a month. It was also time for Becky's birthday and for an anniversary celebration.

With events moving so fast the couple couldn't travel anywhere. It was just going to be dinner and a movie, but Becky knew that it was the thought that counted. But Herb got home later than expected, so the bath water was cold, necessitating a top-off. When it was ready Becky came out to find Herb sound asleep from the exertions of the day. She woke him up and took him to the bath, where he fell asleep again. It was too late to go out to dinner, so she cooked him something instead. He was so sorry. He was simply exhausted from training his men, and Becky understood and appreciated why he was so tired. It was okay. But he still wanted to go to the movies, to make things special. But he fell asleep again, this time while he was eating. There was nothing for it. She kissed him on the forehead and sent him off to bed. There would be time for special dinners and movies some other day. Becky, though, knew enough about war to know that death could come for anyone and that there might not be any more days in life to enjoy special days or movies with Herb. At the New Year's party she couldn't help but look around at the other couples and wonder which of them might be destroyed by Vietnam. But she managed to convince herself that that wouldn't happen to Herb. She told herself that he would return.

The morning of his departure for Vietnam was cold and snowy. She had packed up their meager belongings from the trailer and had stuffed their car to the breaking point, covering everything but the driver's seat. Then she drove to Custer Hill to say goodbye. There were cars and weeping family members everywhere as men clambered aboard the train. But there was no Herb Lind. The parking lot cleared out. The train was full. But still there was no Herb Lind. Eventually a straggler came running past and Becky asked after her missing husband. It turned out that Herb was in charge of the entire troop train and its thousands of passengers. He might not have time for a goodbye. Finally, though, a door to the train slid open and Herb jumped out. He gave Becky a quick hug and a kiss, telling her that he would be home by Christmas.

Their goodbye was short and sweet. And maybe it was better that way. There were no lingering tears, no dawdling. Just a quick military goodbye. As the train chugged to life, Becky turned to her car. It was the only one remaining in the parking lot. It was time to go back to Nebraska to find a new life for a year without Herb. She wasn't quite sure how she would react to the new situation. Now she was used to being married. Would she get used to being single again? As Becky put the key into the ignition she thought that she wanted to get a teaching job again. Picking up that interrupted dream would certainly help to pass the time and ward off the loneliness. She turned the key, and nothing. The car wouldn't start. AAA came and started the car, and warned Becky not to turn it off. It had a malfunctioning starter. Facing a five-hour journey in a driving snowstorm in a car that she couldn't shut off was just too much. Becky set out; she had no choice, but her tears made it even more difficult to see and navigate. She pulled over to a gas station and called her father. Could he drive up and help her bring the car home? She couldn't do it on her own. Her beloved Herb was gone and she didn't know if she would ever see him again.

———— † ————

Aurora Salazar

Meeting Jimmie Salazar had changed Aurora Gonzales. He was a rock in the sea of her despairing life. His family had welcomed her and had become the first real family that she could remember. Both Jimmie and the better life that he represented were intoxicating. Aurora wanted to marry Jimmie and be a part of this family forever, and Jimmie felt the same way. Aurora was young and beautiful, and her maturity belied her tender years. She quickly became his everything, and within months they were engaged. Weddings were a serious business in the Hispanic community of Texas. Regardless of past family frictions or bad feelings, this wedding was going to be a Catholic wedding, and a big one. On the wages of migrant workers and a housemaid there wasn't a lot of money to throw around, but that didn't matter. Weddings were worth the sacrifice. There was so much to be done. Jimmie's parents, Richard and Ramona, joined forces with Aurora's mother, Otillia, and gathered with many of the other members of the extended Gonzales and Salazar families for a bout of wedding planning. By the end of the evening, some of the details were settled, but both families agreed that there would have to be many more meetings before the chore was done and the wedding was ready. As the attendees made their way to their cars, Ramona took Jimmie and Aurora aside. She reached into her purse and pulled out a piece of mail for Jimmie: a piece of mail from the government. She said, "Son, you have a letter here from the army." Jimmie tore it open. He had been drafted and had a week to report for duty in San Antonio.

Aurora was devastated. It seemed like she was cursed never to find any measure of happiness in life. She had finally found something pure and permanent, someone who loved her and would not leave her, and the government was going to take him away. Take him away to war. Vietnam was well known in the Hispanic communities of Texas. Many young Hispanic men had already gone off to serve their country, and many had returned broken or not at all. Although Aurora was young, she knew that Jimmie's draft notice might also be his death knell. Jimmie, though, saw things differently. Perhaps because of his upbringing he was simply much more of a natural optimist than Aurora. Jimmie wanted to serve his country if it needed him. He assured Aurora that he would make it back from Vietnam. He assured her that he still wanted to be married, and to nobody but her.

Aurora was sure that it was the beginning of the end. In training he would forget her. The travel, the work, the new people – Aurora Gonzales would get lost in all of that shuffle. But, once basic training was over, Jimmie came home for a short leave. It turned out that he hadn't forgotten her and that he still wanted to marry her. He was going to Fort Riley, Kansas, for advanced training, but he was sure that he would get another leave before going to Vietnam. He wanted nothing more than to get married to her on that leave. So used to disappointment, Aurora wasn't quite sure how to take the news. So she just fell into Jimmie's arms. "YES!" she shouted to nobody in particular and as an answer to no specific question. Yes, she would get married, and yes, she would have a future.

As the days of Jimmie's training went by, to Aurora it was kind of like a game of marriage musical chairs. When would the training stop so the wedding could start? Nobody really knew, especially Jimmie. From his letters it seemed Jimmie even enjoyed training. The forced marches and endless classes were either tough or boring, but he was getting into the best shape of his life. He was making really close friends with some of the guys, specifically mentioning James Holstein and Mario Lopez. It was plain to Aurora that Jimmie and his Charlie Company pals were becoming close – becoming brothers. She was happy for him; happy that if he had to go to Vietnam he would be going to that dangerous place with people he loved and trusted. Next came a letter with a date – Jimmie would be coming home on leave in October. It was time to get the final preparations for the wedding done. Aurora Gonzales was finally going to get married.

I loved everybody I served with. I loved messing with the California guys. In training we would march all day long, and then we would settle down for the night. They would all get in their sleeping bags. I would crawl out in the dark and get some weeds and rub them together, which made a noise like a rattlesnake. Those fellows would come out of their sleeping bags just hollering. I would just mess with them all the time to keep their morale up. You would get so tired and homesick. You had to keep your mind occupied – you were headed to Vietnam. We had a job to do, and we all knew where we were going. We had to accept it; you couldn't run away. You had to keep going. So I just tried to make the best of it all for the guys. We were so close, so tight, when we left for Vietnam. Sometimes we wondered if we were going to make it home or not, but you had to put that out of your mind. Once you start thinking you might die, then you will. Aurora understood what I had to do, but I missed her, and what I really wanted to do was get married. I had a doubt in my mind that I wouldn't make it back, and I wanted to be married to Aurora and leave my dad behind a grandson to help keep him company.

Jimmie Salazar

Richard and Ramona surprised Aurora with a beautiful white wedding dress. It was the prettiest thing that she had ever seen. The wedding took place at her mom's house, and everyone was there from both sides of the family. It wasn't a particularly big or ostentatious ceremony, but it was the highlight of Aurora's life. Amid the celebration, all fear of Vietnam and of what could be slipped away. Aurora was 16 years old, and she was getting married, with everyone who mattered to her surrounding her. In retrospect Aurora can see that she was too young and too naïve to understand what could happen next. It was only in looking at Richard and Ramona that Aurora realized that something was perhaps wrong. They seemed withdrawn, and less joyous than was warranted by the day. She couldn't quite read it then, but today she understands. Richard and Ramona understood what Vietnam could do to their son, something that was lost to Aurora among all of the excitement of being 16 and in love.

There wasn't really a honeymoon for the Salazars; there wasn't time for it. There was a reception, some music and dancing, and then the young couple settled down to life. But Jimmie was only home for a week, and it was his last visit home before he shipped out for Vietnam. Everyone wanted to see him, to talk to him, to say goodbye. The young couple lived with Richard and Ramona for their week of marriage, which made it more like an odd kind of extended sleepover rather than the beginning of a real marriage. Sleeping in Jimmie's old room, breakfast with the family, people constantly around – it all hardly gave the young couple any time to be a young couple. But Jimmie was joyously happy. Half-jokingly he mentioned that he sometimes wondered if he would make it back from Vietnam, so he wanted to make sure that he left a child behind to bear his name. Amid the constant comings and goings Aurora laughed off the suggestion of Jimmie's mortality; they were too young and too in love to entertain such ideas.

Seven days passed in the blink of an eye, and Jimmie was gone. There were no tears shed; it was more like he was leaving on a short vacation. But when he got aboard that airplane he was gone; just gone. Aurora went back to live with her in-laws and went back to work. She started to write to Jimmie every day, hoping to make the time of their separation go just a bit faster. But it didn't seem to work, and the days while he completed his training at Fort Riley dragged on. It only took a few weeks for Aurora to notice her own physical changes. And a trip to the local health clinic confirmed it – she was pregnant. Even for a love-struck 16-year-old the enormity of the moment became clear. She was a pregnant teenager. She was married to a boy that she knew she loved, but in many ways barely knew. They had lived together as a couple for only a week, and that single week had been so busy that they had really never lived together alone at all. Now the husband she barely knew was off to a year of war, leaving her to face pregnancy and motherhood alone.

———— † ————

Mary Ann Maibach

Gary Maibach had recently graduated from high school and was taking classes at a small religiously affiliated college in Cleveland, which he hoped would aid him in his upcoming career helping to run the Maibach family store in Sterling, Ohio. Very religious and active in the local Apostolic Christian community, Gary returned from college to see that some of his best friends had moved on to marriage. He began to wonder who the Lord had in mind for his marriage, and took the question into prayer – a prayer that was answered. That very night Gary saw Mary Ann Graf, and knew that she was the one. He continued to pray on the matter; after all the two didn't know each other in the slightest. They had never even had a conversation. Gary Maibach took his conviction and belief to his church elder and informed him that the Lord had directed him to marry Mary Ann Graf. Gary and Mary Ann were members of two different congregations, so the elder of Gary's church wrote a letter to the elder of Mary Ann's church, who happened to be Mary Ann's uncle, Rudy.

Mary Ann, who had long since been focused on her nursing career and was resigned to the idea that she might never find love within the church, received something of an odd phone call from uncle Rudy asking if she could meet him at his son's farm. When she got there she was flabbergasted to learn that Rudy was there to deliver a proposal of marriage. He then gave her instructions about how prayerfully to make her decision regarding the proposal. Only after receiving these instructions did Mary Ann find out the identity of her potential fiancé, Gary Maibach. She was able to place him; he was a nice brother in the church, but she had never had any real contact with him. She was flattered, but couldn't imagine marrying someone she barely knew. Skeptically, Mary Ann left the meeting and took uncle Rudy's advice to pray over the question. She prayed for four weeks. She was concerned that there was an age gap of nearly four years, so she read her Bible. The page opened to 1 Timothy 4:12: "Let no man despise thy youth; but be thou an example of the believers, in word, in conversation, in charity, in spirit, in faith, in purity." After further prayer and deliberation, Mary Ann made her decision.

Gary learned of Mary Ann's agreement on Wednesday, May 26, 1965, and the couple's engagement was announced in church on Sunday, May 30, Memorial Day. The engagement lasted seven weeks, during which time the pair didn't actually see all that much of each other, living in two different towns and both busy working at their young professions. There were a few family meals, and some obligatory wedding planning. But the Gary and Mary Ann never kissed, hugged, or even held hands during their engagement. In July 1965 the young couple got married in a simple church ceremony followed by a short reception, complete with cake, punch, and sherbet.

The Maibachs' first stop as a married couple was the local draft board to deliver a copy of their marriage license. Since married men were at a lower draft status, there was little worry that Uncle Sam would come calling. With that out of the way, the Maibachs got down to the hard work that was their married life. One October afternoon, though, Mary Ann opened a letter from the government. It seemed that the draft rules had changed, and Gary was instructed to report to be inducted into the military. Married life was going to be put on hold.

Mary Ann knew exactly what the draft notice meant. As a nurse she knew all too well what horrors weapons could inflict upon the human body. They both also knew that Gary would join the military as a conscientious objector as the Apostolic Christian Church had a long history of non-violence. Its members could not touch firearms, much less wield them in battle. Gary would honor his call to service, which, as it had for so many church members before him, would result in his becoming a medic. And Mary Ann knew that medics were always a prime target for enemy fire in war. The young couple prayed over the future and prepared the best that they could. They both took a short time off of work before his departure and the family gathered for a send-off dinner. Then, on Valentine's Day of 1966, Gary shipped out for basic training. It was only a few days later that Mary Ann discovered that she was pregnant. She told Gary the news in a letter complete with cut-out appliqués of baby clothes. When Gary opened the letter in the barracks of his training facility, the appliqués spilled out across the floor. The tangle of little pictures of booties, diapers, and onesies announced his impending fatherhood for all to see.

After six weeks of basic training Gary was off to Fort Sam Houston for ten weeks of medical training. Having had enough of separation, Mary Ann found an apartment in San Antonio and went to join her husband. She had hoped that Gary would be able to live with her off base, but his training schedule wouldn't allow for that, so Mary Ann found herself alone. Each night Gary completed his training at 5pm. She would go to the base and pick him up, bring him home for dinner, and have to deposit him back on base by 11pm. It was an exhausting regimen that left Mary Ann feeling more alone than ever.

It was traumatic for Mary Ann. She got pregnant just before I got drafted. On the way home from taking me to the bus for training was the first time that she thought that she might be pregnant. Mary Ann is a strong person, a strong Christian, a giving person. Emotionally it had to be so difficult for her. When people still ask her today, "How did you do it?" she answers, "What choice did we have?" It was the way it was going to be, so we had to take it a day at a time. I had tremendous issues with not being able to be there for her. But I also had my training to do, and we found out on day one of medical training how serious it was going to be. A sergeant stood up in front of us and said, "Gentlemen you are about to embark on a course of training at the United States Army Medical Training Center. We will so well equip you to render service to your injured fellow service men that if you come upon a field of battle and carnage in Vietnam you will march up to any individual who may have traumatic amputation of the legs, arms, head, whatever, and you will present him with your certificate of accomplishment from the United States Army Medical Training Center; he will have no alternative but to recover."

Gary Maibach

After completing his medical training Gary was assigned to Fort Riley, and Mary Ann soon followed. The couple moved to Manhattan on July 4 in the middle of a blazing heatwave, and the tiny apartment lacked air conditioning – so life at first was miserable, becoming especially so for Mary Ann as her pregnancy progressed. When her water broke, Gary had to run to the post office to call the hospital, because their landlords didn't allow them to use the apartment's phone. They arrived at Irwin Army Hospital just before midnight, and Mary Ann was the only patient in the entire facility. Because of his training schedule, Gary couldn't stay, leaving Mary Ann to face a long and difficult birth on her own before the safe arrival of their baby daughter Karen.

Four days later Mary Ann was able to return to the Manhattan apartment with her newborn. By the time Gary received two weeks of home leave before Christmas, Mary Ann and Karen were both well enough to travel, and the couple returned to Ohio for a send-off. There were family dinners, plenty of people lavishing attention on baby Karen, and many well-wishers at church. But to Mary Ann it seemed like a pall was hanging over everything. It all seemed strained, because everyone knew that Gary was departing for war. Despite it all, Mary Ann was determined to see Gary off and returned with him to Fort Riley. His train was due to leave at 6am amid a snowstorm, and Gary's mother, Alma, had come along to help. Everyone got up in the pitch dark, bundled up the baby, and drove to Custer Hill for their goodbyes. But the train was delayed; they were told to come back at 10am. So it was off to find some breakfast. But the train was delayed, they were told to come back at 1pm. So they went back to the apartment. All of the back and forth, though, was noticeably wearing on Alma, who was seeing her son off to war. With a deep sigh, and tears running down her face Alma said, "I can't take any more of this." She couldn't bear going back to Fort Riley for a third time. At 1pm the train was finally ready. Gary bent over to kiss Karen, his little sunflower, and then hugged Mary Ann. Clutching Karen tightly in her arms, Mary Ann watched Gary trudge up Custer Hill through the snow, not knowing if she would ever see him again. Mary Ann had been dreading this day for so long, but amidst her tears she realized something. As soon as Gary was on that train she could start counting down the days until his return.

———— † ————

Judy Lilley

While she was still recovering from the tragic loss of her sister Cheryn, Judy Wittman had thrown herself into her studies at both high school and beauty school as a way to get by. One Saturday a friend dropped by and mentioned that her boyfriend had stopped over with a friend of his. She wondered if Judy would like to join them on an informal double date. Judy liked the boy she met that day, Larry Lilley, just fine. He seemed nice, and was a little different than what she was used to. His father owned a Triumph dealership in Lancaster, and Larry was something of a motorcycle racing legend in the area. He had finished high school and was in junior college hoping eventually to study law. Larry was cute, and so different that he intrigued Judy, and the couple began dating. By the spring of 1966 Judy began to wonder if Larry could be something more than a boyfriend, and she went to visit him at his apartment in Lancaster. While he was in the kitchen, she noticed an envelope on the table with "HA! HA!" written on it. She pulled out the letter to see what was so funny and found his draft notice. Now she was sure that the relationship wasn't going to work.

As Larry was about to ship out for basic training he gave Judy a kiss and asked her to write every day. She wrote dutifully, and the couple got to know each other better than ever before through letters. When Larry came home for a short visit after basic training, the couple picked up right where they had left off, enjoying what little time they had before Larry had to return to Fort Riley. It was only when he got ready to leave that second time that Judy realized how special she was to him. He asked her to drive his split window 1963 Corvette up to Fort Riley to visit him. That car was his pride and joy; *nobody* got to drive that car. Judy's mother, June, took a little convincing, but she really did think the world of Larry. Everyone did. So her mom gave her blessing. Judy was off to Fort Riley.

When she finally arrived at the base, Judy had no idea where to find Larry. He was off training somewhere, and she had been lucky just to find Fort Riley at all much less anything or anyone specific. There she was, a beautiful teenage girl cruising a military training base in a slick split window Corvette. Guys came out of the proverbial woodwork to whistle, ogle, and generally admire Judy and her beautiful ride. After a few stops, and besotted conversations, Judy finally worked out where she could find Larry. As she drove toward him, he recognized the car immediately and jumped up and down to flag her down. He stood there with a buddy, obviously excited to see her. With an expectant smile she rolled down the window to greet him. He said, "Hi baby! Pop the hood!" Larry first had to show the Corvette's engine off to his buddy. Reuniting with Judy was a distinct second.

Judy stayed in Kansas for only a couple of days, and Larry was so busy with training that there wasn't much time for them to spend together. But when he was able to get away from the base, he brought his buddies with him to meet Judy. It was plain to her instantly that these guys had become brothers. They all seemed so at ease in one another's company. They all seemed so young. Two of the guys she knew well already, Kenny Frakes and Timmy (Tim) Johnson. They had grown up with Larry and were his best friends in the world. Kenny had been Larry's roommate since high school and had been a fixture in the apartment when Judy had come over to visit and spend time. Somehow they had all been drafted together and were going to Vietnam together. Another guy had joined the group as well, Don Peterson. While Judy didn't know him, he was from the same area and had immediately gravitated toward the other California guys in the unit, where they had also all bonded over their love of cars – especially Larry's beloved Corvette. Lilley, Frakes, Johnson, and Peterson. They were all fast friends – where you found one, you found them all. Judy came to love Larry's friends; they were all such a big part of who he was. And it turned out that Don Peterson was married. Judy couldn't help but wonder what it must be like to be married to a guy who was about to ship out to Vietnam.

After getting to know many of the Charlie Company guys, Judy flew home and went back to work. It was only a few days, though, before she received a call from Fort Riley. Larry was in the hospital with pneumonia. It was so bad that he might die. It was touch and go for a while, but Larry made it and was given a short leave to go home and recover. Once back in California he took Judy aside. Being in the hospital had given him time to think. This whole thing was serious. Vietnam was serious. He was serious – about Judy. He wanted to get married before he left for war. He knew that he would be coming home from Vietnam; that much was sure. And he knew that he wanted to come home to a wife, and that wife was her. It was all quite sudden. She loved him; she was sure of that. But Judy did ask if maybe they should wait until after he got home from Vietnam. However, Larry didn't want to wait. He knew that it was right, and he wanted to do it now.

Larry went back to Fort Riley to finish his training, and the wedding would take place over his Christmas leave prior to shipping out for Vietnam. June never tried to interfere. She loved Larry and was happy for her daughter. Planning for the wedding had to be rushed, but everyone on both sides of the family gathered in the Episcopal Church in Bakersfield on December 16, 1966. There was a big reception in the church following the ceremony, and then Larry's parents took the new family to dinner. Just like that, though, what had seemed like a dream was over. Larry's leave had only lasted a week – including a brief honeymoon at Lake Tahoe – and then he had to return to Fort Riley.

> Training together turned us into brothers. Things that you didn't think you were capable of you just did it in Vietnam because we had become so close. The love of your buddies made you do things you never thought you could. Even with the dangers, there was never a question whether I was coming home. I knew I was coming home. I knew that Vietnam would be like living in a nightmare, but I was so confident that I was coming home. Going to Vietnam was tougher on Judy than it was on me. She didn't know what to expect, what was going on. I figured that I would tell her just enough once I got there to give her some details, but wouldn't really let her know what I was going through.

> *Larry Lilley*

On New Year's Eve Judy got into a car determined to drive to Fort Riley to say goodbye to her man, making it there in the nick of time. Judy waved goodbye to her husband amidst a snowstorm. They had been married for less than a month, and the only time they had spent together was their honeymoon. They were married, sure enough, but most of their relationship had been conducted at long distances of one type or another. How well did they really know each other? As Larry Lilley sat there on the train and watched out of the window as Judy waved, he understood how difficult the whole thing had to be for her. He had only been her husband for such a short time, and now he was headed to war. They really hadn't talked about what war might mean. He had his fears, but he hadn't shared them with her. He loved her with all of his heart, and he felt sorry for her. He vowed to write to her every day. But he also decided to keep the worst from her. She would have enough to worry about in her life without having to be concerned about whatever darkness was gathering in Vietnam.

———— † ————

Esther Windmiller

When Bernie shifted from being a pastor of an Evangelical Covenant church to accepting a ministry as a chaplain in the 9th Infantry Division, his wife Esther wasn't even really sure what all that meant. Military life and the possibility of war were foreign concepts, and the move was just another step in his calling and the faith journey of the Windmiller family. And everything started out well. The military paid to have them moved, their quarters in Fort Riley were better than anything they had ever lived in, and the military community welcomed them thoroughly.

Esther decided that she very much liked her new military life. There were 21 new chaplains at Fort Riley, most of whom had wives and young families. So there was a wonderful support group of wives, a PX to shop at, lots of children around for play dates – Fort Riley was its own, like-minded community. Bernie and the other chaplains were busy with chapel and tending to the spiritual needs of the men, and the wives helped out by baking cookies, hosting dinners, and generally providing the young soldiers a home away from home. It was also an incredibly busy and rewarding time for Esther as a mother. Beth was now ten years old, and, Becky, the youngest, was three. From parties with officers' wives to science fair projects, life at Fort Riley was so fulfilling and busy that Esther really didn't have time to think of what was coming next.

The first time that Esther really let herself stop and think about the future was at the last group meeting of the chaplains' wives. Everyone was going to be going their separate ways soon, with their husbands going off to war. So she asked the group, "How am I going to get through this year?" One of the wives spoke up: "Get a bottle and a box of candy." Another told her to listen to the news every morning for news from Vietnam. If the news was bad, listen to it twice. There seemed to be no other advice – just live with it and deal with it. Regardless of the community that had existed for a short time at Fort Riley during training, Esther realized that during the next year she would be alone.

We didn't know at first that we were headed to Vietnam; they were just rebuilding the 9th Division. I was one of the first two chaplains in the 2nd Brigade. It was all a bit scary for Esther. She came from a very small town, and even though she had gone to college, she was still a small-town girl. She hadn't traveled a whole lot, so the whole thing was an adventure for her. She really did like that larger paycheck, though. It was a big change. And she got to hear me talk about everything. I stayed up all hours of the day and night welcoming the new soldiers as they got off of the busses. I went through much of their training with them, and it was a real eye opener. I had been through training before when I was enlisted, but as a chaplain it's different. One day I was marching out with my troops on a bivouac area. It was a ten- or twelve-mile route march, and I stayed at the back of the pack. And the soldiers started telling jokes and cussing. After a while the first sergeant had all he could take of that knowing that I was there to hear it all. Suddenly he turned around and yelled, "You fucking guys shut your goddamn mouths! The chaplain is here!"

Bernie Windmiller

Bernie drove the family home to Ohio over his final Christmas leave, finding a house for rent outside of Wellington. Esther thought that she would take it well; after all she had been separated from Bernie when he had been in Korea. But it didn't work out that way. She waved at the airport as he left, and the kids hugged their daddy goodbye. Once home, she bundled the children off to their activities for the day. Then it was such a little thing that set her off. She glanced over and saw Bernie's jacket draped over the back of the chair. The way that it hung there made it feel like he was dead, not just gone. The vision hit Esther like a physical blow. She couldn't take it. She fell to her knees in despair and looked to a nearby table where her family Bible sat open. She looked at the page. Psalm 27:14 – "Wait on the Lord: be of good courage, and He shall strengthen thine heart: wait, I say, on the Lord." She wiped the tears away and crawled into bed. She never feared for Bernie's safety again for his entire year in Vietnam.

24 Dec 1966

The days of separation and loneliness have begun.

It was so sad to leave you and the children at the airport, and it wasn't any easier for you I know. All of us are emotional people (I think more than others) and are so close knit as a family – we depend on each other, thrive on each other – we just belong together. All this creates somewhat of a death experience for us. But just think of the reunion! That will be a day!! I feel for you honey, for I'm convinced this separation is much harder for you than for me. How are the children? My heart aches for them. Keith is such a funny little man... The days before my departure he just never seemed to realize what was going to happen. Even on the way to the airport. But at the last moment when I kissed him goodbye, he turned very somber and had that lost look on his face. Perhaps it is just his age. It was a hard experience for all of us, and no matter how long I stay in the ministry it will not become any easier.

[After I made it back to Fort Riley] Jim invited me up to his room. We just sat and talked for a couple of hours. He took me back to my room. When I got out I thanked him and he said, "Bernie, I just couldn't see you sitting alone in your room after you had left Esther."... I've thought so much about calling you tomorrow but decided against it. I don't want to make things harder than they already are.

Well darling I guess that is about it for my first letter. I love you and the children so very much and miss you already. These words you'll hear hundreds of times in the next year. But I mean them from the bottom of my heart each time I write them and they shall be fresh each time they are penned. I'm glad the separation has started, for now we can look to the end.

Your faithful and loving husband,
Bernie

CHAPTER 3

WARTIME

It was hard to build a marriage without Larry there. We had only been married for a couple of weeks before he left for Vietnam. It was a long, hard year for both of us. He probably kept busier than I did. I rode down to Fort Riley with his parents to say goodbye at the train station. My folks drove down separately. We were all at the station, and we waited, and waited, and waited. But they had loaded the soldiers somewhere else, and drove though the train station where everybody was waiting for them and never stopped. That was the hardest part. We were waving at everybody, but the train wouldn't stop. The drive back home was one of the hardest of my life.

Kay Lukes

I brought Lynn up to Louisville to go back to Fort Riley. There was snow on the ground. I cried the whole way home; I was so scared that something was going to happen to him. When we got home I kept my emotions to myself, but I would cry at night when Greg [the couple's son] was asleep. If Lynn hadn't have written me nearly every day I don't think I would have made it. I went back to Albany and lived in the house next door to my mom. It was so hard being a married woman with a child pretty much moving back home. Mom was there all the time, telling me what to do. The house had an outhouse and a well. No running water. I never will forget what Greg said one time. I said, "Greg, go and get me a glass of water." He did, and came back and said, "Mom, can we move next time to a house that has a bathroom and running water?" Boy, don't you think that that just killed me? I said, "Yes, son. We will." That broke my heart. I got a job at the factory. Mom butted in a lot. I had a miserable life that year. It was worse than it was when I lived at home. I had lived on my own for so long that it was a real step backwards. But I never let Lynn know anything about it. I never told him about my hardships. No way. There was no way I was going to tell him about the bad things. I would tell him that everything was fine here. Maybe he knew that I wasn't telling the truth, but anyway. His letters to me were about him being fine, loving Gregory, and when he would be home.

Norma Crockett

May 22 1967

Well I made it here o.k. and have seen some pretty country... I miss you a lot already. I cried a little on the plane, but I tried to be brave.

And I remember that you said keep looking to the future, and it really helped. And I hope you do the same, because when I get back I am going to make you my wife, and the happiest wife on earth. I know it is hard to keep from crying, because I feel like crying now. But that won't do any good. I still have to stay a year, so keep smiling as much as possible. And believe me I will be back to marry you... It's a job that has to be done, and I am going to do it well. And I will feel real proud of you and myself that God is with us and will help us all the way.

Letter from Jim Rademacher to his fiancée Mary Ann

Historians can argue about the efficacy of his planning, and about the sophistication of his tactics, but in 1967 General William Westmoreland, Commander of United States Military Assistance Command, Vietnam, stood ready to take the war to the enemy. Westmoreland had long hoped to use the overwhelming firepower advantage possessed by American forces to bring the Viet Cong and North Vietnamese forces to violent heel, but the American buildup had been slower than he had predicted and enemy resilience had been greater than he had expected. Responding to the call for more men and more military investment, in 1966 President Lyndon Johnson, on advice from Secretary of Defense Robert McNamara and General Westmoreland, had approved a massive troop buildup in Vietnam, resulting in a total draft call during 1966 of 382,010, the largest single yearly draft call of the Vietnam War. It was this draft call that had swept up the young lives of Charlie Company.

The trainees of 1966 poured into South Vietnam, raising US troop levels there first to over 300,000 at the beginning of 1967 and then near to 500,000 by year's end. These men were Westmoreland's mailed fist, ready to put his plans to first search for and then destroy communist forces to the martial test as the war slipped into high gear. From the Mekong Delta to the DMZ, the "Boys of '67" were the shock troops of search and destroy, bearing the brunt of Westmoreland's war. At the macro level 1967 meant seizing the initiative, especially in the area surrounding Saigon, in massive operations from Junction City to Coronado II. 1967 meant the US Marines digging in along the forlorn DMZ, resulting in clashes at Khe Sanh and Con Thien. 1967 meant attempting to sever the Ho Chi Minh Trail and to bomb the North Vietnamese to peace talks. On the micro level, though, 1967 meant the shattering of young lives, and severance of young relationships.

For Charlie Company soldiers, war had first meant a hasty goodbye to loved ones and then a three-week trip to Vietnam on the converted World War II troopship USS *General John Pope*. On January 30, 1967 Charlie Company finally arrived in Vietnam. Sweat poured off of the young soldiers as they made their way to shore and then went by convoy to their new home of Bear Cat just north of Saigon. No amount of training could have adequately prepared the boys of Charlie Company for what they were about to face. The searing heat and relentless humidity packed a combined, and physically draining, punch. Monsoon downpours brought a torrent of rainfall that few Americans had ever endured, leaving soldiers perpetually soaked to the bone. For many, though, it was the smell of Vietnam that was their first memory of the country – a pervading smell of rotting jungle growth, city squalor, cooking odors, and natural fertilizer. The tiny Vietnamese civilians, whether buying and selling rats for dinner, chewing betel nut, or squatting on the side of the road to pee, were the objects of intense curiosity. How did they live that way, and could they be the enemy in disguise? As the convoy whizzed down the streets crowded with bicycles, mopeds, and pedestrians, the boys of Charlie Company couldn't help but wonder about everything they saw, from the grass hooches to the mamasans talking in their sing-song and unfamiliar language.

Within days of its arrival in country, Charlie Company was out on its first operations. While everyone in the unit knew that the enemy could be out there, and feared that he might be, it was just the learning of the ropes of how to be a soldier in Vietnam that first and fully occupied every mind. Hacking through the jungle was different than route marches on the plains of Fort Riley. Muscles ached, skin burned, tempers flared, and sergeants yelled. From searing heat, to biting leeches, to swarms of mosquitoes, it seemed like the country itself was out to get the young American soldiers.

As the wonder of being in such a different country and environment began to give way to the sweltering misery of the daily grind of military life, many in Charlie Company began to wonder what the future might hold. Bernie Windmiller spoke for many when he wrote home to Esther:

> Dick and I were talking today and mentioning how hard it is going to be to one day see some of these boys we have become so attached to and so personal with looking up at us with a lifeless face. Undoubtedly this year will have a major impact on my life.

As it turned out the war in Vietnam was not overly dangerous for Charlie Company just yet. The first month of operations in and around Bear Cat were conducted in a relatively "safe" area and were intended to acclimate the soldiers to their new environment and to teach them how to fight a real war. Digging ditches, burning shit from the latrines, setting night ambushes, calling in marking artillery rounds, burning off leeches – the humdrum of military life; all of these experiences continued the bonding process among the soldiers of Charlie Company. They complained about the tedious labor that was military life, they wondered if the real war would start, and they endlessly cleaned their weapons – but they did these things together. Every playful curse word, every shared picture, every practical joke further cemented deep bonds of comradeship. The military thrives on camaraderie and small unit loyalty. Men risk their lives in battle to ensure the survival of their best friends of their entire lives, not to defend patriotism or a flag. The journey to Vietnam and the first shared experiences of the war in that country transformed the men of Charlie Company from trained individual soldiers into a coherent military unit capable of enduring battle, forging intimate bonds that persevere to this day.

———— † ————

Ernie had gotten his draft notice right after we got married. I had convinced myself that Ernie wasn't going to Vietnam because he was married. So it came as a real shock. We went and had a will made out before he left, but I still just couldn't seem to accept it. I had a job with social services and worked every day to make sure that when he got back we had a little bit saved. I lived with Ernie's mom for six months, and then moved back home to my old room. I read the news every day to try and find out about what he was involved in. I found out everything I could. I didn't go out with my friends anymore; I just didn't feel up to being that happy I guess. I wrote him every day, and every week I sent him a care package with brownies or cookies. He wanted a divorce while he was in Vietnam. Later I found out that he didn't think that we understood what he was going through in

Vietnam. He just wanted out and didn't want to be married anymore. Later I found out that there was some very bad stuff happening to him in Vietnam at the time, but I didn't know it then. He was changing from the man I had married.

Jeannie Hartman

While their husbands were forming perhaps the most meaningful group connections of familiarity and comradeship of their entire lives, the wives of Charlie Company were embarking on a period of intense loneliness unmatched in their adult experience. For the four wives of relatively long-term marriages, 1967 meant losing a trusted partner, someone they had come to love fully and to depend upon for everything from help with the children to deep emotional and spiritual support. For these women half of their lives was suddenly missing, thrusting them into the unfamiliarity of being alone again after having their life defined as operating as part of a couple. It meant playing the uncomfortable dual roles of both mother and father for the family's children – children who were often too young to understand their fathers' absence. For the other wives of Charlie Company, 1967 meant losing a husband that they loved dearly, but in many ways barely knew. Their marriages were young, sometimes only days old, and still full of unbridled passion and the human need to set bonds of intimacy and shared community.

Numerous studies have concluded that the dawning days of marriage are the most important to a couple's continued wedded success. Beyond the simplistic learning of the physicalities of intimacy, the deep complexities of early marriage revolve around the discovery and negotiation of new boundaries. Young couples must first negotiate a secession from the influence of their own parents, often particularly of their mothers. Husbands and wives have to come to grips with new emotions, both shared and singular, and develop a level of empathy unlike any before experienced in their young lives. Within these broader spheres, smaller but no less significant steps have to be taken toward a division of labor within the home, and a unity of household finances. Intellects must meet, arguments must be undertaken, and spirituality must be addressed.[4] These early, heady days of infinite discovery that serve to define marriages are difficult to negotiate in the best of times. In 1967 the vast majority of Charlie Company wives were left to wander alone through these formative milestones of marriage. Like a broken record skipping past the first song, these marriages would actually start only a year later, with much of the formative stage of marriage having been skipped or arrived at by unilateral decision.

Many of the Charlie Company wives were left to move back home with their parents, or to perhaps join their new in-laws while their husbands were at war. These new wives found themselves relegated to bedrooms in houses that were under the control of parents. They were adults. They were married. But it was like they hadn't budged at all. They remained marooned in their childhood beds only masquerading as married adults. The vagaries of the Vietnam-era military draft made it all much worse. The ready availability of draft deferments meant that only roughly 10 percent of the male draft-age population actually served in the military during the Vietnam War, with even fewer seeing combat. This meant that while the lives of the Charlie Company wives were put on hold, the lives of their boomer generational compatriots thundered ahead at full speed All around them, their friends were graduating, getting married, having children, getting jobs, surfing and having fun, going to movies, and generally getting on with life. Charlie Company wives were stuck in their rooms, pining for their next letter from the war zone. Many Charlie Company wives did have jobs of their own, and found fulfilling ways to spend their time while their husbands were away. But even in those cases it seemed to the wives that the war slowed their lives to a crawl, while those around them who did not have a husband in the wartime military threw their lives into high gear. It all left a feeling of being distinctly unfair.

The world of 1967 was a hive of activity; a quick glance at the television or a stroll by the record store revealed a year laden with excitement around every cultural corner. Lunar Orbiter 3 mapped the surface of the moon in preparation for Neil Armstrong's famous "giant leap for mankind." Skirts got shorter than ever before. The whole music world, from Janis Joplin to Jimi Hendrix, seemed to join together in the

Monterey International Pop Music Festival. The Beatles changed the way the world consumed music with their release of *Sgt. Pepper's Lonely Hearts Club Band.* For the politically minded there was everything from an increasing number of anti-Vietnam War protests to the transformative moment of the Six-Day War in the Middle East.

Charlie Company wives certainly noticed the world around them in 1967, buying records and keeping up with fashions like others their age. But, where the glitter, glitz, and endless possibility of 1967 was the lived focal point for others of their generation, it was all just background noise for the wives of Charlie Company. While their friends were studying for college classes, buying homes, or trying to get noticed in mini-skirts, Charlie Company wives were just trying to find out whether their husbands were still alive. While so many other women were marching forward to futures that were brighter than ever, Charlie Company wives had the brakes slammed onto the journey of their lives by war and uncertainty.

> I was almost a senior when I found out I was pregnant and had to drop out of high school. Right after that, Jose found out that he had been drafted. It was so scary. He had to leave for war, and I was at home pregnant. We were married, and then before I knew it he was gone. It was kind of crazy. I was too young. I still lived at home, and my mom was kind of mad at me, so I didn't get much help from her until after the baby was born. It was a very lonely feeling. Belinda was born on February 10, 1967. The Red Cross found Jose in a foxhole somewhere to tell him that he had a baby girl. I wrote him letters once a week telling him all about Belinda. In his letters he never told me what was going on over there. He just said that he was okay. I knew that he was fighting, but that is all I knew. It was very lonely. My grandmother died in April. She and I were so close; it was such a hard time. My grandma was everything. I threw myself into taking care of Belinda, and I knew in my heart that Jose was coming back, because grandma had told me that Belinda had her arms wide open waiting to see her father.

Noemi Sauceda

——— † ———

Amid the wondering and loneliness the wives of Charlie Company had either to keep marriages alive or to construct marriages anew at long distance. For that considerable task, there was really only a single tool – the letter. Husbands and wives alike became inveterate correspondents during Vietnam, often writing to each other on a daily basis. The tool, though, was flawed. Letters often took weeks to deliver, which meant that the news they contained was almost always stale. For their part, Charlie Company soldiers wrote home about everything under the sun, from food, to danger, to love. For California native and 1st Platoon member John Sclimenti there was an especially important issue to discuss with his parents and his fiancée. His girlfriend, Iris Boyd, had gotten pregnant on her visit during John's training at Fort Riley. John was determined to do the right thing, and a marriage was soon in the works. While Iris's parents took the news well, John had some long-distance cajoling to do with his own parents. After learning of his parents' unhappiness during March 1967 John wrote from Vietnam:

> I am not mad. I expected it. I still love you all. I know you don't like Iris. Well, I am still going to marry her. Some how, some way... I am tired of threats. I am sick and tired of doing things behind your backs. I thought you would take the news better. Well I guessed wrong. It sounds like I am pissed. Well, I am... You aren't living with her. I am not ruining my life... I am sorry if I burden you so much... I know you think Iris caused all of this excitement. Well, I guess I did.

After having blown off some much needed steam, John followed two days later with another letter:

> I apologize for that last nasty letter. I was tired and had just come off a mission. I was in swamps up to my butt. I am sorry that I upset you. Try to forgive your wonderful son. I am glad that your last letter was better. It really set my mind at ease.

Drafted out of Detroit, and having completed training in Fort Polk, Louisiana, Jim Rademacher came to Charlie Company as one of its early replacement troops. The draft had taken Jim away from Mary Ann, his bride to be, just before the couple could get married. The high school sweethearts thought it best to postpone a wedding until Jim's return. Rademacher's letters home balanced news from the war with hope for the future:

> We went ashore in a place called the Rung Sat. It is a real heavy jungle. There we set up an ambush and went on small recon patrols. I was the point man, the first man to lead the way. The jungle was so thick that I had a knife about $2^1/_2$ feet long and I had to cut my way through. We walked through mud up to my waist and water was everywhere. To sleep at night we had to cut down small trees and make us a mattress so we wouldn't be laying in the mud, and that was the hardest mattress I ever laid on. Every three hours, I had to get up and guard so no VCs would try to come around...
>
> You keep telling me we should get engaged in Hawaii, but I can't hardly get my R and R in Hawaii, because mostly all the married guys get to go there before the single guys can. The only way we can get engaged is if I would send you a diamond ring, but that won't be very nice. But it would be up to you if you wanted me to. I would like to get married on leave too, just as much as you want to. But maybe we better wait until I get adjusted to the good old civilian life first, because you never know what can happen.

The vast majority of letters were occupied with the mundane details of military life – the weather, the endless slogging through the countryside, and the doings of friends. One constant source of written angst was the horrible food. Soldiers detested C Rations, and were desperate for anything sent from home – and they were so happy when they got it. In June John Sclimenti wrote:

> Well I got the food. It was great! But I stunk out all the guys with the cheese. It was real good. Me and this other Italian kid ate it up!... The beer was good too. It sure had been a long time since I had Coors.

The men also yearned for news from home and the "normal" world that they had left behind. It was almost like they needed to be reminded that home really existed. A rural native of the farmlands of Illinois, 3rd Platoon member Steve Hopper's letter to his parents stands as typical:

> Dad, have you started harvesting the corn yet? Did the crops turn out good this year? Do you have quite a few baby pigs? I hope everything is fine, and I wish I was there to help you with all the work. Now dad, be careful, take it easy and don't overwork yourself. I want you and mom in good shape when I come home so Jen [his fiancée] and I can take you out some night...
>
> Mom, I guess you got my letter concerning Jen's car insurance didn't you? Well mom, would you sign for the money so I can help her out with the car? Mom, let me know if you don't want to, but I sure wish you would. After all, soon it will be both mine and her car.
>
> Jen sure does think an awful lot of all of you. Every letter I get she always mentions you and the girls in it. She told me about the pickled beets you gave them and her and her mother argued over who would get the most.

Letters served many purposes, from sharing to growing to loving – all from afar. But, as the war lingered Charlie Company couples were faced with the more difficult question of how best to communicate the dark side of war.

—— † ——

Jacqueline Bradfield

After their hurried marriage before the local Justice of the Peace John Bradfield had returned to Fort Riley shortly after Christmas, leaving Jacqueline to live with her grandmother Vaselee to await the arrival of their first child. As Jacqueline's due date neared, all of the drama that had engulfed both sides of the family dissipated as if by magic, and the Bradfields and Boyds were united as never before. There wasn't long to wait, with little Barnard making his first appearance on January 8, 1967 – news that reached John after he had already boarded the troopship for Vietnam. The next months were going to be difficult – maybe the most difficult period in Jacqueline's life. But she met those days with determination, deciding that she was finally in control of her own future. And that future was going to be bright.

> We were out on the troopship in the middle of the Pacific, and Ronnie Gangler brought me a message from the Red Cross. I had a son! Another guy named Fred Kenney got the news that his son was born on pretty much the same day. We looked at each other and made a vow that we were going to survive the year and get home to see our children. One way or another I was going to get home to see my son.

> *John Bradfield*

As is the case for any new birth, the days after Barnard's arrival were hectic and passed in a blur of activity. Having Vaselee there as live-in help was a boon to Jacqueline, who was still only 17 years old. Regardless of past frictions in their relationship, Vaselee had much to teach young Jacqueline about motherhood – everything from how to mix formula to how to give baths – and Jacqueline needed the help. And John's mom Varema was there too. Barnard was her first grandbaby, and John had been the apple of her eye – so the connection was immediate and profound. Varema tried hard to be helpful – perhaps a bit too hard. It was all done with love, and with the best of intentions, but a clash of the grandmas developed over Barnard and his future, which caught Jacqueline squarely, and quite uncomfortably, in the middle.

As the grandmothers jockeyed for positions of control and influence, Jacqueline couldn't help but feel like something of a prisoner. It seemed to her that it was her time to be an adult. But here she was living in a room in her grandmother's home. And, although she loved them all the more for their efforts, Barnard was essentially being raised by others. Jacqueline began to dream of a way out. Amid the flights of fancy something else dawned on her. She was married. In the hubbub of having a child and balancing needy grandmas, her marriage had been easy to forget. She was alone, but part of a couple. She and John had never even lived on their own for a day, much less learned what it really meant to be married. What would it be like to live with a man? What would it be like to raise Barnard with a husband instead of two grandmas?

Someone told Jacqueline about a military program that helped to find and subsidize housing for dependents of deployed soldiers. After filling out all of the necessary paperwork, Jacqueline found that as a young mother she was at the top of the list. For once the military bureaucracy seemed to work quickly, and Jacqueline moved out and into an apartment of her own at the very reasonable price of $32 a month for rent. Since John had set up an allotment to send much of his pay every month straight to Jacqueline, she found herself in the very unusual circumstance of having plenty of money on hand to afford both rent and expenses. The excitement of moving out, decorating, and generally being an adult was a real tonic. Jacqueline was determined that she was going to have a real house, home, family, and life waiting for her husband when he returned from Vietnam.

Jacqueline's first step in constructing independence was to join the church. She was lucky, her new apartment was in walking distance of the church and the sanctified women who had changed her life. She attended services every Sunday, with Barnard in tow. All of the women fussed over the baby, providing Jacqueline with a second home. She got baptized and was determined to raise Barnard to love God. With the family's religious future settled, Jacqueline came to her next major life decision. She was going to be a counselor. She was going to help others like those women had helped her – she wanted to reclaim lost lives. But counselors needed degrees, and she had dropped out of school to have Barnard. First Jacqueline made sure that the grandmas would be okay watching Barnard for many of the weekdays, and, after they had gleefully agreed, Jacqueline reenrolled in school. She also got a job working nights. She was going to graduate. She was going to college. Jacqueline was determined to create her own future.

—————— † ——————

Becky Lind

Barely having a chance to say goodbye to Herb as the train pulled out. Stuck in the snow with a car that wouldn't start. Facing a five-hour drive to Nebraska in a car that she couldn't shut off. Facing a year alone without her husband. It had all finally gotten to Becky Lind, so her father had driven to Fort Riley to help his daughter make her way home. Their destination was Weeping Water, Nebraska, a town numbering just over 400 souls, where Becky had located a home for rent. It was a big, lonely old house – the kind of house that they use as haunted houses in the movies. Life rattling around in that old, spooky house was lonely for Becky. She kept it spick and span, but without Herb, it never got to be much like a real home. She didn't even unpack everything. What was the use? He was going to be gone for only a year, and then she would just have to pack it up all again to move to his new duty assignment. Since Herb was at sea with Charlie Company, it was an entire month before his letters started to arrive – letters that made her miss him all the more.

Jan 26

I have been holding off on writing because it doesn't get mailed until we get into Okinawa anyway. I have been seasick all but a couple of days and this trip has been miserable for me. I can tell you that we will probably never take an ocean voyage. The boat is rolling pretty bad

John and Jacqueline Bradfield relaxing on a night out. (© John Bradfield)

Jacqueline Bradfield with her children Barnard (left) and Byron. (© John Bradfield)

John Bradfield and friends crowding round his record player aboard USS *Benewah*. (© John Bradfield)

John Bradfield home from Vietnam with his son Barnard. (© John Bradfield)

Becky and Herb Lind on their wedding day. (© Becky Lind)

Becky and Herb Lind with their son Mark. (© Becky Lind)

Lynn Crockett (left) and Herb Lind. (© Becky Lind)

The Lind family, Becky and Herb with children Mark and Tara on the occasion of Herb's promotion to the rank of Major. (© Becky Lind)

Herb Lind during his second tour in Vietnam standing alongside his South Vietnamese counterpart Major Luc Tam Ky. (© Becky Lind)

Becky Lind at her graduation from Kansas State University with her MA degree.
(© Becky Lind)

Becky and Herb Lind in 2013. (© Becky Lind)

Aurora and Jimmie Salazar posing for a photograph just before his departure for Vietnam. (© Aurora Salazar)

Aurora with Jimmie Salazar in uniform. (© Aurora Salazar)

Aurora and Jimmie Salazar on their wedding day. (© Aurora Salazar)

right now so my writing is not too hot. So far I have done a lot of reading and taken a lot of aspirin and motion sickness pills.

I have been thinking a lot and there is a long time to go but it would be great if it can be worked out for you to meet me in San Francisco and we can take our time in where we go from there. We would probably go some place nice and quiet and spend some time alone just the two of us.

Becky wrote to Herb religiously every day. The ritual of sitting down, organizing her thoughts and committing them to paper, usually in reaction to a letter that he had sent, helped Becky immensely. Reading his letters, and holding a written conversation with him, made him seem more real; more there. And it quickly became apparent that her letters were serving the same purpose for him. Amid the tumult of war, Becky's letters helped Herb remain linked to something more meaningful and pure.

Feb 7

I received your first two letters tonight and it made me feel a lot better. We're busting our butts and really working around here. The camp is starting to shape up a little bit. I am really getting tired though. I start around 6 AM and finish most nights late. Tonight I took off after eight so I could write. I had Sgt. Bunyan take a picture for you and I put it in the envelope.

I really don't know what to write about as we are just working hard in our base camp. There is an operation coming up pretty quick but I'll be staying behind mostly to work on the camp. I also tore a toe nail off walking after dark in my shower thongs. It was my big toe on my right foot so I can't wear my right boot.

I miss you very much. Sometimes I even begin to wonder about the Army.

In reading that letter Becky noticed that there seemed to be something else in the envelope, so she shook it. Out tumbled Herb's torn off toenail. After a bit of an initial shock, Becky came to treasure that toenail. At least part of her husband had returned from Vietnam.

Becky knew that staying busy was going to be one of the best tonics during Herb's absence, so she found a job as a Cass County home extension agent, working to bring agricultural, financial, and nutritional information to rural families. It was the preparations for the county fair, which was always the highlight of the year for many of the rural families, that initially took up most of Becky's work time. Becky had to handle everything from lining up volunteers, to the construction of display cases, to the complex layout of the event. And somehow the county extension office expected Becky to accomplish all of that without a phone.

As life marched on at home, Becky kept Herb fully apprised of local developments on the job and home fronts. She was especially proud of the fact that her pay, when combined with Herb's monthly allotment, meant that the couple had the ability to save some money for the future. Becky loved hearing the news of Herb's day-to-day routine. It made her feel more connected with him. It was through those letters that the couple were also able to plan somewhat for the future, but the theme of their loneliness and longing for each other remained a constant undercurrent.

Feb 25

We are [on operations] at the Ap Binh Son plantation. Not much activity here and it makes a person wonder. Today is just another day and another Sunday. It is getting close to 2 months now out of the way. You see a lot of things here you dislike but can't seem to do anything about. The kids are a bunch of beggars just as you see in pictures of India. We run them off and they come right back or refuse to leave at all. The girls and old women are all trying to sell themselves to the GIs. If an older woman sees a GI looking at a young girl, they will run up and try to sell her to the GI.

I haven't decided on the soldiers' deposits [a way of drafting a soldier's pay into a bank account] but I imagine I'll try to get that taken care of this next month. I want to start getting something built up for a rainy day plus I feel like we should take some vacation next year to really enjoy ourselves. If I get home at the right time and we don't have to rush to get somewhere, we can take a trip down South from San Francisco through New Mexico and up through Texas. We might think about buying some land down around Austin in case we would ever want to retire there.

Becky especially looked forward to the dance that coincided with the county fair. There would be good music, and lots of people, and dancing. It would be a chance to be a 23-year-old woman again. And she had permission from Herb to dance all she wanted. Becky had always loved to dance, but Herb had two left feet and usually sat things out. But he had never minded if Becky danced and had a good time with others. It was just their way. Becky donned her best for the dance, a green, A-line, knee-length dress with fishnet hose and green sling-back heels. The guys she danced with all knew her, but she would always point to her wedding ring just in case. Things were all going so well, and Becky was having so much fun, until there was a break in the music. During the silence a boy asked Becky how she could be dancing when her husband might be lying dead or wounded on a battlefield in Vietnam. She responded by saying that Herb wanted her to dance – to live – while he was gone.

As spring progressed it seemed that Herb was becoming more distant and that both separation and war were wearing on both him and his soul. Becky's days were always brightened when she received a letter from Herb, but his letters of late March and early April sounded notes that made her miss him more than ever:

> I am looking forward to the time when we can meet at Travis AFB and be together again. I doubt very much if we will head straight home. I think if there is time we will try to travel a little bit. Mostly we will be together.
>
> I think by now you know how difficult it is for me to write. I could sit here and write I love you to you all day but a news type letter is something else.

I don't know whether I should send this or not. I feel a little despondent once in a while but I get over it. This war lacks a lot of the motivating forces which were present in previous wars.

As she worried for her husband, Becky took a few much needed days off to go and visit her parents in Saint Paul. She had hardly gotten through hugging Clyde and Nawdean when Herb's dad, Vance, came pulling up into the driveway – driving rather quickly it seemed. Then it hit Becky. How did Vance even know that she was there? Why was he coming to see her parents? Why was he driving so fast? He must have news. News that Herb was wounded or dead. Becky panicked. She ran to Vance's car, sobbing. For his part Vance was shocked. Clyde had called to let him know that Becky was dropping by for a visit, so he had driven over to see his daughter-in-law. There was no news. As far as he knew his son Herb was fine.

It took Becky a while to calm down, and she shared her fears in her next letter to Herb. He had to make sure that she would receive notice first if anything bad ever happened to him. She just couldn't stand the idea of wondering if his parents were going to show up out of the blue one day to deliver the news that Herb had been killed. Herb's response stands as a stark reminder of wartime marriage, balancing the most serious side of war alongside the realities of maintaining a functional marriage at long distance:

Apr 21

On Dad's comment [Vance too had written a letter about the incident] you have explained it very satisfactorily. I will try to help you so you won't go through that again. I have turned you in to be notified if anything should happen to me. They cannot tell anyone else until you have been notified. You will always be the first to be told and will never receive word through either yours or my family.

I am glad the bank deducts the car payment as this just makes it easier. I wonder how much more we owe. It must be $1500 or less. I think it will be paid off in Feb. 68. I forgot about your college loan. When do we start to pay on it?

I live for the day when we will be together again. It doesn't matter so much where we go as long as we are back together.

Although some level of uncertainty remained, as Becky finished reading Herb's letter she reminded herself that it could all be so much worse. Herb's assignment was with the headquarters element of the 4th of the 47th, Charlie Company's parent battalion. That meant that he often didn't have to go with the men into the field. That assignment helped to keep him safe. As a military wife Becky knew that the "wastage rate" of young officers in the field was incredibly high. Nearly all platoon or company level officers seemed to become casualties. At least she wasn't the wife of a line officer.

———— † ————

Aurora Salazar

They were hard facts for Aurora Salazar to face. She was 16, pregnant, and newly married to Jimmie Salazar, a man she loved but only partly knew. Even so, Aurora couldn't help but be excited. She was married, which meant a husband who loved her and being part of a new, and loving, family. She finally belonged and was wanted. And she was going to have a child, someone she could love fully and beautifully. Someone she could raise, comfort, and protect. Someone to whom she could provide the nurturing family that she had never been able to enjoy. At the age of 16 Aurora Salazar was about to embark on adulthood, which was fine by her. She had never liked her own childhood anyway.

Aurora Salazar was young and bright. She knew what wars did. But war wasn't going to take or alter her husband. When he had left for Fort Riley Jimmie had stood there with a slight smile and had told her with a calm certainty that he was coming back. Even as he walked away he was still smiling. He wasn't worried; why should she be? When Aurora Salazar looks back on those days in hindsight she knows that she was simply too young to understand what was going on, what the risks were. She was also too swept up in the vast changes taking place in her young life. Jimmie's place at the family dinner table was very nearly still warm with his lingering presence as Aurora sat down to pen her first letter to him. She promised that she would create a life for them that he would be happy to return to, while making an internal promise to herself to write only positive things in the coming months. War wasn't going to change or spoil anything.

As soon as Jimmie left for Fort Riley, Aurora left sleepy little Johnson City for life with her in-laws in Austin. Her new family didn't have much money, but they had everything else a real family was supposed to have. She shared a room with her new sister-in-law who was almost her age. It was cramped, but fun, almost like some kind of camp-out, and the two soon became fast friends. While progressing through her pregnancy, Aurora didn't work, which was certainly a new experience. So she busied herself by working around the house, helping her new family in any way that she could in a kind of training period to be able to keep her own home once Jimmie returned.

During the months of Jimmie's absence, Aurora Salazar's financial life got better than it ever had been. Jimmie sent more than news home in his letters; he sent most of his paycheck – $97 a month. It seemed like a king's ransom to a poor girl who had started washing dishes on the graveyard shift at age 12. And, since she had the support of her new family, Aurora was able to save most of that money toward her future together with Jimmie. Aurora could hardly believe it. She had money, and an actual bank account. Although she never quite knew how much, Aurora also knew that Jimmie was sending money home to his father. It was only then that Aurora realized the strength of the bond between Richard and Jimmie. It was plain to see that Jimmie was everything to his father.

After Jimmie had gone to Vietnam Aurora tried to stay away from the news as much as she could. If anything really important happened, she was sure that Jimmie would tell her in a letter – if there was a loss, a moment of doubt or anguish; anything really important he wouldn't hold back. But Richard was another matter. He gobbled up every piece of news he could about the war. He would sit and listen to the news a couple of times a day, and devour the newspapers, hoping to find out anything he could about Charlie Company. Some of the news, though, was indistinct or hard to figure out. Was that his unit in the news? Was that the Mekong Delta? Richard would sit with his map trying to piece it all together. The uncertainty was agonizing for Richard. Any newscast could be the one – the one where he learned that his son was dead. Unable to sleep, Richard started drinking heavily to help himself get by. He worried so much that he quite literally made himself sick. Aurora was stunned to see that real love, when mixed with absence, longing, and fear, could be so destructive.

I wrote letters home as much as I could, but I never really told Aurora or my dad much about the war. I didn't want to put any more pressure on them than I had to. There were so many things I didn't tell them. In May, while Aurora was nearing the time to have our baby, I was walking point on a Viet Cong island. I started going over a log that crossed a canal when I saw movement in the water and a guy jumps up with a sub machine gun pointed right at me. I couldn't turn my rifle in time, and he pulled the trigger, but he misfired. I completed my turn and emptied my 20-round magazine into him. My heart was about to come out of my chest I was so scared. You get so scared that you can't think about anything else. But you have to say to yourself that it happened and you can't do anything about it. You have to keep on going to make it home. When that kind of stuff happens you have to take care of yourself and take care of your buddy. If you don't – if you get too caught up in it – you won't make it home.

Jimmie Salazar

It was at a regular pregnancy checkup at the Fort Hood hospital as she neared her term that Aurora learned that her blood pressure had spiked. As the nearest thing that Aurora had for a next of kin, the doctors informed Richard that her situation was so precarious that she might not make it to term and they might have to get to the point where they chose to save her life or the baby's. Since Aurora was underage, the decision was his. But it was no decision at all. Aurora was now his daughter, and he loved her with all of his might. If there had to be a decision, the doctors had to save her.

Even with the comfort of a loving family, the stress for Aurora Salazar was almost unbearable. She was in a hospital – a place that was so foreign. Doctors and nurses were running every which way, and pretty much all of the time. The hubbub was constant and grinding. It made Aurora feel small again. Maybe she had been able to convince herself that everything since Jimmie's departure had been a kind of grand adventure, but the hospital took the bloom off of that particular rose. Was she going to make it? Would the baby be healthy? Would the army send Jimmie home to be with them, at least for a little while? She had so many questions, and so few answers. For the first time in a long time Aurora Salazar felt like a little girl again, lost, confused, and alone.

———— † ————

Mary Ann Maibach

Having seen her husband off to war, Mary Ann Maibach had returned to Ohio with her infant daughter Karen to live in her old room at her parents' house. There seemed to be people everywhere, with a total of eight relatives and one lodger occupying the dwelling. To accommodate the crush of people some rooms were divided into two by drapes, and the back porch was converted into an extra bedroom. At least Mary Ann and Karen had a room to themselves. Mary Ann was an adult mother with an important career. At first the idea of moving back home with her parents had seemed like a step backwards, but the constant hum of human activity proved to be a tonic. The comings and goings of her relatives and friends helped to keep the loneliness and dread at bay – a loneliness that provided the theme of her first letters to Gary:

Jan 9

My heart is so very heavy as I attempt to begin writing this first letter to you, my dear. My thoughts have been with you continuously since Saturday. I hardly think a waking moment has passed that I wasn't thinking of you, wondering how and where you were.

I just love you so much I still can hardly believe that this horrible thing is really happening to us. It all seems like such a nightmare – only the worst thing is I wake up and find out that it's true, and I can't get away from it.

I've got that baby calendar all numbered for my "count-down" calendar. I almost got excited as I hit November & December, just thinking about how near to coming home safely you'll be then.

Mary Ann loved nursing, and she knew that throwing herself back into a nursing career would help her financially and provide a distraction from her own problems. While at work Mary Ann had to be laser focused, giving all of her attention to the travails of her patients, allowing her no time to fixate on her own troubles. And there was always the church. Congregants of the Apostolic Christian Church have long rallied around their servicemen and families, nurturing those afflicted by war. A return to the bosom of her home congregation was bound to provide both Mary Ann and little Karen with solace during Gary's absence. Mary Ann knew that going back to work and to church were the right things to do, but she also wondered how she would react. Everyone at work and church would want to know about Gary, and their well-meaning enquiries and conversations would be a constant reminder of his absence and of his peril:

Jan 15

My precious darling husband I have just finished reading the three letters I've received from you in the past week. It makes my heart ache so, yet does me good to realize how very much you care also, as I love you so very much, my love.

It really seemed strange to me to be at Rittman Church without you. Everyone really made a fuss over Karen. She was awake much more than before, and was real good. You know, honey, I hope this doesn't seem strange or unnatural to you, but I believe I've got such a shell built around me. I'm rather numb. The ache within me is so bad I just can't bring it to the surface and yield to consequences. When people asked me about you, I was as dry eyed as if I was talking about some stranger instead of the dearest most wonderful human being I've ever known, or ever hope to know. I really feel as if my shell is wandering around, going through the motions of living, while my heart is floating further and further away from me.

Honey, I must admit that I really dread going to work tomorrow night, as I feel I don't know what to expect. My papers when I was at the hospital Thursday said charge nurse, so now that [I'm in a position of authority] I'm afraid to think of going and telling people who know what's going on what to do, when I'm in a fog as to what is going on, although I imagine I'll fall back into the groove before too long, at least I hope I will!

For all of the Charlie Company wives, loneliness was the most common of themes during their husbands' absences. From workmates, to mothers, to church friends – each of the Charlie Company wives received an abundance of commiseration in their loneliness. But each new well-wisher, each new expression of concern, each new hug also served to remind the wives of the reason for their loneliness. The longing never seemed to dim, and holidays were often the worst. As Easter neared, a holiday that Mary Ann held more dear than all of the others, she wrote:

Next Sunday, I think, the family is getting together for Grandpa's birthday, and the following Sunday is Grandma Maibach's annual Easter dinner. Your mom has asked me to come to both, but I don't know what to do. I really would rather not go to either, since you can't be there and at times like that I miss you even more, if that is possible, as I miss you so acutely all the time. I don't want anyone to be offended by my not going, but I just really don't know what to do... Honey, I hope that you won't feel bad if I don't go to represent you at family gatherings, but as I mentioned earlier it really hurts to be there when you are so far away.

Like most of the Charlie Company wives, war allowed Mary Ann her first real taste of financial independence. She was driven to learn the arcane details of household budgets, which was often a male purview, and she communicated the learning process often in her letters:

I stopped at the bank on the way, and deposited the money order – so it's now safe and sound in the bank – boosting the total here to $360.61, the most it has been since we were married. I hope to be able to feed it monthly, for either my Hawaii trip, and our 2nd honeymoon when you're home, our 1969 car or whatever it may be needed for. If you make Specialist 4 that will be $40 a month more that can be put into the bank!

It was her daughter Karen who made Mary Ann Maibach's day and filled her with a love so vast that it nearly filled the void of Gary's absence. Like any new mother, Mary Ann hung on Karen's every movement and utterance. Sitting up, rolling over, the shift from formula to food – the many milestones of a baby's first year provided such joy to Mary Ann and brightened her dark moments. Even so, Mary Ann couldn't shake the feeling that she was alone when she shouldn't be. Her husband should have been there as well. Every missed moment – the first word, the first real smile –reminded Mary Ann of how alone she and Karen were, even if they were surrounded by a crowd of loved ones. These moments, and their attendant sorrow, were a constant theme in Mary Ann's letters, which were sometimes leavened with the easy humor that helps to define a comfortable relationship:

Jan 31

Since the last paragraph I've walked around with Karen, and rocked her to sleep for one of her notorious cat naps. She can still be so sound asleep, and in 5–10 min be wide awake again. She seems to think people should want to hold her about 90% of the time she's awake. Quite a gal, that little dumpling of ours is darling. She sure has taken over running this household that's for sure.

One of the hardest things for me is to see so many changes in Karen and not be able to share them with you – other than just by descriptions and sending pictures. Maybe we can revive your folks' old movie camera and take some shots every couple months. She's now on three meals a day. She has cereal & fruit for breakfast & supper, and vegetables & custard for lunch ... She is such a gassy little thing it's really a panic sometimes. Someone will be sitting holding her, and all of the sudden she "toots" a few, and you can hear her clear across the room. There's sure no denying who her dad is!

One of Mary Ann's few demands of her husband's time was that he send a new photo every so often so that Karen would recognize him upon his return. She would sit Karen in front of the photo multiple times every day and explain over and over that the picture was of her father. He was her Da Da. He was coming home soon to help take care of her. And Mary Ann made sure to keep Gary updated on developments:

I must tell you, that in Karen's lesson today she gave your picture the most angelic, beautiful smile, and talked to it. She didn't say Da Da yet, but there's still time for that. It was so cute, but she really acted excited by it – I could just have cried, like so often, if I'd have let myself. If the dam breaks again, or maybe I should say, when, I'm afraid there might be quite a flood once more.

So often when Karen does something real cute, I must think if only Daddy could see this or that. I'll bet that thought goes through my mind at least a half dozen times a day. I really feel sad that you have to miss so much my darling, as I know how much you love her. As long as I live I'll never forget that Saturday morning when you held her the last time in Kansas, and kissed her, remarking that when you saw her again she'd be such a big girl.

Every couple within Charlie Company had to negotiate the most difficult of subjects: How should the husband write home about his war? Should he tell his wife everything about his experiences in Vietnam, including the ugly and soul-shattering side of war? Or was that too much for a distant wife to bear? Mary Ann's letters allow for a rare look into how such a decision was negotiated. For her part, Mary Ann didn't want Gary to hold anything back. If she was going to be able to support him fully while he was away and understand him when he returned, she felt that she had to know the totality of his wartime experience:

Feb 1

I sure do wonder a lot what you are doing, my darling. I'll really be glad to hear how everything seems. Honey, I hope you won't try to protect me from details if they seem bad, because I want to know as much as possible, just what the situation is. I would rather know the worst than wonder if you are trying to keep things from me and maybe imagine things more awful than they really are, although I imagine they're pretty awful there in the sticks where you must try to protect yourselves from weather and foe. Surely God will look down in love on such a faithful child, and ever give His protection and strength to you, dear husband.

Mary Ann wanted to know it all – who were Gary's friends? What did he eat? What kind of operations was his unit undertaking? She desperately wanted to narrow the miles and remain a fundamental part of his life. She kept a map handy to follow his comings and goings as best she could, often quizzing him on his location and what operations might be coming up. She had finally found the love that she once had feared might elude her, and she was determined to be a part of his day, every day, and that he should be a part of hers as well, often writing to him on her work breaks:

March 16

Although you'll probably know the ones you're with much better by the end of the year, do you have any special "buddy," or are you just everybody's friend? When you go out on your 15 man patrols, are you usually with the same fellows? Do all patrols have a medic along whenever they go out? I hope you don't mind the questions, but I really am curious about what my honey is doing.

I'm having the first breather of the evening, so thought I'd try and take advantage of it. I'm the only RN here with 8 patients, so I'm keeping pretty busy, but not hectic, as they're all doing quite well so far. I've only given one dose of morphine so far, so that's a pretty good record. I'm sure wondering what you're doing this Sunday, as it's nearing late afternoon in Vietnam. According to my figures, you're out on patrol today, unless I goofed somewhere in my figuring or they kept you on more than every other day. I'm wondering, often, what the meal situation is for you. Do you get cooked meals when at Bear Cat, and rations out on patrol? I imagine you've tasted about all the flavors of rations by now, and have your favorites, and those that you can hardly stomach. Honey, when you're at home I'll fix you only what you'd like – and whenever you want it – I love you – MORE & MORE & MORE & MORE!

As winter transitioned to spring, Charlie Company shifted from training missions to operations that were designed to result in violence, a change that Mary Ann was easily able to glean from Gary's letters. And soon, Gary had to face his moment of reckoning:

My first contact? We were in the swamps in spring, in deep mud nearly up to our hips alongside a little creek. All of a sudden a whistle blew, and there was an ambush and the Viet Cong opened up on us. You always wonder what you will do when the battle actually starts. What will I do when people are needing help and screaming and there is still fire going on? I remember it like it was yesterday. I hit the dirt when the firing began like everyone else. Then I realized that someone was hollering for a medic. I just picked up and went. I just went toward the sound of that voice, not thinking at all about any danger. The firing didn't last long, maybe measured in seconds. But it seemed like an eternity. I got to him while the bullets were still flying. One of the guys had been shot in the hand and the bullet had gone out of his elbow. I debrided the wound, and did what I could. Nothing prepares you for a casualty situation, nothing.

Gary Maibach

As the situation in Vietnam as revealed through Gary's letters became ever more serious, Mary Ann's own misgivings began to mount. Gary's stress and life was her stress and life – but she felt helpless being so far away and unable to affect events. Gary was in mortal danger, something that Mary Ann realized would only get worse. But all she could do was worry and fret and try to keep a wonderful life waiting for him upon his hoped for return:

March 21

This evening, I picked up the paper, and there right before my eyes was a report that the 9th Division north of Saigon has been attacked by VC troops. Needless to say my heart did all kinds of flip flops, as I imagined what kind of things my darling might have seen and experienced. It really is awful to be here and see things like that – and helplessly wonder what it is all about. I really feel awful about it, and so apprehensive for my love, although I realize it is probably over, at least the worst, by the time I'd read it in the paper. All I can say is that if I'm gray when this year is over you'll know why, and if you are, I'll know why. I pulled out a gray hair the other day, but I don't have too many to spare, so I guess if their population increases I'll just have to leave them there, as I'd rather be gray than bald when you get back.

———— † ————

Judy Lilley

Judy was 19 and very newly married. The only time she had ever really spent with her husband was during their short honeymoon at Lake Tahoe after their December 1966 wedding on his final leave before departing for Vietnam. Judy Lilley was certain that she loved Larry, but their romance had always been prosecuted from long distance, with her visiting him in at his apartment in Lancaster where he lived with his buddy Kenny Frakes; or at Fort Riley, Kansas. Part of the adult side of her brain warned Judy that the relationship had been whirlwind, perhaps rushed. But in the deep recesses of her heart, Judy believed that her marriage was right and perfect, born of a real love that was bound to stand the test of a wartime separation.

Like so many of the Charlie Company wives, Judy dealt with the war and the enforced distance from her husband by throwing herself into her work. Following in the footsteps of her mother, Judy had completed beauty school and now worked in a local salon. It was California in the mid-1960s; everyone wanted to be beautiful. Business was booming, and with long hair becoming fashionable for men, there were more male customers than ever. Living at home with her mother made financial life a bit easier for both women. Judy could help her mom with some of the bills, while stashing away much of her pay – along with the allotment that Larry sent home. Judy's plan was to have enough set aside so the couple could get a real place of their own just as soon as Larry got out of the service. That is when her married life would really begin, and Judy would finally be an adult.

Being married, though, was so new that Judy didn't quite know how to handle herself. Do married women go out to dinner alone, or was it okay to go out with friends? Many of her friends were guys; what would people think if she went out with them to a movie like she used to? Would people start to talk? At a loss, Judy spent much of the first days of Larry's absence working or at home with her mom. Especially after the death of her sister Cheryn, Judy's mom enjoyed and needed the company. But Judy also knew that she couldn't dwell on the loss, or on her loneliness. Staying in that house the whole time Larry was away would only magnify her problems. She had to get out and live.

Seven of Judy's friends from her family's short time in Boron had decided to go to college in nearby Bakersfield. The tiny group of Boron expatriates hung out together and used Judy's home as a gathering place. Especially after Cheryn's loss, June Wittman doted on these college kids. Their presence was a lifeline for June as she navigated the grief resulting from the loss of her daughter, and the group provided Judy with a ready-made circle of friends. And one of the guys stood out. Jim Sommers had been drafted and sent to Vietnam, serving in the US Marines. He had been badly wounded, losing an arm. He was nice. He was safe – he fully understood what being the wife of a soldier meant and completely respected Judy's position. Jim was able to both commiserate with Judy's mounting fear regarding her husband's fate and provide both context for and relief from that fear. Jim Sommers was a godsend for Judy, serving as everything from a sounding board, to a shoulder to cry on, to an advisor on things military. Judy in turn helped Jim. He wondered about his own future. How would he fit back into society? Would women like him with only one arm? Could he put the war behind him? So Judy acted as his sounding board, confessor, and confidant. It was a relationship that both needed to help them prepare for their respective futures.

Judy began to go out, always in groups because she remained concerned about propriety. She went to movies, dinners, and hayrides. She allowed herself to feel young again. The war, though, provided a harsh backdrop to Judy's youthful reality – a backdrop that none of her friends could understand, except for Jim. She watched the news and read the papers in an effort to keep up with where Larry was and to attempt to discern what he might be doing, but the reports were usually so general that they were not much help at all. Most of her knowledge of the war came from Larry's letters. The couple wrote to each other very nearly every day, spurred on by their determination to build a life together. For her part Judy swore never to moan and groan in her letters. Her problems were hers, not his. Her letters were always light and airy, meant to soothe and comfort more than anything else. She also demanded that his letters tell her everything. If she was going to learn how to become a wife the first step was to really get to know her husband. If war was his life, it needed to be hers too.

Larry did his best to fill her in on all of Charlie Company's doings in Vietnam. The first month or so seemed more like the boys were at war with Vietnam itself than with the Viet Cong. Larry wrote about hives of red ants that stung the soldiers mercilessly, leeches that loved to slither up their pants legs to feed, and swarms of ravenous mosquitoes. Some guys had even seen a tiger. Larry hadn't, but he sure believed the stories. The heat was nearly unbearable, the work was backbreaking – slashing through jungle by day and digging fighting positions by night. Some of what Larry told his wife seemed almost surreal:

> We were operating at a rubber plantation and were told that we couldn't shoot at the VC unless they shot at us first. But we could see through the rubber trees on that plantation some VC moving from our left to our right, but they weren't shooting at us. We were operating with a tank unit that day, and I climbed up on a nearby tank and asked the 50-caliber gunner if I could fire his weapon. He responded that we couldn't fire because we hadn't been fired at yet. I said, "Hey, didn't you just hear that round go over your head?" He said, "You know, I think I did." I got on the gun and put maybe 75 rounds out into that rubber plantation in short bursts. Man, did that mess up

some of those rubber trees. The next morning the captain got the unit together and chewed us out something fierce, because we now had to pay the owner of the plantation for all of the trees I had shot up. Dumbest thing I ever heard of. We were playing war, and they were playing for keeps. I knew that it had to change.

Larry Lilley

There really hadn't been much contact with the enemy yet; some guys were even complaining that the war was a bust. But not Larry. The war would get real, but he just didn't know when. Things got more serious as Charlie Company began operations in the Rung Sat mangrove swamp. The boys trudged through knee-deep mud or neck-deep water for days on end searching for an enemy who obviously didn't yet want to be found. Sometimes they found the remnants of a camp – once the rice had still been boiling. It all kept Larry's head on a swivel and seemed to indicate that Charlie Company was headed toward something bigger – it was like a pressure that was slowly building. Something was bound to give in a big way, but when?

What Larry liked to write about most in his letters, though, was his friends. He was lucky. Most of the guys in Charlie Company had arrived in Fort Riley alone. But Larry had his two best friends in the world, Kenny Frakes and Tim Johnson, by his side. It was amazing that the three companions, who had been together since middle school, were first drafted together and then sent to the same unit. Maybe it had been a mistake, but if the army had messed up, at least it had messed up in their favor. So much of Larry's letters were about the doings of his friends. Three 20-year-old guys hanging out together in a sea of other 19- and 20-year-old guys – if there hadn't been a war going on it would have been positively fun. More and more Larry's letters began to focus on the doings of the group's newest member – Don Peterson, whom Judy remembered from her short visit to Fort Riley. Since he hailed from just down the road from Larry's hometown he had fit into the group immediately. Don had that classic winning personality – warm, funny, and wearing a constant smile. He was the kind of guy you wanted to be friends with. He and his wife Jacque had just had a baby before he shipped out, and he was constantly showing his lone picture of his son Jimmy to anyone who would look. The guys looked up to Don – they respected him. And they felt a great deal of sympathy for him, having to leave his wife and child behind. Don had what Larry wanted – a family. Don was what Larry wanted to be. In all of Larry's letters, which often included snapshots of him and his pals, Judy found herself drawn to Don Peterson. Things were bad enough for her and Larry, being separated so early in their marriage. But how much worse were things for Don? He had to leave behind both a wife and a newborn. Judy had gone to church growing up – she was both baptized and confirmed. Church attendance, however, had not survived into her young adult years, even though she retained a core faith. Judy Lilley was not in the habit of praying, but she decided that she would pray that Don Peterson would make it home safely to his young family.

——— † ———

Esther Windmiller

29 December

My Precious, Precious Darling,

Your first letter came today. My first impulse was to come home to you, to do something to be with you. Sweetheart it hurts to see you hurt so very deeply. If I wasn't a servant of the Lord I would never put you through this. We must remember how very much we need and love each other in future disputes and spats we have. This separation ought to teach us something in that area.

I'm glad the children seem to be normal already. It is a bit hard on their daddy's ego to say the least! But I think it is wholesome for you. Life must be lived even in what seems to be the most difficult of circumstances – and it will be lived as long as there is meaning to our living and we have so much to live for!

It ... hurts so very much to see you going through so much agony of heart... We've made each other's lives so very happy in our 11 years of married life and to do something that brings sadness and hurt into your life is the last thing on Earth I want to do. We have talked so much about this year being one of the most useful and meaningful years of my ministry. I truly believe this – that God has called me to something bigger than I even at this moment fully understand. And if this is God's way with us for now then He will give emotional stability and inner strength and peace to cope with the difficulties of our separation. I'm very much concerned about you sweetheart. You know how much I love you and desire to be with you you are much in my thoughts and prayers.

Saying goodbye to Bernie at the Cleveland airport had been difficult for Esther and her four children. She knew that Bernie was off to war, and might not return. But how do you tell that kind of news to your kids? Ranging in age from ten to three, the Windmiller children were smart for their ages, but war and the possibility of wounding or death is difficult even for adults fully to comprehend. Telling children that their daddy might never come home? That is another matter entirely. In an effort to keep her family together, Esther relied on communication and ritual. The communication took the form of a constant stream of letters to and from Bernie, with the children writing to their father at least once a week. Their letters were full of the minutiae so important to young children – the doings of friends, the tribulations of school, and hand-crafted pictures aplenty. His letters were always full of love and support, and sometimes discipline after a letter from mom had spilled the beans on a youthful transgression. The letters helped keep a sense of family normalcy alive for a year of separation and difficulties. Family life went on through the printed word. Checkbooks were balanced, Easter was celebrated, lost teeth for toddlers were tucked away – the Windmiller family survived.

Along with the letters, a reliance on familiar family ritual helped keep the memory of togetherness alive during Bernie's absence. Regardless of how she was feeling, whether stressed or overwhelmed, Esther kept the house running just as if Bernie was there. Breakfast and the ritual of getting children ready for and off to school didn't alter a bit. School and its associated extracurricular activities kept Esther hopping, driving in seemingly every direction at once to keep up with her offspring's busy schedules. There was everything from tests to study for, to practice for sports, to lunches to be made. Being so busy was a tonic for Esther. If she kept working hard – at the limits of her endurance – she could almost forget that Bernie was gone.

As a family of deep faith, finding a new church home was of critical importance. Just being a congregant, instead of bearing the burdens and scrutiny of being the pastor's wife, was a liberating experience. Esther became heavily involved in Sunday School, Bible studies, and women's groups, growing in her faith every day and loving it. She also made certain that religion was a central piece in the daily lives of her children. After the exertions of the day, Esther sat the family down to dinner, just like they did when father was home, but with an open place at Bernie's seat. After dinner was done and the kitchen was clean, everyone would gather around to read a Bible story, and then play games.

Bernie was elated by the obvious well-being of his family:

January 6

Oh how good your letter was – it was you again, happy, content and well adjusted. Now I feel like crying, but for thankfulness to our Lord who is so graciously sustaining you. When I was talking to Capt. Robinson this morning he said "It takes a special kind of woman to be an Army wife." I said to myself, "Windmiller, you've got one!" And I do – the most gracious, wonderful wife a man dare ask for, or could imagine. You know that my heart will throb for you the whole year. I love you so, so much!!... You are so patient to put up with my faults.

How do you do it? Remind me some day to pin a medal on you for your forbearance! You're a gem honey – I love to hear you laughing at life again.

In February as part of the 4th of the 47th Infantry, Charlie Company began to run its initial combat missions. Windmiller, in his position as a battalion chaplain, quickly became acquainted with injury and death. After all, it was Bernie who had to pray for the wounded and write home to the families of the next of kin of the dead. Bernie Windmiller's war darkened more quickly than that of the majority of his men; his burden set in more rapidly. And he needed to share the experience with Esther, even providing her with a topographical map so that she could follow the comings and goings of his unit. And Esther wanted to hear. She was fairly desperate to help her husband in any way that she could. It was her job to support him physically, spiritually, and emotionally. Now that he was facing the biggest crisis of his life, she had to be there. She had to help. But in many ways she felt only like the sad recipient of dire news. She could write letters back; letters that she felt arrived too late to be of any real support. She wanted to know, but she felt powerless to do anything more than worry.

February 4

Darling, would you prefer I didn't mention when I'm going on combat operations and our mission? I don't do it to cause you worry. I'd like to keep you informed so you can follow me around on the map. If it is bothering you please tell me... I'm sorry that my letters brought tears again, but I know this is inevitable when two are so much in love as we are. But I'm not worried about you darling, because I know you have strength from a deep source, our Lord Jesus Christ... Sweetie, you and the children are the most loved and thought of family in the world. Just think, only eleven more pay days to go. How about that!!...

Darling, this operation we'll be on, I don't think is any big deal... Of course there is always the possibility we could run into a good size

"Charlie" force, but I rather doubt it. More than likely we will encounter some sniper fire, booby traps and things of this nature. Of course that is dangerous in itself but no big operation involving large numbers of VC... I'm not really worried at all or afraid. What time I am afraid, then will I trust in the Lord. I'm here to serve these men and I will do so under any circumstances without being foolish or stupid.

Bernie's letters indicate that Esther's reaction to his revelations of war shifted quickly from tears of worry to expressions of support. Regardless of her fears for the life of her beloved husband, Esther realized that tears would do nothing more than worry him needlessly in a potentially deadly situation. She instead focused her communications on her love for him and the interesting doings of their children. Her support needed to be and would be absolute. But then two of Bernie's letters became even more ominous, dealing with the initial woundings and deaths suffered by his unit:

February 10

Late yesterday afternoon we had our first contact here with "Charlie." I was in the briefing tent... when 2 rounds of small arms fire came whizzing into our area right behind us. It was only sniper fire and nothing to get really excited about. But out on the defense line our boys cut loose with machine guns, rifles, claymore mines. You would have thought a whole battalion of VCs were attacking us. The report came in that a sniper round had gotten one of our boys so I left the staff meeting. I came back to the aid station and was there when they brought the lad in. The bullet went in and through his left thigh and into his right thigh. There were no bones broken in the left thigh, but they weren't sure about the right thigh. The boy was in shock, and doc started IVs in both arms, gave him 2 units of blood, bandaged both legs, and called for a "dust off"... I'm thankful that I wasn't afraid and that my thoughts were only of helping that wounded boy. Of course I took no stupid chances. Afterward, when it was over ... one boy said to me, "Chaplain, you weren't even afraid, were you?" I told him that my faith was in the Lord and why should I be afraid.

Darling I trust my relating of these experiences don't upset you. I want you to be fully aware of what is going on, my reactions and feelings. If you ever desire not to be told this, please say so and I'll understand.

February 11

About 0530 this morning Sergeant Onley went to check on the listening post, as is his job. The story I received was that as he approached the listening post the men called "Halt" – to which Sgt. Onley was supposed to stop and give the password. I'm told, instead of stopping Sgt. Onley said, "Shut up" and kept coming toward the listening post. Of course the listening post opened fire on Sgt. Onley and from the looks of the wound I saw, shot him almost through the heart. This is the "hell" of war I detest and can hardly stomach. I knew Sgt. Onley quite well and he was a top notch platoon Sgt.

When they brought him in ... I knelt beside the litter and prayed to the Lord to have mercy on his soul. What does one pray for at a time like this?... This has been our first death, and a needless one at that. I'm aware that mistakes of war will be, but they are extremely hard to accept.

PS The boy who shot Sgt. Onley went into a state of shock just a few minutes ago. I talked to Capt. MacDonald, the CO, and told him that there was nothing we could do for Sgt. Onley, but plenty we could do for the boy who shot him. This boy is young and has a life to live. It is going to be tough for him.

Esther Windmiller was living a double life – a double life that is often the defining trait shared by combat wives. In one way she was more vital and needed than ever before, throwing herself into the lives of her beloved children as both mother and father. In another way she was helpless and adrift, without her husband and unable to be there to help him amidst his greatest danger. Matters only worsened as the public opposition to the Vietnam War began to take hold. Without warning a friend had taken Esther aside and grilled her on the conduct of US soldiers in Vietnam, using a press report on the beating of a Viet Cong prisoner by a US Marine as a bludgeon. She shared her fears and the story with Bernie, who replied:

> One sure has to keep a level head or he could become sour and develop a hatred for these people. Some do – others, the majority of soldiers, are no doubt just indifferent to everything. They have been forced into it, and all they are concerned about is getting out of here alive and becoming a civilian again. This lady who saw a Marine beating a VC. It is very difficult for people at home to understand men's actions in combat. There will always be a small percent of men who are masochistic. We don't try to justify any animal tendencies in our soldiers. But the VC are brain washed, convinced communists and the only way to victory for them is to get rid of what stands in their way. They will mercilessly kill their own people. You don't treat them with kid gloves, or you'll likely be dead. This is war and there is nothing nice about it – there are no gentlemen on a battlefield.

The transition from pastor's wife to the wife of a husband at war was full of change, from serving as both mother and father at school to dealing with the moral questions of war. But there was another aspect of the transformation that perhaps caused Esther the most headaches of all. Bernie had always handled the family finances, but now all of that balancing of checkbooks and paying of bills fell to her. It added another level of unwelcome stress to the year, but it also taught Esther to be financially self-reliant and independent. While there were questions and headaches that were reflected in the couple's letters, Esther came to enjoy handling the financial side of the couple's life. She enjoyed being her own woman. She enjoyed coming out from under Bernie's considerable shadow, even if only for a short time. In a revealing letter, Bernie let it be known that he knew that there was a transformation afoot:

March 13

I'm sure there will be adjustments for us to make when I come home… Obviously after living alone for a year with all men, and you alone with all the responsibilities, there will be adjustments to be made. Me taking back the responsibilities that are mine, you giving up the leadership of the family etc. I'm sure there will be no problems, yet an adjustment.

As worries mounted, and their lives slowly changed, Esther took great solace knowing that Bernie had the support of the many friends he spoke of in his letters about Charlie Company. He wrote of many of the men, and many of his fellow chaplains, but one stood out from the rest. Bernie and Esther had known Lieutenant Charles "Duffy" Black well during training at Fort Riley. As Charlie Company's executive officer, Duffy had cause to work alongside Bernie on several occasions during training, and had often sought out Bernie's religious counsel. A gung ho officer who had once been an enlisted man, Duffy shared many of Bernie's values and much of his outlook on life and on the war. During training Duffy had fallen in love with Ida, the daughter of the 9th Division's postmaster, and had gotten married in the base chapel. Especially as his marriage had neared, Duffy had sought out Bernie more and more for his advice on religion, life, and the military, and Bernie had taken the young man under his wing almost like his own son. Bernie and Duffy had shared a cabin together on the troopship to Vietnam, and life in the combat zone had brought them closer together than ever. On April 4 Bernie wrote to Esther of their growing friendship, "Duffy is a real nice guy – I really like him. I hope that I'm able to stay close to him. I really feel he will be a lifelong friend."

CHAPTER 4

DAYS OF TERROR

I got up in the morning and watched the news. They were interviewing guys coming out of the field and talking about how Company A was wiped out. My mother didn't want me to be upset because I was seven months pregnant. I sat down and watched it with her and said, "Oh mom. Oh my God. I hope Bob is all right." She said, "Honey, don't worry. That was Company A." But I knew if that was Company A, that B and C were somewhere around there too. Then I went two weeks without a letter. They had stopped. All I could do was wonder and worry. It was so hard. It happened around Father's Day. We had driven to Tampa to be with my granddad for Father's Day. I was down there with them not knowing about Bob. It was the longest two weeks of my life. Then I got a letter from Steve Moede [one of Bob's friends]. He said that he had visited Bob in the hospital and that he was all right. He had been wounded, but Steve didn't go into any detail about what had happened. He told me that once Bob got feeling better he would write me. Four or five days after that I got a letter from Bob on Red Cross stationery. The letter took a long time to write, because he was so weak that he could only write six or seven sentences a day. He told me what had happened and about the surgery he had. I was so relieved to see Bob's handwriting on that letter.

Kaye French

I got this phone call at 4 o'clock in the morning. It sounded like a tin can with a string attached. I was told that Ernie was wounded and in the hospital and that they didn't know how bad he was. It was two weeks later before I ever heard another word. I didn't know if he was dead, alive, or how bad he was. Those were the hardest two weeks of my life. I didn't want to go to work, but I had to. Then I came home and stayed in my room. I just cried and cried. The not knowing was terrible. I just couldn't deal with it. Here I am married, and I was in such a bad state that I had to sleep beside my parents' bed in their bedroom. I was so terrified. Until I heard something I slept right beside them on the floor. Isn't that silly? But I was just devastated. I didn't know what to do. I had terrible dreams and would wake up screaming. But I felt more comfortable with them I guess. Then he called himself and told me that he had been wounded but was okay. He was not going back out onto the line. I just sobbed and sobbed. Just knowing that he was alive. He was hurt, but at least he was alive.

Jeannie Hartman

Every time the newspaper came it would have a list of casualties. I was constantly looking, praying that I wouldn't see his name. I was like, "I don't want to see it," but was so scared that I might. I got a call from Ray; actually my dad answered the phone. He couldn't understand the operator, and he thought it was a bad joke at first. Finally I took the phone, and he was calling me from the hospital in Japan telling me that he was hit. He said that he wouldn't let the Red Cross send me a letter because I was seven months pregnant. He was afraid that I might lose the baby. I said to him, "Can you walk?" He said that he could. I said, "Are you lying to me?" I didn't know where he was hit and my mind was going crazy. "Do you have both of your legs? Both of your arms?" He said, "Yes babe, I do." I came to find out later that he couldn't walk for six weeks but just didn't want me to worry. So he didn't tell me all of it.

June Layman

When battle was joined in Vietnam, its imagery was powerful. The smoke puffs and contrails from the launch of a pod of 2.75-inch rockets; the jolt and concussion of 500-pound high drag bombs; the dull roar of small arms fire; the blast of air as choppers thundered in to land. Such images played out on the evening news and gripped the American public. These were battles that Americans could understand, almost an updated version of what had taken place in World War II. But these battles – battles that fit a comfortable societal memory of what war should be – were relative rarities in 1967. For most US soldiers for most of the year, the Vietnam War meant searching for an enemy that really didn't want to be found. It was a war of endless humping the boonies, sloshing through rice paddies, struggling up mountains, and hacking through jungles, in a perpetual search for Victor Charles.

Much of the Mekong Delta, where Charlie Company ran most of its operations, had been Viet Cong territory for many years, meaning that the enemy knew the ground and the people, and had prepared the battlefield. Communist forces in the area wanted to hurt the Americans – wanted to bleed them to help whittle down US national resolve. But the Viet Cong were also tremendously wary of the might of US firepower. Standing in great numbers against American troops was suicidal. So, in 1967, the Viet Cong only sought battle when the situation was perfect, or as a last resort. There were, however, plenty of other ways to hurt the Americans. The Mekong Delta was festooned with mines and booby traps, and there were thousands upon thousands of hidden sniper positions. One land mine that blew off one leg could stop an American patrol dead in its tracks for perhaps an hour or more while medics did their work and a helicopter came and left with the wounded. A lone sniper could kill or wound one or two Americans before making good his getaway, forcing the Americans to stop, take care of their wounded, and reconnoiter the situation. After all, the Americans didn't know if it was a single sniper, or the leading edge of a much larger ambush. And they couldn't afford to blunder forward to find out.

For the Americans it meant sloshing through enemy-controlled territory, surrounded by ubiquitous civilians who might or might not be telling the Viet Cong of your whereabouts, wondering if the next paddy dike was mined, wondering if the next tree line housed a sniper or an enemy battalion or nothing. Operations for Charlie Company in the Mekong Delta were like an endless game of cat and mouse. The vast majority of operations wound up being just a long walk in the hot sun, with maybe a few Viet Cong suspects taken in for questioning. But letting your guard down in the Delta was a lethal mistake. As soon as you got complacent, you would fail to see a tripwire and pay for your carelessness with a leg. Or a sniper round would buzz in and sever an artery. The Mekong Delta was alive with death – death that could be waiting at the next paddy dike or nipa palm. During its year in combat Charlie Company, which arrived in Vietnam with 160 men, lost 26 killed and 105 wounded. The vast majority of the bloodletting took place in staccato, unexpected moments of terror that defined war in the Delta.

There were, however, also moments of the deep, visceral terror of pitched battle. Charlie Company fought four such battles during its time in Vietnam. These battles were initiated by an enemy that had decided that it wanted to be found that day, having both prepared the battlefield and caught Charlie Company at a disadvantage. In each of its major battles Charlie Company squared off against dug-in and well-prepared Viet Cong forces that enjoyed an advantage in numbers of up to five to one. In these battles the Viet Cong tried to draw Charlie Company in as close as possible before opening fire, hoping to negate the American edge in firepower. If Charlie Company was in close, mere yards away from the Viet Cong bunkers, then the Americans would not dare to call in artillery or airpower for fear of hitting their own men.

Even Charlie Company's worst day of battle, though, defied generalization and deviated dramatically from the public image of what battle is and should be. The struggle raged for an entire day, June 19, 1967, killing ten in Charlie Company and wounding 40, while Charlie Company killed an estimated 250 Viet Cong. The battle included all of the accouterments of Vietnam-era warfare – the crash of claymore mines, bomb runs by screaming F100s, the chatter of machine guns, the deep crunch of impacting artillery shells, the metal-on-metal screaming of a helicopter being shot down. But within that symphonic cacophony of sight and sound, even June 19 was intensely individual and personal to its soldier participants. Even while fighting alongside their brothers, while facing an all-too-real foe, June 19 was primal and organic, fought on the level of the single human soul. To survive, Charlie Company soldiers fixated on their immediate surroundings, on the threats to their lives that were the most imminent and pressing. Events more than a few yards away might as well have been taking place on the moon. Combat, and the risk of violent death, focuses the attention like nothing else. That battle provided the men of Charlie Company with the most indelible memories of their lives, but those memories are mere fragments of the whole – brightly colored and intensely vivid, but fragments nonetheless. Their memories focus on their rice paddy dike, the machine gun they were facing, the threat of death. What was the rest of the platoon doing? Who knows? They were busy surviving.

The troglodyte world inhabited by Charlie Company in 1967 belies generalization and didn't jibe well with the common portrayal and understanding of the war as seen in American living rooms on the evening news. Charlie Company's war was personal; whether it was a day of boredom or of stark terror, it was personal. And even while the highs and lows of war were shared with military comrades (the closest friends these men would ever have) the war somehow maintained its intimacy – its distinctly individual understanding. All of that intimate horror had to find an outlet of some sort. Easy in each other's company, the men joked of their experiences with death, sometimes in dark, borderline obscene imagery. But that was sharing with a brother, a soldier. That was sharing within the confines of the abnormal world in which the soldiers found themselves. If they ever hoped to return to normalcy, the soldiers had to share their worst experiences with the inhabitants of the normal world. There was a pressure building up on the soldiers; a pressure that could not adequately be vented into the system. It had to be vented outside, sharing the burden of that pressure with loved ones who knew them not as hardened soldiers, but simply as young men. A son; a brother; a husband. To understand what Charlie Company became; to understand the men who returned to their wives and families; to understand altered lives in a world returned to peace – one must first understand Charlie Company's experience of war. At once a soaring experience; a shatterer of souls; a fount of camaraderie; a cauldron of emotion; a symphonic blend of love, death, laughter, and horror. War was the anvil upon which young lives were beaten and forged anew in a transformation that most of the men barely understood but somehow had to share with those whom they loved the most.

———— † ————

Laughter, grousing about army chickenshit, requests for cookies, queries about health and friends – these still formed the greatest part of the soldiers' collective letters home. But as the war darkened, and death became a given, letters shifted toward loss and a deep longing for normalcy. Drafted out of the Cleveland area, Ray Layman had married his wife June after receiving his draft notice. In April he wrote:

> Ron Schworer was half way across the river when shots rang out of nowhere and bullets hit the water. Schworer went down and never came back up. So come to find out it was [one of our own] choppers firing on us. He was out of his area of operation. He caught hell for that. But that still doesn't bring Schworer back to us.

John Sclimenti, usually the jokester of the unit, wrote home in July:

One of my pals got killed on the 11th. He was from Cleveland and his name is Phil Ferro. Nice guy. His mom wrote to me just before he got killed and sent cookies to us guys. Boy oh boy, what a weird feeling... I know God is with me, and I am glad about that. Just keep up the praying... I just want to get home soon.

For the married men in the unit, their wives became both sounding board and lifeline to a world of normalcy that was slipping away. Like Chaplain Windmiller had already discovered, as the war darkened each man had to ask himself how much should he share about his new and violent life? How much could he share? Could his wife really understand what he was doing, what he was feeling? Would it all change her opinion of him? Could she take it? How each couple dealt with the hard hand of war varied. Some of the guys tried to shield their wives from the worst, hoping that they would somehow return from war unscathed. Others wanted to share every detail of their brushes with death. And the wives varied in their receptiveness to such news. Some, like Esther Windmiller, wanted to be a complete part of their husband's life, which included taking the very bad with the good. For others such letters and information threatened to push them into a haze of isolation and despair. Hailing from North Hollywood, 1st Platoon member Gene Harvey loved to write; he even hoped to take up the pen as a profession one day. The details of his letters to his wife Deana during March and April were especially vivid:

Everyone was quietly awakened. In the pitch black dark we all fired at the noise when it was in front of us. Our massive firepower cut two VC in two and demolished their sampan. Needless to say nobody volunteered to swim out to the sinking sampan and haul it to shore.

So far we have only lost one man in the company. He tripped a grenade booby trap. He's not dead, but was wounded pretty badly. They flew him away somewhere and that is the last we heard of him. A few guys have narrowly missed VC bullets. Actually it hasn't been bad. They say things start to happen when we get down to the delta.

I thought of not telling you, and I discussed with my friends. I finally decided not to keep anything from you, because after all you are my wife. On the other hand this sort of thing doesn't happen very often, so don't worry your pretty little head about anything.

Deana wrote back that she appreciated his forthrightness and honesty, but that the details of the dangers he faced were just too much. She feared greatly for his life, and knowing the full depth of the risks he constantly faced only made it worse for her. She loved him deeply, and wanted to be there for him, but reading those letters left her feeling helpless and alone. At her request, Gene toned down the letters. The Harveys' experience in how best to deal with the realities of combat in letters stands as a prime example. Each couple had to negotiate its own agreement when it came to the husband's sharing of the battlefield reality of his war.

———— † ————

The stories of the Charlie Company wives are so different, set apart by elements as diverse as race, class, geography, duration of marriage, living condition, and number of children. While the guys were a unit, brought together in training and forged in combat, the wives remained individual – physically separate from the other Charlie Company wives and divided by a gulf of experience from their own families and friends. Those differences, and each marriage's distinctly individual nature, has necessitated a written structure that deals with each person and relationship on its own, building narrative walls between the female protagonists of this collective story. Within that structure, though, some commonalities have already become clear. Vietnam was a difficult time, one of separation and longing. One of watching children pass milestones without a father. One of a retrograde movement out of adulthood and back into some hybrid form of childhood, being married but living at home in your old room. But Vietnam was also a liberating time. Goals were set and careers were founded, in part to ready for the return of a "normal" life after the war. Wives took responsibility for finances, cars, education, and the children. Sometimes it was hidden behind all of the loneliness and longing, but the new responsibility was exciting. But the greatest commonality of all for the Charlie Company wives was fear – usually unspoken and sometimes deeply hidden, but fear nonetheless.

The wives of Charlie Company knew full well that their husbands might return from war maimed, changed, or not at all. And they knew that they were powerless to change that fact. For all of their newfound agency in marriage and life, they were helpless in the face of war. They could support their man with kind words, and perhaps a fresh batch of cookies from time to time, but the written word is no match for fear; no match for depression; no match for a bullet. Human beings thrive on control. We rose to the top of the species ladder by seeking to control our surroundings, and control has defined us ever since. But in war, the Charlie Company wives found themselves totally lacking in any form of control. Events controlled them; happenstance controlled them. Try as they might, they could not fundamentally impact their husbands' lives or fortunes in any way. They could only sit back and receive news, and have the war impact them. It was a helpless feeling, and the source of endless anxiety. An anxiety that nobody else can fully imagine.

———— † ————

During March 1967, Charlie Company moved its operations south from the dry area around Camp Bear Cat and into the Rung Sat Special Zone. The vast mangrove swamp, nearly unpopulated and impassable to vehicular traffic, seemed an odd place for military operations, but the remoteness of the region made it a haven for the Viet Cong, who used the area to regroup and train. Intelligence indicated that there were 1,000 Viet Cong resident in the swamp, forces that threatened the Long Tau River, the critical shipping channel that connected the port of Saigon to the outside world.

The vast salt-water tidal marsh, criss-crossed by thousands of large and small streams, was a hellish environment for military operations. With a tidal variance of 11 feet, Charlie Company troopers often operated in knee-deep mud, later only to be assaulted by a chest-deep flood. John Young, a squad leader with 1st Platoon, wrote home to his parents in an effort to describe his new surroundings:

At high tide only the mangrove foliage remains above the water, leaves and branches dragging in the current, like a huge flooded forest during a natural disaster. To be on foot in the swamp during the rising tide is to know a singular helplessness. Dead brown water licks its way over the mud, to knee-level, hip-level, waist-level, and there is no way to escape from it because there is no land, there is only the mud, and soon the water covers it all.

Low tide is the time of mud. At low tide even the big channels are shallow, with long, grey-brown mud banks, and the small streams are empty, steep-sided ditches. Now the mangrove sits exposed atop thousands of piles of mud. The mud is slippery, foul from the eons-worth of dead things rotted and rotting there. The stink is thick under the heavy sun, and there is no breeze to take it away. The mud is everywhere, inescapable, filthy, too thick to wade, too thin for foothold; there is no end to it and no bottom to it. At low tide the world is mud, and a man in it is a panting, straining, futile animal, trapped and useless.

When the tide was in, patrolling meant deep water, weapon and ammunition held overhead on bone-aching arms, tripping over submerged roots, wading through opaque salt water made viscous by the fear of coming under fire while in it. Miserable, agonizing hours of slow-motion movement, when lighting a cigarette or eating a C-Ration meal was a balancing act performed in chest-deep water. Hours of small frights as one foot would slip toward deeper water; sometimes stepping unexpectedly into it. The trick was to turn around underwater and climb back up the bank using your hands and feet. Don't panic, and don't lose your weapon. It worked, when there was no strong current.

But at low tide every step went knee-deep or more into the mud. Each step meant a groaning strain to pull up the trail foot, hands gripping the mangrove, fighting the suction at your boots, knee and ankle joints stretching, thigh muscles going rubbery; falling sometimes, and needing a rope thrown by the men in front to get unstuck. Then take another step and start it all over again. Crossing the empty stream beds always called for the ropes. In an hour a platoon could move 300 feet, and be reduced to gasping, blubbering, spent men, whimpering in a world of endless mud.

Soldiers across Charlie Company wrote similar letters to their families, to their friends, and to their wives. The conditions were so foreign, and so hostile, that they left many at a loss for adequate descriptive terminology, but everyone tried. At times operations in the area seemed almost futile. Struggling through the mud, crossing the seemingly endless number of rivers, swatting at the clouds of mosquitoes that shadowed the unit – Charlie Company made a heck of a racket and moved at a painstakingly slow pace. Everyone was sure that even a half-baked Viet Cong would be able to hear them coming and slip away. The Cong knew the area, dotting it with small base camps, and traveled the streams in tiny, nimble sampans. Sometimes Charlie Company came close, finding a hastily deserted base camp here, and fresh tracks there. But they never found Charlie. On a couple of rare occasions Viet Cong sampans blundered into an ambush, but the VC almost always managed to avoid real battle.

The main worry, other than the mud, mosquitoes, and leeches, was mines and booby traps. The VC seemed to leave them everywhere in order to slow Charlie Company's progress even further. The men always took special care when they found a VC base camp; there were sure to be booby traps all around those locations. On April 8, 1967 1st Platoon discovered a base camp so recently deserted that rice was still boiling above a fire. Platoon Leader Lieutenant Lynn Hunt reminded his men to be on the lookout for booby traps as they searched the area for contact or intelligence. After about 30 minutes of fruitless searching there was a loud THUMP about 40 yards away

– the report of a booby trap. Then the moaning started. Hunt and several of his men moved toward the location of the sound, with Hunt catching sight of one of his enlisted men, Danny Bailey, just as another tripwire tightened around Bailey's leg. The blast peppered Hunt with red-hot shrapnel, and laid open Bailey's left leg to the bone from his thigh to his ankle. Hunt struggled to his feet and walked over to Bailey, who said, "I'm sure sorry sir. I heard what you said about booby traps, but right then I felt something tug. I looked down and it went off. You know, it damn near blowed my ass off."

There had been a few minor wounds before in 1st Platoon, but nothing like this. Gary Maibach, the 1st Platoon medic, rushed to the scene, taking in the sight of Bailey and the more lightly wounded, as he made his way to the location of the first explosion. There he found Lieutenant Duffy Black. From what Maibach was able to surmise from the pattern of the extensive wounds, Black had found a Viet Cong booby trap and had tried to defuse it, only to have it go off in his hands. Black's hands were in ruins, and there were gaping wounds to his torso, neck, and face. Black's breath only came in short, gurgling spurts, and a quick examination revealed that at least one piece of shrapnel had entered the base of Black's skull and had presumably penetrated his brain. Maibach breathed deeply and began to pray for his fallen friend while he patched up the worst of his wounds. It was clear, though, that Duffy Black was going to die. There was nothing that Maibach could do other than stabilize him and hope that the surgeons in the evacuation hospital could work some kind of miracle.

Having done what he could, as others feverishly cut a landing zone into the swamp so a medevac helicopter could evacuate the wounded, Maibach moved on to his other fallen friends. Hunt was easy enough – just stop the bleeding and get him dusted off. Danny Bailey was a different matter. His wounds were ghastly, leaving Maibach to wonder if he would lose his leg. Slapping the pieces of rent flesh back together, Maibach used every field bandage he had – saving that boy's leg became his top priority. Just as he applied the last dressing, the chopper thundered in and the wounded were gone.

Charlie Company's operation went on for two more days, leaving Gary Maibach unaware of the fates of his patients. Once he returned to base, now aboard a navy ship docked amid river, Gary learned that Bailey's leg had been saved, at least for now. Duffy Black somehow remained alive, struggling for breath and constantly hovering near death, but alive. Finally with a respite in his work, Gary wrote of the experience to Mary Ann, sparing none of the bloody details.

As a nurse, Mary Ann knew about blood and loss; she knew that this day was coming. She had already spent more time praying that year than ever before. Her first thought and last thought every day was to pray for Gary – to pray for his safety and to pray that he have the strength and courage to save lives that hung in the deadly balance. When the letter came she set aside *The Hobbit* by J.R.R. Tolkien; flights of literary fantasy had helped to take her mind off of Gary's reality. She cried as she read the letter. Gary had been in such danger – truly mortal danger – and she had not been there to stand by him. But the danger was no longer even fresh; it had passed over a week before. She could not even be there to help him in its wake. He was probably over it and off to the next mission, and she had not been able to help him at all. It all made her feel powerless. But she also fairly glowed with a sense of pride. Her husband had faced a stern test and had passed with flying colors. She always knew deep inside that he would. The mix of emotions was confusing for Mary Ann – helplessness and pride usually don't reside together in the same moment. But in this case they did. Their juxtaposition was odd and uncomfortable, but they were both there. On April 20 she wrote back to her husband, a letter that he would not receive until April 27:

> It surely was awful to hear your account of the patrol ending Apr 10, yet as you said, it was rather expected to happen sooner or later, but is hard anytime. I'm glad Lt Black didn't expire while you worked with him, yet we both are well aware that such a thing could very well happen sometime, or many times before the business is over, May God protect you from as much of such awful happenings as is possible. May He give thee grace and strength to bear whatever the cross may be.

It sounds as if you did a real good job, and kept your head as I expected you would – such an organized person as you are, my dearest love. I read your account of the incident to everyone at the supper table, and honey, the boys, especially, were really impressed by it. I could tell by the way they acted. Mom cried, and the girls, except for Karen, who squealed on and off, just shook their heads in distaste. Since it had to be thus, I'm glad you wrote as you did.

Bernie Windmiller had not accompanied Charlie Company into the field that day. He had instead remained behind to work to ready the chapel and his sermon for the coming Sunday service. Then the call came in from headquarters. Duffy Black was in the hospital and was not expected to live. Even with his deep faith, Bernie couldn't help but question and wonder. Just four days before he had written to Esther about his affection for Duffy, about their growing friendship, and about their future. And now Duffy, one of his very closest friends, was hovering near death? Bernie hurried to the hospital to be by his side, and to pray for and with the other Charlie Company soldiers who had been wounded in the incident. Bernie chronicled the experience in his letters home to Esther:

This has been a full day, a day of joy – and tragedy. [At chapel] I felt the power of the spirit so much, and it was a delight to preach the gospel... When I went to chow at noon, I received word that four of our men in Charlie Company had gotten wounded by a grenade booby trap – one of them was Duffy Black. He was seriously injured. I told Bill to get the jeep so we could get to Long Binh to the 24th Evac Hospital... When we arrived Duffy was in surgery. I talked to the three other men ... they had found a base camp and were searching through it when Duffy tripped the booby trap. A few minutes later the other three tripped another. You can't see these trip lines because they use very thin fishing line and often lay it right on the ground and cover it with mud. Then when you step down your boot sinks into the mud and the line sinks too, pulling the pin from the grenade.

At 1715 I got a chance to talk to one of the surgeons ... and he indicated that it was going bad for Duffy and he had several nasty head injuries. Poor Duffy. I have been praying all afternoon for God to spare him. Duffy and I are close and it really hurts to think he might not make it. Again, this is part of becoming emotionally attached to these men... I pray for his life for Ida's and Duffy's love. This is not wrong. They loved so little – they haven't had a chance to even know each other yet. O Lord, for the sake of love, stay death.

I've never been in the midst of such heartache and sadness. Strong, young men suffering, dying, and I'm sure the worst is yet to come. There will be more suffering – more deaths – more visits to hospitals – more letters to mothers, fathers, and wives to write.

Esther had come to know both Duffy and Ida at Fort Riley, where the young couple had turned to the Windmillers for friendship and guidance. Esther admired the young couple for their courage in choosing to marry amidst the threat of war. And now it all seemed to be over so suddenly. The next day, though, there was hope:

Praise be to God! Duffy has pulled through... Although he is very lethargic and responsive only for a brief period, he is going to make it. He knew me and said in a very loud voice – "Bernie, I almost got zapped!" Sweetheart, I've never prayed so hard for a guy in a long time – and prayer has been answered. The only regret I have is that Duffy will no doubt be out of my sphere of influence before long, as he will be headed back to the States in a week or so. But I do feel that I have created a relationship with him that will be life long.

Sadly, though, Duffy's turn for the better was only momentary, and two days later the end came:

Duffy was in surgery again. He began hemorrhaging, apparently from the brain, so they went in to see if they could find it and stop it... Poor Duffy is just deteriorating away and only an act of God can save him.

After surgery the doctor said that his condition was grave and that he could offer us no hope of recovery. Said he had done all he could and it was now out of his hands. They've operated 3 times on Duffy and the Doc said they could operate again and save his life but it would mean a vegetable life for Duffy – and he couldn't do that. Duffy's father-in-law [who was also in Vietnam with the 9th Division and who had also arrived at the hospital] took this report very hard, so we both walked outside. We stood in the silence of the night, trying to find some answer – trying to find some cohesion to our confused thoughts. I walked over to Sgt. Acevedo [from 1st Platoon] and put my arm on his shoulder – and said nothing for a few minutes. What can one say? Then I assured him that I had prayed earnestly and that we had to prepare ourselves to give him up. I assured him that God understood our confusion and was acting in accordance with what He allows, even though we don't understand. Sgt. Acevedo is a real great man, of few words, but of depth. He put his arm on my shoulder – said nothing, but we felt and understood each other's feelings perfectly.

I felt the need of prayer, so I walked the short distance to the chapel and knelt at the altar. I found myself arguing with God for Duffy's life – I was struggling, not willing to accept the end... Duffy was like a spiritual son to me – there is something of me in Duffy and I didn't want to let go of it... When I submitted to what God might want and what I wanted, peace came over me – a relief of soul. At that point I felt someone beside me – it was Duffy's father-in-law kneeling in prayer also.

Sgt Acevedo and I slept about 2 hours ... and at 0400 the neurosurgeon woke us and said that he had abandoned all hope and death could come at any time. His pupils (Duffy's) were dilated and fixed and there were no voluntary responses. Poor Duffy, he just lay there, a hunk of flesh breathing.

Duffy's loss, and Bernie's attendant mental anguish, hurt Esther Windmiller deeply. She was a nurse, and a convinced follower of Christ. It was in her makeup to strive to ease the suffering of others. But April 1967 found her at a profound loss, unable to be there for the man she loved and for a fellow combat wife who needed her so. Bernie's letters over the succeeding days are reflective of responding to a woman who was undergoing a crisis of confidence. After dealing with Bernie's departure, Esther had squared her shoulders and dealt with every new challenge without complaint.

In April, though, all of those manageable challenges got mixed up with the swirling angst that was part of the escalation of war and loss. Those stressors seemed to have pushed Esther very nearly to her limits. In his letters Bernie reacted to Esther's growing fears that she was not going to be able to continue to persevere against all of the challenges of her life. Those challenges had even led Esther into a rare argument with Bernie's parents about the best way to care for the family. Bernie knew that Esther was a strong woman, but she had never been outwardly argumentative, especially with relatives. Her letters even went so far as to wonder if it would be better if Bernie came home, at least for a short period, to help set things right. She was so worried for him and for his health, perhaps his mental health most of all amid the accumulating loss. Bernie realized that he had to do something, and managed to find time on a long-distance phone line – an expensive and rare commodity – phoning Esther in the middle of the night. In their conversation the two were able to talk things out in a way that letters could never match. Just the sound of each other's voices was a tonic. After the conversation, Esther's crisis of confidence had passed. Her life wasn't about to get any easier. After all Bernie still had nine months to go in Vietnam, and the war only seemed to be getting worse. But even with all of that, Esther was sure that she had been to the edge but had come back; that the future would be different. April, and the events of Duffy Black's death, had forced Esther to grow in ways she had once believed to be unimaginable.

———— † ————

For the next month the letters home from the men and husbands of Charlie Company returned to normal, pausing to note a shift in location to a new base camp at Dong Tam. Made of reclaimed mud from the bottom of the My Tho River, Dong Tam was perpetually damp and smelly, which became a common refrain of the letters, but operations had returned to normal, with a significant level of wastage associated with booby traps and snipers – wastage that was becoming so common that it was beginning to change the outlook of many of the boys of Charlie Company.

We had red ants everywhere that would bight you something fierce. The mosquitos sounded like kamikaze planes coming in. You would cover yourself with a poncho to keep them off, and they would slap into it so hard that you could hear it. With the trees and roots everywhere, you could hardly see anything. Every chance I got I would always walk point for my squad. Every time you put somebody new on the point they would get hurt. So I always walked point. I just hated to see guys, often the new guys, take their turn and the first thing you know they are getting hit or walk into a boobytrap. I was used to it by now and good at it, so I just kept walking point all the time. The losses, like losing Lieutenant Black, really got to some of the guys mentally. But you get to a point where you just say to yourself, "It happened, but you couldn't have done anything about it," so you just keep on going. You gotta take care of yourself, and your buddy. If you stop to think too long you might not make it home. Sometimes you really worried whether you would ever make it home. You had to stay alive.

Jimmie Salazar

On May 15, Charlie Company headed out into its first search and destroy operation in the Mekong Delta proper. Intelligence had indicated that the Viet Cong 514th Provincial Battalion had retreated to recover its strength after a recent sharp battle with the 3rd of the 47th to the area between where the Rach Ba Rai and the Rach Tra Tan streams branch off from the My Tho River. Everyone was just a bit more nervous than usual as Charlie Company entered the rice paddies in search of the Viet Cong, sending out a reconnaissance squad each time it made ready to cross an expansive open area. The area's paddy dikes were festooned with bunker complexes, any of which could house a Viet Cong ambush. Any open area was a potential death trap – better to risk a single squad to ambush than the whole company. It was nearly midway through the day when it fell to Depew, New York native Dave Jarczewski's 2nd Squad of the 1st Platoon to serve as the recon element. The rest of Charlie Company took the chance to drop their packs, light up a smoke, and take a short breather as Jarczewski's squad moved out. But when Jarczewski, who was known to most simply as "Ski," and his men reached the middle of the open area, all hell broke loose.

The Viet Cong had prepared the battlefield with care, catching 2nd Squad in an L-shaped ambush. From their bunkers dug into the rice paddy dikes, Viet Cong gunners had Jarczewski's men right where they wanted them – stranded in the open too close to Viet Cong positions to allow for the use of heavy firepower and too far from US positions for 2nd Squad to receive any help. Small arms and machine gun fire tore across the rice paddy, and 2nd Squad took losses almost instantly. Jarczewski barely had time to yell "Get down" before Charlie Company's lone Native American member, Charlie Nelson, was shot through the chin and also had his kneecap blown off. Jarczewski crawled over to see what help he could offer only to be shot himself, with the bullet entering through his shoulder, cutting through his midsection, puncturing a lung, and breaking five ribs before exiting through his back. Carl Cortright, a new replacement to the unit who had never even had the opportunity to fire his rifle in anger, was shot through the spine and paralyzed. With his buddies being shot to pieces all around him, Don Peterson knew what he had to do. He shouted, "Get ready to run like hell and I'll cover you!" Then, after waiting a few seconds to make certain that his words had been heard and understood Peterson jumped to his feet, firing his M-16 on full automatic toward the VC bunkers. An instant later Viet Cong bullets stitched across his midsection and Peterson toppled back into the rice yelling, "My chest! My chest!"

Charlie Company's 2nd and 3rd platoons did what they could to help, with 3rd Platoon attempting to move onto the Viet Cong flank and taking heavy losses of its own. For the remainder of 1st Platoon, though, the ongoing battle was pure mental agony. That was their 2nd Squad out there. Those were their friends, their comrades, being blown away right before their eyes. And there was nothing that they could do to help. They did their best to lay down covering fire, but it had little impact. The Viet Cong hail of bullets continued, and their buddies kept screaming. Everyone in 1st Platoon wanted to get out there into that paddy to help their friends, but the platoon leader – a replacement who was only with the unit for a short time – wouldn't let them leave cover. To move forward, he said, was suicide. The news hit nobody harder than Gary Maibach. Those were his men out there wounded. It was his job to get out there and save them. His medical bag was in his hand and he was half-way across the paddy dike when he felt the lieutenant's hand on his shoulder holding him back. He wouldn't let Maibach go; dead medics don't do anybody any good. All Maibach could do was watch in utter helplessness, hoping against hope that his opportunity would come.

It was hours before 1st Platoon was able to launch a desperate attempt to retrieve its wounded. Men zig-zagged through the rice to find their fallen friends, dragging them back across the cover of a tall paddy dike where Maibach was finally able to get to work. He had to deal with all manner of injuries from the extensive shrapnel wounds suffered by Texas native Don Trcka caused by the explosion of a grenade, to Nelson's dangling kneecap. There was little that he could do for Dave Jarczewski, who had a collapsed lung and a sucking chest wound. Ski was already turning blue, and his breathing was only shallow gurgles. He was probably going to die. It was Cortright, though, that affected him the most deeply. Maibach saw a clean entry and exit wound smack bang in the middle of Cortright's spine and the lad couldn't feel his legs. Maibach patched the wounds as best he could and got Cortright some morphine to dull the agony. But Maibach knew that the 20-year-old Cortright would never walk again.

Loaded aboard the chopper, the wounded were off to the hospital, where they were met by Chaplain Windmiller. He wrote of the experience to his wife Esther:

> Today I had 22 of my men wounded and one KIA... Charlie Company ran into some VC bunkers that had machine guns in them. The VC pinned them down so they couldn't move and then there were VC snipers up in the trees who shot down at them. It is pathetic to see these guys come in. I went right into the admitting ward and talked with them as their wounds were being dressed... One had a chest wound and his lung was filling with blood. Another had been hit in the side and it looked like it went into the spine. He couldn't move from the waist down. He was in a lot of pain and I held his arm and he just squeezed my arm so tight until they gave him a shot to ease the pain and relax him... It was sad, sad... So this is the beginning of what will no doubt be a long and bloody eight months. Charlie is really down here and he can really fight.

It had been Charlie Company's first real battle in Vietnam. A few men cowered; a couple shit themselves; but most fought hard and well. Their training kicked in. Their love for each other kicked in. Their desperation kicked in, and they fought. They had seen their friends cut down. They had become killers, and they had survived. It was the most important day of their lives. The test had come, and they had not been found wanting. The battle filled the pages of letters written home – everyone needed to tell their families what had transpired. A letter home from 1st Platoon member John Young summarized the day's bloody events:

> We went out four days ago on a two-day operation, and it finally happened: contact. Our platoon was crossing a rice paddy when we began drawing fire from a treeline to our north... My squad got back ok, but the 2nd Squad began drawing machine gun and automatic rifle fire from another treeline to our east... One of the men from the 2nd Squad crawled all the way back and said that there were four

wounded lying out in that open rice paddy, under intense fire and a 120 degree sun... We fired our machine guns until both barrels burned up; we fired grenades at every possible target; we fired thousands of rounds of M-16 ammo; we fired anti-tank rockets at the bunkers... Around 1630 A Company began moving into the northern treeline and Charlie started to run, and we started to drop them. One of our machine guns cut down 4 or 5 who were running single file along the trees... When a half dozen or more VC jumped into a haystack we fired another anti tank rocket at it, and got a direct hit, which blew it all to hell. For an hour or longer we shot VC like targets at a shooting gallery... At the end of the day my platoon had one man killed and 7 wounded. The dead man was in 2nd Squad ... and there were 110 dead VC out there.

---------- † ----------

Don Peterson's body was too far from the 1st Platoon lines to be retrieved during the fighting. It was only after the firing had finally died down that Doug Wilson and John Bauler of 1st Platoon were able to go out into the open rice paddy to Peterson's fallen form. Although he had two large bullet holes in his chest, somehow he looked more asleep than dead. The two spread out a poncho and rolled Peterson, who most of the guys knew as "Pete," into it, and then carried him back to the dike that 1st Platoon had sheltered behind for most of the day. From all around, the men of Charlie Company froze in place as the sad procession passed by. Pete had been larger than life, everyone's favorite. He had the most of anyone to live for – a beautiful wife, a new child who everyone knew was going to be a football star one day. And he was gone. Since night was already falling after the day-long battle, it was too dangerous to bring in a helicopter for a dead man. Don Peterson would remain with his brothers of Charlie Company for one more night.

The men laid Don's body in front of Gary Maibach. There was nothing that the medic could do, but it seemed somehow proper to take Don to Maibach's side. Everyone knew of Maibach's deep faith, and everyone knew that prayer was needed. It fairly broke Maibach's heart. The few married men in Charlie Company shared a common bond. Maibach prayed and mourned Don's death, mourned for Jacque, and mourned for their young son Jimmy. Maibach gave Peterson a quick inspection, and then affixed a killed-in-action (KIA) tag to his friend. It was his duty. He didn't want a doctor in some faraway hospital or morgue to be the one who did it. Don Peterson deserved a friend at his last moment with the unit.

Maibach wrote of the crushing experience to his wife Mary Ann. She wanted to share the bad times with Gary; wanted to be there to help him in any and every way. Seeing him have to go through such difficulty was agonizing. She wanted to be there for him, but all she could do was read a few words, and jot a few words of her own on paper, often substituting a heart for the letter "O" in her writing. And written hearts seemed somehow to fall so piteously short of the mark. All she could do was weep and hope:

> Dearest, it is with a very heavy heart, aching so for my precious husband, that I write this letter. To think of that horrible May 15, and realize how many similar situations my beloved may be in in the next 6–7 months makes me so heartsick. Surely God has promised to be with His children even to the ends of the earth, and I can't hardly help but think it sounds almost as if that's where you are, and surely He is with you, ever giving strength to go on, and to bear the horrors that you must see. I love you so much darling, I just feel so awful about all you must see & endure. I got those pictures out, and found two of Don Peterson. I think it was really thoughtful of you to write his wife, but then that's my darling, so wonderful in every way.

——— † ———

For two of the Charlie Company wives, Don Peterson's death was intensely personal. Judy Lilley had met Don Peterson at Fort Riley, where Don had become close to her husband Larry and his two best friends Kenny Frakes and Tim Johnson. The guys had bonded over

Larry's Corvette and a shared community feel since they were all from the valley north of Los Angeles. Once they had played football against each other; then they found themselves in the same unit at Fort Riley. Judy was drawn to Don since he, too, was married and even had a child. Don and his wife Jacque had what Judy wanted: a family. As Larry's letters had begun to flow in from Vietnam, they focused more and more on Don Peterson. He was the glue that held the guys together. Plainly Larry looked up to Don. He was doing such a difficult job, all while missing his son Jimmy. Larry was pulling for him; and Judy had found herself praying for him. She almost felt like she knew Jacque and Jimmy by following family news in Larry's letters. Then, without warning, the letter came announcing Don's death. The battle had not been on the news. There was no forewarning. Everything in Vietnam had seemed fine for Larry's close circle of friends, and then, without warning, one was gone.

Don Peterson was the first guy from the valley area killed in Vietnam, and his funeral in nearby Arroyo Grande attracted mourners from all over. Flags everywhere seemed to be at half-staff. Don had been a local football hero – but to Judy it was more than that. Don had represented hope – the hope that Charlie Company might somehow make it home unscathed from war. If anyone had something to fight for it was Don Peterson, but now he was gone. Death was real, and it could come for any one of the men of Charlie Company at any time. The funeral had an open casket, so Judy followed the line and paid her respects to Larry's dear friend. She had never been to an open casket funeral before and was surprised by the sight of Don lying there in full uniform, looking so peaceful. Judy then took her position near the rear of the crowd, not wanting to get too near or bother the grieving family. The 21-gun salute startled her; it was like the sound pierced her very soul. Vietnam was for real; it was for keeps. Which of the other guys would be next? Would it be Larry? Would it be her husband whom she hardly knew?

Steve and Karen Huntsman had lived with Don and Jacque Peterson during Charlie Company's training at Fort Riley. Since the guys had been away training most days, the wives all got to be best friends, sharing cooking tips, shopping money, and pregnancy hints for Jacque. It had all been like some kind of adventure, teens learning how to be homemakers and wives together. When training was complete, Karen and Jacque had swapped addresses and gone their separate ways, but they had written letters and remained in touch as the months passed.

Karen was devastated to learn of Don's death. The news came in a letter from Steve, and was followed a couple of weeks later by a letter from Jacque that included a snapshot of Don's funeral. Crying, Karen put the photo into a scrapbook she was making for Steve of his year in Vietnam. As she wiped the tears away Karen looked off into the distance lost in thought. How sad it was that Jimmy would never get to know his father. What was Jacque going to do? How hard could it be to be a war widow and single mother at 19 years of age? It was that same night that the dreams began. Sometimes Karen dreamed that she was in Vietnam, helping Steve to survive. Being meaningful for the man she loved. The other dream was of him marching home through the mist wearing his uniform. Karen knew that Steve would make it home. Don Peterson had not made it, but Steve was going to come home to her.

———— † ————

On May 15 the bullets were flying all around. I was in a little creek and not caught in the open. Smitty [James Smith] was caught out there, and laid down with his arms in front of his head. He got shot in the right forearm; if his arm hadn't have been there he would have been killed. That firefight was a test of courage. One guy froze up, wouldn't get up because he was afraid he was going to die. I actually asked myself, "Why am I not afraid?" I really wasn't afraid at all. After the firing was over, I felt good about myself. The reaction is not one I would have expected from myself, but I felt like a warrior. I'm no hero, but I never really felt fear. I just figured if I was going to get hit or killed it was going to happen. My mom had given me a small Bible. I used to say that verse all of the time, even at night. "The Lord is my shepherd; I shall not want. He maketh me to lie down in green pastures: He leadeth me beside the still waters. He restoreth my soul: He leadeth me in the paths of righteousness for His name's sake. Yea, though I walk through the valley of the shadow of death, I will fear no evil: for Thou art with me; Thy rod and Thy staff they comfort me. Thou preparest a table before me in the presence of mine enemies: Thou anointest my head with oil; my cup runneth over. Surely goodness and mercy shall follow me all the days of my life: and I will dwell in the house of the Lord forever." I would recite that and know that I would make it through the next day.

John Bradfield

On May 15, that is when I got hit. A sniper got me in the left wrist. We were getting hit and couldn't tell where the fire was coming from. I had my guys shoot at the tops of the trees, because there were snipers in them. We kept running out of ammo, and I had already been back to the Command Post once to carry ammo forward. I had to go back again to get some more for the men. On my second trip back with ammo all of a sudden I felt like someone had hit me with a sledgehammer. Knocked me back about 15 feet. My arm jumped away from my body like in a football game, and I thought, "Man, I've got a million-dollar wound." They took me out of there on a helicopter to the hospital at Dong Tam. They got the bullet out and patched me all up; kept me there for two weeks. Then I was on light duty for a couple of weeks more. I wrote letters home, but really didn't write about the war. It was the Red Cross that notified the family that I had been shot. My dad was so shocked that he had a heart attack. I didn't want to put pressure on my family by talking about the war. Aurora was getting ready to have our baby. They didn't need any more pressure on them.

Jimmie Salazar

After the battle of May 15, life for Charlie Company in Vietnam went on as normal. There was constant patrolling, usually three days on and three days off, and a host of search and destroy missions, continuing the effort to corner and destroy VC units that called the Mekong Delta home. The VC went back to being elusive, with a sniper attack here and a few mines and booby traps there. The war was a dull roar, not a gigantic cataclysm. But even the dull roar of war could be devastating, resulting in experiences that were life-changing in a host of ways for the boys of Charlie Company.

On June 1 we were patrolling Viet Cong Island in the middle of the My Tho River. We were walking down a well-beaten path when I felt the tripwire tighten around my leg. The boobytrap went off a few steps behind me, and blew my trousers off. I can still hear it and smell it. I can smell the blood, and feel the hot metal hitting the backs of my legs, my buttocks, and my lower arms. I had a flak jacket on, so there was no damage to my back. Doc Elijah Taylor ran over to help me, cutting the rest of my trousers away. Turns out those were his trousers; I had to borrow them for that day, but he didn't seem to mind much. I couldn't sit down because Doc had to dig that shrapnel out of my legs and buttocks. Sergeant Joe Marr and Alan Richards were wounded in the same blast – Marr in the groin and Richards in the jaw. I still blame myself for their wounding. They took us by helicopter to the hospital at Dong Tam. I had 30–40 shrapnel wounds.

Steve Hopper

Hopper wrote home about the incident, telling his parents bare-bones details of what had occurred. His letter included instructions not to share the news with his fiancé Jennifer, and for his parents only to reassure her that he was fine and was looking forward to the day he could return home and marry her properly. Hopper also told his family that, while there might be racial strife on the home front, there was none in his corner of Vietnam. The war was deadly serious and when death waited in the next tree line, the next rice paddy, or the next step there was no time to worry about the color of your comrade's skin. A letter home to Hopper's family and to Jennifer outlined his thoughts:

> So many times I think about all the fighting going on at home. If all the people realized what they were doing I'm sure it would make a big difference. Over here my feelings towards a black man are the same as they are towards my buddies back home. Maybe people don't like me feeling that way, but you never know when you'll save his life and he'll thank you for it or in turn when he may save my life and I know I'll thank him for it and thank God for putting him on this earth. Maybe someday people will wake up, but I'm afraid it will be too late then.

———— † ————

As Jimmie Salazar, Steve Hopper, and dozens more recuperated from their wounds, at the beginning of June some new intelligence came in that the 5th Nha Be Main Force Viet Cong Battalion had been located near the village of Can Giouc south of Saigon. The plan was for elements of two US battalions, including Charlie Company, to encircle and destroy the 5th Nha Be. The operation resulted in a day-long battle on June 19 that left 38 American dead and 101 wounded, including ten dead and 40 wounded within Charlie Company. The Viet Cong suffered even greater losses, losing 250 killed in action. It was a battle that changed everything for Charlie Company. So many had been killed or wounded that the core of the old unit that had trained together and shipped out to Vietnam together was simply gone. Nearly everyone had lost a friend. Some had lost several friends. And nearly everyone had become a killer. In military terms Charlie Company was now "blooded" – a unit that was fully battle tested. But in human terms it had all hurt so much. The battle was the subject of many anguished letters home, with Bernie Windmiller describing the series of events to his wife Esther in especially eloquent terms:

> How should I begin this letter? It will no doubt be one of the most eventful letters I will write. Maybe if I mention Operation Concordia

it may make you aware of the situation I have been in, that is if the news has reported this battle, and I'm sure it has. And a battle it was, one that will be stamped on my conscience forever.

We hit our Landing Zone at 0700 and jumped off into waist deep mud, spread out and covered the 1,000 meters without incident, other than trudging through the mud ... it looked so desolate and strange, kind of eerie... Charlie Company sent our Blitzer element up along a small stream, with two small boats alongside them in the water with four men aboard each... As our Blitzer element reached upstream they received fire from across the river. Then the VC opened up on those two small boats and literally blew them out of the water. We never did find the bodies of those fellows and they are listed as Missing in Action.

The VC initial burst of fire wounded 3 men in our Charlie Blitzer element. So I dropped my pack and started up along the rice paddy dike to reach those wounded men. I was scared but kept my head. I knew I had to help those men. I would run like crazy and then dive behind a dike, run and dive. I made it to a shack and took cover behind it. [Two of the wounded] were right out in the middle of the rice paddies. After a couple of minutes the medic [Gary Maibach] came and we both took off running out to the 2 wounded. We threw ourselves beside them and hugged the ground as the bullets went zinging over our heads. We got them bandaged. One boy had a chest wound and the other one was hit in the right wrist, left upper arm and left ankle. He had some broken bones and was in a lot of pain. I stayed with them for about an hour flat on my stomach, with bullets still zinging over my head ... I was able to talk with these boys to assure them of God's presence and that all would be well... One was yelling with pain, but there was nothing else we could do since we were starting to receive heavier fire. The chopper came and we got him aboard. I crawled back behind a little mound of dirt in the rice paddy, which was enough to shield myself and one other fellow from VC fire.

But we could not move. Every time we tried to they fired at us. I don't know if you remember Lt. Shulman [Platoon Leader of Charlie Company's 4th Platoon] or not. Well, Shelly, as we called him, came walking to my front about five yards, standing up. I yelled to him to get down. He took about five steps and got hit. He died right there about 45 minutes later before we could evacuate him. Several fellows got hit all around me, and we called for another dust off... A chopper came down to take our wounded out. We loaded about five aboard it, and he started to take off and was about six feet in the air when the VC shot him down. One of the pilots was wounded. This took place about 10 yards behind me. In fact when the chopper fell the guy next to me and I thought the big rotor blade was going to hit us [Windmiller and Gary Maibach]. We took the guys off that chopper and put them on the ground. One of the gunners no sooner got out and laid down, right behind me, when he got hit.

In about 10 minutes a med evac chopper came in and we loaded the wounded aboard it. He took off and was about 20 feet in the air and turning when the VC opened up on him with 50 caliber machine guns and the chopper came crashing to the ground on its side. Some men that were closer to it than I ran over and pulled the pilots out. They were badly beaten up, but alive. One of the wounded was thrown out and killed; one of the crewmen had his legs pinned under the chopper, but they were able to lift it up enough to get him out. One of the wounded, who had actually walked to go on the chopper, was pinned under and was dead. We tried later to get him out, but couldn't. As soon as that chopper went down two others came in and took all the wounded aboard them... I said a prayer over one dead soldier ... and one of the wounded guys crawled up next to me and just grabbed my hand and clung to me. I was able to talk with him and minister to him, and he seemed to quiet down.

All this time they were having air strikes with 500 lb. bombs and machine gun fire; and artillery was firing. It was all so close to us; the bombs just lifted us off our stomachs, and the shrapnel of the artillery fell in on us. I got hit several times, but it had lost all its steam each time. It scared me the first time it happened. They were pieces about the size of quarters and half dollars, some bigger. But the VC were dug in so well and their bunkers so thick even all this did not knock them out. They kept firing at us.

We knew we could not cross that stream to go in after them because they would zap us in the water. So we ran back to the ATC's and they moved us over across that little stream and we jumped off and went after them. This time I stayed in the rear with Captain Lind as the boys were assaulting the VC positions.

I know that telling you all this will frighten you and cause you to worry. These kind of battles will come again, but this is what our faith in Christ is for. We must trust Him. I do what has to be done and nothing foolish... I guess we all consider ourselves lucky to be alive – but mine is not luck. "The Lord is a present help."

June 21

[Writing about visiting men in the hospital] I'm sure you can imagine it was a sad sight to see all these men with various type wounds and of degrees of seriousness. Some I knew well – others were just acquaintances. But they are my men, and it hurts to see each one. There were about three with serious head wounds who were not responding. One of my dear friends, a fine Christian, had his left arm blown off, head and face wounds; he looked terrible and could barely talk. As soon as I saw him he said, "I was talking to the Lord all the time and He heard me." I prayed with him before I left and could not hold back the tears.

One of the boys I had reached in the middle of the rice paddy said, "I knew you would come, Chaplain." They all wanted to know about their buddies. Some of them cried when they heard their best buddy got killed, and all immediately and anxiously would say, "Chaplain, what about so and so?" If he had not been wounded or killed, they would usually say, "Oh, thank God." If they had been killed it was usually deep silence or they became teary eyed and choked up...

In all I saw 57 and 15 I could not find... Now I have 72 letters to write to wives and parents.

The man at Windmiller's side for much of the day was Gary Maibach. Having started the day in his usual position as 1st Platoon medic,

Maibach had asked for and received permission to go and help the wounded of 2nd Platoon after he had learned of the death of that platoon's medic, Bill Geier. Grabbing his medical bag and sprinting toward the scene of the fighting, Maibach had bumped into Windmiller, and the two spent much of the afternoon patching up the fallen. There were several, including Lieutenant Schulman and Bill Geier, that Maibach couldn't help, and it broke his heart. He had never seen anyone die on the field of combat, and it happened more times on June 19 than he would ever care to remember. One leg had been shot off; another patient had a sucking chest wound; one poor guy had been hit five times, while his rescuer was shot twice. Two men had severed arteries. Maibach's day was a sea of blood and moaning. And then the chopper had gone down, and Maibach had watched in horror as Forrest Ramos, who had been shot clean through the elbow and had stood in the door smiling, tumbled from the aircraft and fell to the paddy below prior to the aircraft crashing onto his body. For all of his deep faith, Maibach was shaken to the core, and he, like Windmiller, shared his experiences with his wife.

Mary Ann could hardly believe her eyes as she read the letter. She had known that death would come – after all, Gary had already faced the loss of Duffy Black. But she had never imagined that death could come in such a gruesome and comprehensive manner. First she wept and then she prayed for her husband. It was plain to see that he was hurting, that his soul had absorbed a physical blow. He was in such pain, and she was powerless to help. She chronicled the ebb and flow of her feelings in her next two letters:

> I've just finished re-reading your letter about the battle and again my heart aches for you darling, and I feel all choked up with love for you. Wanting so very much to be able to take you in my arms and comfort you, my one true love. Surely the love I feel for you is so overpowering as to cause such a concern for you.
>
> I can surely imagine your anxiety over going out again so soon after that fateful patrol. Surely it must take much faith and courage to

go out each time, but especially so after having such an unfortunate experience as you had on the 19th. I'm praying with all my heart you may be spared many more experiences such as that. Honey, although I know I can't really know how wretched the things you experience really are I want you to know how much unhappiness it brings me to think of what you must endure, yet I am so thankful that you do write it as it is. May God give you an extra measure of grace for the horrors that you must endure.

Just two weeks later Mary Ann was working a quiet afternoon shift at the hospital, serving as head nurse. Caring for her patients and the minutiae of her labors helped to take her mind off of things and made the days go faster. And after June 19 she needed to be distracted from wartime reality. In the back of her mind she knew that Gary had to be out on another operation. There had been a gap in his letters, and that always happened when he was out. She looked up from a chart to see two well-dressed military officers heading her way, asking for the head nurse. Immediately she knew the news that they carried. Gary had been killed; the letters had stopped because Gary was dead. By the time they reached her Mary Ann was shaking with fear. But then they merely asked for the room number of the friend whom they had come to visit. Barely able to collect her thoughts, Mary Ann gave them the proper directions. Then she found an unoccupied room where she sat and cried for an hour.

———— † ————

Nearly everyone lost a friend on June 19, but the situation was worst for Larry Lilley. He had started the day by kidding with his best friend Kenny Frakes. Lilley's 1st Platoon had to slop through the rice paddies all day, while Frakes and 4th Platoon had things easy, spending the day in the unit's plastic assault boats and gliding along the rivers and canals in comparative comfort. Larry couldn't help but wish that he was floating along on one of those boats as he watched them turn a corner in the small stream that ran on Charlie Company's flank. But then the firing had started. Two 50-caliber machine guns ripped the tiny boats to pieces, cutting through their occupants and tossing their bloodied bodies into the water. Lilley was not near enough to the scene to see that Kenny had gotten hit, but he knew in his heart that nobody could have survived.

The boats had been nearing the frontage of 3rd Platoon when they were hit. Larry Lukes remembers the scene, in terms that he wasn't able to write in letters home then or share fully with his wife Kay to this day:

> The weapons platoon was aboard the plastic assault boats, and the VC opened up on them. Then I saw Kenny Frakes floating by in the canal; he had a shoulder wound that I could see. I crawled up over the dike, lying in the mud, and I grabbed him – had a hold of his webgear. The bullets were just banging all around hitting in the water and in the mud. All I saw was him floating there; the shooting didn't even hardly register. That look on his face – it was pain and fear. He just looked up and said, "Let me go. Just let me go." His right shoulder was all bloody and his arm, but I never knew how badly he was hit. I really liked Frakes; he was a hell of a nice kid. I was just shaking, but I let him go. I was just crying, tears running down my cheeks. I started thinking "Why did I let go? Why didn't I keep pulling him?"
>
> *Larry Lukes*

The fighting had gone on all day, with Larry Lilley continually moving closer to 2nd Platoon and the site of the demise of the plastic assault boats. But in all of the firing, helping the wounded, and trying to stay alive, Larry Lilley never again caught sight of his best friend Kenny Frakes. His body wasn't discovered until the next day, having washed a good bit downstream. Later that night, as things had finally quieted down, Lilley paid absent attention to the report of a stray sniper round. He hoped that nobody had been hit. What a way to go, being hit after the battle was over. It was only the next morning that he learned that the sniper round he had heard that night had struck Tim Johnson,

Larry's other best friend in the world, smack between the eyes, killing him instantly. The opening burst of fire in the battle of June 19 had taken Kenny Frakes; the last round fired had taken Tim Johnson. Bookends to the worst day Larry Lilley would ever know.

My best friends in the world were Kenny Frakes and Timmy Johnson. We had grown up together, and I was living with Kenny when the induction notices came in. My mom took us all to the induction center together, and we were so nervous about going to Vietnam. As we were crossing this big rice paddy, Kenny was in one of those little boats with maybe eight guys. They were going up this little tributary to my right, maybe 50 yards in front of me. I turned to the lieutenant and said, "I thought that they were supposed to be behind us." He said, "They are! Get on the horn and get them back here!" I squawked them on the radio and they answered. I yelled, "Turn that goddamn boat around and get back here!" In the process of turning the boat around the Viet Cong set off a claymore mine that was the size of the bottom of a 50-gallon drum. Damn. Everybody in that boat died, and the boat circled out there for maybe 25 minutes. Kenny Frakes' mom absolutely refused to believe that her son was dead. I had to describe to her how he died, and she still would not believe it. His car was parked in the family driveway for 30 years until his mother passed away. That night one last round came in, and it snapped past my head; it cracked when it went by me. I thought, "Holy shit, I thought we had killed everybody in that tree line!" Then someone screamed out that Timmy Johnson had been hit. I found out the next day that the round had hit Timmy Johnson right between the eyes. On one level I was happy just to be alive. After so much firing it just seemed like nobody should have survived. But I did. But I was also so shocked to have lost both Kenny and Timmy. That was a shock. There is not a day that goes by that I don't miss those guys. You are slapped in the face by reality and think, "This can't get any worse. This can't happen." But I saw it happen. It makes you tough inside; tougher than you want to be. You can't pretend that it didn't happen, but you have to put it on the back burner and get ready for the next patrol. It was a humbling experience. Why was I going home and my buddies weren't? But you have to live with it. It makes you quiet inside.

Larry Lilley

Once back at Dong Tam, Lilley knew that he had to sit down and tell his wife Judy what had happened. But somehow he just couldn't write it. He had to come to terms with it all himself before he could write it. And he just sat there, staring. Understanding wouldn't come. Acceptance wouldn't come. Words wouldn't come. Back home Judy lived through another of those times when there was a gap in receiving any letters. But this gap suddenly turned different. Rumors swept the valley. There had been a battle in Vietnam, and four boys from the valley had been killed. Four soldiers from Lancaster. There was a frantic call from Larry's sister. "Have you gotten a letter from Larry?" Nothing new. Then Larry's mom called, crying. "Are you sure that a letter hasn't come?" Then they told her the rumors. If Larry had been killed the army would notify Judy first as his wife. She had to be on the lookout. The soldiers who carried the notification of Larry's death could arrive at any time. A day later a letter from Larry finally arrived, full of agony over the loss of his best friends. The emotions that struck Judy were so full of contradiction. Larry, her husband, was alive – joyously and fully alive. But his two best friends were gone: two guys she knew better than almost anyone else in the world. Judy felt a great sense of relief juxtaposed in an odd balance with a crushing sorrow.

Judy had known Tim and Kenny for as long as she had known Larry. Wherever he was, they were. Whether it was hanging around the apartment, tinkering on cars, or training at Fort Riley – they always seemed to be together. Tim and Kenny were so young, so fun loving, so full of mischievous energy. And Kenny was so damn funny. It wasn't like he told jokes; it was more like he was just a riot at everything he did. Judy also knew Kenny's girlfriend. He wasn't serious yet, at least that is what he said, but Judy thought Kenny's feigned disinterest in commitment was a bluff. But now it didn't matter. Both Kenny and Tim were gone. Just like when Don Peterson died, the whole town turned out for their funerals. But not Judy. She had endured all of the sorrowful funerals that she could bear. Seeing Don Peterson in his casket had hit far too close to home. Seeing Kenny and Tim might just push her over the edge into a real despair from which extrication might prove impossible. Larry was still over there. And it seemed like the war was out to get the boys from the valley. Was he going to be next? Dwelling on such thoughts threatened to break her.

———— † ————

Mary Ann Simon had known Jim Rademacher much of her life – he lived nearby, they were in the same grade school, and they rode the bus together nearly every day. Maybe it had been just a natural thing that they had gotten together. She had been 15 when they first kissed. It was Jim's first kiss, or so he said. At a high school football game on September 25, 1964, while the couple strolled past the goalpost, Jim reached into his pocket and pulled out his class ring, asking Mary Ann to go steady. She gave a little scream, quickly said "Yes," and ran over to tell her girlfriends before cutting some angora to make the ring fit her much smaller finger. The couple especially loved dancing – there were dances every Friday night. Mary Ann loved the fast songs – "Dance, Dance, Dance" by the Beach Boys; "Lipstick on Your Collar" by Connie Francis – but she danced those with the girls since Jim only liked to slow dance. After graduation Mary Ann got a job working for the state of Michigan up the road in Lansing and Jim worked framing houses. The idea was to put aside enough money to get married and start a family. But in November of 1966 his draft notice came in. The couple decided to wait to get married until he got home.

Jim's eyesight wasn't all that great, so the couple hoped that his trip to Fort Leonard Wood would be a short one. But it seemed that the army was hard up for men, and Jim was inducted. After basic training Jim went first to Fort Polk, Louisiana and then to Fort Knox,

Kentucky. At the conclusion of his training cycle, Jim came home for a final leave before shipping out to Vietnam. At his going-away party Jim's World War II veteran uncle caused a scene. Thoroughly drunk the uncle had begged Jim to go to Canada, to do anything other than go to Vietnam. Wars were hell and would consume Jim one way or the other. Family members whisked the drunken uncle away, but a pall hung over the rest of the evening.

Jim sent Mary Ann a steady stream of letters chronicling his journey to Vietnam. His letters were newsy, full of information on things like the climate and the people and full of wonder as to where he might wind up and with what unit. On June 15 the mystery was solved – Jim Rademacher had joined Charlie Company. Jim went on his first mission on June 17 and followed with a letter on the 18th:

We go out for another mission tomorrow morning at six o-clock and I guess it's supposed to last for six days, so I won't be able to write you during that time because they don't have mail boxes out in the field and I can't carry paper and pen with me. It probably would get all wet and muddy anyway.

You keep asking me how it is out here... I wrote already that we went on a two day mission, and I told you we didn't see any VCs. Well A and B company lost about four men killed and I saw one man dead and about ten injured. I guess one guy had both legs blown off. So as you can see it's no picnic over here, and a man can only take so much and how much I can take I don't know. So far I have been lucky and haven't seen any real action yet. But I got the feeling we are going to get it one of these days just like the other companies on this ship... And now going out for six days we are eventually going to run into something, and most injuries come from the traps the VC have and they have a lot of them. So if I am at the right place at the right time I will get it also. I will never know and that's what gets on my nerves all the time is who is next in line, me or one of my buddies.

Jim Rademacher was badly wounded in the battle of June 19, his first real action with Charlie Company. Shot through the chest in the opening phase of the fighting, Rademacher crumpled to the ground in agony. He was caught in the open, with Viet Cong bullets impacting all around. He could hardly move. All he could do was yell for help and hope. A few minutes later a form crashed to the ground beside him, asking if he was okay. It was Chaplain Windmiller, followed quickly by Gary Maibach. With help having arrived, Jim blacked out.

For Mary Ann the wait back home started out okay. Jim had warned her that he would not be able to write for maybe six days. But then that turned into two weeks. What could be happening? Mary Ann was frantic, but she really couldn't share her fears with anyone. Nobody would understand. Then, finally, the letters began to arrive.

> I hope you're not mad because I got shot. Well today is the best I felt since I have been hit so I figured I could write you.
>
> Well I am doing real good and will be all right in a month or so. I got hit in the left hand and then the bullet just went to the right of my heart and came out of my right side so God was with me out there.
>
> The doctors also put a few extra holes in me. One hole in my right side is so the infection can all drain out which is still open. I will have four marks on my belly. One is about a foot long where they cut me open to fix up my insides like my liver and a few other small items inside. I also got a cut on my left arm just above the elbow where they had a tube in me so I could eat. Well I can eat all right all by myself.
>
> I don't know what my left hand is like because it is all bandaged up and I can't see what all is wrong with it. But it sure looks funny. But the doctor said it will be all right also. So I will be as good as new before I know it. I got my Purple Heart. It really looks nice but I would rather not have gotten one the hard way.
>
> I never hurt so much in my whole life. It hurt so bad at the time that I wanted to die. But now it don't feel too bad anymore. It still hurts only when I laugh. So I never laugh. The doctor might send me

to Japan unless he changes his mind. I was hoping maybe they will send me back to the states. I will just have to keep hoping and praying that they do send me back home.

Mary Ann burst into tears at the news. There was relief that Jim had not been killed, but also despair that he had been hurt so badly. Needing to compose herself, Mary Ann stepped outside. Her dog – she loved that dog – walked over to see what was the matter, and in her frustration Mary Ann kicked it out of the way. Desperate for more information the family called their local representative and the Department of Defense in Washington DC to see what they could learn regarding Jim's condition. By the next day their representative got back with the news. Jim had been taken off of the critical list and had his condition had been changed to serious. Hoping for more, the family went to the post office. The local postmaster was a World War II veteran and understood their desperation all too well. He promised to call to let the family and Mary Ann know when Jim's next letter arrived so that they didn't have to wait for mail delivery to their homes.

There was a second agonizing wait between letters, with the next communication from Jim dated July 4:

Well it's been sixteen days ago since I got shot and I am doing real well. They have been moving me around the last couple of days. They flew me to the Philippines where I stayed one night. Then I took a jet to the air base in Japan and stayed there over night. Then I went on a helicopter and flew to Camp Zama Japan where I am at right now in an Army Hospital.

I got a couple of broken bones in my left hand but I guess it will be all right. It's just a matter of time. My chest wounds are just about all healed up. I am sure a lucky man to be still alive today.

I will probably stay here for now until I get all healed up. Then they probably will send me back to Vietnam, which I don't want to go back there as long as I live. I had enough fighting even if only there a couple of days and my first big battle. I never did get to shoot my rifle.

I never got a chance to. The VC got me the first couple of minutes before I could get to some cover to hide behind. Well honey you can write me. I guess my address is on the envelope so write as soon as possible. I haven't got any letters since I got shot. Well that's about all I know for right now so good bye.

P.S. I love you very much and wish you were here by my side and don't worry because I am going to be all right.

Jim's wounding was big news in their tiny town of Fowler, Michigan. The local gas station bought a big get well card, and everyone dropped by to sign. Everybody asked about him, gave Mary Ann hugs, and wrote notes that they asked to be passed on to him. Everyone was supportive, but Mary Ann was still taking it hard. At work her boss was understanding, giving her all the time she needed to compose herself. Mary Ann went to visit Jim's parents every day. She needed their support, and they were there for her every step of the way – even offering to let her move in if that would help. As time moved on, so did Mary Ann. She began to accept the change, and accepted that Jim would actually be okay. In any small town there were rumors. One group of folks was sure that Jim had lost an arm. Another group was sure that he had lost another, perhaps more meaningful, appendage. They never said such things in front of Mary Ann, but she heard the rumors just the same. Mary Ann knew that she had passed her own personal crisis point when she found the rumors to be funny, and she told everyone to rest assured that Jim was hurting, but still all in one piece.

It was in August that Mary Ann received news that was like a double-edged sword. Jim was getting better quickly and was about to get out of the hospital. His recovery had been so fast that there was no need to send him to a stateside hospital. Instead he was being reassigned to Okinawa. There were so many things to unpack from that letter! Jim was getting better, which was wonderful. But he wasn't going to come home for part of his recovery, which was a real let-down. He wasn't going back to Vietnam. That was the best news of all. He wouldn't be in danger anymore. Mary Ann would never again worry about receiving a letter about Jim's wounding or death. That particular news was like having an albatross lifted from her shoulders. But even then there was a downside. Since Jim was being reassigned to a non-combat position, his stint in the military would keep him overseas for two years, not the expected one. Jim was going to be okay, but his life with Mary Ann was going to be put on hold for yet another year. All of her friends were getting married and moving on with their lives. But she had to wait for another year. It all seemed somehow so unfair. Mary Ann was overjoyed that her future husband was going to be safe, but she was going to have to wait even longer for the future to arrive.

———— † ————

June 19, 1967. Outnumbered and caught dead to rights by a dug-in and determined foe, Charlie Company and its sister companies engaged in a full day of desperate life or death struggle. After witnessing his command pinned down and taking crippling losses for most of the day, Captain Herb Lind was ready to do anything to save the situation. A nearby monitor gunboat, with US Navy Commander Dusty Rhodes at the helm, volunteered to venture into the narrow stream that separated Charlie Company from the Viet Cong positions to bring its 40-millimeter cannon in the bow turret and the 81-millimeter mortar amidships to bear on the Viet Cong bunkers. Lind got to his feet and walked alongside the monitor as it unleashed a fury of fire, shattering the Viet Cong bunkers and throwing mud, concrete, and entire trees off in all directions. Jimmie Salazar remembers watching the spectacle and thinking that it was the most beautiful sight that he had ever seen. 1st and 2nd platoons then crossed the canal and assaulted the stricken Viet Cong positions, unleashing a chaos of death as enemy soldiers popped out of the ground all around while attempting to flee their compromised positions. Herb Lind's quick thinking and personal bravery had saved the day, but he never wrote home to his wife Becky about the battle; he didn't even inform her that he had taken command of Charlie Company.

Having won a considerable, if costly, victory, Charlie Company dug in for the night. The next morning, though, was perhaps even more dreadful. A few hundred yards away, Charlie Company's sister unit, Alpha Company, had stumbled into a U-shaped ambush on June 19. With fire pouring in from all directions, and with no cover, Alpha suffered nearly 90 percent casualties – most in the first few minutes of firing. With so few survivors, it fell to Charlie Company to clear the dead from Alpha's battlefield. The events of June 19 and 20 are seared into the minds of every Charlie Company veteran – events that served to shape the lives of these men and their families for decades.

What I saw on June 19? Those guys on the boats didn't have a chance at all. They were hit with a claymore and all kinds of fire. They didn't jump off of the boats, they were blown off of the boats. When the navy monitor came up the canal later in the day to take out the Viet Cong positions, the bodies were still in the water. When that monitor came by you could see it churning the bodies in the water like a mixer. Later in the day we had to go into the canal to try and haul the bodies out before the tide took them away. We all had friends in Alpha Company. We had to pick up all of their bodies, weapons, and webgear and haul them all over to the boats. It was tough. You had to walk through puddles of blood that had already congealed. The bodies had been out there for a while, and the blood. It was a strong odor that you can never forget. There were a lot of people who had been hit and had just bled to death. You had to haul their body up out of the sticking blood. I just thought, damn. But it had to be done. We went through hell, but I don't regret it. If it had to be done again, I would.

Jimmie Salazar

On June 19 the fire started we all got down, but Forrest Ramos yelled, "John, I'm hit! I'm hit!" He had been shot through the elbow and had a million-dollar wound. I looked over to my right just in time to see another guy hit with a 50-caliber round. I was close enough to hear it slap through his flesh. He screamed and I saw a hunk of flesh fly off of his thigh. We were so happy when Ramos got on the medevac chopper; he was going home. Then to see it shot out of the sky and him fall out; in the middle of it all I just started crying. Sometimes you can't help it. I just started crying. At night I was in a little hooch, and saw Timmy Johnson's body lying there wrapped up in a poncho. He had been shot between the eyes.

At the time of the June 19 battle I was still just 20 years old; this adventure was no longer fun anymore, the war hit me in the face and body like a blast furnace at Cleveland's Republic Steel plant, and I was made over again, I remember during the battle that I could not believe what was happening; it was so surreal. I saw myself as someone I did not know. I was three dimensional, standing outside of my body looking at this warrior gone mad. I saw me as a creature I did not recognize; I really wanted to fight and kill anything that was responsible for my buddies dying and getting all mangled up. I remember looking in the river beside me and seeing dead bodies of comrades floating in the strong current, one guy's dead body with nothing on from the waist up floating down the river, I will never forget the face, but I did not know the soldier. You ask how did I deal with the losses on that day? I still have not, and they still live in my memory and will always have life as long as I live.

John Bradfield

When Forrest Ramos got hit, he was all smiles telling me that he had a million-dollar wound – "I'm going to Washington; I'm going home!" When the chopper came in for the dustoff, he got in and it got shot down. We were still under very heavy enemy fire. He fell out of the chopper as it crashed and it came down on top of him. We tried to dig him out, but the chopper was so heavy that we couldn't get it off of him. The skid pushed him down into the rice paddy water, and he drowned. I was the one who wrote to his family and sent home his belongings. I felt really bad, and I keep reliving this every day of my life, but I made a promise to him that if I got out alive I would better myself in his memory.

Jose Sauceda

———— † ————

Even after events as momentous and life-changing as those of June 19, Charlie Company's war simply went on. The men had little time to process their grief, pausing perhaps to note all of the empty bunks on the barracks ship, or all of the unoccupied seats at breakfast, or the pile of bloody gear gathered from the corpses. Some wondered if they had become nothing more than animals. Some reveled in still being alive against all the odds. Many mourned the loss of friends. Some wondered if they could have done anything differently to save their friends. Some shared such thoughts in letters home, but many hid those thoughts away even from themselves. But the war just kept rolling on as before. Missions had to be run, replacements had to be trained, and life had to be lived. The fighting and dying, though, if anything seemed only to increase in tempo. Only three weeks went by before Charlie Company fought its next major battle. Soldiers, wives, and families had only just begun the mental process of inching away from the memory of June 19 when it happened all over again.

The tactical situation was eerily reminiscent of Charlie Company's first battle on May 15. This time 2nd Platoon was in the lead and sent Sergeant George Smith's squad out to recon a tree line across an open rice paddy. Within a few yards of their goal, all hell broke loose once again. A dug-in enemy battalion had opened fire, hitting machine gunner Frank Schwan in the chest and dropping him to the ground. Schwan struggled to the safety of a paddy dike, throwing up blood and passing out several times, but he realized that three other members of the squad were caught even further out into the paddy dead to rights. Simultaneously, on Charlie Company's right flank, Fred Kenney, 3rd Platoon's point man, was hit square in the chest with a burst of machine gun fire and killed instantly. All across the battlefield, Charlie Company troopers hit the dirt, scrambling for whatever cover they could find. There was a furious exchange of fire for the remainder of the afternoon before darkness quickly began to set in. Unlike June 19, though, there would be no cathartic conclusion to the battle. It frustrated Captain Lind. They had the enemy locked into battle, but the lead elements of Smith's squad and 3rd Platoon were too close to enemy lines to allow for the calling in of artillery fire or air support. All an outmanned Charlie Company could do was sit tight and exchange fire with an unseen and numerically superior enemy force.

Making matters much worse – there was no way for the remainder of Charlie Company to rescue its stranded recon elements. Any move toward Smith's squad or Kenney's position drew heavy incoming fire. Lind and his platoon leaders had to assume that the company's lead elements were dead, and it was no use to waste lives on attempts to save the dead. The men, though, were restless – determined to go and try to save their friends, only to be held back by their officers. It was worst during the night. Charlie Company troopers could hear the Viet Cong out there among the fallen, executing them, ransacking their bodies. As dawn gathered, there was one minor miracle. Frank Schwan had survived, hobbling along with the help of uninjured squadmate Henry Hubbard. The duo, who were part of Jack Benedick's 2nd Platoon, had barely escaped a harrowing night of Viet Cong patrols and uncertainty:

I had just rotated point squads when 3rd Squad headed off into that rice paddy. They were within 25 yards of the Viet Cong tree line when the fight started. That is when I lost four guys. I could see them when they got hit and went down and everybody hit the ground. It is hard to talk about, but they didn't all get killed at once. Harold Wayne King was the machine gunner, and he got hit in the neck, but he fired all of his ammo before he died. He kept shooting until he died. You could tell by the spent ammunition lying all around him when we found his body the next day. Everybody tried to get out there to them, but it was too dangerous. We were taking too many casualties. We were badly outnumbered, and there was just no way to get out there to them. Sergeant George Smith was a pretty happy go lucky guy. He was a good soldier and had been through Officer Candidate School. He wasn't afraid of anything. Butch Eakins was an early replacement; he was a farmboy from Missouri. Phil Ferro was one of the many guys drafted from California. He had won a Bronze Star on June 19. King was a country boy from Virginia. Real quiet, but really did his job. Such a good guy. When we went to police up the bodies the next day, they had all been shot in the top of the head by the Viet Cong. I was mad. It was time to get even.

Jack Benedick

But there was nobody on whom to exact vengeance; the Viet Cong had fled in the night. Then came the grim task of collecting the dead, made all the worse by the lack of enemy dead. Charlie Company had suffered, and had dealt no suffering in return. Bernie Windmiller wrote to Esther of the experience:

[On July 11] We moved across the river and started northwest. We got about 1500 meters when we came under heavy fire... The 2nd Platoon had a point squad out in front of everyone else – 6 men, and 4 of them were killed in the first 10 minutes of the fight, one right through the head. One of them was [Phil] Ferro, the boy whose mother had sent me a box with such a nice letter. Now I have to write and tell her her son is dead.

That point squad was out there all night long. No one could get to them. Frank Schwan of the point squad was hit in the stomach and the bullet exited his back, and he was hit in the shoulder. Hubbard was not hit at all. Just at dark they crawled back about 25 meters in some tall grass. Shortly thereafter the VC came out and stripped our 4 dead guys of their weapons and gear. They never mutilated their bodies. Schwan and Hubbard crawled back about 500 meters to a dry spot and stayed there all night. The next morning we found them and brought them back to our command location. I talked with Schwan. He could hardly walk, he was so weak. He was covered in mud from head to toe, having laid in it for most of the battle and the night. He said to me, "Chaplain, I lived through the night. I'll make it now I know."

The experience of July 11 was the most difficult of the entire war for Charlie Company commander Captain Herb Lind:

We don't have any idea what damage we did, if any, to the VC that day – there was no body count to substantiate it. The 2nd Platoon was on point that day, and they had a squad caught out in the open, and had four killed almost immediately. We tried several times that day to get out to them, not knowing how many were wounded and dead at the time. But we never got out to them that day. If I had ordered a full mission to get them out we would have taken double that many casualties to rescue dead people. This battle still bothers me more than June 19 does; I just wish we could have gotten out there to them. I don't know how many died instantly and how many bled to death. We tried to get them. But you still wonder, "What could I have done? What personally did I not do right that caused this?" The reconnaissance squad was a good 600 meters in advance of the main unit in a wide open rice paddy. If they hadn't been out that far the whole platoon would have been wiped out. That is hard to accept, but the point element was a sacrifice. Their purpose is to trigger an ambush before the main element gets into the kill zone. It is a hard trade off to accept, when you know that someone could lose his life.

Herb Lind

Many of the men of Charlie Company felt an odd sense of liberation after July 11. Since death was such a regular and maddeningly random occurrence in the new world of their reality, many men now believed that they were not going to survive the war. In that surrender to death, though, there was a type of freedom. They knew what their end was going to be and no longer had to be scared. None, though, wrote home to their wives of such things. How could they? How would their wives ever understand the visceral meaning of brutal loss? How could their wives understand the depth of friendship the men had developed, only to see that friendship ended as bodies were ripped apart, heads were blown to pieces at close range, brothers were drowned under downed helicopters? The men couldn't fully understand these events themselves, much less meaningfully explain them to their wives. The men became acquainted with death, but the wives did not. Death would always be there separating the husbands from their spouses – a critical life experience that could not be expressed or shared. In the wives' world of waiting and wondering amidst a sea of normalcy, the news of battle, even if incompletely reported by letter, always came as a nearly debilitating shock. The wives tried desperately to understand, perhaps realizing that they never would. Mary Ann Maibach spoke for many when she wrote:

> I was, as always, so unhappy to hear of your unfortunate patrol again, though am ever so thankful that once again God protected you from all the danger around you on every side. I'm always so distressed thinking of my precious husband in such a situation, with bullets flying around, and having to load the wounded and dead, yet surely, I think, God gives you an extra measure of grace & strength in these times of such great need. That assurance really helps me so much my love, and I pray even harder for your protection from danger & evil – I love you so much... We will continue to hope my darling, that before too very long you may be relieved of such a rough schedule and job – and trust that God knows best, and will supply for you each and every need.

———— † ————

Each of Charlie Company's losses that day hurt badly – each in its own measure. But one loss perhaps stood out above the others. Like Don Peterson before him, Fred Kenney had so much to live for. The conclusion of Bernie Windmiller's letter to Esther about the battle made the point:

> We also had one boy Fred Kenney from the 3rd Platoon whom we could not reach until the next morning – also married. The VC had stripped him also and taken his wedding ring and watch. We got a chopper in the next morning and got the bodies out. Sgt Smith was one of the 4 killed from 2nd Platoon of Charlie Company. He is the one I laid with for so long in the battle of the 19th of June. He and I had helped some of the other wounded... It was not the large type of battle we had on the 19th. But when you're getting shot at every battle is big...

As I've said before, these operations do not get any easier, and I don't relish getting shot at every time we go out. But if the Lord can keep me for the next 5½ months, and He can I know, then I'll make it... Missing you is more and more pronounced each day. Sometimes it just seems I can't take another day without you.

Once again, Windmiller's words cut his wife Esther to the quick. Realizing her husband's continuing danger and the losses and grief that he faced on such a regular basis left Esther feeling lost and incapable – incapable of being there to help share the burden for the man she so loved. She spoke of her fears in her letters, to which Bernie responded:

As I reread what I had written and relived the experience of July 11 again, I was moved to tears. I know how you must feel when you know I've been in combat, the fears, anxieties, etc. Know that I feel them with you. But I'm sorry to have to see you going through these hard days. If it were possible to spare you these experiences, you know I would. Again and again I commit my life to the Lord – there is nothing else I can do or want to do. I confess that my faith is often weak, but in moments of crisis even a weak faith is not to be despised. You asked if I snap back after these operations. I do, especially when we have two days off.

Known to one and all as "Cool Wig" due to his wavy blonde hair, Fred Kenney was a gregarious surfer kid from California. Everyone knew that he was married and had gotten to know his wife Barbara through her letters and care packages. And there was no doubt that everyone knew that Fred was a father. His son Fred had been born while Cool Wig was aboard the troopship to Vietnam. Upon receiving the news that he was a papa, Fred had jumped so high that he had turned his ankle and whooped so loudly that nearly everyone had heard. Fred didn't even get a picture of his son until he arrived in Vietnam, and then he went from bunk to bunk at Camp Bear Cat showing that thing off – everyone got a look at little Freddie. And

Cool Wig never had tired of showing off each and every new picture that he received. Mail call probably meant a new picture, which probably meant a visit from Cool Wig.

Everyone mourned the loss of Fred Kenney. But Captain Herb Lind never wrote home about such things. Lind was sparing in his language on the best of days, and he had also made the decision to guard his wife Becky from the truth of Vietnam. Becky had long taken solace in the fact that Herb spent most of his time with headquarters company, and was not leading troops into the field on a daily basis. But just before the battle of June 19 Captain Rollo Larson, who had commanded Charlie Company, had shipped home, and Herb Lind had taken his place. Herb was very concerned that his new assignment would cause Becky to worry, so he simply hadn't told her about it. He told both his father and his brother about the new development, but he did not tell Becky. In Herb's letters home the entire battle of June 19, his personal heroism, and even the receipt of a Silver Star had gone entirely unmentioned. His letter home following the battle had read simply: "Just back in from the field and I am really bushed. We were out 3 days and we were really pushed. Yesterday we covered twice as much ground as we are supposed to in a day." Becky had to discover that Herb had been in a battle by watching the news and had quizzed him in her own letters, learning only bits and pieces of the truth of that day. But July 11 was different. Of all of Charlie Company's battles both big and small, of all of the many losses – in Captain Herb Lind's letters home only Fred Kenney's loss receives mention:

July 30

We are back in from the field. We only stayed out 3 days but they were bad in that we never knew where they were going to send us next. I don't think it was too well planned in advance. The whole operation got ridiculous the way they bounced us around. Well I'm back in and just tired out.

I have a letter to answer from the wife of a man who was killed on the 11th of July. It is going to be tough to answer because she wants to know just how her husband was killed. I liked the kid real well and it has bothered me ever since the 11th.

Terse and to the point. Such was Herb Lind's way. But Fred Kenny's loss had touched Lind deeply – so deeply that he violated his own unwritten rule in his letters home. Fred's loss touched everyone:

> I was about 15 yards behind Fred Kenney. It was Cool Wig, then Richard Rubio, then me. The Viet Cong had just opened up on 2nd Platoon, and we were nearing a tree line in front of us. Fred was maybe 20 yards from the trees when they opened up on us. They hit Fred right away; Rubio dropped behind a dirt clump, and I was behind a paddy dike. We tried to get to Fred, but we couldn't and had to fall back. At night you could see the Viet Cong out there crawling around with brush tied to them for camouflage. It wasn't until the next day that we found Fred. I can remember how excited Cool Wig was when he got the Red Cross letter that told him that he had had a son. That was such a sad day; everybody liked Fred. His death affected us more than anyone else. He was such a good kid. That day changed us all. We didn't treat people quite so nice after that. They took his watch, wedding ring, and gear. The Viet Cong yelled at night, "Come and get me! Help!" pretending like they were Fred and trying to get us to come out. It was all we could do to stay back. Finding Fred the next day, pulling him up out of the water, and watching the water come pouring out of the holes in his chest – I just sat down on the dike and cried. Every one of us had tears running down our cheeks. He was such a special person. He will be my hero until the day I die.
>
> *Larry Lukes*

The loss of Fred Kenney had indeed touched the lives and souls of Charlie Company, but his loss was catastrophic for a little family in California that was eagerly awaiting his return home to meet his son for the first time.

CHAPTER 5

LOSS

A FRIEND AND ALWAYS A BROTHER

Sitting in the rain and trying to figure a way out,
Half an hour before, my friend and I stole some beer and ice.
We tied my poncho and laid some beer inside,
Covering the beer up with ice we chopped up,
To get the beer cold.

Wouldn't you know... It started to rain,
My friend who helped in the deed
Saw that I was in need and called me over.
He shared his poncho and he solved my need.
Later, everyone drank cold beer
And gave us a loud cheer.

The next day, everyone went out on a mission
Including my friend and I.
After awhile, between the sounds of bullets and bombs,
You take a hit and go down.

My friend comes around and asks if I could run.
I yell, "Hell yeah!" My friend covers for
Me and I take off.

I turn to leave my friend behind.
He yells out, "My chest!"
I know he's been hit.
He is gone now, but this I know
He will always be
"My Friend and My Brother."

Poem by 1st Platoon trooper Charlie Nelson about the loss
of his friend Don Peterson

CONFIRM DEATH OF SERGEANT LOST IN BATTLE

Official notice from the U.S. Army has confirmed the news of the death of Sgt. Elmer "Fred" Kenney whose mother lives in Chatsworth. He had been reported missing in action earlier.

He died of gunshot wounds inflicted while engaged in a firefight in action near the Mekong Delta, Vietnam. He was a member of Company C, Fourth Battalion, 47th Infantry, Ninth Infantry Division.

Funeral services are pending but will be held locally. His mother Mrs. Mary L. Kenney of Chatsworth received word Wednesday confirming the news of his death. His wife Barbara of Canoga Park, now living with her parents near Redding, Cal, also was notified.

A 5 month-old son Frederick also survives, whom Sgt. Kenney had never seen.

Besides his widow and son he is survived by his mother, four sisters, Mrs. Mary Lou McGinnis of Costa Mesa, Miss Susan Kenney of Santa Monica, Mrs. John Stein of Chatsworth, Mrs. Ross Turen of Del Mar, and three brothers Tom, Charles, and Gordon of Chatsworth.

He attended Chatsworth Park Elementary School, John H. Sutter Junior High School, and graduated from Canoga Park High School in 1963.

Local newspaper story

There are 58,178 names etched into the black granite of the Vietnam Veterans Memorial on the mall in Washington DC. At first many derided Maya Lin's design as a black gash of shame that would tarnish both the landscape and the memory of the fallen. Since its opening, though, the memorial has gained an iconic status among Vietnam War veterans, becoming a site of memory, mourning, and catharsis. It is in looking at the etched names – those endless names marching off in their carefully regimented lines – that the memorial gains its greatest meaning. The vast majority of the names on the wall remember young men, in the prime of their lives – with everything to live for – 30,096 of those killed were aged 18–21. While mines, booby traps, grenades, and illness all took a toll on American soldiers in Vietnam, most of the names on the wall were victims of small arms fire – accounting for a total of 18,518 American dead.

Every man who died in Vietnam left behind parents, cousins, and friends who fervently desired to the depths of their souls that their loved one would return safely from war. Their earnest prayers, though, were in vain – prayers ripped to profane shreds by a knock on the family door. Early in the war, the next of kin received news of a loved one's death via impersonal and inscrutable telegram. As casualties mounted, however, the military decided that it needed to humanize the learned reality of death, establishing casualty notification teams across the country to deliver the painful news in person. Normally at least two military officials, clad in dress uniforms and with at least one being of higher rank than the deceased, would arrive with the solemn tidings that the family's loved one had been killed in action in the Republic of Vietnam. As often as they could, military officials would remain on hand until other adult family members arrived to assist the next of kin in their time of need.

Military deaths touched off a flurry of bureaucratic activity. Normally within 24 hours a casualty assistance officer would arrive to begin the labors of dealing with insurance benefits, delivery of the body, and the details of the funeral. Family members could choose to handle all of the details themselves, but generally most funerals for American soldiers killed in Vietnam had a military element, often including a military honor guard, a 21-gun salute, the playing of Taps, and the handing of the folded flag that had adorned the casket to the next of kin. Many found a type of solace in the crush of funeral minutiae. Filling out forms, planning flower sprays, choosing music, greeting loved ones – all of the mundanity of death – at least provided distraction. It was only after the solemn ritual, and the departure of relatives and well-wishers, that the parents, siblings, and assorted kin – those who had loved the slain most dearly – truly had to try to move on with their lives. It was when things were quiet and normal, that the next of kin had to face the dead in stillness and silence. Somehow, though, even though their world would never again be full and complete, those left behind had to try to live.

——— † ———

Some of the names on the wall stand for an even greater level of tragedy and loss. Of the total number of US dead in the war, 17,215 were married, leaving behind widows and young families. The love of a wife for her husband is both visceral and profound, a different kind of love than that of parents for their children. And the love of children for their father is different yet again, something at once almost primal and sparkling pure. The severance of the silken ties of marriage by violent death in war has long been understood to represent a type of loss that is so powerful that it very nearly defies both imagination and characterization.

Tragically there were several Charlie Company marriages that were cut short by violent battlefield death. Of the 26 members of Charlie Company killed in action during 1967, seven were married. Due to the happenstances of time, I was only able to locate and interview two of the Charlie Company widows. The others had either passed away or become lost to the surviving members of the unit and could not be located. In many ways the stories of these women are much like the others chronicled here – they were young boomers with wonderful hopes for their futures who fell in love with and married men who served in Vietnam. But the similarities end there. The random lottery of battle changed the lives of these women forever, setting them apart from their generational compatriots in myriad ways. These stories – stories of loss and resilience – need to be told, but they are separate. At the considerable risk of interrupting the flow of this book I choose to tell the stories of Jacque Peterson and Barbara Kenney here. Lives interrupted.

Jacque Peterson

Jacque's mom Harriet was a firebrand: a woman with a real zest for life – a blur of nervous energy. Her dad, though, was mellow. He was handsome, a tall, well-sculptured Native American who had the patience of a saint with the whirlwind that was Harriet's life, but Harriet didn't quite see it like that. She needed more – more excitement, more activity, more everything. So the couple split when Jacque was in the 1st grade, leaving her with only few memories of their lives together in Yuma, Arizona. Harriet remarried after meeting Deloy McMullen, who was a radar technician for the Air Force. Harriet was repaid for her decision by almost immediate activity, as the family first moved to Biloxi, Mississippi, for a year and then to Lorraine in France. Jacque didn't mind bouncing around; it meant new adventures every time, and France was her favorite. She grew up on a bicycle meandering the open country lanes and winding village byways, picking up baguettes for sandwiches and picnicking in the meadow below the village's castle, which doubled as the very unofficial playground for the local children. In winter, wooden shoes served as skis on the icy cobblestone streets, resulting in wonderful speedy fun, but also bruises, welts, and cuts.

When the family finally landed in Santa Maria, California, while her stepfather was stationed at Vandenberg Air Force Base, Jacque was a high school freshman who was adaptable, resilient, fluent in French, and just a bit different than all the other local kids. She had never lived in one place all that long, so she was from nowhere and everywhere all at the same time. Even though she was shy, Jacque had a knack for making friends quickly, and was just as good at losing them quickly. Jacque was popular, in part because she was gorgeous, and also because she was so down to earth and accessible. She loved watching movies, especially those of the teen heartthrob variety. She loved pop music and dancing until her clothes were drenched in sweat. It was California and it was the beach, so there were dances and teenagers everywhere. This was the epicenter of boomer life and culture, and Jacque McMullen ate it up. She did well in school, keeping her grades respectable enough to go to college if that was her decision. But she really hadn't thought that far ahead. Endless summers, music, cruising, and friends were enough for now.

The McMullen home was on Grover Beach, which meant that Jacque went to the beach nearly every day. Walking along the beach on one spring day she came across a group of kids her own age, and struck up a conversation. One of the group caught her attention immediately. Don Peterson was tall, rugged, handsome, and shirtless. He seemed to be with another girl, a redhead, and Jacque figured that they were an item, but that didn't concern Jacque. If she wanted his attention, she knew she could get it. The next time she saw Don was in study hall at school in Santa Maria. She was in the back row and he in the front, and the timing was right because the Sadie Hawkins dance was coming up. One of her friends, an older guy named Harry Herr, saw Jacque steal a lingering glance at Don. Did she like him? When Jacque finally admitted that she did think that the new guy was cute, Harry egged her on to ask him to the dance. In true high school fashion, a nervous Jacque scribbled a note: "Do you want to go to the dance with me?" After the missive had completed its hand-to-hand journey, Don turned around and looked at her quizzically. She gave him a kind of nod to let him know for sure that the note was from her. A grin broke out across his face, but he remained silent. No nod in return. Harry quickly looked away. Suddenly Jacque was nervous; the kind of nervous that only a high school girl can feel when she has publicly opened herself up to embarrassment and potential ridicule. After study hall Don met her in the hallway and accepted. It turned out that Don Peterson was a great dancer, and the two were soon an item – he the popular football star, she the beautiful, younger girl that nobody quite had a bead on yet.

The days of their romance were idyllic. Maybe it was because he was a middle child, but Don was more mature than all of the other boys. He got into typical teenage boy kinds of trouble, but he also had a serious streak. He was actually interested in Jacque, her likes, dislikes, hopes, and loves. He listened to her. The couple spent a great deal of their time together on the beach. Jacque loved to lie in the sun and tan, always getting darker than the other girls due to her Native American background. Don would come by, seemingly perpetually shirtless, wearing boots, and handsome. Often he would have some beers that he had talked an adult into buying for them and then the couple would head to one of the Pismo Beach dances. Don did have a temper, though, and woe betide any boy who looked too long at Jacque.

Jacque especially enjoyed surfing. It was a perfect way to lose herself, a needed respite as her mother spiraled into alcoholism. Her stepfather drank too, in the boozy manner of good fellowship often expected in the military at the time, but he did not slip into the alcoholic haze that had taken her mother. Deloy did his best to ignore Harriet's problems. Don also had a difficult situation at home, which brought him and Jacque even closer together. They could relate to each other. Don's parents were both alcoholics, and their marriage disintegrated in spectacular fashion during his junior year in high school. His mom remarried and moved with her new beau into a trailer park. Don gravitated toward his father, Pete, helping him with his contracting business. But Pete's drinking also got ever further out of hand.

Don graduated high school in 1964, while Jacque still had two years to go, so the couple decided that it would be best that they continue dating, but not exclusively. Don went on the road with his father, riding up and down the California coast painting houses, so he couldn't commit to much of a relationship. Jacque was in love with him, but began to wonder where they were headed as a couple. Was Don leaving her behind? She got the answer the night of her junior prom, the social highlight of the entire year. Don was coming back to take her, and it was going to be just like old times. But he didn't come back, leaving Jacque sitting in her prom dress on the front steps awaiting a date that never arrived. As it turned out, Don's father had failed to pay his rent and had gotten evicted. Drunk and spiteful, Pete decided to steal a car that was on the property, an old 1940s-era Ford. He forced his two older sons to help him steal the car, tying it to a truck and towing it away. The whole thing, from the missed prom date, to Don being gone so much, to his troubled relationship with his parents, made Jacque wonder if Don Peterson was going to be a part of her future.

One night changed everything. Pete roused Don from bed to accompany him to a local bar. Don was tired, and didn't want to go. But you didn't argue with Pete when he was in one of his moods. While Pete was in the bar, and the music seeped out of the doors, Don sat in the car trying to sleep, but he was so angry that it was impossible to drift off. As the drinking and cavorting continued indoors, Don decided that he had had enough. He took the keys and drove off. His dad could find his own damn ride home. Minutes later, Don lost control of the car and crashed, coming to rest upside down in a ditch as water began to pour in the windows. Try as he might he couldn't get his seatbelt off, and he began to panic. He thought that he was saved when he saw a man and woman looking at him through the windshield, but they just walked away. Eventually the seatbelt gave up its grip, and Don slithered out of a door that he wrenched partially open. He was alive, but terribly shaken. The next time he saw Jacque he related his ordeal to her, with big tears rolling down his cheeks. That couple had left him to die. He swore that he would never do that to anyone else. He would die himself before watching someone else die who needed his help.

Don's brush with death left him a changed man. He wanted more from life. His dad was a drunk; his uncle was in jail. Don didn't want that. He wanted to live right and to make his life matter. And he wanted to do those things with Jacque. In March 1966 the couple wed in a small ceremony in the home of Don's grandparents. They were his positive role models – gentle, loving, together, and always there for him. Jacque was 17, Don all of 19. Although the newlyweds could only afford a spartan apartment, life together was wonderful, beyond what they could have hoped. Don worked hard, still painting houses with his dad, while Jacque began to learn to keep house. They were going to make something of themselves. Even though the doctor had told Jacque that it wasn't possible, by May Jacque suspected that she might be pregnant. After the test came back positive, Jacque nervously wondered how her husband would take the news. When she opened the door she found Don standing there with a letter in his hand – it was his draft notice.

Jacque Peterson was 17 and newly married to the man of her dreams, a man with a newfound level of maturity and love brought on through adversity. And now that man could well be headed off to war. The Petersons sat down and talked it all out. Some folks were running off to Canada. Jacque was fluent in French; maybe that would help with immigration? But that pipe dream went by the boards quickly. Don wanted to serve his country if it needed him. It would be an honor. Jacque was from a military family. Her uncle had been a prisoner-of-war in Germany during World War II. Her stepfather had been lost at sea twice in the Atlantic. Even with all of that bad luck, they had come through their experiences fine. They were klutzes and had survived warfare with nary a scratch. Don was an athlete – trim, fit, and well coordinated. If her uncle and step-dad could blunder through the world's biggest war safely, then there was no way that Don was going to get hurt in Vietnam.

———— † ————

Barbara Kenney

Barbara was born on the Pine Ridge Reservation of the Oglala Lakota in South Dakota. Her mom, Marilyn's marriage fell apart quickly, though, and she whisked Barbara and her older sister off to California. After a short stint in Santa Monica, Marilyn got married to Eddie Tobin, and the family moved to the San Fernando Valley. It was the perfect place to be a middle-class boomer girl. Barbara was a decent enough student, sometimes thinking that she might even go to college. Often, however, she wondered if being a stay-at-home mom was her future. Barbara was quick to soak up the lessons of domesticity – from cleaning, to cooking, to organizing. But thoughts of the future were usually driven away by the breezes of the present. From cruising, to surfing, to music by Credence Clearwater Revival – the valley had everything that a young person wanted in the way of distractions.

Beautiful and smart, Barbara was quite popular at Canoga High, and she could virtually have had her pick of the boys. But she had already made her choice. From the beginning of school she dated Don Hill, who was popular in his own right and cut something of a dashing figure as a skilled surfer and dirt bike rider. Those were important skills for kids in the valley, and Don had them both. Like so many young relationships, though, Barbara and Don's was full of drama. They both had forceful personalities, and often clashed in epic teenage arguments. Hot and cold best described their ongoing courtship, despite a high school engagement.

One of Barbara's best friends was Ruthie Kenney. As soon as they had met the duo had known that they would be friends forever. In the wake of another breakup with Don just after her high school graduation, Barbara was hanging out at Ruthie's house when her brother Fred returned from a trip to Europe. The two fell for each other immediately and completely. Barbara loved hanging around with Fred and his family. They lived on a 5-acre orange grove that was mainly used as a dirt bike track. There were eight Kenney siblings, and they all seemed to have a host of friends, so there was always something fun going on at their house. It was a hub of teenage activity. Fred was one year older than Barbara, and paid her so much attention, without any drama.

It was a whirlwind romance. Within months Fred had popped the question, and Barbara had accepted. Fred had taken a job as a carpenter on home construction sites and joined a union. With Fred bringing in good money, and with Barbara working in retail, they figured that they could make it on their own, and the couple wed on December 10, 1965. There was one minor hiccup on their wedding day, though, when the preacher asked Barbara if she took Elmer to be her wedded husband. At first she hesitated, wondering who Elmer was, because Fred never went by his given first name. After the minor gaffe, the rest of the ceremony went off without a hitch.

The couple spent their first few wedded months moving from apartment to apartment, searching for the right place to start their new life together. After finally coming to rest at a perfect apartment in Chatsworth, Barbara was busy unpacking the last moving boxes when the mail arrived with Fred's draft notice.

———— † ————

Jaque Peterson

After Don Peterson was drafted, his wife Jacque, who was newly pregnant, traveled to Biloxi, Mississippi, to live with her mother and stepfather, a situation that their alcohol abuse made difficult. Jacque lived in a travel trailer outside of her mom's mobile home. Without a working shower or air conditioner Jacque found her new living conditions to be primitive, bordering on unbearable. Don started sending letters from basic training. He actually liked it a lot. He excelled at the physicality of it all, and was making some great friends – especially Larry Lilley, Kenny Frakes, and Tim Johnson. Jacque could hardly believe that three friends from the same high school had been drafted together and were all in Charlie Company. They had all lived only one town over in California from Jacque and Don, and they had so many friends and experiences in common it was like they had all grown up together. The fact that Don was thriving and making so many good and new friends, though, made Jacque all the more lonely. After basic training, Don received a short leave and visited Jacque, and the couple decided that, regardless of the difficulty, they had to be together. After Don's return to Fort Riley for Advanced Individual Training (AIT), Jacque packed the couple's few things and made her way to Kansas. With little money to spare, Jacque and Don moved into a three-bedroom home that they shared with two other married couples from Charlie Company, Don and Sue Deedrick and Steve and Karen Huntsman.

Even though conditions were crowded, with the Deedricks and the Petersons sharing the sole upstairs bathroom, and their husbands gone for long stretches of training, the three young brides bonded as they worked the best they could to set up the perfect household. Often stranded in the house, since only the Petersons had a car and the boys usually used it to get to Fort Riley and back, the threesome chatted, drank coffee, and tried to have a hot meal waiting on the table when their husbands came home.

All in all life in Kansas was good fun, and something of an adventure. Jacque took in ironing and hired herself out as a babysitter to make more money. When the boys were home, the two Dons would pop open a beer, prop up their feet, and watch sports on television. The Huntsmans wouldn't join in on the drinking, due to their Mormon beliefs, but everybody got along famously amid the shared adversity of cramped living and nonstop training. Karen and Sue seemed entranced by Jacque's advancing pregnancy. They both wanted to become moms as well, and helped Jacque in every way possible as she moved through the processes from morning sickness, to grudging comfort, to being too big to wear anything but Don's shirts.

As AIT gave way to unit training, and Vietnam lurched ever closer, the mood in the house began to darken. Karen, Sue, and Jacque noticed that the amicable chats over beers were getting fewer, and that strain had begun to show in each marriage. Over a dinner conversation one night one of the guys admitted that he was scared, indeed petrified, of going to Vietnam. They all feared that their wives might wind up war widows. Each of the couples talked the issue out, but there was really nothing for it. All the wives could do was offer their unflagging support and promise to be there with a wonderful life awaiting their husbands on their return.

The Petersons retreated to their tiny room. Both Don and Jacque were convinced that he would make it through the war just fine. But, just in case reality had something different in mind, the couple concocted a failsafe option. If Don decided that Vietnam was becoming too dangerous he would encode a message home. The tip-off would be if he asked Jacque what she wanted for Christmas. That would be the signal that he had had enough. She would then write back as inflammatory a letter as she could muster, including perhaps lurid details, demanding a divorce. If the letter was convincing enough, and Jacque swore that it would be, Don would put in for a hardship leave to save his marriage. Once home, with the ruse complete, they could run off to Canada together.

At the conclusion of training, Don and Jacque made their farewells to their new friends and boarded a train in Fort Riley bound for Montgomery, Alabama. Jacque's stepfather, Deloy, was stationed at nearby Maxwell Air Force Base, and the couple thought that it would be best if Jacque lived with her mother and stepfather while Don was away in Vietnam. In order to board, Jacque had to lie and say that she was only seven months pregnant, since the train conductor evidently wanted no part of helping to deliver a baby on the journey south. After two days of travel, the couple got off in Montgomery, where Jacque's parents met them, and three days later Jacque went into labor.

The delivery was long and difficult, eventually resulting in 9-pound baby James being delivered by C section. In those days hospitals, especially Air Force hospitals like the one at Maxwell, did not allow fathers and babies into the same room. The dad could only gaze at the child through the glass of the nursery room window. Don was able to visit Jacque, but whenever the nurse brought James into the room, Don had to leave. Given the situation, it was little wonder that Jacque began to suffer from post-partum depression. Jacque was delighted that James had been born in time to meet his dad – but she wanted him to really meet his dad. She had just given birth, her husband was off to war, and she was looking at living for a year with a new baby while stranded in her mom's house – a living arrangement that had a difficult history even when she was single, much less learning how to care for a child. Jacque wanted to have both her husband and baby in the room at the same time, and she didn't think that it was too much to ask. By the third day of the regimen of having to give up little James every time Don entered the room, Jacque was done.

After Don had been shooed from the room for James's feeding, Jacque began crying hysterically while holding James, and a nurse rushed in and asked how she could be of help. Jacque yelled, "Go and get my husband!" The nurse went to take the crib away, but Jacque held on, still crying, and said again, "Go get my husband!" Finally the nurse shook her head, left the crib behind, and summoned Don to the room. For an hour and a half, Don got to hold and play with James, and even had the opportunity to change a diaper. With both of them together, Jacque was able to notice that James was the spitting image of his father, who bragged about how well this big baby boy was going to be able to play football one day. He would take him out in the backyard of the house that they were going to buy together and teach him how to throw and catch. All too soon, though, their idyll came to an end. The nurse returned, and Don had to leave to get ready to return to Fort Riley.

The next morning, Don and Jacque's stepfather Deloy returned to the hospital to say goodbye and were shocked to find Jacque up and dressed. Don had to say goodbye to James in the hospital, but Jacque was determined to accompany her husband to the train depot for his send-off. With Deloy hovering in the background, Don and Jacque spent an hour together talking on the platform while waiting for the train to arrive. Jacque had never once laid down the law to Don, but she did now, saying through her tears, "Don't run out and be any kind of hero. Keep your head down. We need you." As the train pulled into the station, Deloy slipped Don a bottle of booze to help dull the pain of the trip back to Fort Riley, and Don held Jacque in a long embrace before jumping onto the train car at the very last minute. As the train pulled away, Jacque sat on the platform and sobbed. Deloy, a crusty old Air Force NCO, didn't quite know how to react, so he just sat beside his stepdaughter who buried her head into his chest and cried for half an hour.

———— † ————

Barbara Kenney

Fred Kenney was anxious to make the best out of a bad situation. He had just moved into a new apartment to start his life with Barbara when everything had been interrupted by his draft notice. The draft had netted quite a haul in the Los Angeles area, and Fred was sure that he was going to be inducted with a good many of his friends. Fred was certain that one of his Canoga High classmates, Richard Rubio, had been drafted. Both of them also knew Larry Lilley, Kenny Frakes, and Tim Johnson – the trio drafted from nearby Lancaster. Barbara was happy that Fred would know people in his unit, but she was terrified of losing him. Losing him permanently was less of an issue than losing him for two years. They were young and in love. Death seemed so distant. But two years was a very real thing. They had just found each other; had just started life together. And now it was all going to be interrupted by training and war? It was all such horrible timing. Fred sat Barbara down in their meager living room to talk. There was nothing for it. His nation had called, and he would answer. Everything would be okay. His pay would be pretty good, and he would send nearly all of it to her so that she could save and they could really start their lives together with a bang when he got back. On that day things would be better than they had ever been before.

Hoping to use what time she could to save extra money, Barbara did not follow Fred to Fort Riley. It would have meant moving again, twice, and he would have been spending so much time at training that they would have had very little time together. She would have been essentially all alone in a very strange place. So Barbara opted to move back in with her mom and to stash as much money away toward her married future as possible. Fred was barely gone, though, when Barbara started feeling ill in the mornings. Her mom knew what was up before she did, and a pregnancy test proved it. Barbara was expecting. The world slowed to a crawl. Maybe she should get a job, but what was the point when she would have to quit in a few months? She could and did continue to hang out with the Kenneys and their wide circle of friends, often spending the night at the Kenney house. They all seemed so busy moving forward with their lives. Barbara's life by comparison seemed stuck in neutral. Sure, she was pregnant, which she loved. She and Fred had talked about having eight children. So in that way she was moving forward, but without Fred it seemed like she was not nearing her own future. Everything was on hold for two years.

The couple began writing while Fred was at Fort Riley – happy, forward-looking letters. Fred Kenney was in the crowded platoon bay one afternoon after drills toward the end of basic training when he opened a letter from his wife Barbara that he thought was just going to be full of the normal, mundane news and gossip that were staples of a long-distance relationship. Instead he leaped for joy when he learned that he was going to be a father, after which he went around poking the letter into the faces of whoever happened to be around, clapping them on the shoulder and announcing his impending papahood. His subsequent letters focused on the houses of their future, the other children they would have, and on family life in general. Barbara was happy and knew that Fred was going to be a great dad. Barbara's mom, though, had moved north to Cottonwood, a little nothing of a town as far as Barbara was concerned, so she arranged to live with Mary-Lou, one of Fred's sisters. It would mean sleeping on the couch and sharing a tiny apartment, but it would be worth it to be around so many family members and dear friends.

In what seemed like the blink of an eye Fred was home for his final leave before shipping out to Vietnam, and the Kenneys hosted an epic Christmas and going-away party for Fred. In the middle of it all someone produced a camera and snapped photos of the happy couple. But all of the merriment somehow seemed forced. Barbara had begun to understand what war meant, what it could do. And she was deeply troubled, something that she found difficult to hide. She was very pregnant – due in only a few weeks. Something that Fred marveled at. His baby was in there kicking; he could feel him (and he was convinced that it was a him). Everyone agreed that it was such a damn shame that the baby was going to be born right after he left. Maybe he could get a leave from Vietnam to come home and see him? Nobody knew.

After the passing of so many years, Barbara can't quite recall the day that she took Fred to the airport for his flight back to Fort Riley. She is certain that she cried, and a lot, but that is about all that she can recall. The events were hazy then, and remain hazy now. A few days later the well-meaning photographer gave Barbara the snaps from the party. There she was, posing with her handsome husband. But there was no joy in their faces, only a deep sorrow. Still, the photos were a memento of a singularly important night, so Barbara enclosed them in a letter to Fred – a letter that met him in Vietnam. In one of his first letters to her from Camp Bear Cat, though, Fred sent the pictures back. The pictures just didn't look right. Their sadness was too great, a melancholy that threatened to cloud his memory. He wanted happier memories of Barbara to cherish over his year in Vietnam. Barbara looked at the discarded pictures again and agreed. There would be new pictures that they would take together – happy pictures that would mark the real beginning of their married and parental lives.

Nearly two weeks into his 21-day voyage to Vietnam a civilian bearing a Red Cross telegram wandered into the 3rd Platoon area in search of Elmer Kenney. At first the men did not know who the man wanted. There was no "Elmer" in their midst. They did have a Fred Kenney, though. Figuring out what was going on, Fred ran over and tore open the telegram. Barbara had given birth to a boy – his son – Frederick. Risking injury on the pitching and rolling ship, Fred jumped for joy. He was a papa and couldn't really even begin to believe it. For the remainder of the trip, Fred didn't stop talking about his son. What was he like? Was he big or little? He was bound to be cute, right? All babies are cute. Fred finally saw a picture of little Freddie when Charlie Company arrived at its home base at Bear Cat. It was everything he had hoped for. Now he could start to tick off the days on his calendar to when he would be able to go home and meet Freddie in person.

———— † ————

Jacque Peterson

After Don's departure, Jacque spent a couple of more days in the hospital and then took Jimmy home with her mom and stepfather. The living arrangements there, though, remained strained, perhaps even more so with Jacque negotiating the tasks of learning to be a mother amid the constant strain of her deeply flawed relationship with her own mom. Jacque had always heard that learning how to be a mom was hard, from lack of sleep, to figuring out how to swaddle, to striking the best balance between formula and natural feedings. But to learn all of those things, and so many more, without a husband around to help, being worried for your husband's future, and living with a controlling mom – the heaped stress quickly became too great. Jacque decided to move back to California to live near Don's grandparents. She knew that they would be helpful without being intrusive, which is just what she needed. Jacque was receiving Don's military allotment, so she figured that she had enough money to get by in a small apartment. When she informed Don of her decision in a letter, he originally objected. He wanted her to save the money so that she could visit him in Hawaii for an R&R. But, once he realized the depth of Jacque's misery, he relented.

Jacque drove her old beater of a car cross country with Jimmy next to her in a car seat and moved into a one-bedroom apartment just a block from Don's grandparents. Things were finally good. Jacque settled into full-time motherhood, drowning any fears or worries about Don in a sea of parenting. Jacque had never really paused to think about what it might be like, perhaps because of her imperfect relationship with her own mother, but Jacque fell in love with all aspects of being a mom. There was a level of love there with Jimmy that she had never before understood or experienced. And she just couldn't wait for Don to discover that love. She knew how deeply it would hit him, and she knew that he would be a great dad. With grandma and grandpa offering what help she needed, Jacque thrived as never before, and her elation with her new life was evident in her letters. She wrote to Don constantly, informing him of all of the changes that Jimmy was going through, not wanting Don to miss anything. The letters that he sent back were full of questions about the mysteries of babies and parenthood. He seemed at ease with the idea, and calm about the goings-on in his own life in Vietnam. Don's letters were all happy – things in Vietnam were good. The people were nice, the surroundings were fascinating and the boys in the company always said hello.

Then came a letter, dated May 10, that caught Jacque short. She remembered the code that they had agreed on at Fort Riley. If things were getting too bad he would write and ask her what she wanted for Christmas, sparking a letter from her that was full of anguish and demanding a divorce. But the letter she received was blunt and frightening, dropping all pretense of a code. He simply wrote, "Please honey, get me the fuck out of here. I'm going to die." The letter shook Jacque to the core, and it was only much later that Jacque learned the truth from Don's platoon mates. He had seen so many of his buddies get blown up or shot. He had seen how random yet pervasive death was in war. Those losses affected Don Peterson so deeply that he told several of his buddies that he had experienced a premonition of his own death. He had even shaved off his mustache that he had grown in Vietnam, because he knew that Jacque didn't like him with a mustache, and he didn't want her to see him in his coffin with one. But all of that Jacque learned only decades later. At the time she only knew that Don was in distress and deadly serious. She had to get him out of there. Frantic, Jacque called her Air Force NCO stepfather. Should Don shoot himself in the foot or something? How could they get him out? Deloy heard the depth of despair in Jacque's voice. It was against every military regulation in the book, but he promised to try to reach Don in Vietnam to see what he could do to get him home. But it would take time.

———— † ————

The firing was coming from everywhere. I was shot through the chin. I could put my fingers through the holes and touch them together. First I screamed, "You motherfuckers! You shot me!" Then I thought, "Nelson, you are dead." They had us dead to rights in an ambush. One of the guys yelled, "Medic!" But I figured, fuck the medic. He is too far back to help. Pete knew the score. He looked at me and said, "Can you run?" I said, "Hell yeah, I can run!" Pete said, "Get ready to run like hell and I'll cover you!" I had just started running when I heard firing and Pete yelled, "My chest! My chest!" and fell back into the rice paddy. I was shot through the knee; Jarczewski through the chest, Scott through the shoulder, and Cortright through the spine.

Charlie Nelson

What a horrible day. We got all of the wounded out on one chopper as night fell, but there wasn't room on the chopper for Pete. He was going to spend one more night with us. I filled out the KIA tag and placed it on him. It was something that I felt I needed to do. This was our buddy. This was our Pete. I didn't want some doctor at a rear area who didn't even know him to fill out that tag. Pete was kind of the glue that held the unit together. Great guy; tough as nails. Do anything for you. A pall fell over the whole unit, especially with our platoon.

I was devastated. He was always there, always working. I have so many pictures of him. But now he was gone.

Gary Maibach

As Don Peterson yelled "Get ready to run like hell and I'll cover you," in a forlorn Vietnamese rice paddy in the Mekong Delta, Jacque Peterson was lying in bed with Jimmy after celebrating her first Mother's Day. Other than holding Jimmy closer than usual, the day hadn't been all that different. She wanted to save the real Mother's Days for when Don got home. No doubt there would be many such days; maybe Don and Jimmy would make her breakfast in bed? But even if she really didn't want to celebrate, other folks did. One of her sisters-in-law wanted at least to get together, so a few days later Jacque took Jimmy and went over to enjoy a late Mother's Day celebration with her. Suddenly then there was a loud knock at the door, and a friend burst in and told Jacque that she had better get home in a hurry. When Jacque reached her small apartment, she was surprised to find three military men taking up her entire couch.

The men all stood in unison as she entered the room. Jacque was a little mad that these strangers did not have the decency to allow her to sit with her baby, so she asked them what they wanted. One stepped forward and bluntly stated, "Mrs. Peterson, I am sorry to inform you that your husband has been killed in action in Vietnam." Jacque was incensed. "Why are you bothering me with this? Can't you see that you have the wrong Don Peterson? There is another guy named Don Peterson in Delta Company. This message was meant for his wife. My Don Peterson is fine." The military men, though, never missed a beat. Their leader informed Jacque, "Lady, we don't make those kind of mistakes. Your husband is dead. We have to go because we have other stops to make." At that point she glanced down to see Jimmy on the floor. She didn't remember putting him down, but she must have. The men left, informing her that they would come back the next day. She told them in a fury that someone could come, but it had better not be them, and that tomorrow she would get a letter from Don telling her that it was all a crazy mix-up.

Jacque had to talk to someone, anyone. Even though she refused to believe that her husband was dead, she had to pass on the news. With no phone in her apartment, Jacque went to her landlady's and called her mother in Montgomery, Alabama. When there was no answer, she called the Montgomery Police Department who had to break down the door, because Jacque's mother was passed out drunk. Jacque then called Don's father, Pete, who, when he heard the quaver in Jacque's voice responded, "My son is dead, isn't he?" Pete said that he would be there as quickly as he could, and the two agreed not to let Don's grandparents know anything until he had arrived. The news would crush them, and they would both need to be there to help them cope. Hanging up, Jacque returned to her apartment and clung to Jimmy, feeling desperately alone. She knew it had to be a mistake. They had the wrong Peterson. Maybe her husband was MIA or wounded or something, but he would turn up soon.

A few days later, Jacque received a call from the mortuary; would she come down and identify Don Peterson's body? She dropped Jimmy off with a friend and went in alone, shaking uncontrollably. The director of the funeral home asked her what she wanted to do, and she replied that she wasn't sure. Seeing her obvious distress, the director told her that he would open the casket and leave the room to allow her time alone. After the funeral home director departed, Jacque cautiously inched toward the casket, and there he was. It was her Don Peterson after all. He looked so calm, so beautiful. He didn't seem to be hurt at all. Somehow she couldn't cry; she just sat there with the casket and talked to Don, talked to him about everything – their son, the house they would have, everything – talked to Don for four hours straight. Worried that she had not returned, the friend with whom Jacque had left Jimmy finally came and opened the door and told her that she needed to come out. Jimmy needed his mother. Jacque was only barely able to make herself leave Don's side, turning to say "I'll be right back" as she left.

It then fell to Jacque to arrange the funeral, as relatives and friends began to gather. Several friends brought over outfits for Jacque to try on. None of her clothes fit anymore because she had hardly eaten since she had received the tragic news. Just three days later, Don Peterson was laid to rest in Arroyo Grande with full military honors. Don was the first from the area to die in Vietnam, so the ceremony attracted great interest, complete with local television coverage while school flags were flown at half-mast for 50 miles around. The military guard informed Jacque that she was to sit in the place of honor with Don's family during the ceremony and that she was to remain seated to receive the folded flag and to await the 21-gun salute. Jacque nodded her head in understanding, but everything was a blur. Everything was wrong. On the way to the funeral, Jacque rode in the lead vehicle with Richard, Don's younger brother, who was disconsolate. He could not believe that Don, his idol and best friend, was really gone. The two were hand in hand for most of the ceremony. After Don's casket was lowered into the grave the crowd let out a gasp as Jacque stood up her tallest to receive the flag. She shook the guard's hand and with tears streaming down her face simply said, "He is my husband." Jacque then turned and gave the flag to Don's mother before resuming her seat. At the ceremony's conclusion Jacque was in a haze of despair. She knew that everyone meant well, but she had to be alone. Leaving Don's parents to the job of receiving the condolences from Don's many friends, Jacque walked through the crowd to the limousine. Having had all she could take, she told the driver, "Just take me home." After picking up Jimmy from the babysitter, Jacque took him to their tiny apartment where she held him close as she cried for hours. What were they going to do now?[5]

———— † ————

Barbara Kenney

After Fred's departure for Vietnam, Barbara continued living with his sister Mary-Lou, but that couch kept getting less and less comfortable. The company was certainly fun, but Barbara wasn't getting any sleep. For the last few weeks of her pregnancy, Barbara's mom came down from Cottonwood and the pair stayed in a hotel room together. Freddie's delivery went off without a hitch, and then Barbara made the decision to move to Cottonwood with her mom. It was a small town north of San Francisco, so it was a long way from any of her friends. But living there with her mom had its great benefits. Barbara was a new mother with a husband off fighting in a war, so she needed her mom's help. Living in such a small town, however, and living at home under the watchful, though helpful eye of her mom made Barbara feel all the more alone. Before Fred's departure for Vietnam her life had been so vibrant, and her future so clear. She and Fred were always surrounded by a circle of friends – the Kenney circle of friends – in the San Fernando Valley. She longed to be with them and to be part of their lives, but she needed her mother's help with little Freddie. Raising a baby was a full-time job, which Barbara threw herself into wholeheartedly. It was all new to her. What did a 102-degree fever mean? Do you take them to the doctor or wait? How could she best get Freddie to sleep, even when he didn't want to, which seemed to be quite often? It was a steep learning curve, one that Barbara began to enjoy more and more.

Unable to be with his new family in person, Fred expressed his love and happiness in letters, in which he launched into dreams about the life he, Barbara, and Freddie would embark upon when he returned home – the kind of house they would buy, the kind of sports Freddie would play, even the number of grandkids they would have one day. To Barbara today her correspondence with Fred strikes her as immature and goofy. But that is exactly what Barbara and Fred were, 20-year-old kids, full of restless energy and stuck in that goofy first stage of love. For his part, Fred mostly hid the hard hand of war from Barbara, filling his letters with the doings of his many California friends, especially Forrest Ramos. Some pages in the letters were entirely taken up with a recounting of Forrest's most recent pranks. He also sent home several pictures of the group of friends clowning around together. By and large the letters were teenage love letters, written by a young couple that missed each other dramatically.

Two negatives stood out from all of the positives in Fred's letters. First was the loss of Don Peterson – a young father from California, just like Fred. Fred's letters, though, didn't linger on Peterson's loss for long – perhaps it just struck too close to home. It was after June 19 that Barbara Kenney noticed a distinct change in the tenor of Fred's letters. He continued to ask questions about little Freddie. Was he sitting up yet? When would that happen? Would Freddie be walking before he got home in January? Fred also still mused about what their lives would be like as a family once he came home. But his letters also sounded an unfamiliar note of despair. The fighting of June 19 had been difficult for Fred, especially the horror of watching his friend Forrest Ramos fall to his death out of the dustoff helicopter. He couldn't shake the vision from his mind. He had to get home. He just had to make it home safely for Freddie, but he wasn't sure anymore if he would make it out of Vietnam alive. Barbara was worried for her husband, but covered it up in her own letters. He would be fine. The loss was fresh now, but he would get over it. As long as he kept his head down and wasn't a hero he would get home safely, their little family would have a happy life, and Vietnam would fade into a distant memory.

On July 11, while Barbara was writing another letter designed to lift Fred's spirits, Fred Kenney was sitting in an Armored Troop Carrier showing off a picture of Freddie to Tom Conroy, one of his best buddies in 3rd Platoon. A replacement whom nobody seemed to know wandered by to see the picture, looking first at Kenney and then back at Conroy and then back again before asking whether the two were brothers. Both Kenney and Conroy got a good laugh at that as they disembarked and headed off toward their objective. As Kenney made his way to the front of the file, slated to walk point later in the mission, Conroy watched him go. Newly married himself, Conroy couldn't help but wonder what it was going to be like when he became a dad like Fred.

Kenney's squad was walking point for 3rd Platoon. Richard Rubio had been walking point for much of the day, and Fred took over just before we were about to get near to another tree line. I was an RTO [radiotelephone operator], so I was further back in the file near Lieutenant Hoskins. Seconds after Fred had taken over as point man, all hell broke loose. Fred was hit instantly and fell backwards yelling for help. It seemed like he yelled for hours, but it really wasn't long at all. We were in a firefight for the rest of the day, and Lieutenant Hoskins was shot and injured trying to get us up there to where Fred was. We pulled back and the tide came in. The next day we were working our way across the battlefield and someone yells, "Over here!" They had found Fred. I ran over and saw that he was dead. We had to get him out of that flooded rice paddy, so Tim Fischer grabbed his legs, and I took his arms. When we picked him up water poured out of a hole that went right into his heart. Then blood shot out of the wound and hit me in the face. I nearly lost it. I was in shock. Fred Kenney was the nicest guy in the world. He would do anything for you. I will always remember that day. It still hurts.

Tom Conroy

That moment forms Tom Conroy's last coherent memory of his time in Vietnam. He remained in country until January 1968, and fought in more battles, but after the shock of that single, horrific moment, the rest of Tom Conroy's tour is just a haze.

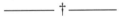

Meanwhile, back in Cottonwood, to have some fun, Barbara's mother suggested that they all drive to San Francisco to see her grandparents. The day started well enough, and it was a pretty drive. But they arrived to find Barbara's grandparents in tears. They had just received a telegram that Fred was missing in action. Holding on to Freddie tighter than ever, Barbara felt her blood run cold. Missing in action? That meant that there was a good chance that he was still alive.

Together the family drove back to Cottonwood to await news. It was the longest drive of Barbara's life; the hours passed in silence, uncertainty, and fear. She still can't remember if she slept that night or not. The next morning there was a knock at the door, and Barbara opened it to find two officers in their dress uniforms. They regretted to inform her that her husband, Elmer Kenney, had been killed in action. The whole family began to weep as Barbara slumped into the nearest chair. Fred, her Fred, was gone. He had been everything to her. Now he was gone, and he had never even had the chance to meet his son. She then looked at Freddie, mercifully asleep, and despaired that her son was going to have to grow up without his dad. It all settled on her like some great weight. She was now 21, had a five-month-old son, and was alone.

In a fog of grief Barbara Kenney did what she had to do: return to Canoga Park, go to the funeral home, and help plan the funeral. People came from all around to pay their last respects to Fred Kenney. It was a beautiful service, and the military honor guard presented Barbara the folded flag with great dignity and respect. Barbara could not stand to leave Canoga Park again. She had to be near Fred and those who shared his memory. It dulled the pain to have someone with whom to share it, someone to talk to about Fred and the good times. At first Barbara and Freddie moved in with Fred's sister Mary-Lou into a small trailer on Paradise Cove. Life in the trailer, though, seemed both forced and cramped. Maybe the hustle and bustle of moving kept her busy, and kept her mind off of things. Whatever the reason, after only a few months Barbara moved again, this time to live with her own sister just down the road in Woodland Hills. Barbara was among friends and family, people who had known and loved Fred, but still she felt so terribly alone. All of her friends were planning their lives, had relationships, were thinking of marriage, and were looking to the future. But for Barbara life seemed to be over. She wanted normalcy and happiness, not only for herself but especially for her son Freddie. But she was not sure how she would ever be able to find normalcy and happiness again.

———— † ————

Jacque Peterson

As the weeks went by, Jacque Peterson still could not reconcile herself to the loss of her husband. She waited on pins and needles for a letter to arrive, or for a knock on the door. Don had to be coming home. It had to be a mistake. It couldn't all end this way. As days turned to weeks and weeks to months, the mailbox remained empty and the front door silent. Reality, a confining reality like those movies where the walls close in on the victim, was becoming clear. But it was a reality that Jacque still rebelled against. She decided that she had to move – there were too many reminders of Don's continued absence everywhere. Friends, family, places, beaches. Don not being in those groups, in that scenery, continually called his loss to mind. In her desperate loneliness Jacque moved to a farm that her family owned outside of Dinuba, California, near Fresno, where she and Jimmy were able to find some solitude. Solitude was lonely, but it was a different kind of lonely, where she was not constantly reminded of absence. While there, Jacque watched from a distance as several of her relatives and friends came home from tours in Vietnam. Loved ones were coming back to everyone but her. She still waited for the knock on her own door, to see Don again, but the knock never came.

Alone, and in hope of finding a future for both herself and her young son, Jacque met and married David Bomann, who promised to love and take care of Jimmy like he was his own. In some ways, David loved Jacque and Jimmy too much, and that is where the trouble started. And it had to be difficult for him to live in the considerable shadow of the ghost of Don Peterson. Jacque did her best never to mention Don to David, never to compare. But even her silence spoke volumes. To move toward a Bomann future and away from a Peterson past, David decided that he didn't want to be Jimmy's stepfather; he wanted to be his dad. He wanted to adopt Jimmy as his own. It pained Jacque greatly, but she went along with the charade.

To avoid confusion, the couple cut all ties with the Peterson family and never spoke of Don Peterson. Down deep Jacque knew that Don Peterson was the irreplaceable love of her life, her soulmate. But for the good of her family she had to put him and his memory into the past. It was for the best. It would give both Jimmy and herself a new life. Jacque bundled up all of Don's letters and pictures and sent them to her mom.

The rural life of the Bomann family, which quickly grew to include two more children, seemed idyllic. Jacque spent much of her time toiling as a housewife, raising her growing family. In that sense her life was typical for many women of her age – just because it wasn't the life that she had dreamed for herself didn't mean that it was atypical or bad. And there was lots of work to keep her busy outside of the home as well. The land had acres and acres of grapes, beehives that helped with pollination and produced honey, and also chickens and pigs aplenty. Jacque had never once dreamed of being a farmer, but that is exactly what she had become. For his part Jimmy enjoyed roaming the vineyards and going to the small local school. But as he grew up, Jimmy began to notice something odd. It didn't hit him all at once, but built slowly over time. A vague hint here, an unexplained oddity there. His father, David, didn't seem to treat him the same as he did his other children. The more he thought about it, the more curious it all became. He didn't look like David. He didn't think like David. He didn't walk or talk like David. Unsure of so much, Jimmy began to rebel – he drank and he got into trouble at high school. Jacque didn't know the exact nature of the problem, but she had a pretty good guess. As her eldest son questioned his place in the world, Jacque came to her own realization that she had erred. She had tried so hard to make her marriage work, especially for the children, but she now understood that losing Don had left her incomplete. She had tried to fill the gaping hole that his loss had left in her soul – she had reached out for love and a future. But it had been a mistake. Nobody could replace Don Peterson. As her marriage to David crumbled, Jacque knew what she had to do. She had to tell Jimmy about his real father.

It was all so much for Jimmy to take in; David wasn't his father? He had a different dad who had died in Vietnam? There were so many questions. Who was he? What was he? Suddenly being Jimmy Bomann didn't make sense anymore. And the guy who could help him make sense of his life wasn't there – he was gone, lost when he was only an infant. Jimmy felt nothing but sorrow for his mother, who had plainly loved this man named Don Peterson so deeply, but who had been forced to push even his memory away so far. But he also felt betrayed and conflicted. Betrayed by David posing as his father and forcing his real father into the past. Conflicted because he loved and respected David. David was the only father he had ever really known. Two fathers warred for his soul, but one was only a faint whisper on an un-remembered breeze. Jimmy had to learn, had to go back into the past and rescue Don Peterson.

As her divorce from David Bomann became final, Jacque decided to do all she could to help Jimmy on his journey by moving her family to Pismo Beach, where he could be reunited with the Petersons. For Don's parents, his siblings, and the entire extended family, watching Jimmy walk into the room was wonderful but heart-wrenching. At age 16, Jimmy was a carbon copy of his father. It was as though Don had come back to them whole and young – unchanged – after so many sad years of absence. There were tears for what had been missed, but there was also great joy at a family reunited. Jimmy went to a much larger school now, a school that offered him more chances to indulge his rebellious side, and he was a constant presence at the doors of the various Petersons. He wanted to learn everything he could about his father. What had he been like? Was he athletic? Was he an artist? Was he a surfer? Everything. He heard all of the stories about his dad, comfortable and well-worn stories that other families swap over Thanksgiving or Christmas dinners to nods of group remembrance. But to Jimmy they were all so new. The thing that was most obvious was that the Petersons loved Don deeply and missed him dearly. After nearly 16 years their pain was still fresh, so near the surface and so constant. Vietnam to them was not the past but a living, organic part of their beings, and the shared agony of the

Petersons' unhealed scars opened new wounds in Jimmy. Instead of finding closure, finding a father, he was more confused than ever. The one person who could make sense out of his life was not there, and never would be. Everyone said that he looked like him, that he walked like him, that he talked like him. But how the hell was he supposed to know? Jimmy felt deceived. He felt angry and lost.

For Jacque it was like starting over yet again. In what turned out to be a fairly messy divorce, Jacque lost the land and farm that her family had given to her. It was back to living in a tiny apartment, living on minimal child support and Don's survivor's benefits. With three children to care for it wasn't nearly enough, so Jacque made a decision. Casting her mind back into what now seemed a distant past, Jacque remembered that at one time, when the world seemed brighter and more full of promise, she had dreamed of becoming a nurse. She had been hospitalized a few times in her life for illnesses, and the nurses that had taken care of her had been so wonderful. In their jobs they cared for people and they mattered. If her future was to be her own, instead of a man's, she wanted to care and matter. So nursing it was. But it wasn't easy; her classes to become a Licensed Vocational Nurse were difficult, even more so when she had to juggle studying with taking care of her children. Jacque Bomann's life didn't have a spare minute. In one of the proudest moments of her life, Jacque finally graduated as an LVN in 1985. It was all her own accomplishment. That degree was Jacque's.

Jacque had planned to go straight on and take the necessary classes to become a Registered Nurse. But she decided that she couldn't do that to her family. To put herself through the LVN program had required going to school all day, while working any job she could find at night to pay the bills. Her children deserved a mom who was at home and had time for them. So Jacque took a job as an LVN, finally working regular hours, and only took classes from time to time to move toward her RN degree. Along the way, she slowly drifted apart from the Petersons again. Although they had never said as much, they were bound to blame her for taking Jimmy from them for so long. There was an underlying tension there – the tension of shared loss.

With her new degree in hand, and a new life waiting, Jacque made the decision to move again, from Arroyo Grande to Santa Maria. Her new town was just a bit further south; close enough to remain geographically familiar but without all of those sights, sounds, and people that were constant reminders of Don's absence. Jacque threw herself into her work and her family. Initially she worked as a hospital staff nurse, and loved it. After slow but steady work she gained her RN and moved to another batch of rewarding positions, ranging from labor and delivery, to surgery, neuro-trauma, and psych. Each of the positions had its rewards and its tricks of the trade. As her children grew, graduated, and moved on to jobs of their own, Jacque Bomann could finally count her life a success. She was alone, but she enjoyed it. It was a comfortable kind of solitude. Her career also moved into home health nursing, something that she enjoyed deeply. So many of the patients she cared for were elderly and greatly appreciated her company. The pace of life had slowed, and that was just fine by Jacque. She was her own woman, and she had value.

As Jacque's life moved forward, Jimmy found that his still needed direction. The confusion that was his life, and the drinking that played an ever-more important role in his daily routine, were threatening to get the best of him. Before he had even graduated from high school, Jimmy enlisted in the navy. He hoped that service would give him the discipline and the focus that he lacked. But his two years of service were a rough ride. He was still rebellious, not a trait valued by the military, and still liked to drink. He did, however, gain some focus and maturity. Jimmy took back the last name of Peterson and decided to embark on a career in the music business. But there was still a hole in his life. He had collected bits and pieces of his father, learning much from his dad's family. But he still didn't know his father, and somehow he had the feeling that getting to know his father was a key to his own future.

The future finally arrived when Jimmy received a phone call; some guys named Jim Dennison and John Bauler had found his name in a phone book. They had known his father, served with him, and had been there the day that he had died. They were going to have a reunion, and they wanted to know if Jimmy and the rest of the Petersons wanted to go. Jimmy didn't have to think long. These guys knew how his father had died, a story that neither he nor Jacque had ever learned. When Jimmy, accompanied by much of the Peterson clan, walked into that reunion, their acceptance was immediate. Since he looked so much like his dad, everyone recognized Jimmy instantly. A crowd formed around Jimmy as everyone moved to greet him.

Over a period of days at that first reunion, and then at subsequent gatherings, Jimmy soaked it all in, sitting with men who had for decades been rehearsing what they would say to him about that tragic day in 1967. Although his father's friends often wept when recounting the story of his days in Vietnam, it was evident that these men were overjoyed to see him, and that in telling their stories to Pete's son they gained some kind of closure, a sense of completeness. For Jimmy it was painful to hear how his father had died, to hear of the love that these men had felt for him and still felt so long after his death. But in that pain was true understanding, a sense of who Don Peterson actually was. Don Peterson had been good, had fought through the adversity in his own life to become the kind of man everyone in the assembled family of Charlie Company admired. Don Peterson, his father, had been loved. Was still loved. As the stories piled up, Don Peterson in Fort Riley, Don Peterson showing off Jimmy's picture to everyone, Don Peterson talking about how he and Jimmy would play football together one day – for the first time Don Peterson came alive to his son. Jimmy finally felt a sense of closure, mixed with the pain of loss. He finally felt like he knew his dad, but lost him at the same time. And the loss stung, leaving Jimmy to wonder. Clearly Don Peterson had been loved. But Jimmy had never had a chance to love him. He had been denied that chance. Had Don Peterson made it home alive, Jimmy wondered how his own life might have been different. Jimmy couldn't help but think that on the day his father had died he had been robbed of some of the better parts of his own future.

Jimmy went home from one of the reunions determined to tell his mom something; determined to tell her how Don Peterson had died.

Jimmie Salazar with M60 at Fort Riley. (© Aurora Salazar)

Aurora and Jimmie Salazar in 1985. (© Aurora Salazar)

Jimmie Salazar with his grandchildren. (© Aurora Salazar)

Gary and Mary Ann Maibach on their wedding day in 1965. (© Gary Maibach)

Gary and Mary Ann Maibach during Gary's training as a medic at Fort Sam Houston, Texas during 1966. (© Gary Maibach)

Gary Maibach posing in his uniform. (© Gary Maibach)

Jerry Specht (left) and Gary Maibach. (© Gary Maibach)

Gary and Mary Ann Maibach with their children Karen, Mark, David, and James. (© Gary Maibach)

Gary and Mary Ann Maibach. (© Gary Maibach)

Larry Lilley (right) and Bill Reed during Charlie Company's training at Fort Riley, Kansas. (© Judy Williams)

Judy and Larry Lilley on the couple's wedding day while Larry was home on Christmas leave from Fort Riley. (© Judy Williams)

Ben Acevedo (bottom left), Larry Lilley
(bottom right) and Kenny Frakes.
(© Judy Williams)

Larry Lilley (left) and Tim Johnson.
(© Judy Williams)

Mekong Delta action brings death
to three Antelope Valley soldiers

Burial with full military honors will be accorded three young Antelope Valley men who fell victim to North Vietnamese gunfire in the Mekong Delta, South Vietnam, last week.

All three were reportedly members of the 47th Infantry Division serving in Vietnam and were believed killed when a 134-man company was nearly wiped out in action last Monday.

Dead are Kenneth Frakes, 21, and Timothy A. Johnson, 21, both of Lancaster and Monte Harper, 20, of Palmdale. All three held the rank of Specialist Fourth Class.

(See—CASUALTIES Page 2)

KENNETH FRAKES

TIMOTHY JOHNSON

MONTE HARPER

The local newspaper's announcement of the deaths of Kenny Frakes, Tim Johnson, and
Monte Harper; all were killed in the fighting on June 19, 1967. (© Judy Williams)

Esther Windmiller on her graduation from nursing school. (© Esther Windmiller)

She had avoided that story for 40 years. It was time for her to know how it all ended. It was time for her to know of Don's heroism and sacrifice. For Jacque Bomann, a mature adult with grown children and a thriving career, it was like being dragged back into the past. Along with Jimmy's sad story, a tide of memories came rushing back, threatening to overwhelm her. It wasn't too long after she had learned of how Don had died that I first made contact with Jacque to arrange for an interview to learn her story. The words of that interview encapsulate the experience of a wife's wartime loss of her husband in far more eloquent terms than I could ever muster:

> Hard to believe that 43 years have gone by. I do not have any pictures of Don other than his high school picture. When I tried to move on, I left all my memories of Don with my parents. They have since died and I do not know what they did with any of them. All I have is what I remember.
>
> These interviews have not been easy for me and have started all the nightmares up again. All of the sadness has returned, I bring his pictures up and stare at him. Each new picture I find that someone puts up on the internet is a new treasure for me. I miss him.
>
> He was my best friend. We had great plans. He was the man of our little family and was doing such a great job. To this day I resent having to play out this life thing all by myself, without him. It's not fair.
>
> I found later that I had transferred all those feelings I had for Don for the first person I met after his death. Somehow I felt I deserved being treated badly for letting my husband die. I realize now why I did the things I did, made the choices I made. I realize now that thrill of having a relationship like I had before is gone, of the complete contentedness I at least had in my life for a short while. In a little corner of my heart I am so sad I am alone. When I openly talk about Don I seem to sit in that corner where all my feelings truly are.
>
> My husband's memory keeps me happy.

———— † ————

Barbara Kenney

It was the worst period in Barbara Kenney's life. Although she remained friends with the Kenney family and had support from her own family, Barbara was alone. Through it all her one link to something outside of her melancholy was Freddie. He was her everything – a tie to the past, a love deeper than she had ever known, and a hope for the future. She loved being Freddie's mom, but she needed a lifeline. In high school Barbara had dated Don Hill before she had met Fred. Don had been drafted right after Fred, had gone on his tour of duty in Vietnam, and was headed home. Shortly after his return a mutual friend had a welcome-back party for Don, and invited Barbara. Don was still her friend, and he had made it home from war. She decided that she should go to the party.

Don Hill had never gotten over his breakup with Barbara. Having learned of Fred Kenney's loss, he told some friends that he was going to marry Barbara and take care of her and Freddie. He told her as much at his welcome-home party. At first Barbara didn't quite know what to make of it. On one hand it was sudden, and jarring – so near to Fred's loss. On the other hand, it was like a life preserver for a drowning person. Barbara craved nothing more than normalcy and a loving family for Freddie, and Don was there – a good man. A man she had known for much of her life. The couple started dating again, and suddenly something like normalcy returned to Barbara's life. Don was good with Freddie, gentle and understanding. All of her friends were coupling up and getting married; it just seemed like the natural next step. There were some red flags, though. Barbara and Don had always been that couple in high school that constantly broke up because they were fighting. And it seemed that the fire was still there – arguing was part of their relationship. But, in her need to provide a secure family life for Freddie, Barbara decided that it was worth the gamble. She decided to get married again. She talked her decision over with the Kenneys. They knew and liked Don Hill, and fully supported Barbara's desire to get married and to start her life over.

A few months later the couple wed. Don Hill was a good father and worked hard on his relationship with Freddie. Don also did his best to understand Barbara's grief; after all, Fred had been his friend too. The little family even kept a picture of Fred Kenney on the wall to keep his memory alive. When Freddie turned five years old, as soon as they thought he could process the information, Barbara and Don sat him down and told him about Fred – his real father. Freddie sat through the explanation as best he could as tears began to roll down his cheeks. It all left the boy with so many questions. Don wasn't his real dad? His real dad had been in the army and was dead? It broke Barbara's heart to see Freddie so distraught and so confused. Looking at that picture and learning of his real father are Fred Kenney's first memories from his childhood. He remembers crying – for two reasons. He wept for a father he never knew. He also wept because that meant Don Hill wasn't his real dad – he loved Don. Don was great to him. It was all very confusing for a mere five-year-old. For Barbara, telling Freddie about his dad was like losing Fred all over again. She and Don both helped Freddie deal with his sorrow and questions as best they could, and, over time, he seemed to come to peace with the pain. As the years passed and Barbara and Don had four other children of their own, Freddie learned to balance a fatherly love for Don Hill with a growing curiosity about his real father. In the process, Freddie came to know and become close with his Kenney relatives and developed a fierce pride in both his father and his sacrifice.

Along the way, the Hills moved to Simi Valley, with Barbara living the life of a devoted homemaker and Don working a variety of positions for Kraft Foods. Outwardly it was all a picture-book middle-class marriage and family life. Don and Freddie often went dirt biking together, and Freddie became a fixture on the local beaches, surfing every afternoon once school was over. Beaches, drinking beer, girls. It was a thoroughly fun high school experience for Fred. He also got into music, enjoying the punk scene of Los Angeles in the 1980s so much that he even began headlining his own band.

As time passed, though, Don and Barbara began to grow apart. Perhaps it was simply due to the many strains that so often doom marriages. Perhaps, though, the end of the marriage was rooted in its beginnings. There was still love there, and both parents cared deeply for their children, but the couple divorced in 1986. Although Don did his part to provide support, Barbara was once again alone – and without a job – but this time with five children. The important thing in her life was caring for her "babies," but to do that she had to go and find work. Within a few months, Barbara was lucky enough to find a position with a friend who worked for a title company, a job that she would hold for 22 years. It was tremendously hard work for Barbara, raising five children and working full time. Don Hill lived close by and was involved, but Barbara's new life was her most physically demanding yet – leaving her with little time for herself or to dream about what might have been.

As he got older, Fred Kenney got more and more curious about his father. From the Kenney family he heard story after story about him; Fred Kenney seemed to have been a great guy. It made Fred stop in his tracks. His dad had been universally loved. He felt cheated that he had never had a chance to meet him. That one day in Vietnam had changed his own life so much. And he wondered how different his life would have been had Fred Kenney lived. Ever more curious, Fred read his dad's letters home to his mom. Those helped, but they didn't tell the whole story. Fred Kenney wanted to know more.

———— † ————

Vivian Conroy

As Fred Kenney sought to learn more about the truth of his father's life and death, the events of June 11, 1967 haunted the relationship of another couple. Vivian Maxwell hailed from the tiny town of Palmdale, California, where her father Edwin worked as a truck driver and her mother Kathleen was a housewife. It was a thoroughly middle-class upbringing, in a small-town setting. Vivian and her younger sister Elizabeth both did well in school, and her parents supported their educations fully. Vivian hoped maybe one day to become either a stewardess or a secretary, but for now she enjoyed her new record player. As she grew, Vivian's love for music transformed into a love of dancing. There always seemed to be a band playing in the local roller rink on the weekends, which was a great place to meet boys. Vivian met Tom Conroy by chance at a football game when she was 14, and within a few weeks they began dating. They were going steady by age 15, and when Vivian was 17 they had an engagement party – not an unusual event in a town where if you weren't married by 20 folks wondered what was wrong with you.

Tom left school in 1965 to get a job and to start making his own way in the world, and Vivian graduated in 1966, right after Tom had received his draft notice. Vivian wasn't about to put off her marriage until after a war, so just as soon as she could arrange things, the couple wed in a beautiful ceremony at the local Catholic church, and then Tom was off to Fort Riley. Vivian followed him there, where the young couple shared a house with Bill and Sue Reed. Living there was almost fun, experiencing life as a married couple for the first time. Everything was new, and she had a friend in Sue to share it all with, but she knew that it had to end, because the boys were off to Vietnam soon.

While Tom was in Vietnam, Vivian lived at home with her mom. She got a job working at a local finance company, and, between that pay and the money Tom sent home, she was able to save a good nest egg. She couldn't help feeling a little proud of herself, because by the time Tom got home she had gotten a house ready for them – three bedrooms and near to their parents to boot. She and Tom wrote letters religiously while he was in Vietnam, and everything seemed fine. He didn't write about the bad stuff, so Vivian was surprised when the Tom who returned from Vietnam was greatly different than the Tom who had shipped out only a year before. He seemed more distant, and he jumped at loud noises. It was the anger, though, that was the most noticeable change. The Tom she knew did not seek out or continue confrontations. The new Tom did. Whether being cut off in traffic or dealing with an issue at home, the new Tom could blow into a rage at a moment's notice. It was difficult for Vivian, always walking on eggshells around Tom, never knowing what might set him off.

Vivian had a feeling that Tom's issues were in some way tied to Vietnam, but Tom refused to talk about the war. She had to hope that this somber, dark time in Tom's life would pass – that his wounds would heal on their own. Tom worked hard to put the war behind him, and, like so many veterans, thought he was doing a reasonable job of hiding his pain. But Vivian knew him too well and could sense his suffering. The couple had three children, and Tom worked hard to support his burgeoning family, first in a chicken-rendering plant and then as a truck driver before settling down to work in construction in the Los Angeles area until his retirement in 2000. Along the way, Tom began to hear more and more about something called Post-traumatic Stress Disorder (PTSD), but he knew one thing for sure. He didn't have it. Finally, though, a fellow veteran handed Tom a pamphlet on PTSD. Mainly in an effort to please his well-meaning friend, Tom leafed through the brochure and, to his great surprise, discovered that the symptoms he was reading described him perfectly. Nightmares, quickness to anger, hyper-alertness, dislike of crowds, feelings of guilt; they were all there.

With Vivian's full support, Tom Conroy went to the VA to receive counseling, where he shared his experiences in Vietnam with another person for the first time. It had all been bottled up in him for decades, festering. The doctor encouraged Tom to confront his fears. Remembering Vietnam was a good thing, not a bad thing – remembering led to healing. Slowly, tentatively Tom Conroy began to explore the memories of his past, memories that conjured horrible images and brought such pain – it hurt, but he kept trying, kept moving forward. The doctors at the VA encouraged Tom to share his experiences with Vivian. Sometimes the discussions were short and terse, others were long and full of obvious anguish. It meant a great deal to Vivian that Tom was finally confiding in her; it meant that he trusted her completely.

As Vivian and Tom Conroy came to grips with the past, and unraveled its grip on their present, they both came to understand.

If Tom was going to conquer Vietnam he had to come to terms with what he had done there. He had to remember everything. In his voyage of rediscovery Tom Conroy got back into touch with some of the many Charlie Company veterans who lived in the Los Angeles area. He even began to write poetry about his wartime experiences. As he began to piece his Vietnam experience back together, Tom realized that there had been one critical moment in his life. There was one image that was burned into his consciousness that he had to confront. He had to confront the memory of Fred Kenney. Tom first tried to confront this most painful part of his past through poetry:

> I saw your name upon The Wall and I cried so many tears
> It seems just like yesterday, but it's been so many years
> I saw so many faces of veterans with welting eyes
> We never told you how we felt, or got to say our goodbyes
> Your memory etched in our minds, you were so brave and bold
> Stories of your young lives still need to be told
> You were eager and full of life, and waiting to go home
> I'm sorry for not getting to you while you were lying all alone
> I've cried so many tears my friend, I cannot forget that awful day
> I heard your cries and screams for help, but then you heard God say
> You're coming home to be with me, I'll guide you through the light
> Your life was gone, you had gone home and I cried through the night
> My life has been filled with sorrow to remember how you died
> But I know that you are in heaven and looking down with pride
> When we meet again someday, I hope you will take my hand
> For we will be Brothers again and together in the Promised Land.

But the ghosts of his past would not leave him be, so Tom got out the phone book.

————— † —————

Barbara Kenney

The younger Fred Kenney had since married and had children of his own, three daughters – Cheyne, Olivia, and Emilee. He was at his home in the Simi Valley one evening when the phone rang. A voice on the other end asked, "Is this Fred Kenney, the son of a Fred Kenney who served in the 9th Infantry Division and who died in Vietnam?" After a short pause, Fred answered that he was. The man identified himself as Tom Conroy and said that he had served with Fred's father. They had been friends, and he had been with him the day he died. Conroy expressed an interest in meeting Fred, and his mother Barbara if she was still in the area, to talk about what had happened that day. Fred took Conroy's contact information and said that his mother did indeed still live in the area and that he would talk to her about it. After Conroy hung up, Fred called his mother, and neither was at all sure about what to do next. They both wanted so badly to know about Fred's time in Vietnam and about his friends. But could they bear hearing the story of his loss? After several conversations, Barbara and Fred decided that they shouldn't pass up this opportunity.

A few days later, Barbara and Fred Kenney met with Tom Conroy, Bill Reynolds, and Stan Cockerell. To the Charlie Company veterans it was like a moment frozen in time. Barbara still looked just as beautiful as she had in the pictures that Fred had delighted in showing off, and in Freddie they saw the image of their long-lost friend. For Barbara and Fred, the meeting was a cathartic experience. These men had clearly loved Fred Kenney. They remembered him so fondly and spoke of him in a way that almost seemed to make him come to life again. There was a shared joy in the room, until the men began to talk about the events of July 11. The details brought everyone to tears – with some reliving old pain while others absorbed it anew. During it all, Barbara noticed something. It seemed to be making Conroy, Reynolds, and Cockerell feel better to speak to her – like they were finally transferring a burden they had carried alone for so long. Finally delivering a message from the past that had weighed on them so heavily. Although hearing of the manner of Fred's death was difficult, the knowledge was tempered with a feeling of calm. Fred had died surrounded by friends; friends who cared so much about him that they still held his memory dear after so many years. While Barbara sat detached from the conversation going on around her as the three men spoke further with Fred, her memories strayed back to the day she had first met Fred Kenney. There he stood, young and good looking. It was love at first sight. They were supposed to have had such a good life together, but he had fallen in that rice paddy so far away in Vietnam. The love of her life was truly gone, and she would never find someone so thoroughly nice ever again.

———— † ————

Jacque Bomann and Barbara Hill are now doting grandparents, each with their respective flock of grandchildren constantly hanging around the house. Both look back on lives that were ripped from their courses in 1967. May 15. July 11. Those days put a stop to everything and started something new. Each woman reached out to attempt to reconstruct the love that she had lost. Their new relationships led to the births of more beloved children. Their new relationships in some ways saved them. But their new relationships were doomed by Vietnam. For Jimmy and Freddie, those terrible dates in 1967 robbed them of their fathers. Both have gone on to productive lives, both choosing careers in the music industry. Both have children of their own – and have relationships with those children that are wonderful, yet complicated by their missing relationships with their own fathers. Both Jimmy and Freddie have wondered on many occasions how their lives might have been different, if their fathers had been there when they were growing up instead of being names carved in the black granite of the Vietnam Memorial.

CHAPTER 6

WAR'S END AND HOMECOMING

I knew that Jose was coming back, because Belinda [their infant daughter] had her little arms wide open waiting for him. So I really believed that. I tried to show her pictures of him while he was away. I got a letter telling me that he was coming home. But when he got home she was very angry at him. Here is this strange man kissing me in front of her, and she didn't like that. He was a stranger to her. I told her, "He's your daddy!" Jose moved in with us with my mom and my dad. And then the nightmares began. I didn't even know what was going on. My mother was in the kitchen and she dropped a whole bunch of pots and pans. I looked back and Jose was on the floor. He would hit me in the middle of the night. I would wake up with bruises on my face and on my arms. I didn't know why these things were happening, and he didn't want to talk about it. We went to San Antonio to ask for help from the VA, but they turned him down. He had an appointment and they told him that he was okay. You can go home. This was as soon as he got out of the army. I really didn't understand what was going on, but I knew that he had some kind of a problem.

Noemi Sauceda

Gregory knew that his daddy was gone. I would talk about Lynn and read his letters to him, and I would say "It won't be long until daddy comes home." He would just say, "I want my daddy; I want my daddy." It was hard, especially around Christmas. The protests bothered Lynn. He wrote in a letter saying. "If someone spits on me, I won't make it back. And you will just have to take care of Gregory. Because I will kill them." It was big talk, but he was just so mad that they could treat his guys this way. We went to pick him up at the airport, and since he was still in the military we went down to Fort Knox. We stayed there until he retired in 1973. Lynn would have nightmares and talk about Vietnam in his sleep. But he never would talk about it; he just kept it all in. And I think that is worse. We bought a farm right after he got home to get ready for when he wasn't in the military anymore. One of his friends asked him, "Why are you buying a farm? You got into the army to get off of a farm." Lynn said, "Well, a lot of water has gone under the bridge since then." Lynn retired and went farming. We had about 500 acres and raised cattle. He worked long, hard days. But he was a good farmer and loved it.

Norma Crockett

Charlie Company had arrived in Vietnam as green as grass. Some of the men had resented being drafted, some had carried a chip on their shoulders, and others had seen the war as some kind of grand adventure. Some enjoyed getting an extra paycheck, while others were convinced of the need to save the world from the advance of communism. However, neither the men nor the officers of Charlie Company had known what to expect from violent combat. Many understood that they might get wounded in Vietnam – perhaps a picturesque bullet wound in the shoulder while firing from the hip before being given an obligatory smoke by one of their buddies – wounding as experienced in the World War II movies of their youths. Most, as is so common among the young and vibrant, had arrived in Vietnam believing implicitly in their immortality. Effectively unable to conceive of the possibility of their own violent deaths, these young soldiers had been certain that they would make it home physically and mentally unscathed. Life – marriage, children, success – was going to continue as normal once their year of service had come to an end.

The brutal reality of war, though, had intervened. Death had come – sometimes to those who had the most to live for like Don Peterson and Fred Kenney. Death and wounding weren't like in the movies. Helicopters crashed on friends, spines were shattered, and limbs were blown off. Perhaps the most frightening thing of all about war was its shocking randomness: its unpredictability. The very best of soldiers, the brave men who did everything right, might suddenly get blown to bits before your very eyes, their bodies little more than unidentifiable chunks of meat. Powerlessness in the face of the destructive force of modern combat came as a shock to many of the young American soldiers who had arrived in Vietnam – leaving them to grapple with questions of their own mortality at an age when most civilians of the same age were wondering what girl to date or what party to attend.

As Charlie Company became a blooded and battle-tested unit, perceptions about the war and their place in it changed for many of the men. For some soldiers combat simply made them meaner; they became killers, often seeking vengeance for their fallen brothers. Others fixated on survival, certainly their own and perhaps that of their closest circle of friends. They had lost so many brothers to war that they were not sure that they could bear to lose any more. They focused their main energy on survival, on reaching that magical day when they would board the freedom bird for home. Nothing else mattered. Many who had once believed in the cause of the war began to wonder whether the whole thing was worth it. Was Vietnam – dirty, smelly Vietnam – worth the sacrifice of so many young American lives? Was an ephemeral struggle against communism worth your best friend never getting the chance to go home and see his child? The brutality of battle in a year of war that seemed to drag on and on was a heavy spiritual and emotional weight for the boys of Charlie Company.

All of those things leave you emotionally cold. Death is death; we're all going to die. You develop a closeness to death. I don't know whether that is good or bad. Everyone had to deal with loss in their own way. And the losses brought those of us who were still there closer together than ever before.

Larry Lukes

It all made us a little meaner, and we were pretty mean already. But nothing made us lose our edge, because if you lost your edge you were dead. And we were a real band of brothers – a band of brothers born in Fort Riley, and a band of brothers until we die.

Jimmie Salazar

It all made us so angry – angry soldiers. We didn't understand a lot, but we understood that our friends were dead. It all made us into harder people. We were angry, not just at the enemy, but it was an anger that would last on beyond the war. We wondered who was responsible for all of this, for our pain? I had made plans to visit Forrest Ramos after the war, and now he was gone. Unless you are made of stone you have to think of these things.

John Bradfield

—————— † ——————

After the battle of July 11, Charlie Company still had five months to go to complete its tour in Vietnam. More killing and death awaited the unit, with Benny Bridges lost to a sniper on July 29, and with others from across Charlie Company being maimed or wounded often on a near-daily basis, either shot by snipers or hit by booby traps – Jim Nelson losing an eye, Joel Segaster getting shot through the gut, Ernie Hartman shot through the leg, Alan Richards shot through the midsection, Ronnie Gann nearly paralyzed by a bullet wound, a replacement named Brookins who was so new that nobody remembers his first name losing a foot to a land mine. The drums of war continued their deadly beat. The wounds, ghastly wounds, were too many for anyone to remember. In any other circumstances any of these events would have been life-changing, but in Charlie Company's Vietnam War they were becoming the norm. For those closest to the events, each elicited deep reactions and anguished letters home.

On October 6, a familiar refrain repeated itself. Steve Hopper, who was due to get married as soon as he returned home, led 3rd Squad of 3rd Platoon, which was walking point for Charlie Company that day. It was nothing unusual. Moving with care, Gale Alldridge and Danny Burkhead, two new replacements who both had only 30 days left on their tours of duty in Vietnam, had led the men forward, about 100 yards in advance of the main body of troops. It was just another recon of just another open paddy while nearing just another tree line. It seemed that the Viet Cong had been avoiding major battles since July, so nobody had any reason to believe that this day would be any different. Everyone was still on full alert, though; snipers and booby traps could be almost anywhere. But nobody expected anything major. Realizing that the day was almost at its end, the men had even chatted a bit about sharing C Rations that night as Alldridge was the first to make his way over the last paddy dike before the tree line, followed closely by Burkhead. Their turn as the recon element was nearly done. Suddenly fire blazed in from both the left and the front. The Viet Cong had them badly outnumbered and were impossibly close. Hopper and his men had been caught near the corner of an L-shaped ambush.

> My squad moved maybe 50 to 100 yards, and the enemy opened up on us. In looking back, the entire time we had been moving out across the rice paddies we were being watched by the enemy hidden in bunkers strategically placed within the dikes. We were badly outnumbered by an enemy expertly hidden in reinforced camouflaged bunkers, which offered them phenomenal cover.

When the initial burst of enemy fire occurred, Danny Burkhead and Gale Alldridge were out in front across the paddy dike immediately to my front and into another paddy. When the VC opened up on us, we all hit the ground. My RTO [radiotelephone operator] was wounded in the initial fire so I took the radio off his back and strapped it onto mine. I ordered my squad to seek cover with the only cover being the dikes directly in front of us where the enemy had just fired from.

I couldn't believe it; the VC bunker that was trying to take us out was only about 30 feet to my left. Before I knew it a Viet Cong inside the bunker had thrown a grenade out at me. It landed 3 or 4 feet from me and splashed into the water. I was in between the grenade and my RTO, but all I remember at that point was pulling him close to me and curling up into a ball thinking to myself, "If I stand up I will be shot; if the grenade goes off at least it will get me and not my RTO." I waited, and the grenade never went off. I thanked God.

At this time Burkhead crawled up from across the dike and reported, "Sergeant Hopper, Alldridge is dead! I believe he was killed in the opening burst of enemy fire." I was stunned and thought to myself, "This guy was 30 days from going home." At that very moment a rifle shot was heard, and as Burkhead raised his head to tell me the news, he was shot in the head. He slumped down against the dike across from me, literally inches away, and all I could do was reach for him in an effort to provide some comfort. I remember two things at this point. I prayed, and I was mad. I could not believe I had lost two of my men. As I collected my thoughts I loaded a clip of tracers into my M16. When Burkhead was shot, I had seen where the shot came from – another bunker just ahead of us and to the left. I always carried 20 rounds of tracers in one clip, and it was at this moment I vowed to seek revenge using those tracers. I quickly loaded the clip and laid my M16 across the dike and then purposely started some movement to get this bunker to open fire on us again. When I moved, the enemy responded by firing. Knowing this guy killed Burkhead and probably Alldridge as well, I pumped every tracer round right into the hole that he was firing out of. Then the bunker remained quiet.

Not knowing how many other bunkers were yet to be discovered, I started calling in artillery. Once the marker round was fired and adjustments made I asked for full effect and began walking artillery rounds towards us to take care of any remaining bunkers. As I walked artillery closer and closer to us, I remember knowing the general vicinity of where Alldridge was in the rice paddy. Suddenly I thought, "I cannot harm his body with artillery. He was a good soldier who paid the ultimate sacrifice." I held such respect for him. I therefore purposely kept artillery away from his location. I felt that was the least I could do for Alldridge and his family at home.

Steve Hopper

Jennifer Powell had grown up in the tiny town of Greenfield in the lush corn belt of middle Illinois. Her high school was so small that she had done everything from play saxophone in the band, to star on varsity sports teams, to compete in beauty pageants. At small schools, kids just did it all. She had met Steve Hopper in the lunchroom during her freshman year. He was so mature that he even had a five o'clock shadow, and Jen wondered where he had been all of her life? How could she have missed him in such a small school? Steve, however, had already noticed Jen. At a football game Steve butted in on Jen's date with another guy, which she didn't mind at all, and the two instantly became a couple. Her parents quickly came to idolize Steve – he was smart, hard working, and good looking. After high school the couple began to talk about marriage, Steve got a ring, and the families had begun to discuss wedding dates just before his draft notice arrived. After much back and forth, the couple held off getting married, figuring that they would get Vietnam out of the way first. While in Vietnam, Steve had been relentlessly upbeat in his letters, always talking about the good things, especially plans for their wedding. Even Steve's letter home about the October battle that saw him receive his second wound maintained a positive air. Jen was worried for him. Who wouldn't be? But if he could remain confident, then she resolved that she could follow his example.

It was the constancy of human wastage and deadly threat that weighed most heavily on Steve Hopper, causing his optimism to waver, and his letters home took on a darker tone:

We got back from a mission yesterday. Everyone was so damn tired because we walked around 14,000 meters in three days in this area that was so thick at times you couldn't see ten feet in front of you. We had to use machetes all the way and we ran into booby traps, punji traps, and sniper fire all the way also.

God I hope all of us make it home for Christmas. We only have around 30 guys left in our company that came over here the same time I did. We came over with 160 or something like that and we have only 30 left.

I think if I hear about much more fighting I'll lose my mind. I'm so sick and tired of hunting and being hunted. All I want is to come home and lead a normal life.

Sometimes the tension gets so great that I feel like I'm going to lose my mind. Oh well, maybe it will be the last time something like that happens. That's what I said last time too, though.

You wouldn't believe the tension that builds up inside a person over here. Sometimes you feel like saying, "The hell with it" but then I think about my family.

John Sclimenti had a number of important things to write home about as the months passed in 1967. First he had navigated the difficult waters of a rushed marriage, having to return home in March to marry Iris, whose unplanned pregnancy was beginning to show. John had written about his hopes for fatherhood in many of his subsequent letters. But most of all, John Sclimenti liked to have fun. He was the most well-known comedian in the unit, and his letters home reflected his buoyant tendencies, constantly ribbing his parents and his bride. Rarely did he mention the downside of war, even though he often asked for his family's prayers. But as the war continued, and the price paid by Charlie Company rose, darkness penetrated even the letters of jolly John Sclimenti:

I don't feel too cheerful. One of my buddies got killed and I ain't up to writing. After this month it might quiet down I hope. Elections are coming up and the VC want to raise all kinds of hell. I feel bad because you guys worry about me too much and I wish you wouldn't... I'm really getting to be a nervous wreck.

Although John's correspondence quickly returned to a more confident frame of mind, his letters got shorter and contained fewer flights of humorous fancy. He stuck to the news, and what he needed, pausing just over a month later to note: "Hello folks. Well I am a POP. A BOY! John James. I just got the word. He was born the 29th. I sure am happy!" As a husband and a new father, John Sclimenti had more reason than ever to want to get home safely, and caution was the new watchword. He had to get home to meet John James.

There were losses to mourn. Steve Hopper had a wedding to plan. John Sclimenti had a baby about whom to enquire. While those events sometimes formed the centerpieces of individual letters, the correspondence of Charlie Company in general remained dominated by the minutiae of wartime life. They missed home, they longed for their wives, they hated the food, they joked about their buddies, they wondered how the home sports teams were doing, they asked after old friends, and they griped about the service. Amid the constant written banter of normalcy, though, the moments of scribbled angst became more common and more worrisome. While the majority of letters home remained upbeat and focused on the future, the Charlie Company wives did not have to be sleuths to discover that a crisis of confidence lurked beneath the placid surface of their husbands' correspondence. As the chaplain and a man of faith Bernie Windmiller often wrote of trust and of hope in his letters home, along with the mundanities of buying a camera, car payments, and care package cookies. As the war rolled on, though, doubt and fear became prevalent themes:

Aug 3

I've been tense these last few weeks. I just seem so shaky at times and so tensed up inside... I am surprised because I always believed that I was strong enough and close enough to the Lord to take anything calmly and in stride, without it shaking me. In some ways I'm disappointed in myself and wonder about the depth of my own trust in the sustaining grace of the Lord. War is a strange thing and does strange things psychologically to people. When you are out in the field on operations and in combat I as well as all of us do our job, usually without question. It has to be done and one does it day after day – it is part of our routine just like yours is getting up in the morning, dressing, and feeding the children and getting them off to school and then going about your daily duties. That is your life and you do it because it has to be that way. Yet here, when one gets a break in the routine of war, you begin to realize what you have really been through and it dawns on you what has really taken place... Darling please don't let it worry you, I'm not a nervous wreck in any sense of the word nor really losing my balance mentally or spiritually. I know it is easy for you to allow my feelings on paper to grow out of proportion in your own mind.

Aug 23

It has been a while since I've been in a hospital. Some of the fellows I had a hard time talking to – knowing what to say. What do you say to a young lad from St. Paul Minn with both legs amputated just below the knees? "I'm sure you consider yourself fortunate to be alive. How do you feel today? Even though you've had this great loss, life can still be useful and have meaning for you. Medical science can do wonderful things for you. God bless you and give you strength." Boys with tubes in every opening of their body and some where openings have been made with the knife... I came out kind of shaking literally and I just had to light up a cigarette. I know I don't need them under normal conditions, but these kinds of experiences just get to me.

Sept 10

I am writing with a very sad heart. Late yesterday afternoon we had 4 men wounded and 2 killed. One was a dear friend Lt Dennis Loftheim. He was reconnaissance platoon leader in Echo Company. No more fine brilliant boy, with such a promising future ever lived. As his platoon was moving across a rice paddy dike, one of his men set off a booby trap, wounding 4. Denny ran to the front immediately to care for this one lad. As he was bent over him tending his injuries a second explosion was set off and blew his and another boy's body 20 feet in the air. The two bodies were mangled, almost beyond recognition. They were the worst I have ever seen. His arms and legs were a tangled mess of bones and muscle – his skull was ripped off from the forehead. The other boy was blown in two – his body brought in wrapped in a poncho, a heap that only took up half the litter. They never knew what hit them. I ministered to both bodies and then had to leave. I retched at the sight – and wept. Then went back to the pre-op ward and helped calm the four wounded. Honey I'm too emotionally involved to be objective about this war. The one boy who was Dead On Arrival had a young wife expecting twins in a month. I can't see that these lives are worth it!! I wrote the letters to the next of kin this morning. What can words do – what can one say? That makes 62 KIAs since coming to Vietnam.

As with so many of the wives, the shared pain of her husband's letters weighed heavily on Esther. For many months, family, faith, and work had sufficed as armor to protect her psyche from the hammer blows of war, and Esther had thrived. Her children were prospering and she shone brightly in her career as a nurse – tasks demanding enough in their own right to challenge the strongest of women. Like her Charlie Company sisters, by sheer dint of will Esther had kept her hectic home front life balanced with the demands of a distant war that threatened to engulf her husband. But the stream of cruelties from Vietnam flowed relentlessly on, chipping away at Esther's considerable resolve. Bernie had his men; Bernie had his ministry – Bernie had community. Esther and the Charlie Company wives, though, had no one who really understood. Everyone around them meant well, but they couldn't understand. How could they? The only person who really understood was in Vietnam, fighting for his life. How could the wives share their emotional need with their husbands without adding to the wartime difficulties that already threatened their very lives? Like the other Charlie Company wives, Esther began to waver, sharing her own fears with Bernie, which was poignantly reflected in one of his mid-September letters home:

> Darling I know you must feel as though every ounce of energy has been drained from you and you'd like to collapse. Sweetheart you know I'm coming home. Live one day at a time and lean heavily on His grace. We've only 105 days left, 4 pay days. We'll make it because we must.

The steady drumbeat of war was even reflected in Herb Lind's letters home – taciturn and stoic Herb Lind, who had only noted the carnage of June 19 by stating, "Yesterday we covered twice as much ground as we are supposed to in a day." The war was wearing even on Captain Lind:

> August 23

> This will be a short letter as it is already 2:30 AM. I'm tired and pissed. I feel that I have really been taken advantage of. It seems that they think they can call on Charlie Company every time they need some help. It has gotten to the point that they don't realize that there are other companies. I'm usually not one to complain so much but it is getting bad. I feel that the Battalion has gone to the devil.

> I'll sure be glad when this tour is over with. I am getting tired of the way things are being done. We really haven't gained a hell of a lot. I can see some rough times ahead. We won't win over here for a long time. I don't feel that many of the people are on our side.

September 15

Many more days like today and I'll do like Cpt. Larson [his predecessor who had left the military]... I swear that everything is a crisis and I'm sure that the way they operate is going to kill a lot of troops. There is a big battle going on right now and we are feeling it but not as an active participant. The US forces involved are not faring very well. They are being misused and misguided in my opinion.

November 3

We don't seem to get too much of a break as we go out at 0130 this morning. It will be for 3 days which will seem like a long time I'm sure. It seems to me they are very hard on the troops. They push them to the ground. I feel that it is because they are all blood hungry. They are all pushing for heavy contact and I feel that they forget about the welfare of their troops... I am really upset lately. I know that it is probably because I want to go home.

———— † ————

The wives of Charlie Company dealt with the accumulating strain of war in different ways, and each wife communicated her feelings to her husband in a different manner. Becky, like her husband Herb, was sparing of words and direct. Deana Harvey tried diligently to help her husband Gene, but tended to steer the conversation away from the worst of war and toward more happy times. Mary Ann Maibach often spoke in terms of her deep faith, but her letters to her husband Gary as the war continued to grind away at the couple's dwindling supply of physical and mental energy stand as representative of a difficult time. The letters reflect two distinct types of pressure that were building on the Charlie Company wives as the war dragged on. One pressure was represented by the wear and tear evident in their husbands' psyches. The other pressure was one born out of hope. The end of their war was nearly in sight. Could they dare hope their husbands could make it that long? Could their marriages and families hold out for just that little bit longer to see it through to the end?

June 28

I love you with all my heart and yearn for the time when this year long nightmare is over – when you are home again, and when these trials come upon us, we can comfort and console in person. Oh how I long to take you in my arms, hoping that gesture so full of love could help just a little to alleviate the sorrow and pain you are feeling.

July 14

[When she found out that Gary's R & R was being delayed] Sometimes I'd just like to take this whole army business and shove it up the you know what! I'm on the verge of an explosion and can hardly take any more of this Army crap. It ain't fair and that is all there is to it. I feel bad for me, honey, but I feel much worse for you as you are the one who must keep up a hectic patrol schedule and bow down and let them take anything they want from you. I'm fed up from the top of my head to the tips of my toes. Maybe we are still lacking in patience – the way I'm spouting off I'm sure it's apparent I am, but I don't know how many more "tests" we must be able to endure. I want to bear my cross willingly, but honey it goes so hard for me sometimes – and I grope for little bits of encouraging information to cling to, trying to keep my courage up to face each new day as one closer to being together.

August 3

My love, how I wish I could take my poor discouraged husband into my arms, put his dear head on my breast and assure him everything will be alright – that he just had an awful nightmare about a bad Army experience. As I began reading your letter my heart just started aching for you, and I felt such a longing to be able to console you even before you mentioned your need for the same.

October 29

Today seems to have been an especially "lonesome" day for me, as I miss you so much. I drove down here after dark this evening and Karen was tired and trying not to go to sleep, and really cross, and she cried and I tried to comfort her and at the same time watch the road, I wanted to cry so much myself – for you, for her, and for me. I felt so fed up with this way of life, and it seems as if I can hardly stand not having you here, when I love you so much, and have such a great need for you, my precious darling. I love you. The days just can't go too fast to suit me. I need you.

November 5

Darling, as far as I'm concerned this week, the next two months just can't go fast enough... I am so discouraged, so tired of the way of life I'm leading – the running around between different houses, the letter writing each day – the observing of our dear daughter and longing feeling that you, too could share the experience. Darling, I love you so very much – and I need you badly.

November 18

So help me, sometimes I think the nearer this year comes to being over, the nearer I come to driving everyone crazy with my sighs, and groans etc, etc. Some days I just feel as if all inside of me is wound up in a tight little ball... I've got to stop this nonsense, and yet don't seem to be able to.

——— † ———

As the calendar turned to November, and their time in country got "short" each member of Charlie Company, and every wife back home, began to focus on DEROS, or Date Eligible for Return from Overseas Service. While everyone in the unit knew that the return home was looming, nobody knew quite when they would ship out, and DEROS became the prime subject of wild rumors. Some thought that Charlie Company had fought and suffered so much that they would be given a break and sent home in time for Christmas. Others swore that the army was so short on men that they would be shipped home at the exact last minute, and not a moment before. The uncertainty, and the ebb and flow of rumor, led to hopes both raised and dashed on both sides of the Pacific. The stress became palpable and had a powerful focal point. After all they had been through, nobody wanted to die with home in sight. After all they had been through, both husbands and wives dared finally have a real hope of survival. After all they had been through, nobody wanted to be the last name on the wall.

Steve Hopper had to balance the thrill of helping to plan his marriage to Jen on one hand against the sheer desire to get home quickly and safely on the other, writing:

> I'll pay for the rehearsal dinner and I'd like to have it up at the Ranch House if that's fine with everyone else. Can't wait till I get home so I can see everybody again. It'll be so great to get back in the world and see everyone again. I only have 24 days left over here and that's about 25 too many. Oh well, I guess time will pass soon enough.

While Hopper had managed to retain a philosophic air concerning the irony of war's end, John Sclimenti couldn't help but note a change in the demeanor of Charlie Company and in his own motivations. To this very day John Sclimenti is the life of any party, but war had changed him and altered the perceived path of his future:

> Well the guys in the company are jumpy as could be. There is a lot of tenseness in the air... I'll tell you I think I have aged about three years over here. When I get back home my ideas have all changed. I just want to work and settle down. I don't need all that fancy stuff I thought I wanted before. You really realize what life is all about. I think that everybody in the United States should be in a battle at least once. That

would straighten things up. I want to come home so bad it hurts...
Please pray extra hard this month.

For Bernie Windmiller, the looming end of his combat tour was a cause
for introspection. Married longer than his Charlie Company compatriots,
Bernie had better cause than most to understand that his absence had
been transformative not only for him but also for Esther. He could
hardly conjure up in his imagination how difficult things had been for
her back home during his absence. In a letter home on November 14, he
wrestled with the idea of coming home to a loving, yet changed wife:

> I can tell by your letters and experiences that you have grown a lot. I'm
> sure I have too, but sometimes it takes suffering to teach us lessons we
> would never learn otherwise. Honey, no doubt we have gained a
> greater independence, which is not all good. I'm sure it is not the
> wrong kind of independence. It may take some adjusting but I'm not
> afraid of it and I'm sure that it will cause no difficulties.

Confident that he and Esther could navigate the challenges of being
back together after such an intensely individual year of pain, growth,
and change, Bernie's letters went on, first to deal with the tremendous
fright of a near miss and then to a chronicle of yearning as the
uncertain date of reunion drew nearer and nearer:

Nov 20

> Patrolling a bunker complex. I had just stepped over the bunker when an
> explosion went off 3 feet behind me. I didn't know what it was, but
> I immediately hit the ground. When I looked up, the Sergeant right behind
> me was laying on the ground. He had stepped on a pressure type booby
> trap. I had been walking around it just seconds before and had not stepped
> on it. No one saw it and it was just buried in the ground. It was a concussion
> type booby trap and therefore no shrapnel or I no doubt would have been
> wounded by the shrapnel too. I ran over to him and luckily he only had a
> broken foot – didn't even break the skin. You can believe I was shaking. We

got him dusted off and about ten minutes later we heard another explosion up the line. When I got up there a guy had stepped on a pressure type fragment grenade and it blew his foot all apart. I'm sure that he lost the foot. We no sooner got him dusted off when another guy stepped on another one just a few feet in front of me – got a real bad bruise and sprain I tell you. I am afraid to put my foot down anywhere.

November 24

I've been so "antsy" all day, finding it hard to settle down to anything. I'll be a nervous wreck when I get home. I listen to a lot of stereo music; it is relaxing.

I do get 30 days as soon as I hit the states. No, I'm not going to run off and leave you while I go visiting – don't worry! We'll have so much to do and have lots of fun in those 30 days.

December 10

It is a cause for gratitude to God for our wonderful love, when you see so many unhappy people married to unhappy people. I've thanked the Lord more than once for you and the children when I've seen guys getting "dear John" letters from their wives and divorce papers. How fortunate we are. May these experiences always cause us to love each other more, be more considerate of each other, and more dependent upon Christ. Your words brought me to tears – you are so dear and I'm so proud to be the man in your life. You are the most precious person to me too, honey – you are simply beautiful in every way.

December 25

I'm longing to get home to you. Just 7 more days. By the time you receive this it will be only 2 or 3 days. It hardly seems possible!

As the commander of Charlie Company, and a professional soldier, the close of Herb Lind's tour in Vietnam was different, which was reflected in his letters and in the reality of his immediate future with Becky. While the men of Charlie Company were concerned with their survival and with that of their comrades, Herb Lind had the responsibility of military effectiveness in battle on one hand weighed against the welfare of those under his command on the other. The lives and fates of his men hinged on his every action. Excerpts from two of Lind's letters in November offering his characteristic brief summaries of his military doings for Becky made the tension clear:

> Back in from the field and happy. The operation was a success as far as I'm concerned because we didn't get anyone hurt.

> Back in after a more or less uneventful operation. We really didn't get close to anything. A lot of time was spent just moving and searching. In my books the operation was a success but I guess militarily it didn't accomplish much.

Amid the hustle and bustle of lives reclaimed; amid the detail of the concluding paragraph of war for Charlie Company, Becky Lind was able to see the man she loved hidden within the tightly buttoned up captain. She knew Herb well, and knew that he was both sparing with his words and not apt to dwell on issues of emotion. The words were few, but they were there. And the fact that he opened up so rarely made the words all the more special:

> I am just waiting for the end of this tour. It is mostly from missing you... I don't really know what we'll do when I'm home but I would just like to do as we please. We might do some traveling and sightseeing. We have a trip to make to the Black Hills together sometime and any place else we feel like seeing. I want to be independent so we can just do whatever we feel like... I only want to be with you for a while when I first get home... I want to be together. We have had so little time together that it will almost be like a new start.

———— † ————

The Charlie Company wives knew that they had changed, grown, and persevered. And they all realized that the experience of war had changed their husbands. But the greatest and growing feeling from November and December of 1967 was a real sense of excitement and building joy. Some, like Esther Windmiller and Norma Crockett, were looking forward to the return of trusted marriage partners – the other side of their relationship coin. Others, like Becky Lind and Nancy Benedick, were ready to welcome home men to whom they had been married for over a year. But the majority of Charlie Company wives, from Noemi Sauceda to Sue Reed, awaited husbands whom they really only knew through letters. These wives waited with boundless hope to begin their marriages. With a young daughter at home, and a marriage that was barely two years old, with much of those two years having been devoured by training and war, Mary Ann Maibach occupied something of a marriage middle ground. She knew her husband Gary well, but they remained in the almost giddy, explorative early stage of marriage. Her letters to Gary spoke volumes regarding the highs and lows of waiting during those two hopeful, yet interminable, final months:

November 6

I'm so thankful and happy to be your wife – and I'm so anxious for the time when once more we can live together as husband and wife are meant to, rather than being 12,000 miles apart and having to resort to writing some of our thoughts of love to each other – and our frustrations.

I've been thinking so much about your homecoming, and am wondering so when it will be – and decided maybe you should write "Important" on the envelope informing of your rotation date, to add a little more excitement knowing as I opened it how very important the news it contained was.

November 15

As I watched Karen, my heart longed so for you to be able to observe this dear little creation – so perfect of mind and body. Honey, I really

237

can't tell you enough how dear she is, and how anxious I am for you to get to see her – and love her as a real person instead of a little girl of many pictures and stories traveling over the miles to you, and I'm also very much looking forward to her learning to know you.

I almost cried tonight as I played with Karen while giving her her bath, as I wanted so for you to be able to be there too, and enjoy her. I feel thankful for a great many things honey, but I still must try, so hard, to keep these bitter feelings from coming into my mind, as it seems as if they're always wanting to take over whenever I lower my guard for the least little bit of time. It sure is a constant struggle.

Dec 18

I'm making plans to stay home tonight, and every evening this week – in case you call – I love you so much, my darling, and if at all possible I want to be here if – and when – you call. I don't know if it's because I know that you'll be home, at least within the next month, but anyhow it just seems as if Karen is getting cuter – as well as more spoiled – with each day that passes.

I'm still hoping to have you home long before this letter would get to Nam, though I've no assurance to give such hopes.

I'm sort of on pins and needles, one minute reconciling myself to the fact you won't be able to come home, and the next all excited hoping just maybe, somehow, in 5 days from NOW, or less you'll be here.

—————— † ——————

Homecoming

Gene's letters frightened me. He had completely lost touch with reality over there; this violent world was his reality. He didn't have any clue of the impact his letters were having on me. He did tell me about the good days too, but it all had a real impact on me. There were many nights that I just couldn't sleep. When he came home and got off the airplane there was a big anti-war demonstration. They were so angry about our guys, thinking that they shouldn't be over there and thinking that they were killing innocent people. It was terrible. People were hollering horrible things. I couldn't think what is wrong with these people. Gene had been over there risking his life for his country.

We all went to the airport to meet him, his mom and dad and I, and his sister. To my dismay he was the last guy off of the plane. I was so happy to see him, but a little shocked. He didn't look like the same person who had gone over there. He was extremely thin and looked a little worse for wear. But he had a big smile on his face. Gene was a little bit different. He would hit the floor at loud noises. Frequently I would wake up and find him on the floor. But he wouldn't talk about it. He didn't talk about Vietnam with me at all when he first came home. He was home now and he wanted to put Vietnam behind him. But I got a little concerned, because he had a tough time relating back to reality.

Deana Harvey

When Bill came back from Vietnam he was in his uniform and just walked up to the front door of his mom's house where I lived. Needless to say we were all happy about that. He had to go to Fort Hood, Texas to be discharged. When we got back to California is when I found out I was pregnant, which was a really good thing. But we weren't really settled into life yet. Bill had to rush to find a job, and we didn't even have insurance. We were so happy, but everything was happening at once. I really believe that he had a lot of adjustments he had to make that he was never able to tell me about. Our son was born with Highland Membrane disease, which is premature lungs. He only had a 50 percent chance of living. It was traumatic, and we had no insurance to pay for it all. Our son pulled through, and is now a big, strong grown up. It had to have been such a hard time for Bill to come back from Vietnam. He didn't talk about Vietnam to me. I wish that he had. I think that he had some serious issues with coming back from Vietnam. He was a lot different. He wasn't the same person who had left. The guy that left was a really, really good guy. The guy that came back was still a good guy, but had a lot of problems.

Sue Reed

Larry called me from Los Angeles to tell me that they had landed, and my folks drove me up to Omaha to meet him there at the airport. It was pretty much just us at the airport, and I jumped into his arms. It was all over. I was so happy to get him back. We struggled a bit because things were so different and new, and he had changed. He wasn't the same easy-going guy as he was when he left. He was a little more difficult to be around. A bit impatient. Something like that had to change everybody. I knew that I had to be patient. It really took years to work through it – the stress and feelings of resentment about what had happened there and how he was treated when he came home. He didn't talk about the war much with me; it was when he got with other guys that he would really talk about it all.

Kay Lukes

The boys of Charlie Company, now veterans of the Vietnam War, returned home during the first weeks of January, 1968. Where they had shipped out to Vietnam together on a troopship, though, the guys returned in ones and twos aboard commercial airliners. For every one of the survivors, the return to "the world" was emotionally complex. There was considerable joy – the joy of survival; the joy of returning home to loved ones. There was also a tinge of guilt – survivors' guilt. They could get on an airplane, go home, and hug their wives again, but so many of their friends had been denied that chance. Too many had died in that forlorn country – a place that would haunt the dreams of so many. There was even more guilt in that the war was not done. Victory had not been achieved. And there was a sense of loss. The men of Charlie Company had become brothers, even closer than brothers. Months of training and a year in the crucible of war had forged the tightest of bonds and the closest of friendships. Once aboard that freedom bird, though, those friendships came to a screeching halt. The boys went their separate ways – to Cleveland, to Minnesota, to Louisiana, to California. Some swapped addresses and promised to write. Others swore that they would visit each other, no matter the distance. But down deep the guys knew that such promises, no matter how well intended, were the kind that are made to be broken. Charlie Company was no more.

When the boys of Charlie Company had been drafted out, Vietnam was one of the most popular wars ever in American history, but that had all changed. While Charlie Company was first training and then enduring its year in combat, events had conspired to sever much of America from its support first of the war and then of its warrior protagonists. While in Vietnam the boys of Charlie Company were aware of the events that drove public opinion, and they knew much about the fractured results. But, even in their most disturbed dreams, the boys of Charlie Company could not imagine what faced them societally when they came home. Their freedom birds touched down on the eve of the Tet Offensive, at the dawning of America's most divisive year since its bloody civil war.

Instead of being greeted by well-wishers, Charlie Company was met with protestors, jeers, and taunts. The level of vitriol varied, with some making it through their landing terminal essentially unnoticed in a crowd while others had garbage tossed at them and were called "baby killer." The results were devastating. The United States had tired of its Vietnam adventure. The war would not be won. There would be no cathartic victory that brought meaning to the lives of Charlie Company's fallen brothers. Vietnam veterans were too often societally marooned, alone in a mass of people who neither understood nor valued their service. America was hell bent on moving on, and leaving the veterans behind. Charlie Company had once been the tightest of human communities. Born of the white heat of combat, Charlie Company was a place where men relied on, valued, and understood each other. The members of that community, though, were now scattered to the American breeze. There was no new community that could truly understand the life-changing, soul-rending events of their violent military past, leaving the men of Charlie Company to rely almost solely on their wives and families for support. Amidst the pressure, some marriages were forged into something even stronger and more meaningful, while others shattered.

Just as the men could not really fathom the changes that had been wrought in American society during their absence, the Charlie Company wives could not fully grasp what had happened to their husbands both physically and emotionally during their year abroad in combat. In fact, many of the men were quite unaware of the extent to which they had changed. Exposure to the constant threat of death, the reality of death, a permanent state of alert, learning that closeness only led to a deep hurt when that closeness was ripped away – the lessons of the troglodyte world of combat had come on only gradually. Infinitesimal in their slowness, the emotional alteration was like looking in a mirror every day. You never seem to change; you are used to the vision. But the changes are there, and especially visible to those who haven't seen you for a year. In January 1968 the realities of dramatic personal change that faced each couple were a part of an undiscovered future. In January 1968 there was only joy for a husband returning, a father returning, a lover returning. There was only joy at reuniting well-worn and comfortable marriages; joy at discovering what new marriages really meant. In January 1968 there was only a comforting sense that finally everything would revert to normal. But for many of the Charlie Company marriages, normalcy was gone forever.

————— † —————

By the time I rotated home I didn't have any of my original officers left. Almost everybody had already rotated out or home. Charlie Company was still a well-oiled machine, but I missed the old hands.

Leaving Charlie Company was like leaving a family. It was family:
kindred spirits. Those guys never left me. It made me what I am today.

Herb Lind

Becky Lind drove from Nebraska in her Chrysler Newport, a car she
didn't particularly like, to California to meet Herb's flight in San
Francisco. A snowstorm hit in the middle of Wyoming, but that New
Yorker just kept plowing on. Once in the San Francisco area
everything slowed to a crawl. She knew that Herb was coming home
soon, but not exactly when; so she waited. Finally the call came that
he was expected at 5am the next day. The early morning hour meant
that there was really nobody in the airport except for the military
men returning home from Vietnam. There were no hecklers, only
embraces. After kisses and hugs, Becky was hoping for a leisurely car
tour through the vineyards and vistas of California to allow for
reacquaintance after so long apart. Herb, though, had other ideas.
He had been car shopping by letter during his last days in Vietnam,
and he wanted to get to Nebraska to buy his preferred car. Herb Lind
was not going to be denied. The couple gathered some provisions
and drove to Nebraska in two days, stopping only one night for six
hours and using empty food containers in the car in lieu of bathroom
stops. As the couple motored relentlessly on, Becky took in some of
the changes in her husband. Outwardly it was easy to see – he had
lost a great deal of weight while he was gone, down to a mere 125
pounds. But, as she sat there looking at him, Becky wondered about
the changes to him that were hidden inside. She wondered what her
future life with Herb was going to be like. He was no longer the
calm, cool Herb Lind of her memories. That Herb had been replaced
by a wired, goal-driven man she had never met.

The couple moved to the Fort Benning area for a short period
while Herb trained. There they bought a new boat for the water
skiing that they both enjoyed. Being on the water was calming,
almost letting the old Herb shine through a bit. Wives couldn't get
jobs on such short tours, so Becky contented herself with opening a

sewing center to teach more of the wives how to make their own clothes. It was at Benning that Becky got the welcome news that she was pregnant. Next followed two equally short stints in Augusta, Georgia, and Fort Bragg, North Carolina. Eight months pregnant, and with very swollen feet, Becky was happy to get to the new apartment outside Fort Bragg. The couple wouldn't be there long enough to get their furniture out of storage, but she was sure that she could make the apartment feel like home all the same. But the place was a mess – fleas everywhere, tattered furniture, broken blinds. By the time she had cleaned it well enough to allow for living, it was time to head to Fort Bliss, Texas and entirely new living arrangements. And these arrangements were going to be equally short lived – Herb had received orders for Vietnam once again. Becky was so close to her delivery date that the military doctor almost didn't let her on the flight to Texas, but with a little convincing he allowed it.

As it turned out Mark Lind was a bit reticent to make his first appearance, being three weeks overdue before his birth on July 3, 1969. It all had been such a whirlwind since Herb had gotten home. One duty station after another, one move after another, and a new baby. There had hardly been any time really to be a couple again, and now there was only time for a short visit to New Mexico before Herb shipped out. For Becky and Mark it was back to Nebraska to live in a house owned by her parents. Her confidant, pal, and older sister Gay lived in the basement apartment with her husband and three children. The living arrangements, though cramped, worked out well. Becky was able to leave Mark with Gay during the day and took a job teaching Home Economics at the local public school. Between her new job, serving additional duty as freshman class sponsor, and learning how to be a mom for the first time, Becky found herself more than busy. It also helped that this time around she was sure that Herb did not have a combatant assignment, and she made more than certain just to check up on that from time to time in her letters to keep him honest. Becky Lind had been through it before. She knew what separation was like; she knew what the life of a military wife was like; and she knew that her husband was in no more than a passing danger. This time she knew how to deal with Vietnam.

———— † ————

I left Vietnam on January 1. I made arrangements for Esther to fly to Chicago from Cleveland to meet me. We wanted three or four days to ourselves and then to go home to focus on the children. I got into Travis Air Force Base about 10 o'clock at night. Once we were processed I went and got an airline ticket to Chicago. The flight was taking off in a few minutes, and they didn't think that I could make it. But I wanted to try. I got to the counter just as the plane started to back out. But they called and held it for me. I was the last guy off in Chicago. I stepped off ready to grab my wife into my arms, but there was no wife! I looked all over and couldn't find her. I had her paged and then stood back off in a corner to watch. And sure enough she walked up, all spiffied up, and I walked up and tapped her on the shoulder and said, "Are you looking for somebody?"

The ministers of the local community asked me to come by and give a presentation on my ministry in Vietnam. I gave an hour-long talk with slides. As I was packing up I heard two people behind me crying. It was two young college girls. They asked me if I would meet with them. There were about 25 college students and their professor from a nearby university. Boy they started raking me over the coals; so angry. They were so upset that a man of the cloth could have been involved in the Vietnam War.

Bernie Windmiller

Esther Windmiller got the tremendously welcome news that Bernie was going to arrive in Chicago from the west coast. He was, however, only able to give her the date, not the time. She was supposed to go to O'Hare International Airport and meet every airplane that arrived on January 7, 1968. Bernie would be on one of them. Her parents put her on a flight from Cleveland, wearing a nice new dress, a Kelly green coat, and a mink hat. Esther wanted to look just right for their reunion; she wanted to see him, to run from the crowd, and she wanted to kiss him. Just like you see in the movies. She had done her homework. The first flights from Oakland and San Francisco arrived at 7am, so she sat there all night waiting for those flights. But she met all of those flights, and couldn't find Bernie. She sat down in tears, wondering what to do. Who could she call? Then she heard the announcement, "Esther Windmiller, please come to the United desk." She jumped up. Somehow she had missed Bernie in the crush of people. As she ran to the desk, she felt a tap on her shoulder. It was Bernie. He was thinner, fitter, sporting a crew cut, but it was her Bernie. It wasn't at all like the movies, but it was kind of perfect.

The Windmillers spent their first night back together in a nearby hotel, where Esther had to leave the radio on. The sounds of combat in Vietnam had been so loud and so constant that Bernie couldn't sleep in the deep silence of the hotel room. The Windmillers linked up with their children and the rest of the family when they returned to Cleveland and New London. Esther next held something of an open house so that Bernie could meet all the new work and life friends that she had made while he was gone. Like Herb Lind, Bernie remained in the military, and shortly thereafter he had to report to Fort Campbell, where part of his assignment was counseling. At first he thought that the sessions were for him to learn how better to help the Vietnam veterans who would soon fall under his spiritual guidance. But it wasn't that kind of counseling at all. Instead it was counseling for him – aimed at helping him better come to grips with how he might have changed in Vietnam.

That first year after Bernie's return home was difficult for the Windmillers. He had changed of course, but so had Esther. Somehow the dual differences were jarring. The love and devotion were both still there in abundance. So was faith. So was family. But a connection had gotten lost and needed to be reworked. For 12 years Esther had been content to live in Bernie's shadow. But a year on her own, a year of growth, independence, and self-reliance had been transformative. Esther knew that she would never again be truly fulfilled by going back to life as it had been before. She couldn't return to the type of marriage that her parents once had, where the wife is a secondary helpmeet, getting her husband to work on time and making sure that dinner is ready. The Windmillers had to find a new balance for their marriage, almost like starting over as new people. Bernie and Esther began to see the counselor together and they talked frankly about how they had changed and how their marriage needed to adapt to who they had become. Their marriage had to turn into a marriage of equals and a marriage of deep friendship. The process took time, as one might imagine, but Bernie and Esther were able to fall in love all over again and their new marriage proved even stronger than ever.

Life went on for the Windmillers, but Vietnam remained a stealthy part of that new life. Bernie would sometimes have nightmares, or startle at loud noises. But neither of them understood his reactions as a leftover shard of war. Bernie didn't talk about the war, and Esther didn't ask. She had read his letters and thought that she knew. Even so, Vietnam was still there, a silent partner in their refurbished and thriving marriage. Vietnam had been a year in his life, and Esther knew that it had been life-changing for them both, but neither knew how much. It helped, though, that Bernie remained in the military community. At Fort Campbell Vietnam veterans recognized each other, and valued each other. Esther also found community, forming close relationships with other wives, taking cooking classes, walking her children to the pool at the end of the block to swim with the children of other Vietnam veterans. Vietnam was there for the Windmillers, but with such a tightly knit support group Bernie's experiences of war were relegated to a comfortable corner of their lives. Vietnam was there; Bernie would have it no other way. But it was not dominant as the Windmillers looked forward to a bright future.

———— † ————

We stood there at the airfield outside Saigon and the airplane came in to take us home. It was full of replacements. We all stood silently as they walked by; we felt such great sympathy for what they were going to go through. I flew through New Jersey. We were on the air base there, so there were no protestors or anything. There we saw a room of brand new recruits. They hadn't even had their haircuts yet. I often wonder what happened to them. The next morning I met my wife and parents. Second only to the joy of seeing Mary Ann and my folks again was getting reacquainted with my daughter Karen. She had been born when we were at Fort Riley in November before we left in January. Now she was 14 months old. She didn't look like the snapshots. Now she was walking. I was so happy that she let me pick her up. She was used to having lots of people around, and I was just one more new person.

Gary Maibach

On January 3, 1968, Mary Ann Maibach finally got the welcome news. Gary was headed home. He really had no idea when his plane would depart, or when or where it would arrive. But he heard that he was going through Alaska, so he would call her from there with details. The phone rang in the dead of night. He was coming into McGuire Air Force Base in New Jersey. Mary Ann's mother, Louise, watched Karen, while Gary's parents drove Mary Ann to McGuire. Since it was at a military base, Gary's out-processing was a bit different. There were very few civilians around, and certainly no protesters. And there was no joyous reunion at an airport terminal gate. Instead, Gary had to go through the military rigmarole of inspections, forms, and health checks before he emerged to see his family. There were hugs and kisses all around, before the car full of Maibachs headed for home, making it as far as Harrisburg, Pennsylvania before having to stop for the night. It was bitterly cold, with a few lingering flurries in the air, and Mary Ann couldn't help but wonder how Gary was coping. After all, he had been in the tropical heat for the entire year. But Gary's smile said it all – he was coping just fine. Once into the hotel room, Mary Ann noticed something that she had first detected in the car. It was an odor; something she had never smelled before. She had thought that it was a smell from the car, but it had followed them inside. It turned out that it was Gary. He still smelled like Vietnam.

The next stop was Stirling, Ohio, where Mary Ann had lived with her family while Gary was away at war. Mary Ann's mother had everything ready – a piping hot dinner waiting on the table, the aroma of freshly baked bread hanging thick in the air, while supportive family was everywhere to be seen. Amid the joy, though, Mary Ann and Gary felt an undercurrent of concern. Karen had been but a babe in arms when Gary had departed for war. Now she was a 14-month-old toddler who wouldn't know him from Adam. How would she react to seeing her dad again after so long? Initially Karen looked at the strange newcomer quizzically, not sure at all what to think. The room fell silent as everyone awaited the child's next move. Mary Ann fretted. She had shown her daughter pictures of Gary every day, repeating "Da Da, Da Da," but somehow it hadn't worked. But the house had been bustling with people for the whole year, with parents and copious numbers of siblings and in-laws around pretty much all the time. Karen was acculturated to crowds, and to strangers. Gary was just another stranger, so she toddled over to him just like he was any other visitor. Gary picked her up for the best hug of his life.

The small town of Stirling, and its supportive group of Apostolic Christians, once again became Gary and Mary Ann's community. There was no discord over the war, only a supportive radio interview and well-wishes all around. Gary slipped back into life, like putting on a comfortable old shoe. He went back to being an usher at the local church and began working again at Maibach's, the family's store in town. Mary Ann kept on working and enjoying her nursing career. There were so many willing family members around to help out that balancing two careers with raising a daughter didn't pose much of a problem at all.

The Maibachs had another child, Mark, in 1969, after which Mary Ann decided to work only part time. With two children around the house it was becoming harder to balance motherhood with her career. Such was the way of things. Gary kept moving up the ladder at the family store, taking on more of the day-to-day operational aspects of the business. At the same time he became more deeply involved in the life of his local church. Through it all, Vietnam was there. Mary Ann had a fairly good idea of what Gary had been through from his letters, but she knew that she could never truly understand. Even so, she wanted to understand and help, and Gary was completely open; ready to talk about Vietnam at any time. He startled at loud noises, especially fireworks. He had bad dreams, often of being drafted again and having to leave his family. They talked about why these things were; about how they both had changed. And they both turned to faith. The scriptures taught that trials and tribulations were strengthening moments – moments that imbued a strength that could be utilized to help others. There were hard times, bitter times. Times in which Vietnam loomed large. Times in which arguments came too easily. But in those times especially the couple turned to Romans 8:28: "And we know that in all things God works for the good of those who love him, who have been called according to his purpose." In 1971, as Mary Ann was first thinking about quitting her work to become a full-time mom, Gary was elected to the ministry. The Maibachs decided that it was a chance to put Vietnam to good use. Mary Ann understood that Vietnam had changed her husband and would always be a part of his life. Now he could preach the good news and use his experience of war to reach out to those veterans who had had their faith dimmed by war and had become separate from God.

———— † ————

When we landed at LA, the seatbelt rule went out the window. As soon as we touched down there were guys all over the plane, jumping up and down, hugging each other. It was an exciting moment to be back home. We got in at midnight, and the airport was almost empty. We out processed the whole night, but nobody went to sleep. They made the announcement the next morning that we were ready to go. We had spent an evening together reflecting. We went, got our new uniforms on, said our goodbyes, and off we went. It was like, I'll see you next week or something. Here are guys you spent almost two years with. You said goodbye to them, stepped out the door and into a cab, never to see some of them again. I remember going to the airport and thinking that I hadn't gotten any of their addresses or phone numbers. I started asking myself questions that I wished I had asked a year earlier. It hit home all of a sudden that I might not see these guys again, my best friends.

Steve Hopper

Jennifer Powell was on pins and needles waiting for the war to end. She and Steve Hopper had delayed their wedding for the war; a wedding that was now planned for January 27, 1968. Steve would barely have time to get home before he had to pick out his tux and recite his wedding vows. She had seen changes in Steve in his letters, becoming perhaps a bit more fatalistic as his time drew short. But there was always the laughing, wonderful Steve shining through in the written word as well. However, at the beginning of December she had received a letter that had stopped her cold. Steve was thinking of reenlisting, which would keep him away for an additional year. His brother, Bill, had been drafted, and Steve hoped that by reenlisting he could keep Bill out of Vietnam. That was Jen's Steve. So nice and always thinking of others. But she was going to have none of it. Their future as a couple had already been put off for a year. Steve had done his dangerous part for his country, witnessing death and being wounded in the bargain. It was time for him to come home. The wedding invitations were printed, the rings were bought, and the church was booked. And there most certainly was going to be a groom at this wedding. Steve's next letter agreed: he was coming home.

Like all of his Charlie Company buddies, Steve had no firm details on when he would be arriving home. As the family prepared for his return, Jen was surprised when her World War II veteran father, Joe, said that he wanted to talk – which was a comparative rarity. And he wanted to talk about war; something he had never done before in his life. He took his daughter aside and told her that war changes people, and that Steve would have seen things in Vietnam that he would never be able to forget. He told her that Steve would never want to talk about those things and that she should not ask him questions about what he did in the war. If he wanted to talk, he would, and she should listen. But she should never ask.

Left to wonder what her father's words might portend, Jennifer was at work at the drive-through at Farmers State Bank when the call came in. Steve was about ready to board a flight from San Francisco to Saint Louis. That phone call touched off a flurry of activity. Jen's mom, Joan, rushed into the bank to take Jen's place at the teller's window. Jen hurried home to take a shower and to put on the new outfit she had bought for the occasion. Then came the drive to nearby Saint Louis, accomplished in plenty of time. Still two hours of waiting to go before the airplane landed. There he was! At the top of the stairs getting off the plane! As soon as Steve got into the terminal Jen screamed in joy. Steve looked her way, and she ran to him. She wanted to jump into his arms, and he was ready with a hug – but it wasn't the kind of hug Jen was expecting. Steve just looked around and said, "Let's go get my luggage." Jen worried that maybe he wasn't excited to see her. Maybe everything wasn't right. It was years later before she found out the simple truth of that moment. Steve felt overwhelmed. The sights and the sounds. Jennifer. These were things he knew and recognized. But he didn't know them anymore. This world seemed the same – seemed like it had been locked up in a time capsule waiting for him to return. But he had changed. He had just left his comrades, maybe never to see them again. He had just left the most transformative and violent period of his life. All of that had come to a screeching and sudden halt. This moment meant that something brand new was starting.

Jen offered to let Steve drive, but he turned her down. He wasn't quite sure that he remembered how to drive. And he found the lights to be quite disorientating. He hadn't seen that many lights on at night for a year. Somehow all of that light meant peace, something else he had to take in. Then it was off to Jen's parents' house for a home-cooked, Midwestern feast. All of the Powells and Hoppers were there – such a crowd. Through it all, Steve was smiling and outwardly happy, but Jen sensed that he was still on his guard; that he was still wrestling with his old yet new surroundings.

The Hopper wedding in First Baptist Church in Greenfield was packed with well-wishers, and even though Jen's dad got a bit tipsy before the ceremony everything went off without a hitch. The newly married couple bunked in Jen's room at her parents' house for an uncomfortable few days before Steve went to Fort Leonard Wood, Missouri to finish out the bit of time remaining in his military hitch. Then it was off to Peoria, Illinois, for a real beginning to married life. Steve had landed a coveted job at the Caterpillar factory, and the couple got their very first place – a tiny one-bedroom apartment. To many folks that dinky apartment wouldn't have been much to talk about, but to Jennifer Hopper it meant the culmination of a dream. Her time of waiting had ended, and her real life had begun. She got a job at a local bank, and the couple began to save some money for their future. Steve had a few nightmares, but the distance that had been in their relationship and in his eyes since that day in the airport had diminished. Sometimes he would startle, or wake up in the night in a cold sweat. Jennifer would ask him about those times, but Steve just said that he was remembering things from Vietnam and that it was no big deal. She would then ask him if he wanted to talk about it, but he never did.

———— † ————

We flew into LA. At the airport there were some protestors. It pissed me off a little bit, but they were just dumb people who didn't know what was going on. They didn't want war, and I understand their reasons, but I had believed in our government. I remember being so excited to see my son John James for the first time. I was worried about picking him up, because I thought that I might break him.

John Sclimenti

Iris Boyd's Vietnam experience had been a bit different than that of the others. She found out that she was pregnant in February, 1967 – something she knew would make her the talk of the town. Her fiancé John Sclimenti came back for a quick leave from Vietnam in March so that they could marry. The ceremony was in Las Vegas, with only her mother, father, and brother in attendance, as John's disapproving parents refused the invitation. Just like that Iris Boyd was Mrs John Sclimenti, and her husband was back on the airplane for Vietnam. Iris got fired in July from her job as an office clerk; they didn't want pregnant women working there. Married at 18 and awaiting her first child, Iris lived with her mom and felt a bit trapped. She took up knitting, but that didn't seem to help much. So she hung on John's letters from Vietnam and mentally constructed her future life with him. It was John's sense of humor and his zest for life, along with his dancing skills, that had attracted Iris to him in the first place. And his letters let her know that the John she remembered and counted on for the future was alive and well in Vietnam. The circle was completed in October when John James was born. It might be on hold, but Iris's future was set.

It is only in retrospect that Iris came to understand the pressure that John Sclimenti must have felt when he got off of that airplane in January 1968. When he had shipped out to training in 1966 he had been a teenage boy. When he stepped onto the tarmac he did so as a veteran, a husband, and a father. That type of transformation would have been difficult to negotiate in the best of times, but Vietnam had not made for the best of times. John wasn't turning a page after the difficult experience of war; he was starting a whole new book. Iris had been afforded time to look to a future; John had not. That she depended on him to make that future possible just put that much more pressure onto his shoulders. As she stood there hugging him and dreaming of white picket fences, Iris couldn't see that both the present and the future had locked John Sclimenti into a stranglehold.

It didn't take long for Iris to notice the differences. The cool and funny John had been replaced by a nervous and jittery John.

Humor had been replaced by agitation. Iris had no idea that the culprit was Vietnam; that the culprit was the intense pressure of an uncharted future. She figured it was a phase, something that would pass. Like many wives of her time, Iris tried to be supportive. She hoped that her support would hold things together until whatever it was that darkened their marriage had made its exit. The couple never even thought to talk about the war. It was the past. The present was the problem. Iris thinks now that if they had known to talk about Vietnam back then everything could have been different, but they didn't. Outwardly everything seemed fine for the Sclimentis. John got a good job working at the post office. Even though he found his labors to be rather tedious, the position paid well. They bought a duplex in Reseda, California, had two more children, Steve and Christopher, and lived the middle-class life. Iris stayed at home to raise the children, and money was tight, but the future had come just like she had thought. Still Vietnam remained a part of her new life.

———— † ————

Like their other wartime sisters, Jacqueline Bradfield, Aurora Salazar, and Judy Lilley also worried and waited for their men to return even as their lives dramatically changed.

MY GOD coming home was a BITCH! I have never seen anything like that in my life and never want to see it again. After fighting for so long and facing so much we were hated in our own country. I could not believe it! It was like living in hell on earth. Thank goodness for a mother's love. I wore my uniform one time to church with her. Man I looked like General Patton with all the medals displayed on my chest. But even in church the uniform was a source of embarrassment, but my mom was proud of me no matter what. I never wore the uniform again. [Later in life] I would sometimes make the drive over to the Vietnam Memorial late at night when no one else was around. There I could find peace and comfort with the spirits of the Memorial. I would always go to Panel 22 and sit there with Forrest Ramos, Timmy Johnson, and Fred Kenney. At night there it felt like they never left you.

John Bradfield

Jacqueline Bradfield

Moving out of her grandmother's house and getting active in the church had been a tonic for Jacqueline Bradfield. She was 17 and a new mom. Her husband, with whom she had never even lived, was off in Vietnam. Those kinds of things floored other folks, but they were full of positive power for Jacqueline. Her childhood had been hard, hopeless, and friendless. But now she had little Barnard, the love of her life. She had a house of her own, bought with military benefits. She had her faith. And she had a husband – a husband who was far away, but a husband whose letters made it clear that he cared deeply for her. She finally loved and was loved.

Jacqueline was impatient; she was ready for that bright future to happen now. It was an impatience best held at bay by constant activity. With the grandmas pitching in to watch Barnard, Jacqueline first got her new house in spick-and-span order, then she rectified her past by graduating high school, and then enrolled at community college. For a girl from whom nothing was expected, Jacqueline couldn't help but feel a bit proud of herself. While her relationship with her grandmother Vaselee had been fraught with difficulties, from her upbringing Jacqueline had certainly learned responsibility. It was a lesson that served her well in 1967. Even though she wasn't a good writer, she kept up a steady correspondence with John, who never really wrote home about the bad stuff – even when he was wounded by a booby trap in August.

When the call came that John was headed home in January 1968, Jacqueline had everything ready. She had even saved enough of the money that John sent home to buy a car. But she was also nervous. She hadn't seen John in so long, and so much had changed. There was a child and a house. He had been through war, and she had moved forward in life so much. But something in the back of Jacqueline's head reminded her that they were both still so young. She was just a teenager and John was just embarking on his 20s. Could they possibly succeed where their own parents had failed? Then the knock came at the door – she didn't quite know when he was coming in, so she had waited at the apartment. And, just like that, there he was. All fears suddenly gave way to excitement. Her John Bradfield was back home, and their real life could begin.

John and Barnard hit it off from the beginning, just like two peas in a pod. The topic of Vietnam and what John had been through never really came up, except for wondering when his record collection was going to arrive from its trip overseas. As usual, John Bradfield was a man of action. It was his maturity and no-nonsense attitude that had helped attract Jacqueline to him in the first place. Within two weeks of coming home he had landed a good job at the post office. Even though he never talked about it and she never asked, Jacqueline got the feeling that the post office was a place where lots of Vietnam veterans landed, and that there was a good support network there for John. She wanted to stay in school, and John was wonderful about it. He pitched in with Barnard, often drove her to school, and then went to work the afternoon shift. Then a second son, Byron, came along. Since she spent her mornings at school and he spent his mornings with his dad, Byron bonded especially closely with John. Taking the bus to school in the mornings Jacqueline couldn't help but daydream. Growing up, she had never known love – had never been able to define it. This new life, though, just had to be love. Didn't it?

———— † ————

We almost froze to death on the tarmac at Travis Air Force Base. Then we took a school bus to the San Francisco Airport. There were a bunch of people calling us baby killers and stuff like that. All I could do was look straight ahead, get the hell in there, and forget about those people. As soon as we got inside they called my flight to Dallas. I ran to try and get there in time. Lieutenant Colonel Tutwiler, our battalion commander, was on the same flight. I was the last one there, and this captain tried to bump me off of the flight. Tutwiler turned around and chewed that guy out left and right and made him apologize to me. I was so happy to get home. And that was it. I never heard about anybody from Charlie Company again until 2002. I never let anybody know that I was coming home. I didn't want anybody making a big thing out of it. So I just took a taxi to my mom's house. It was about six in the morning when I got there. I knocked and my wife came to the door and started hollering when she saw me. It was the first time ever that I saw my son. When I first held him in my arms, I felt free. I felt like I was tied to something before, but when I held him, I knew that I was free.

Jimmie Salazar

Aurora Salazar

The time in the hospital had worked for Aurora Salazar. Her blood pressure came down, and baby Richard was born in June 1967 with very little difficulty. It seemed like a miracle to Aurora. Both she and Richard were healthy, even after the doctors had been so worried. The first thing that Aurora did once home was to snap a picture and scribble a quick letter to Jimmie – he was a dad! That letter made its way across the Pacific and found Jimmie at Dong Tam preparing for a mission. He was elated, and let Aurora know that their life together once he got home would be different. Different than she had ever known. They would get their own place. They would both get good jobs. Their kids were going to have family, love, and a future. And he did mean kids. There were going to be more! And that is the way that it went with the Salazar letters. Aurora kept Jimmie up to speed on what Richard was doing, marking each passing milestone with a special letter. And Jimmie's letters never much spoke of Vietnam. They spoke of the wonderful normality that was going to be their future together. Sometimes he sent pictures, or wrote of the doings of his buddies. But he never dealt with battle. Never dealt with death. Jimmie had been wounded in the fighting on May 15, shot through the arm, necessitating two weeks in the hospital. He wrote to his parents about the incident, but gave them explicit instructions not to tell Aurora. She was still pregnant at the time, and he didn't want to worry her.

Aurora Salazar didn't worry. She was young, not even 17 yet, had a child and a husband, and had a future that was brighter than she had ever dared hope. Vietnam seemed more a place that Jimmie was in, rather than a war he was fighting. Jimmie was sending home most of his paycheck, much of which Aurora was able to save. But she decided that the future owed her more. Aurora's in-laws, Richard and Ramona, were happy to watch the baby while Aurora went job hunting. Lacking a high school degree, Aurora was pretty sure that she was going to wind up a waitress again, but she was determined to at least try to find something better. Almost miraculously one of her first jobs – a dream job – hit. It turned out that the Internal Revenue Service in Austin didn't require a high school degree, or even a GED – a General Equivalency Diploma. They just hired her on the spot as a file clerk. A real paycheck and benefits. Working for the government. Now she could really put some money aside and be ready maybe even to buy a house when Jimmie got home.

By December 1967, Aurora was counting down the days. Aurora had spent a bit of every day preparing for Jimmie's homecoming. Each evening she had taken out Jimmie's photograph and showed it to little Richard, repeating "Papa, Papa." Aurora couldn't imagine what it must have been like for Jimmie never to have seen his own son, and she tried to make their meeting as smooth as possible. In January 1968, everyone knew that Jimmie was due home soon, but there were no exact details. He had promised to phone, but no call had come. It was early in the morning, with breakfast cooking on the stove. The doorbell rang and Aurora went to answer, absently wondering who would come calling so early. She opened the door and screamed – it was Jimmie! Behind her she heard a noise. It was Richard chugging his way across the floor in one of those circular baby walkers. He was burbling "Papa, Papa!" Aurora Salazar had done her job.

At first the Salazars still lived with Richard and Ramona, until Richard kick-started the future by telling Jimmie that it was time to be the man of his own house and to move out and get a place of his own. And Jimmie did just that, remaining in the Army Reserves and getting a job as a mechanic with the Lower Colorado River Authority. And then the future hit with a vengeance. Two more children followed quickly, Gary and Jimmie Junior. Amid the family growth, tragedy struck. Jimmie's father Richard had never quite gotten over the worry of his son being gone to war and continued to fade, passing away in 1971.

Maybe it was the stress of losing his father. Maybe it was the way that he had been young one day and then found himself with a job, family, and three kids almost the next. It had to be something, but nobody ever suspected Vietnam. Aurora had noticed signs that Jimmie had changed almost from the minute that he walked through the door on that January morning. He was not that happy-go-lucky boy that she had fallen in love with at age 14. There was something different, darker about the new Jimmie Salazar. The simplest part of the change was that Jimmie had become a heavy drinker. On the surface Jimmie seemed to be doing everything right. He was a great, if sometimes distant, father to his sons. He worked hard and didn't spend profligately. To their neighbors it must have seemed that Aurora, Jimmie, and the kids were living the American dream. But Aurora knew that something was haunting Jimmie; something so powerful that it had changed him. However, she didn't know what it could be.

Try as he might, the drinking couldn't seem to keep Jimmie's pain at bay. Most visibly to others, Jimmie sometimes hit the dirt at loud noises. More personal to Aurora, though, were the cold night sweats, the whispered voices of friends who had been killed, and the terrible nightmares. Sometimes Jimmie would wake up in the middle of the night screaming and punching Aurora. When he came to, Jimmie was horrified. How could he be hitting his wife?

He loved her. What the hell was he doing? Aurora didn't know what to do. She was just beginning her 20s, she was holding down a job while raising three children, and the kind and happy boy she had fallen in love with was gone. The new Jimmie still cared for his family deeply with a love that almost ached with tenderness, but his life was tinged with a constant sadness, a new and volcanic temper, and ever-present alcohol. Aurora and Jimmie still loved one another; they both would do anything for their children, but something was tearing them apart. Aurora turned to her faith and went to speak with the family priest, while Jimmie went to see a physician. Surely someone would understand their troubles, understand the darkness that threatened to engulf Jimmie's life. But in the 1970s there were no answers. Both the priest and the doctor remarked that many Vietnam veterans seemed troubled, but neither could offer much advice other than telling the young couple to remain strong. There were no answers, and the required strength was fading. There were only questions and confrontation. With her happy future lost to an unknown assailant, in 1974 Aurora Salazar filed for divorce. Both she and Jimmie wanted to make it work – the love was still there. But they just could not find a way to live together any longer.

———— † ————

I had played my part and served my country well. I was proud of what I had done. I came into San Francisco not knowing what to expect. But I wasn't approached by anybody; I wasn't harassed. I was just kind of ignored. My wife came to pick me up at the airport. It was a quiet and uneventful homecoming. When I had left for induction, my dad would not come out. Wouldn't even say goodbye. But when I got home it was a whole other story. He was happy to see me and wanted to know all about what had happened. Veterans were pretty much ignored. I don't think that anyone even acknowledged that I was a veteran. It was around 2000 finally when a local newspaper reporter came in and asked if I was a Vietnam veteran and wanted to talk about my time in the war. We hadn't received any recognition for so long, and to have a guy call me out of the clear blue sky to do an interview and to thank me for what I did. It blew me away. It was more than 30 years since I had come home. The first recognition I got.

Larry Lilley

Judy Lilley

Judy Lilley was still doing her best to navigate her limbo world. She was married, young, living at home, and learning that it was okay to still act young even though her husband was away at war. More than most of the wives in Charlie Company, Judy had good reason for concern. Larry was very open in his letters, in part because he had so much that he needed to work through. His entire circle of close friends had been killed in Vietnam. Don Peterson on May 15, and both Kenny Frakes and Tim Johnson on June 19. How could one man be forced to go through so much? And each of those losses had a reflective impact on Judy. She had known all of those guys. She had idolized Don and Jacque Peterson; they had the strong relationship and family that she hoped to have. But Judy's connections to Kenny and Tim had run even deeper. She had known them as long as she had known Larry. Kenny and Tim were vibrant, important parts of Judy's life – and now they were just names on headstones and memories.

In a way it was the best letter that Judy had ever received when she found out that Larry had been injured. He had been jumping across one of the endless small waterways in the Mekong Delta when he had heard his knee pop. Then it had swollen up and refused to bend. Although Judy was sure that it hurt, she knew that Larry's banged-up knee was going to keep him out of combat for a while. And a while was pretty much all he needed before he came home. Judy could almost feel her heart rate drop. Larry was going to make it.

Judy drove up to San Francisco to meet Larry at the airport. She really can't remember much about that homecoming, except for the crying. First there was a visit to see Larry's parents, and then Judy went in to quit her job. Larry still had a few months on his military hitch and was off to Fort Campbell, Kentucky. And this time she was going with him. The couple rented a single-wide trailer near Fort Campbell, and had a television the size of a bar of soap. But still they felt lucky. They were together. Judy did her best to make the trailer as homey as possible, and found that she enjoyed married life. She couldn't detect any differences in Larry's demeanor; he seemed to go about his work just like everyone else. Their relationship seemed to be going just about like everyone else's too. But even if Larry had been different – had been changed by Vietnam – Judy couldn't have noticed it. The couple had spent so little time together before Larry had shipped out that they really didn't know each other at all.

After Larry finished out his military obligation, the Lilleys moved back to Lancaster, California. Both began to look for jobs, and money was tight. Her short stint of being a housewife had been fun, but now it was time for Judy to get back to work. For his part, Larry spent a bit of time looking for something new and different before taking his father up on the offer of a job at the family Honda store. Judy had plans to open her own beauty salon; a process that would take about a month. In the interim she also went to work in the Lilleys' Honda store, doing bookkeeping. And somehow that job just stuck – first working with the books and then selling motorcycles. Judy was good at the work, and really enjoyed it. And, while some couples find working together to be difficult, Larry and Judy got along famously at the shop. At home Judy got the feeling that Larry was pretty controlling, that his word was the law. But she figured that is how marriages work and just rolled with it. He was the love of her life, and no doubt some bad had to come with all of the good. The bad got worse when Judy received a call in 1972 that her mom, June, had suffered a stroke. After driving to the hospital, Judy, who was just about to have her first child, learned that there wasn't much the doctors could do for June other than make her comfortable. June's slow death put great stress on the families, both the Williamses and the Lilleys. For Judy it was one of the most sorrowful and transformative moments of her life. She had been so close to her mom, especially after her sister had died. Now she was gone too. Judy Lilley wasn't sure what to do next.

———— † ————

Nancy Benedick

It was April 30, 1969 on my second tour, and we were moving along a tree line. I walked out into a rice paddy to see what was around the bend. I stepped up onto a rice paddy dike, and BOOM! I went flying through the air. When I hit the ground I had my hands on my crotch to make sure that the family jewels were still there. I knew that I was hurt bad. One leg was gone, and the other one looked like ground hamburger. I directed them to take care of the other wounded guys first, and they went out on the first helicopter. I was the last one medevaced out. The guys were kind of shocked about how I took it. I was just cussing because my fighting days were probably over, and I was worried about getting my injured men out safe. I was conscious the whole time, and they took me to the hospital at Dong Tam. I was not a very cooperative patient. They hauled me in there and there were half a dozen doctors, and I kept sitting up to see what they were doing. They kept telling me to sit back down, but I just sat there and said, "No. I want to see what you are doing." They finally gave me a shot that I knew was going to knock me out, so I reached up and grabbed one of the doctors by the throat. I yelled at him, "If you cut my fucking knees off, I'll kill you." When I woke up the next morning I still had my knees, so I was a little happier. I decided right then that I wasn't going to sit around and be a cripple.

Jack Benedick

Nancy Rolle grew up outside Kansas City where her father, Don, worked for Kresge's Five and Dime and her mother, Elizabeth, was a homemaker. Elizabeth had grown up an army brat, and talked about military service often and quite favorably. It was a typical middle-America upbringing. Regarding her future, Nancy had been torn as long as she could remember. She admired her mom and wanted a family of her own. But in her town it was pretty much expected that a girl should go to college, with nursing or teaching being the careers of choice. Since it was expected, Nancy did it. She went off to college, where she found that she had a real passion for education. The learning and independence were great fun, and she had bumped into a cute guy in World History class – Jack Benedick.

Jack was everything that Nancy wasn't. He was overt, brash even – a real man's man, while Nancy was cool and cautious. They say that opposites attract, and it was fully borne out in the case of Jack and Nancy. They got along famously, and had a wonderful time together, even though Jack wasn't the type for commitment. As they got more and more serious he swore that they weren't ever going to get married. Jack's parents had suffered through a very turbulent marriage, often in conflict with one another and with their children. Regardless of his troubled relationship with his parents, though, Jack had idolized his father, who had been a military man. Jack had grown up playing war and was determined to follow in his father's footsteps.

Nancy got a job teaching after graduation, and Jack joined the military and was soon tapped for Officer Candidate School (OCS). By then Jack had overcome his aversion to marriage, and did things the Jack Benedick way. Quick and direct. He sneaked out of OCS, met Nancy in Savannah, Georgia, and there was a basic – but deeply meaningful – wedding in front of five guests. When Jack had taken her hands during his recitation of the vows, Nancy was sure that he was looking through her eyes and into her soul. It was fast, it was all Jack, but it was both right and permanent. Then it was back to OCS for Jack, and back to Nebraska to teach for Nancy. But it turned out that she couldn't hold down that job for much longer, because she was pregnant. After training the Benedicks moved to Fort Leonard

Wood, Missouri, and set up a home together for the first time. Jack's dad had to wire the couple some money to buy basics for the apartment like toothbrushes, dishes, and diapers for Jack Junior who had just recently been born. They all lived in a nice little duplex, and married life was off to a pretty good start. But then Nancy learned from a friend that some of the guys, including Jack, were off to Fort Riley to train for Vietnam.

The training at Fort Riley had gone by in a flash. Jack had been so busy, and was so dedicated to his men, that he was only home for short stretches, often using that time to play with Jack Junior. Nancy dedicated most of her time to learning how to be a mom and how to raise a child. They were hectic days, but good ones. The kind of days that you look back on later in life as some of the best ever lived. When Jack left for war, Nancy moved back in with her parents. It was another good time in her life. Jack was Jack. He was indestructible, so she was sure that nothing was going to happen to him in Vietnam. And she really enjoyed being at home. Jack Junior bonded with her family quickly and thoroughly, especially with her father Don. Even though it was physically crowded, that year at home with Jack Junior gave Nancy room to grow. She was able to take on responsibility. People relied on her. She was becoming independent – a mature, responsible adult and parent. And the fun thing was she knew that she was changing.

In her letters, Nancy was always breezy, filling Jack in on the latest doings of the family and especially of Jack Junior. For his part, Jack's letters were full of adventure. Vietnam and his men were important to him. It was important that he was able to get to the edge of life and look down without being frightened – calmness in the face of war was dearly important to Jack Benedick. Vietnam made him. The only worries he ever expressed in his letters involved being transferred from Charlie Company to a rear echelon position during the fall of 1967. It was standard practice in the Vietnam-era military, but it still rankled. Jack Benedick wanted to be in the field with his men. Jack eventually returned home in January 1968, meeting Nancy and Jack Junior in Fayetteville, Arkansas. It took a while for Jack Junior to become comfortable around his father again, but Jack took back to parenting like a duck to water. It helped that he was assigned back to the familiar territory of Fort Riley where he had pretty easy duty as part of the post-operations section. He had plenty of time off to be with Nancy and Jack Junior. The pair romped and played, sometimes earning Nancy's good-natured wrath. It was fun for her to watch as Jack Junior came to idolize his dad. The young family settled down into a comfortable routine, and even wondered together what civilian life would be like after Benedick's military career ended in May 1968.

Future idylls were shattered when Jack Benedick received a phone call from the parents of his best friend John Hoskins. From the time that they had first met in Fort Riley in the spring of 1966, the two young Charlie Company platoon leaders had formed an inseparable bond despite their differences, Hoskins the warrior-poet graduate of West Point, Benedick the hardscrabble OCS graduate. The pair had shared everything in Vietnam – victory, sorrow, and pain. The Hoskins said that their son John, then a company commander serving his second tour in Vietnam, had died, killed by the detonation of a land mine he had been trying to disarm. It was while he was serving as one of Hoskins' pallbearers on a dreary, gray afternoon at West Point that Benedick made his decision. He wasn't going to leave the army. He was going to go back to Vietnam to get revenge for his fallen friend. There was no chance at all that he would catch Hoskins' killers, but even an impersonal revenge was better than doing nothing at all. Nancy was not happy with her husband's decision, but in her heart of hearts she had been expecting it. Even she couldn't really see Jack Benedick as a civilian. He was a military man. It had been nice to dream about playing house together and having a normal life, but she had always known deep inside that he would return to Vietnam.

There was a brief period of family normalcy while Jack underwent some refresher training, and then he shipped out back to Vietnam in January 1969. Nancy and Jack Junior moved back with her parents for a second time. For a while everything was good again, but this time Nancy was under no illusions. She had been part of the military world long enough to know how dangerous Vietnam really was. She had known of the dangers of war during Jack's first tour as well, but had not been able to admit it. This time, though, was different. This time she was worried.

On May 1, 1969, Don and Elizabeth had gone out for lunch, leaving Nancy and Jack Junior alone at home. They were on the floor playing with some cars when the phone rang. It was the Western Union man. He had a telegram, but couldn't find their house. Nancy almost fell to the floor. She gave the man directions, but dreaded receiving the telegram that he carried. She can't remember if she met the Western Union man on the porch or if she waited for him to knock. The words on the telegram hit her in bursts. Land mine. Traumatic amputation of both legs. Hospital. Nancy Benedick was sick, physically sick. She was desperate for more information. Jack was alive – but what else? Her parents rushed home to help as soon as they received the news. But Nancy was inconsolable. And it only seemed to get worse. She had to call Jack's parents and let them know, and, while his father took the news rather stoically, his mother dissolved into tears. There were no letters from Jack over the next days to allay her fears. He was too badly wounded to write. So Nancy took the bit between her teeth and contacted the Pentagon. Her husband was wounded somewhere in Vietnam and she needed information now! From this point forward Nancy received a telegram each week outlining Jack's progress. It slowly became clear that he was going to survive, but it also became clear that his injuries had been catastrophic and life-changing. Her Jack – the man's man who was always defined by the physical side of life – was coming home with no legs.

Jack Benedick's second homecoming from Vietnam was dramatically different than his first. Nancy drove to Colorado to meet him at Fitzsimmons Army Medical Center. She was able to lean over and give him a hug and kiss, but Jack was too weak to reply in kind. He had lost a great deal of weight, in part due to having contracted malaria on top of everything else. His legs were gone below the knees, and, even though he had already undergone several major surgeries, his wounds were not yet bound up. Bone still protruded from the stumps of both legs, left that way to help ward off potential infection. Jack was also a little shocked at how Nancy looked. She had been so stressed by the situation that she had not been able to eat much, and had lost an alarming amount of weight. Jack cracked a smile and mentioned that they both should start eating better and taking better care of their health. Nancy spent every day at the hospital with Jack, arriving at 10am each morning and remaining until they kicked her out at night. It didn't help matters that Nancy was pregnant with the couple's second child, but at least she could kid with Jack that she felt sicker than he looked from time to time.

With Jack Junior safe back home with her parents, Nancy could make caring for Jack, and the progression of her own pregnancy, her full-time jobs. It was plain that he was going to be there for a hell of a long time – they first had to close up his wounds, then there were the skin grafts, then he had to recuperate and gain strength, then there were prostheses, and then there was learning how to walk. The doctors predicted that it would all take about a year. So Nancy bit the bullet and rented a house nearby. She was going to be by Jack's side for every damn minute of that year. She and Jack made some great friends during their time at Fitzsimmons, developing common bonds with several of the other amputees and their families. In their communal loss, they all shared something special. And Jack found something else that he needed – a nemesis. Nurse Goodheart was a stickler for every regulation in the book, and Jack Benedick loathed regulations. They went round and round nearly every day, sometimes seriously, but mostly in a playful way.

After months of healing, it was finally okay for Jack to move into the house with Nancy. He just had to report for physical therapy twice a day every day to get his strength back up, weakened after having been in a bed for so long. Jack wore long pants to physical therapy, in part to get strange looks from the other patients. One kid even asked him, "Mr. You don't have any legs. Why are you wearing long pants?" But Jack took it all in stride. He seemed to love crawling around the house to work his strength up. It was almost like having a giant baby around. Oddly, Nancy felt like that time living in Colorado was one of the best of her life. She was needed – and being needed feels good. It was her job not to feel sorry for herself, her family, or her husband. Other folks could do that. If she started feeling sorry for their situation, it could all end badly. It was her job to make everything that was so abnormal feel and seem normal. It was needed, it was nurturing, and it was liberating.

Once he was strong enough it was time for Jack to try on his prostheses. And that moment was pure Jack Benedick. The orderly gave the unwieldy devices to Jack and helped strap them on. Then he told Jack that he needed to get into the wheelchair to report to the doctor for his first steps in training to walk again. Jack mumbled something like, "To hell with that," hopped up and walked out. Nancy just trailed in his wake. There was nothing for it. Jack did have the decency to pop his head into his doctor's office to let him know what was up. The doctor's eyes shot open wide at the sight of Jack Benedick standing in the door. Flustered the doctor stammered, "You can't do that! We have to teach you how to walk again!" Benedick calmly replied, "Well sir, I didn't forget how to walk." The doctor spluttered for a moment and then replied, "But what if you fall down?" To which Benedick answered, "Well, I didn't forget how to get up either." Nancy grinned at the doctor as she left. Her Jack Benedick was back.

Once he had his new legs, there was still a lot of physical therapy to go before Jack was going to get his release, and he bore the regimen about as stoically as he could. Seeing that Jack was about at the end of his tether, a hospital nurse suggested something new. How about skiing? Jack and Nancy had skied a few times before on a tiny slope outside of Omaha. But this was a real mountain they were talking about. Nancy knew what the answer was going to be even before Jack opened his mouth. This was the exact kind of challenge that her husband needed to keep going. Jack agreed, and took to skiing like a natural. The motion, the speed. It was all addictive, and it all made him feel physically whole again. In the evenings Nancy and Jack would sometimes talk about the future, what kind of jobs they both might have. They spoke of the future of their growing family now that baby Mike had joined the mix. Things were like a real family again. Jack

Junior had also come to join them. Jack was busy being his idol again. It got so normal that on one occasion Jack jumped up from the couch to help Jack Junior with something, only to come crashing to the ground. He had forgotten that he didn't have any legs.

In typical Jack Benedick fashion, Nancy's future came into better focus one day when an officer dropped by with some Social Security disability forms that needed filling out. Jack was about half-way through the tiny mountain of paperwork when he made an offhand comment. "Hey. I can still collect this while I'm on active duty, right?" The young officer looked over his glasses and replied, "Well, no. You can't stay in the army." That set Jack off right then and there. Goddamned if he wasn't going to stay in the army? Who the hell was going to kick him out of the army anyway? He could do just as good a job as anyone else, with or without legs.

Nancy Benedick had done her job – she couldn't even help thinking that maybe she had done it too well. This was normalcy. Jack Benedick had overcome the obstacles and was as irascible as ever. Whether he would ever admit it or not remained to be seen, but that gentle presence that had always been there pushing him over those obstacles was Nancy Benedick. The woman who stood there by his side with a smile on her face as he fumed and cursed at the stunned military functionary. It looked like Nancy Benedick was in for some more of the military life.

CHAPTER 7

LIVING WITH VIETNAM

For Steve Vietnam never really had to come up in conversation. It was like he had been there and it was done and over with. He didn't talk about it, and I didn't ask any questions. We were just sort of removed from what life had been like before. In 1972 Steve got a call from one of his buddies from 3rd Platoon, Tim Fischer. He had found Steve and was so excited to have found him. From then on Steve talked about it a little bit more. But still not a lot. I do remember him waking up from time to time with night sweats. Maybe holler out in the middle of the night. You couldn't really tell what he was saying; he would just wake up from a nightmare. I'd ask him about it, and most of the time he wouldn't want to talk about it. He would just say, "I'm remembering stuff." And I would ask him if he wanted to share it, and he would say, "No. I don't need to. I'm okay." Vietnam never affected our relationship and didn't seem to affect him in anything he did. It wasn't a big to do in our life. He had just done what he had to do. He could have let it bother him, but Steve just put it far enough back to where it didn't affect his life. And so it didn't affect me.

Jennifer Hopper

Vietnam changed Ernie so much, but I couldn't ever leave Ernie. I just love him so much. You can't just give up on that. I try to find out as much as I can on PTSD. I read everything I can get my hands on. I'll watch anything. I can't get enough learning about PTSD. But sometimes I wonder who am I supposed to get help from? Who am I supposed to go to? The war drastically changed my life that I thought I would have growing up. Never would I have thought that I would have this life. This PTSD stuff is so sad. People just don't understand it. I'm trying to, but it's not always easy. I know that there are times when Ernie's friends thought I was horrible, but they don't live with him. When he goes out he is happy-go-lucky and can't buy enough drinks. But when he gets home he can turn very quickly. And his friends just don't see that. One of his friends told me the other day, after they had been out drinking and gambling, he said, "Jeannie; I have to give you a lot of credit. I have never heard you render any doubt."

Jeannie Hartman

55 years old to me was too darn young to be gone. Every day I miss him. Ray didn't talk about Vietnam much, but I did ask him about the Agent Orange. I remember his answer distinctly. He said, "Babe, it's like somebody threw tons of talcum powder on you; that's just the way it looked. And then the foliage would be gone in practically moments." The biggest thing that aggravated him was when he got kidney cancer. The government wouldn't admit a connection to Agent Orange. He breathed it in; it was everywhere. When he got bad one of his doctors asked him if he had been out of the country, and Ray said that he had served in Vietnam. The doctor just shook his head like this is it. Ray felt like, "I went over there and served my country, and now I have to get this?" It was kind of a rip-off. There were no ifs, ands, or buts about it. Even 15 years after his death I am still fighting the government on this. I have filed everything. I don't think about it all the time or it would drive me crazy. It's extremely frustrating and gets me ticked off sometimes. The cancer took Ray from me, from his grandkids. You just want to say, "Are you kidding? These are the men

and women who have fought for your freedom and you don't give a rat's you know what for them." And there's not a darned thing I can do about it.

June Layman

When Steve got home from Vietnam we seemed to fight all of the time, which we didn't do before. I didn't know he was drinking, and this probably caused some of our fights. I just thought it was my fault because I always took everything personally. I tried to understand. When I would go and try to get some help, he would get mad at me. It was kind of a catch-22. I thought well if you can't beat him join him. So I joined him and started partying with him. The thing is that didn't work either because he still got mad. He just drank and drank, and he didn't talk about Vietnam. I used to talk to my sister about it and she suggested it might be Agent Orange that affected him. I would say something to him and he would say it was not. I went to a counselor and he got mad at me for that and I talked to my doctor and he got mad at me for talking to him. I talked to the preacher at the church. I just couldn't figure out why he was so ornery all the time. I guess that was his way of letting it out without actually talking about it. If I tried to ask him, he just yelled at me. So I just shut up. In the end that's when I said I have done everything, I have been good, I've gone to church, I've not gone to church and partied with you and now you're still yelling at me I am done, and we got a divorce. Steve is a good and brilliant man, but Vietnam changed him and we never talked about it. Now he does talk about Vietnam a lot more. I think that if we had talked about it more back then, things might have been different. I was telling this lady I was with last night if we knew then what we know now, we probably would have stayed married.

Karen Huntsman

Americans have long had something of a schizophrenic relationship with the Vietnam War. Sometimes the war is forgotten, languishing in the public memory in the shadow of more palatable societal moments like World War II or Kennedy's Camelot. On other occasions Vietnam is the subject of acrimonious debate, with scholars and movie makers dueling over the soul and meaning of the war and its era. The often bitter relationship between Americans and their lost war in Southeast Asia has greatly influenced the public's view of Vietnam veterans and how those veterans see themselves and their society. As the result of this complex interplay there exist generalized, and sensationalized, public images of the Vietnam veteran; images informed less by reality and more by movie portrayals including Robert De Niro's magisterial performance of the unhinged veteran Travis Bickle in *Taxi Driver*.

The result has been a mythologized common vision of the American veteran experience. Everyone knows the initial stereotypes: the veteran who joined Vietnam Veterans against the War and tossed his medals on the steps of the Capitol, the veteran loner, the veteran ready to go off any minute, the homeless veteran. It was only after the Persian Gulf War that those stereotypes began to fade as Americans rushed to right the historical wrongs perpetrated upon the Vietnam generation of soldiers. Now there exists a new vision of the Vietnam veteran – as a man approaching his 70s, proudly wearing a "Vietnam Veteran" ball cap, receiving belated thank yous and invitations to march in parades. Through it all, though, the Vietnam veteran has remained a cardboard cutout – an assigned societal vision – a victim. The truth of the matter, though, is far more complex and infinitely more human. Vietnam veterans were not simply what society assigned them to be; they were instead individuals, young men returning from brutal conflict determined to get on with their lives.

Over 3 million Americans returned home from service in theater in the war zone that was Vietnam; of that number, though, only slightly over 1 million were combat veterans. Those who had seen combat accounted for only roughly 3.3 percent of their generation. While their generational compatriots had gone to college, begun families, landed jobs, and moved forward in the "real world," combat veterans had watched their friends die and meted out death to others.

They had lived on the razor's edge where even a misplaced step could mean going home in a body bag. The uniqueness of their experiences left combat veterans virtually alone in the crowd. Nobody seemed to be able to understand them, and they, all too often, failed to understand society. For some combat veterans the lack of true empathy became a simple fact of life, for others it became an ever-broadening gulf, leaving them alone and adrift.

The crushing sense of isolation combined with the powerful and tragic nature of combat proved a toxic blend. Published in 1990, the massive *National Vietnam Veterans Readjustment Study* found that over 800,000 Vietnam veterans suffer from some level of Post-traumatic Stress Disorder (PTSD). Surrounded by its own mythology, PTSD is most often badly misunderstood. Combat is traumatic, a world of death and horror that is outside the norms of human experience, and the nearly unimaginable rigors of battle put extreme stress on the psyche. As Victor Frankl, a concentration camp survivor, stated, "An abnormal reaction to an abnormal situation is normal." There is no less normal situation than combat, and soldiers emerge from combat often irrevocably changed. All too often alone in society, swept under the cultural carpet, too many Vietnam veterans were unable adequately to heal from their experience of combat. That experience, the death and suffering, became an integral part of them; Vietnam would always be a major presence in their lives. That enduring presence is PTSD. At its furthest limits PTSD is crippling – a world of flashbacks and depression. But for many more combat veterans PTSD is something to be lived with – an inability to trust, controlling hyper-alertness, quickness to anger, emotional distance. For most veterans who suffer from PTSD, Vietnam remains part of who they are but does not dominate their lives.

——— † ———

Since there exists no "typical" Vietnam veteran experience, the postwar stories of those who served in Charlie Company, 4th of the 47th Infantry, cannot stand as representative of any greater whole. However, investigating the lives of Charlie Company veterans can help add much needed depth to the rarely told and oft misunderstood story of how American combat veterans and their families learned to live with the Vietnam War. Charlie Company's war certainly had contained many elements of trauma, for both the soldiers and their loved ones. During its time in Vietnam, Charlie Company suffered 26 killed and 105 wounded – a rate of attrition that both left indelible imprints on the men and shaped their futures. Based on my interviews with nearly 100 Charlie Company survivors, I believe that numbers can provide something of a window into understanding how the accumulated trauma of war interacted with a soldier's humanity. For 30 percent of Charlie Company veterans, protesters were their first welcome home from war, an experience that had a profound and lasting impact. The soldiers felt alone and unwanted – as if the sacrifice of so many of their friends had been in vain. But whether welcomed home by protestors, or met only by apathy, 70 percent of Charlie Company veterans felt cut off from society, like outcasts because they were veterans.

Caught between trauma and abandonment, Charlie Company veterans were left alone to deal with Vietnam. A total of 60 percent of Charlie Company veterans suffer from some level of government-identified PTSD. The numbers could well be higher, but some veterans of the unit refuse to seek any treatment. 23 percent of Charlie Company veterans are 100 percent disabled with PTSD.* Comorbid disorders often accompany PTSD, the most common of which is usually alcohol abuse. In need, many turn to booze to cover their symptoms or merely to sleep. 35 percent of Charlie Company veterans identify as alcoholics. The numbers don't lie. There is a darkness associated with war – a darkness that can last for years. But there is a risk of assigning too much agency to PTSD. Much like war itself, those who don't suffer from PTSD find it difficult to understand. The name, especially the term "disorder," carries a stigma. Those who suffer from PTSD must be "crazy." Nothing, though, could be further from the truth. PTSD is infinite in its complexity. It is perhaps not surprising that all of those veterans who are rated

---

* A 100 percent disability rating assigned by the Department of Veterans Affairs indicates that the veteran is unable to work.

100 percent disabled with PTSD in Charlie Company identify Vietnam as the most important event in their lives. It is surprising, though, that all of those same veterans identify Vietnam as one of the very best events of their lives. Certainly the war involved trauma, but it also meant growth, camaraderie, and love.

It is of critical importance to understand what PTSD isn't, and to do that requires some background. At the time of their drafting, Charlie Company was overwhelmingly drawn from the working class. The Charlie Company of today, though, is much different. 11 percent of the unit have become members of the upper class, including at least three millionaires, a much higher rate than the 6 percent nationally who claim upper-class standing. An astounding 78 percent of Charlie Company veterans claim upper-middle or middle-class status, as compared to 45 percent of the nation at large. 12 percent of Charlie Company falls into the status of lower middle class, leaving only 2 percent of Charlie Company – only one of the respondents – below the poverty line, compared to the national average of 15 percent.

The numbers are compelling. The boys of Charlie Company raised themselves up from a 42 percent poverty rate before the war to a 2 percent poverty rate after. Certainly some were struggling with other issues of reintegration, but even they made American success stories of themselves. They went back to school or held down well-paying jobs, they raised families, and they generally beat the odds while outperforming American society as a group. Some had problems with alcohol, and some could not keep their marriages together, but they moved on with their lives nonetheless. They often found niches that suited their abilities and foibles, including working as truck drivers, correctional officers, and post office employees – jobs that either allowed them to be alone or in which they were surrounded by others with similar experiences. Regardless of the difficulties and personal idiosyncrasies, Charlie Company succeeded.

———— † ————

For the married veterans of Charlie Company, including those who married long after the war, their wives and families were a critical part of success. Wives tried to understand and console, they cared for children, they got jobs of their own, they pushed wheelchairs, they too often cried alone at night. Being the wife of a Vietnam veteran meant marrying the war, marrying your husband's comrades, marrying trauma, and marrying strength. If the veterans felt alone within postwar society, their wives had it even worse. They tried hard to understand, only to be told that they shouldn't. They tried hard to help, only to be told that they couldn't. For so many wives of Vietnam veterans, the only person with whom they could share their burden was a man who shut down at the mere idea of sharing. That shutting down was often in a misguided attempt to shield the wife from harm, but it was isolating all the same. Although they had not been to war themselves, that war hurt the Charlie Company wives deeply. Psychiatrists label the problem secondary traumatization. Suffering from war, the veteran husband shuts down, or is emotionally distant, or perhaps even violent. Those actions reflect the trauma of war onto their partners and cannot help but become part of their lives as well. In many such families the wife has to take on more of the spousal burden, from handling finances, to taking the kids to school, to earning a greater share of the pay. Termed caregiver burden by mental health professionals, the unequal shift in family care can place great strain on the veteran's partner and their marriage.

What God had brought together, though, has often been put asunder in American society. The common perception that marriages in earlier years of recent US history were longer lasting and that divorces were rare is actually misguided. After hovering in the teens during the 1930s, divorce rates in the 1940s spiked, reaching a high of 43 percent in 1946, indicating the difficulty of keeping marriages alive during the stress of war and its aftermath. During the 1960s, when the boomers' parents were dealing with raising high-school children, divorce rates dropped to near 22 percent. For the baby boom generation itself – the generation of the women of Charlie Company – the story of divorce worsened. With a change in the law during the 1970s no-fault divorce became an option as did citing irreconcilable differences as a ground for divorce, which made ending marriages easier than ever before, with divorce rates jumping to 50 percent by 1980. For women married in 1966, the year most commonly associated with marriages in Charlie Company, 38 percent of all trips down the aisle ended with visits to the lawyer's office to file divorce papers. That the marriages of 1966 fell apart, though, was not for lack of trying, with 78 percent of the marriages begun in that year persisting for at least a decade.[6]

The aftermath of war played out in myriad ways in the marriages of Charlie Company. Of the 22 total marriages examined in this study, five ended in divorce and a sixth involved a divorce and a subsequent remarriage. There is little doubt that the unimaginable strain of war played a major role in the dissolution of these marriages. That being said, though, these Charlie Company marriages ended in divorce at a rate of roughly 25 percent, which is actually a good deal lower than the overall divorce rate for other marriages begun in 1966. Many of the Charlie Company marriages began at a relative disadvantage, with the wife being married as much to a war as she was to a man – and with some left alone to deal with the birth and care of an infant. That these marriages survived at all is almost miraculous; that they survived at a rate greater than others of their time is a true testament to the women and men who were part of these marriages.

————— † —————

It is the way of war – young people, many with young marriages, go off and do the fighting and dying. Oftentimes the husbands (and increasingly combatant wives) return from war changed, leaving wives to feel alone, helpless, and abandoned. Their love for their husband is still there, but nothing else seems the same. What was true for many of the wives of Charlie Company still holds true today. But the wives and families of veterans were not alone in their experience then, despite their isolation, and they are not alone now. There are other wives out there that feel the same way. And there is help available now.*

---

*   If you are reading this book, and the stories are striking too close to home, contact the US Department of Veterans Affairs, National Center for PTSD at https://www.ptsd.va.gov.

For the wives of Charlie Company who took part in this study, being married to a Vietnam veteran was a complex undertaking. For almost all of the wives there were hard times in learning to live with Vietnam. There was also tremendous personal growth. For some, cherished dreams were tucked away in surrendering to the realities of the moment. For others, doors previously unknown were opened. For many, there was a lack of community, only later to be replaced by a wonderful community of brothers and sisters once Charlie Company began to have reunions. For all, there was a surprise. All of the husbands and wives of Charlie Company had understood that the war would steal a year of life. But, once that year was over, they all believed that normal life would resume. War, though, had other ideas. That single year changed everything. Vietnam might slide further into the past, but it never went away. For both good and ill, even half a century later, the veterans, wives, and families of Charlie Company are still living with Vietnam.

———— † ————

Jacqueline Bradfield

John had become somewhat distant, there was no doubt about that. And he liked to stay out late, there was no doubt about that either. Jacqueline even began to wonder if some "bad habits" had made their way back from Vietnam with John, but there was nothing for it. Boys would be boys, and men would be men. But there was so much good going on. Jacqueline had almost finished community college, something she had never really dreamed would be possible. John had been great with the two boys, Barnard and Byron. Jacqueline spent the mornings taking classes, and John went to work the evening shift at the post office, which sometimes kept him there until quite late. Between school, work, and raising two small children, there really wasn't that much time to be worried about the small stuff. Just like Jacqueline had planned, she had an apartment and a car waiting for John upon his return from Vietnam. But as the years drifted by, and the kids grew, the Bradfields needed more room to stretch their legs.

John wanted a house – home ownership was a sign of success. He began to take classes of his own at the community college and took on a second job. He was determined that the Bradfields were going to have that house. When Jacqueline finished her degree it seemed only natural that she would pitch in on the financial front, so she found a job at a local bank. She hoped that it would only be a stepping-stone to something bigger and better, but it was a start. Perhaps John was a bit old fashioned. Perhaps it was because he had generally been more on edge about things since he had returned from Vietnam. Whatever the cause, John hit the roof about Jacqueline's new job. Making matters worse, Jacqueline now needed a car of her own. First the fact that she wanted to learn to drive and then to have her own car, and then the matter of financing, sparked a new, volcanic round of arguments. Jacqueline couldn't believe all the fuss. She had learned independence while John was off at war, and now that independence seemed to be paying real dividends. But that independence also seemed to bother John greatly. He had never been like this before, and the anger drove a wedge into their relationship.

The arguments started to get out of hand. John tried to stop the bank from financing the car, and then threatened to get rid of the thing once it was bought. John still reveled in his family, and still seemed to enjoy the thought of being married, but he and Jacqueline were drifting further and further apart. It was like they were living separate lives in the same house. Maybe it was because they had started off so young. Maybe it was because John had changed in Vietnam. Maybe life and the war had forced them both to grow, but they had just grown in different and competing directions. More likely it was a combination of everything. John thought that Jacqueline was seeing another man; she thought that he was seeing another woman. One thing that Jacqueline was sure of, though, was that she was becoming more independent just as John wanted to control her more fully. That was the heart of the matter – the couple could not share control.

Suddenly the Bradfields' lives were full of lawyers, arguments over who would keep the house, and custody matters. Jacqueline and John still loved each other, and both certainly loved their children, but they just couldn't manage to live together any longer. Money-wise Jacqueline didn't ask for much, just a bit of child support and no alimony. It was time for her to be on her own, an independent woman. She realized that her new life would be financially difficult, so she saved every dime that she could and moved over to a new job selling insurance. Jacqueline really took to sales, and her salary was enough to keep the family finances solid. But then came the news that her company wanted her to move to Texas. It was one of the biggest decisions of her life, but Jacqueline knew that she had to get away from Cleveland, where there were so many memories tying her to a past that she hoped to move well beyond.

The move to the Houston area was difficult in more ways than Jacqueline could have imagined. There were all of the usual problems, from finding a new house, to going to a new school, and to having to make new friends. The move also greatly troubled Barnard and Byron. They loved their dad, to the point of idolizing him. They missed him greatly, and often blamed Jacqueline for moving them so far away. Such feelings are quite normal for the children of divorced parents, but her sons' angst threatened to tear Jacqueline to pieces. The one thing that she wanted for her boys was a family – the type of loving family that she had been denied. And every angry word from them hit her in the heart like a dagger. Jacqueline and John tried hard to make matters right by their boys. Both children tried moving back to Cleveland with their father for a while, but there was considerable tension on that end as well. Jacqueline remarried for a short time, still trying to find love and to build a nuclear family.

Seven years after the divorce, John got remarried to Esther Stone, a work colleague who was single-handedly raising two children of her own. The adjustment to being a stepmother had its ups and downs, and the children – her Jason and Kayce and John's Barnard and Byron – had their own difficulties in navigating their relationships.

But, even though there were some heated times, the family made it all work. Esther knew from the very beginning that John was a Vietnam veteran, and could tell right off the bat that he needed to talk about his experiences. John would have bad dreams, full of blood and horror. He would sometimes fly into anger at a moment's notice. Sometimes he would watch Vietnam War movies and be sullen for days. Esther had been hearing a lot about PTSD, and she knew its warning signs. John had them all. He didn't want to talk, but Esther knew that he needed to and pushed him to go to counseling sessions, and John agreed.

> I was diagnosed with PTSD when I was working for the postal service. At first they rated me at 30 percent, but in 1988 I had a nervous breakdown, later found to be PTSD related, and I am currently rated 100 percent and am receiving therapy at the VA. In 1988 I was bunkered down in my basement suffering the ills of PTSD, I was a dues-paying member of the Vietnam Veterans of America Association and got their magazine every so often. By chance I came across an announcement of a reunion of Charlie Company to be held in Vegas. I almost fell out of my chair. I thought that we had long been forgotten about! I am surviving cancer at the present, and there are good days and bad days. Today is a good day.
>
> *John Bradfield*

Esther has attended several Charlie Company reunions with John, and sees the good that they do for him. John retired in 2001 and immersed himself in his hobby of riding motorcycles. Esther had to retire to help care for John when he was diagnosed with colon cancer in 2008. John has since recuperated, and he and Esther live together in a Cleveland suburb where John still very much enjoys riding motorcycles and Esther works closely with a neighborhood church.

After her split from John, Jacqueline worked hard to keep her little family afloat, which took up a great deal of her time, including most of her weekends. Her new marriage fell apart in nearly record time, and her children remained deeply conflicted about the divorce and their move to Texas. Jacqueline really had no friends or family she could talk to about it all. She was as thoroughly alone as she had been even when she was young. But Jacqueline had never lost her faith, and as the darkness of her new life threatened to engulf her it was faith to which she turned. Jacqueline attended New Faith Church every Sunday, still trying to emulate the well-dressed and sanctified women who had rescued her when she was young. It was at New Faith that Jacqueline was first called to the ministry. Perhaps because she needed help herself, Jacqueline was determined to try as best she could to help others. The church needed a leader to build up its women's center, and Jacqueline, with people skills built over years of sales, seemed to be the perfect choice. The pastor told Jacqueline that there were many young women who were alone and in need in the community who needed her help. It hit Jacqueline like a jolt of electricity. There were young women out there who were just like she had been when she was young. There were young women who needed their own well-dressed, sanctified women to come into their lives.

Jacqueline had found her passion. She wanted to help women who were living without love and means like she once had. In confronting their present, she was able to come to terms with her own past. Jacqueline Bradfield was finally able to forgive the past and able to understand who she really was. Her self-worth came from within, and was inspired by faith. Nothing, neither the tribulations of war nor family problems, would ever be able to take that away from her. In 2006 Jacqueline received a call from her oldest son Barnard, who now was grown and had children of his own. One of his children, Donovan, was sick, and he needed his mom's help to get by. Jacqueline prayed on the matter, and then went to spend a week with Donovan in the hospital. After his recuperation family matters necessitated that Jacqueline look after Donovan for several more years. The two became fast friends, the preschooler and the grandmother. Donovan accepted Jacqueline fully and completely and didn't pass judgment of any sort. And she loved that child like life itself. Even after Donovan was able to move back home, he constantly called grandma, asking if she was okay. And she kept him at least one day a week. Now Donovan is in school, and it is Jacqueline who often walks him there and helps to take care of his homework. As the duo walk to the front door of the school, hand in hand, Jacqueline looks down at Donovan's smiling face and is so thankful that she finally has the family and the love she always craved.

———— † ————

Becky Lind

When Herb Lind returned from Vietnam for the second time, the family took a long trip through New England and down to Washington DC, with Mark, who was a toddler, spending most of the trip perched on Herb's shoulders. Military life soon came knocking once again, though, and it was back to Fort Riley, where the couple bought their first real home and welcomed their second child, Tara. Although she was no longer a teacher, Becky very much enjoyed her new life; being a mom and homemaker seemed to fit her well. The Linds' finances were solid, in part due to raises given by the military to help keep men in an increasingly unpopular army.

Herb thrived in his career as a military man. Being surrounded by people who valued and understood his service really mattered. Herb had a community of like-minded people who helped him through any postwar difficulties. There was also a military community support group for Becky. Everyone around seemed to be an officer's wife, and everyone seemed to know and understand what military life and war really meant. Her favorite part was helping the wives of new officers and enlisted men. They needed to know everything from where to shop to what to expect from war. Becky volunteered to help those families who needed her most, the lower-income families that were just starting out life together.

Herb's next duty assignment took the Linds to Germany, where both Mark and Tara learned to ride bikes, zooming around with their German compatriots. Becky biked with the kids to school, and the German moms were amazed that Tara, who was only three years old, could ride without training wheels. Next followed short stints in Virginia and Georgia before the Linds returned to Fort Riley in 1981. Becky enrolled at nearby Kansas State University and graduated in 1984 with an MA in Food and Nutrition and a dietician's license.

Becky found a job in Kansas State University Union Food Service shortly after graduation and quickly rose to become cafeteria manager, where she managed 250 employees and the food delivery and diets of tens of thousands of students. The new job carried with it a feeling of accomplishment and independence. Becky was no longer just an adjunct to Herb's life. Becky mattered, and she liked it. As much as she enjoyed the independence, Becky experienced a great deal of stress while balancing her job and home life, but learned to cope, as she always had. After retiring from the military in 1985 Herb took a job in auto supply sales that allowed him to travel to small garages in towns all over Kansas, a regimen that he enjoyed. But Herb never seemed to be able to replace the military. His new life didn't provide him with the same sense of purpose. For some veterans such a major life change brings Vietnam screaming back to the front of their memories in full force. Not so for Herb. There were some moments – leaving the movie *Top Gun* early since it brought him too close to war; folding up his chair one night and hurrying back to the camper – that time of night was when snipers were at their most deadly in Vietnam. Sometimes he woke up and couldn't get back to sleep, wondering what he could have done differently in battles back in 1967. But those moments were few and far between. Vietnam was a very manageable thing for Herb and Becky Lind.

After a bout with bladder cancer in the 1990s, which necessitated constant interaction with the VA, Herb moved to the job that he liked best after the military, serving as maintenance supervisor at the First United Methodist Church. Having taken time off to care for her ailing husband, Becky took a challenging new position with the Area Agency on Aging, working to feed the area's elderly. Life was vibrant and full of activity on all fronts. There were now grandchildren running around at the Linds' beloved ski weekends and camping trips. And the Linds greatly valued Charlie Company reunions – Herb got a chance to see the most important people from his life, and Becky was able to learn more about both the war and her husband. Life had hit a comfortable stage for the Linds.

> I never really talked much about Vietnam, but since the reunions have begun I have talked more. Since the reunions Becky has gotten a lot more involved and interested, mostly she says because she didn't want to ask before. Now she likes to talk about it and feels a part of it, which is good. From a long career, for me Vietnam and Charlie Company stands out. I would do it all again. It was a positive in my life. More and more people want to talk about the Vietnam War, which I very much welcome.

> *Herb Lind*

In 2000 Herb's bladder cancer made a reappearance, necessitating a second surgery, which went well, and in 2009 prostate cancer first popped up, resulting in another operation. Herb remained in very good spirits, and the doctors were sure that they had gotten it all. In 2014, though, the prostate cancer was back again, and the doctor said that it was the most aggressive prostate cancer that he had ever seen. This time there were chemotherapy treatments, which took a great physical toll on Herb. A follow-up surgery in October resulted in the discovery that the cancer had spread across Herb's abdomen. Becky broke the news to Herb – he had only a few months to live, and maybe less than that. Herb had never liked to see Becky cry, so she was determined that she wasn't going to cry now when he needed her the most. She spent her time in the hospital working on a project gathering together Herb's pictures. But then she needed a break, and said that she needed to go home to mow the yard. She spent those three hours crying on the riding lawnmower.

Determined that Herb would live his last days in the comfort of his own home, the Linds left the hospital the next day, and when she got home Becky realized that she didn't have any way to get Herb up the stairs and into their house. It involved a walker, using a belt to pull him out of the car, and an office chair with wheels, but Becky got him inside. After a few days Becky got better at the regimen of helping to care for Herb – he was so weak and frail that he needed help with very nearly every aspect of life. But neither Becky nor Herb was going to quit. Becky took Herb to church, on trips, and to visit the grandchildren. They were determined to live life. By the spring of 2015 Herb was going downhill and was put on hospice care. But Herb was a fighter, and just refused to give up. His extremities were cold, and he could hardly eat, but he just kept right on fighting. On May 6, 2015, Becky said to Herb, "I don't know what I will do without you." He replied, "You will enter another phase of your life, and you will do just fine." Those were Herb Lind's last words. He lingered on for a few more days before Becky whispered to Herb that he just needed to stop breathing, because his body had finished its job and he couldn't go on.

Herb Lind died on May 10, 2015. Becky kept right on working, throwing herself into funeral arrangements and then into a busy life as a grandmother. Tara had married Pete Newcome and had two children, Lindsey and Tommy. Lindsey is now doing well in high school and Tommy is prospering. Mark is now divorced, and his children, Theron and Diana, are doing well – Diana in school and Theron in the University of Nebraska. All of those things help to keep Becky Lind occupied and vital, and she has become the custodian of Herb Lind's memory.

--------- † ---------

Aurora Salazar

Her divorce from Jimmie in 1974 had pained Aurora Salazar more deeply than she would admit to anyone. So much of her own young life had been wrapped up in family disappointment that divorce, no matter the cause, seemed like a personal defeat. Jimmie's drinking and

Vietnam were to blame, but Aurora had lost her dream of family. Her dream for her own family. Somewhere down deep she knew that Jimmie loved her and the children deeply, but sometimes the anger and booze just kept that love from showing through. Nevertheless she knew that it was there. And Jimmie knew what he had lost. He desperately wanted to be a good father, so he started to get his drinking under control and began dealing with his own bad times. Jimmie had recognized that he had problems and was working on them. Aurora keenly wanted an intact family and still loved Jimmie deeply. Those twin forces brought the couple back together. The couple remarried in a small church, and Aurora was now convinced that the grass was not greener somewhere else or with someone else. Jimmie was her man, this was her family, and they were going to make it work.

Aurora had moved from her IRS job and gone to work for Motorola in the early 1970s, and, together with Jimmie's salary as an insurance salesman, the Salazars were firmly middle class. Being far better off financially than she ever had been growing up, Aurora was determined to keep it that way. But life threw a considerable curveball at the Salazars in 1988. Aurora received word that her older brother, Jessie, had passed away. He was divorced, and he had left just a single letter behind – a letter saying that he wanted his three youngest girls, Jamie, Annette, and Molly, to live with Aurora and Jimmie's family. Suddenly the Salazars had a real houseful, with children ranging from grade school to the later years of high school. In some ways it was like starting a family over again. And everything the Salazars thought they knew about family had to be relearned.

Facing a new situation, Aurora retired, but, since the family needed the money now perhaps more than ever before, she also opened a bar and ran two taco trucks. Jimmie pitched in across the board, when his insurance job allowed him the time. His drinking was pretty much gone – a couple of beers during the year on special occasions was about it. There remained anger issues, though, and he was diagnosed as a diabetic. Although he remained a bit distant, and had never opened up about Vietnam, it seemed that Jimmie had gotten his relationship with his past under control, and the Salazars prospered.

It was in 1992 that Jimmie suffered his first heart attack. The doctors said that the war and the strains of its aftermath had taken a devastating physical toll on Jimmie, and that his heart might never fully recover. Jimmie did everything in his power to recover – diet, exercise – but further heart attacks followed in both 1994 and 1996. With his heart failing, Jimmie had to give up his job – and, without either work or alcohol to serve as buffers, Vietnam came back into his life full-force and unbidden. The nightmares, the anger – it was all there. But this time there was an added and all-pervasive feeling of hopelessness. Jimmie Salazar had a life sentence. Aurora felt helpless as she watched her husband slip away a second time; often he would just sit in his chair and stare at the walls for hours. Although he didn't talk about it at all, at least this time there was a name for his problem and the couple's pain – Jimmie was diagnosed with PTSD. Jimmie gravitated toward other veterans, becoming active in local veterans' groups like the American Legion and the Veterans of Foreign Wars, and he became involved in a PTSD support group.

About two months after I got home I went to the church to check on my nervousness. Whenever there was a loud noise I would drop to the ground. But they couldn't help me; nobody knew about PTSD back then. I would go to sleep and then wake up beating on my wife. I would think, "Goddamn, what the hell is going on?" I don't do that anymore. If I have nightmares I go and sleep in another room. So many people lost their lives over that place. So many lost so much. My PTSD really kicked in hard when I had my first heart attack. Reoccurring nightmares, night sweats, hearing noises, seeing shadows, getting angry for no reason. I don't like being with many people. I get nervous as hell when I am around a lot of people. If somebody says something, I can get mad real quick. I have PTSD meetings every week. The doctors mean well, but I haven't seen any changes in my PTSD. My wife and family standing by me made the difference.

Jimmie Salazar

As her daughters neared the end of their high school careers, Aurora Salazar was ready for a new challenge and opened El Mague Restaurant in Johnson City, Texas. Her tacos had been such a hit, and she loved to cook so much, that the idea of opening a full-time restaurant seemed natural. It took a great deal of work, and some investment, but hard work and perpetually moving forward were Aurora Salazar's two chief traits. However, just as the restaurant began to flourish, Jimmie suffered a massive heart attack – one he was not expected to survive. As the doctors made ready for an emergency quadruple bypass, Jimmie apologized to Aurora for all the pain that he had caused her. She did her best to calm him, and then he said something that shocked her: "My only regret is that I never got a chance to see my brothers again." Aurora had no idea what he could mean. All of his brothers were there at the hospital. Jimmie shook his head, he meant his brothers from the Vietnam War. His brothers of Charlie Company. It was only then that Aurora understood what Vietnam had meant to Jimmie, and how deeply Vietnam had affected both of their lives.

Jimmie Salazar survived the surgery, only to be diagnosed with diabetes so severe that it resulted in neuropathy from the waist down, leaving him with badly deteriorating function in both of his legs. With mounting physical problems, in addition to his ongoing PTSD, Jimmie went on 100 percent disability. He was almost a prisoner in his own house, but Jimmie Salazar knew what he wanted to do. He was determined to live, which meant finally talking about and coming to terms with Vietnam. Jimmie was going to get well in every way he possibly could, and there was only one way to do that. He had to find Charlie Company. He wasn't quite sure where to start looking for his old friends, so the process was slow. However, with Aurora's help in 2002 Jimmie hit pay dirt. He located a website for the 9th Infantry Division – a site that was full of pictures of his old friends. There they were, all so young, all so vibrant. There was Fort Riley; there was Dong Tam; there were Kenny Frakes and Tim Johnson; there was – everything. Somehow sure that it was too good to be true, Salazar fumbled for the telephone to call the number listed on the website. The "Hello" came from a voice instantly recognizable even after 35 years – Bill Reynolds, Salazar's old friend from 2nd Platoon. Reynolds couldn't believe his ears. The boys from Charlie Company had been looking for Jimmie for years – how the hell was he doing? The chat went on for nearly an hour as memories of the endless mud of the Rung Sat, the steaming heat of the rice paddies, the sudden fear of stumbling across a Viet Cong sniper, and of lost friends all flooded past. Then Reynolds gave Salazar the best news of all. Charlie Company was having a reunion, and he ought to come. It didn't take Salazar even a minute to decide. Heart attacks, diabetes, and neuropathy be damned. He was going to Las Vegas to see his brothers once again.

Amidst all of the work of owning and running a restaurant, Aurora was delighted to see her husband reaching out to his friends about his war. She went with him to that reunion, and what she found there was life-changing. Jimmie had never shared the memories of fallen friends, of night ambushes, of killing with her. But at that reunion she heard those stories and learned of her husband's role in Vietnam for the first time. It was in Las Vegas that Aurora first learned why her husband had been hurting for so long. It was in Las Vegas that Aurora Salazar learned of the pain that Vietnam had inflicted on her own life.

Jimmie improved as a result of finding his friends once again, and was open about the troubles of his past. But his physical problems began to mount up, resulting in Jimmie being placed on a hodgepodge of medications that needed careful monitoring. Fate had also intervened to make Aurora a mother again, this time raising two of her grandchildren, Jimmie (whom everyone calls Bumper) and Tristan. The combination meant that Aurora was needed full time at home once again, so she gave up the restaurant, even though it was doing a thriving trade. She did take on one last part-time job, though, being elected to the City Council of Johnson City. And, just because she wanted to, Aurora got her GED at age 72. From living on her own and holding down a job at age 12, Aurora Salazar had come one hell of a long way. She was financially independent, living in a beautiful home on the "right side" of town. She was a council member. She had an expansive and wonderful family.

Jimmie now spends much of his time doting on his grandchildren, and they love him deeply. Jimmie's namesake idolizes his grandpa and wants to be just like him, having joined the Young Marines in an effort to emulate his hero. Basking in the glow of a successful life, Aurora Salazar works full time now alongside Jimmie with the grandkids. There have been many successes in Aurora's life, but the one that gives her the most satisfaction is to hear her grandchildren say, "Maw maw. I want to grow up to be just like you."

———— † ————

Mary Ann Maibach

Gary Maibach was 26 years old when he was chosen as a minister of the Apostolic Christian Church. It was a wonderful honor, for which Mary Ann knew her husband was well suited, but it also carried a great burden of faith. The church in Stirling was and remains a very active one, and the calling to help care for the spiritual, mental, and physical well-being of so many special souls was profoundly meaningful for Gary and the entire Maibach family. The ministerial position was unpaid – a true calling. There were two services on Sunday, and one mid-week, to a congregation that initially had a Sunday morning attendance of over 700. When the congregation ballooned to over 1,200, it was time to build a second church. The position also sometimes involved travel to preach in churches that did not yet have a permanent minister. On days when there were no services or travel, there were still all manner of duties expected of a minister, from hospital visits, to counseling, to aiding in the physical and spiritual care of those congregants who were shut in.

Gary often found himself preaching from his experiences in Vietnam and from his life as a veteran dealing with the fallout of war. He sought out contact with other veterans as a way to reach out to those who did not have a strong background in faith. While in Vietnam Gary had been deeply saddened when comrades came to him and asked him to pray for them, because they were too far gone to pray for themselves. Gary and Mary Ann were blessed with a strong community of faith in Stirling, and with a community of believers that valued and understood their experiences. But they were painfully aware that others were not so lucky. Many soldiers returned from Vietnam lost in a wilderness of faith, and Gary tried as best he could to be the spiritual lighthouse for his old friends.

Gary also worked full time at the family store, taking over more and more of the managerial aspects of the business and working long hours. Once their second child, Mark, was born Mary Ann was conflicted. She wanted to be a full-time mom, but she also loved her career as a nurse and the personal satisfaction and sense of independence it brought to her life. So she compromised and decided to work three nights a week while Gary pitched in to watch the kids while she was at the hospital. The Maibachs remained deeply and passionately in love, but sometimes it just seemed like they said hello to each other while one was headed in and the other was headed out.

In 1974 things got just a bit more with the arrival of David, the couple's third child, and Mary Ann quit work to become a full-time mother. Two years later baby James was added to the mix, leaving Mary Ann to deal with four children, ranging from Karen, the eldest, at ten, down to two who were still in diapers. Through it all Gary's responsibilities at work only continued to mount, as he rose to become president of the family store. At the same time Gary's ministerial calling also conspired to take up more and more of his time. Gary was so busy that he missed out on time with the children, something that Mary Ann and he both regretted, but it could not be avoided. Mary Ann's father had been a minister in the church, so she was aware of the challenges of being a pastor's wife. Life had a certain quality of being watched all of the time – being called to help care for the souls of others invites judgment regarding one's family life. While Mary Ann dealt with living in a glass house graciously, the regimen had its difficulties for the children, who sometimes resented being held to a higher standard than their friends.

With only one paycheck coming in, and with four ravenous children to feed, the Maibachs were on the lower end of middle class. There was a bit of a mend-and-make-do and hand-me-down regimen, but the children never really wanted for anything. And they never complained – in part because they knew that there was real, desperate need out there in the world. Even with their busy schedule, the Maibachs always found time to give of themselves to the community. It was their spiritual and moral obligation. Mary Ann worked with a women's group in the church to visit the sick and to bring lunches to needy families in the area, and it was always a great way for the children to pitch in with the making and delivery of lunch buckets.

By 1983, when her eldest, Karen, was 17 and her youngest, James, was seven, Mary Ann decided to get back to work to help alleviate the family's financial burden. So the family bought a second car, and Mary Ann took a job working in an office. With Gary continuing to work hard at what amounted to two full-time jobs, and Mary Ann being both a mother and working full time herself, the years passed quickly and were jam packed with the milestones of life, from elementary school graduations to band concerts, to high school graduations. As life altered, so did Gary. Vietnam became something more of an issue with him, but not one that anybody else but Mary Ann could see. He developed diabetes that the VA associated with his wartime service, and was rated for PTSD. Gary went to support groups for PTSD, where he tried to use his experiences to help others who were more thoroughly entangled in their own memories of the war.

The scripture teaches us that the things that we go through are strengthening us so that we might use our experiences to strengthen others. I was always so frustrated when I was in Vietnam that there was so little that I could do. I have felt frustration like so many others. Everybody wants you to tell them your story, but nobody wants to hear your story. They can't empathize. It is just a story. But when you know God and how much He has done for you, it all comes into better focus.

It is so sad, but there is a God-shaped hole in a lot of these Vietnam veterans. They would be much better off if it was filled the way it needs to be. There is a lot of peace to be had there that is so freely offered by a loving God. I would like nothing better than to sit and have a deep spiritual conversation with veterans who are lost. There is a phenomenal source of strength there that isn't available any place else. So many of the guys in Vietnam were far away from God, and many remain so today, and it breaks my heart. I still pray for them and love them.

Gary Maibach

Gary retired from the Maibach family store in 2006 in order to devote himself more fully to the demands of the ministry. He remained a fixture at the pulpit, where everyone in the congregation knows Charlie Company from his sermons. What new free time he had, though, was quickly consumed by more community service and with the parental and grandparental needs of the burgeoning Maibach family. Gary also became ever more active in the doings of Charlie Company, attending reunions and serving as a sounding board for so many of the men who called when they needed to get something off of their chests. Gary even ventured back to the battlefields of Vietnam with many of his Charlie Company buddies, including Steve Hopper and Larry Lilley, in 2015 and 2017 – journeys that involved traumatic memory but infinite healing. Mary Ann retired from her office job in 2014, and now devotes time to service projects and to a wonderfully large Maibach family, which includes 13 grandchildren, two grandchildren-in-law, and three great-grandchildren. When I called Mary Ann for our interview, some of the grandchildren were plain to hear in the background – I can only imagine the hubbub of holidays at the Maibach home. Gary was off to deliver hand-churned ice cream to the relief center, and Mary Ann was taking time away from making a quilt for World Relief. Later that day she had to cut the interview short to go to sing at a nursing home and to take some of the patients out to run errands. Mary Ann and Gary Maibach had a life that was interrupted by the

Vietnam War – a part of Mary Ann's life that she had forgotten was so difficult. But the Maibachs persevered through the challenges Vietnam had to offer, and turned the travails of war into moments of continued learning and growth.

———— † ————

Judy Lilley

Losing her mother June long before her time had broken Judy Lilley's heart. The loss was made all the more poignant because June had just missed meeting her first grandchild. Not long after her mother's funeral, Judy gave birth to Jodi, opening a new chapter in her life. Passing on to a new generation the dreams and lessons that June had once instilled in her seemed like a perfect way for Judy to honor her mother and what she had meant in her life. June had been a wonderful example of motherhood – always there to teach her the little lessons of life even while fate conspired to require hard work outside of the home. The situation for the Lilleys, though, was somewhat different than it had been for Judy's family. Larry's job, and later the couple's part ownership of the Honda dealership, made for comfortable living. Even after the arrival of a second child, Keith, in 1975, Judy decided to be like her mom. She could have the best of both worlds, being a mom while continuing to work keeping books at the Honda store.

Larry was dedicated to his work. He truly loved everything about motorcycles – he loved building them, riding them, racing them, and selling them. There seemed to be motorcycles everywhere both in the shop and at home. The business expanded, eventually coming to include the ownership and operation of three motorcycle dealerships. With each new acquisition, Judy's workload went up a bit. But neither seemed to mind the escalating time investment. Hard work just seemed to come naturally to both Lilleys.

As much as Vietnam had cost them both with the loss of their dear friends Kenny Frakes and Tim Johnson, neither Judy nor Larry ever really mentioned the subject. Judy didn't notice anything at the time, but in retrospect she wonders if Larry worked so hard and doggedly in part as a distraction – so Vietnam would remain in the background where it belonged. He was different than when he had left. How could anyone fail to be affected by what Larry had seen? He was more domineering; but maybe that trait had been part of his character all along and Judy had just never had the chance to notice it during their short pre-Vietnam courtship? Larry certainly seemed to value and prize life dearly after what he had seen. And, since there were other Charlie Company veterans living nearby, Larry did have the chance every once in a great while to chat with his wartime buddies. But, all in all, life seemed to be progressing just fine for the Lilleys.

Maybe it was because they had married so young and had known so little of each other. Maybe it was because they had both grown and craved a level of independence that the other could not provide. Maybe it was because of the many unstated hurts and conflicts that normally conspire to scuttle healthy marriages. Maybe it was in some ways related to Vietnam. Whatever the causation, under the outward veneer of middle-class perfection the Lilleys had irrevocably grown apart. At the heart of the matter Judy felt too controlled, that Larry's domineering tendencies had placed her in a straightjacket that did not allow her the ability to be herself. She loved Larry Lilley, and down deep she knew that she always would. He had been the first love of her life, and would always remain part of her life. But she just couldn't live with him any longer. After a lengthy separation, the Lilleys divorced. He kept the jointly owned business, and she kept the house. Judy got custody of the children, with Larry taking on the role of a rather distant father.

In her early 30s, Judy Lilley had never really had a chance to be alone before. Her children were, of course, still there. And they needed her like never before, having taken the divorce very badly. Jodi was 12 – a time apt to be a tough age for a girl in the best of circumstances – and she was devastated by the family's rupture. Judy was there to offer to support to Jodi and Keith, the same way that her mom had once been for her. But, even with the pressures of family, Judy was really alone. Independence, though fraught with difficulties and responsibility, was a tonic. She felt that she should be scared of facing an uncertain future on her own, but she wasn't. It was actually exhilarating, and it was a time of personal growth. She took a job as a bookkeeper at a local masonry store, where her bosses were great and appreciated her deeply. It was the perfect job, one that Judy would hold until she gave up work altogether.

Mark Williams was Kevin's youth league soccer coach, and his first meetings with Judy were just that of parents dealing with the minutiae of children's soccer – cleats, twisted ankles, and diving saves. After a while, though, Judy and Mark figured out that they were attracted to each other more than just at the level of coach/mom. Having both been through the marriage wringer once before, the couple were cautious, dating four years before thinking of marriage. But when Mark popped the question, Judy couldn't help but say yes. He was a great guy, and he was wonderful with the kids – and they seemed to like him, which was of paramount importance. Before she accepted his proposal, though, Judy had to talk to Mark about Larry. As the father of her children, Larry Lilley would always be a part of their lives. But it went deeper than that. In divorce Judy and Larry had remained close. As childhood sweethearts they shared so much in common that they needed one another, and the shared loss of Vietnam caused them to continue to need one another. Whatever the cause, Judy told Mark that Larry Lilley would still be a part of their lives. And if that was okay, then she agreed to marry him.

Judy got married to Mark in a ceremony in Hawaii. Mark had a good job at Southern California Edison, and Judy kept her bookkeeping position. The couple built a new house in Lancaster, California. As her children were making their ways through the southern California teenage years that she remembered so well – cruising and the Beatles were well in the past, but surfing was still there – Judy and Mark began to reap the benefits of their hard work and penchant for savings. Mark was able to retire at age 55, taking a job working on a golf course to occupy his now considerable time. And, although her bookkeeping job at the masonry firm had served her so well, Judy retired too. The children both graduated first from high school and then from Fresno State University, with marriage and grandchildren following soon thereafter.

Through it all, Judy kept in touch with Larry Lilley. Sometimes the calls were about mundane matters that distant parents have to deal with in raising children while separated. But they also talked just to talk. Larry had lots to share about his life over the years. The motorcycle business had continued to prosper, and he had married again in 2000. His new wife, Patty, knew that Larry was a Vietnam veteran, and was aware that he had a stubborn streak a mile long. But since this was Patty's third go-round on marriage, she was pretty sure that she could handle anything Larry had to dish out.

It was now Patty's turn to go to work with Larry in the family motorcycle business, a job that she did well and came to like. Their marriage, like any other, wasn't always wine and roses, but they made it work. In 2014 Larry finally retired, and that is when things began to darken somewhat. As Judy had once suspected, Larry had used hard work to cover up Vietnam. Or maybe it was just a crisis of confidence that often comes with retirement. Whatever the reason, though, Larry got more moody and depressed after retirement. It was around the same time that Larry first got involved in Charlie Company reunions and even took a trip back to Vietnam in the company of Gary Maibach and Steve Hopper. With that, the memories from 1967 came flooding back. Don Peterson, Kenny Frakes, Tim Johnson. Along with the memories came a battery of emerging health problems related to his service in Vietnam, including severe hearing loss. Patty does her best to help Larry, including urging him to get tested and counseled for PTSD. She is happy, and so is he. But managing Vietnam has become a new part of their lives.

I had put Vietnam on the back burner for years. I didn't talk about it or boast about it. Nobody wanted to hear about it frankly. It kind of faded into the sunset. I didn't talk about the war with my kids until they were maybe 17 years old. Just never talked about it. For my business I had breakfast rides every Sunday morning so folks would ride their motorcycles. One Sunday morning I saw that a nearby town was hosting the travelling Vietnam Memorial. I told my son to lead the breakfast ride, because I had something else to do. He kept asking me why, so I told him. He wanted to go with me, so we wound up taking the whole breakfast ride to the Vietnam Memorial. We got to the desk where they asked if you knew anybody on the wall. When I responded that I did they asked, "Did you see some action over there?" I told them that I had and that is why I was there. My son was standing with me at the panel for June 19, where my friends had their names on the Wall. He pointed to the names and said, "What happened to that guy?" I just busted up crying like a baby and could not talk. Later at lunch we were decompressing and my son asked me when I was going to tell him about it. I told him that I couldn't. I was just so emotional and couldn't understand it. Eventually I shared it with him, and just busted out crying like a baby.

Larry Lilley

Judy Williams might be retired, but she hasn't slowed down one bit. She is using her time to live life to the fullest, enjoying golf, camping, and playing cards with groups of her friends. And she hears a good deal from Larry Lilley. He didn't talk about the war when he came home in 1967, and maybe that was a real pity. Perhaps their lives would have wound up differently had they just talked about Vietnam. But he is now, finally, talking. He tells her of reunions, of his trip to Vietnam, and of his friends – both living and dead. Larry Lilley is finally letting go of Vietnam.

———— † ————

Nancy Benedick

The military officer had let Jack Benedick vent about his future, but then told him that the decision was out of both of their hands. The army just didn't need double amputees. Seconds after the officer had departed, Jack Benedick was on the phone with his old battalion commander, Colonel Guy Tutwiler, who, in turn, called his old brigade commander, General William Fulton. The two men knew Benedick well; they knew that he was about the most hard-charging soldier they had ever met. If he said he could still serve without legs, they believed him. Tutwiler and Fulton placed a few phone calls and pulled a few strings, and Jack Benedick received his orders. He was off to Fort Benning for the advanced officer training course in preparation for his new command. Jack Benedick was the only double amputee in the active military.

His Fort Benning classmates looked at Jack Benedick with a sense of awe – especially impressed when he decided to go on runs while wearing short pants. After training, Benedick, now a captain, reported to Fort Carson, Colorado, to serve as a company commander in the 1st Brigade of the 4th Infantry Division. He walked in the door at brigade headquarters, where the major who served as brigade executive officer was seated at a desk reading his personnel file. The major glanced down at his legs, and gave him the bad news. There was no place for a double-amputee officer in the 1st Brigade. Benedick looked the major square in the eye and said, "Give me a chance. If I can't cut it, I'll retire in six months. You have my word." Shaking his head and grimacing, the major replied, "All right. I'm going to hold you to it." A few months later, it was the major, not Jack Benedick, who retired. Before he left, the major sent Benedick a formal letter of apology. Not only had he been able to hack it, Benedick had proven to be the best company commander in the entire outfit.

Nancy had resigned herself to a continued military life – Jack was her husband and the military was his future; thus it was her future. The couple bought their first house and lived in Colorado Springs. Nancy got Jack Jr and Mike enrolled in school and got busy working with the military wives of Fort Carson and as a volunteer at the children's schools. The physical regimen of an officer's life put great strain on Jack's legs, resulting in more surgeries and near-constant infections to his skin grafts. Even so, Jack never talked about an emotional impact of war, and had little time for those who did. He did talk about Vietnam – a lot, usually in the company of fellow officers over drinks at a local bar. As the booze flowed and the guys shared their wartime tales, often filled with dark humor and expletives, Nancy realized full well what was really going on. Those guys were Jack's support group. They had experiences like his; they valued and validated his experiences; they all cared. And for Nancy, being around the other officers' wives was a tonic. While their husbands did not share Jack's physical challenges, these wives understood her. Unlike many of the other Charlie Company wives, Nancy Benedick was not alone in trying to cope with the meaning of her husband's wartime experiences.

Jack and Nancy kept up a very active social life, one that came to focus on sports. Although he was sometimes distant and was a rather strict disciplinarian, Jack seemed to enjoy helping to coach his sons' baseball teams. But Jack's true love remained skiing. He had taken to the sport as part of his physical therapy while at Fitzsimmons Army Medical Center, and, since he was now stationed in Colorado, he decided to hit the slopes with a vengeance. Jack worked closely with patients at Fitzsimmons, both past and present, and organized a disabled ski club – the Rocky Mountain Disabled Ski Association. In 1973 Jack was named president of the Rocky Mountain Handicapped Sportsmen's Association. Disabled sports was in its infancy in the United States, and it was Jack Benedick who led the charge.

The disabled sporting events provided the Benedicks with community, where it was normal for the kids to have fathers who took off their legs at night. While it was Jack who was rising in prominence, it was Nancy who did much of the work to make the events possible. For every event in which Jack garnered applause for a motivational speech or for a flawless run down the slopes, Nancy was in the background making things happen. The other skiers and athletes took to calling her "Saint Nancy." And, while Nancy certainly didn't think of herself as a saint, she was glad that Jack's friends took notice of her tireless efforts.

Esther and Bernie Windmiller on their wedding day in 1956. (© Esther Windmiller)

Bernie and Esther Windmiller (in rear) surrounded by family at Bernie's retirement ceremony. (© Esther Windmiller)

Fred and Barbara Kenney on their wedding day. (© Barbara Hill)

Fred and Barbara Kenney, shortly after their wedding. (© Barbara Hill)

Barbara and Fred Kenney at the airport on the day he departed for Vietnam. Barbara sent Fred the picture in Vietnam, but he returned it with the note "too sad" written in the margin. It was the couple's last picture together. (© Barbara Hill)

Barbara Kenney with her son Freddie. (© Barbara Hill)

Jacque Peterson high school graduation photo, 1966. (© Jacque Bomann)

Don Peterson (left) and Doug Wilson aboard ship. (© Jacque Bomann)

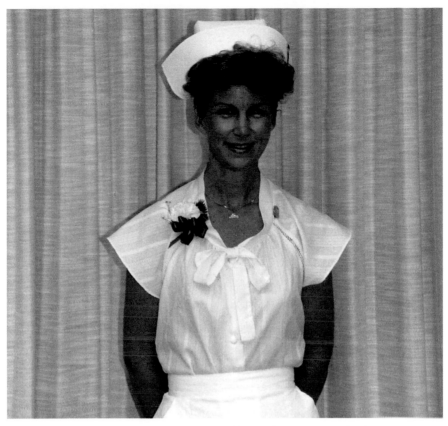

Jacque Bomann (Peterson) on her graduation from nursing school 1985.
(© Jacque Bomann)

John Sclimenti on a smoke break outside Camp Bear Cat. (© John Sclimenti

Nancy and Jack Benedick. (© Nancy Benedick)

Jack Benedick Junior kissing his father's picture goodnight while Dad was away in Vietnam. (© Nancy Benedick)

Nancy Benedick and Jack Junior during May 1967. (© Nancy Benedick)

Jack Benedick (left) during 2 Platoon operations outside Bear Cat. (© Nancy Benedick)

Jack Benedick skiing. (© Nancy Benedick)

After nearly six years in Colorado, Jack was assigned to attend Command and General Staff College at Fort Leavenworth, Kansas. After receiving promotion to the rank of major, Jack transferred to San Francisco to work in the Office of the Inspector General. While adjusting to the new position, Benedick received jarring news. A cordial officer informed him that a change in regulations meant that remaining on active duty put his eventual military disability benefit in jeopardy. As the young officer closed his briefcase Benedick responded, "What. Does this mean that my legs will grow back? What a nice surprise." Jack and Nancy discussed the decision for hours. Leaving the military was his decision, and his alone. But Nancy told Jack that she would very much support retirement should that be the case. And, just like that, Jack Benedick's military career was over. Financially things got better right away since Jack could now claim retirement pay and disability benefits. And, unlike some retirees, Jack and Nancy knew right where they were headed. It was back to Colorado and the world of disabled skiing.

Jack Benedick again became a fixture on the ski slopes of Colorado, at the same time that local resorts, business sponsors, and the international sports world were coming to realize the importance of competitive sports for disabled athletes. Benedick became a tireless advocate of disabled sports, skiing competitively from 1979 to 1986, helping to create the US Disabled Ski Team, and winning a silver medal in the Winter Paralympics in 1980 and two bronze medals in the World Championships in 1984. In 1986, Benedick was appointed Director of the US Disabled Ski Team, a position he held until his retirement in 1995. He was also a member of the United States Olympic Committee from 1984 to 1988 and was instrumental in having disabled skiing added to the 1988 Winter Olympics in Calgary as a demonstration sport, where the US team won four of the available six medals. Benedick also served as director of the able-bodied cross-country ski team and was team leader for the 1994 Winter Olympics in Lillehammer.

For all of the adventures, meetings, competitions, and accomplishments, Nancy Benedick was there – still being "Saint

Nancy," the quiet organizational and physical force. For Nancy Benedick the new civilian life in Colorado was right where she had always wanted to be. Nancy hadn't wanted to follow any certain career path, she had just wanted to be a mom. And finally, after so many years of military life, Nancy could do just that, be a mom. Like so many of the Charlie Company wives, Nancy found herself balancing the life expectations imposed by her generation, with the reality of postwar readjustment of a veteran husband, and the necessities and realities of her own life and dreams. Jack Jr was entering high school, and Mike was making his way through elementary school, so it was the perfect time for Nancy Benedick to throw herself into motherhood and everything that it entailed. As she volunteered more and more at the children's schools, Nancy found herself entranced by teaching and education. She had always known it from her own past, but it was only by being there in her own children's classes that she realized how profound a difference good teachers can make in the lives of students. And Nancy Benedick decided that she wanted to make a difference.

Drawn by their inclusiveness and intellectual freedom, Nancy began teaching in a local Montessori elementary school in Evergreen, Colorado. Nancy dearly loved Jack, she loved her children, and was ferociously serious about her job as a mother – but in her teaching career Nancy found a level of personal fulfillment that she had not known to be possible. Nancy worked as a full-time teacher for 22 years, often remaining in touch with her students long after they left her care, and even teaching multiple generations from the same families. As her career progressed, Nancy also took on the task of mentoring the younger teachers, helping to train them for everything that they would experience in the modern classroom. Jack Jr and Mike finished school and embarked on their own adult lives and careers, with Jack Jr headed off to the military and Mike to college. Through it all, Nancy kept right on teaching, until, in her 70s, the regimen became a bit too difficult, and she retired. But the teaching bug was still there, so Nancy continued to teach art part time, twice a week. And she will continue to do so, just as long as she can.

Amid the forward rush of a full life, Nancy and Jack were to face their greatest challenge. It first came on as an odd feeling of imbalance while Jack was skiing during the Winter Olympics at Lillehammer. While the odd feeling did dim over time, it never completely went away, and sometimes came back even worse than before, so in 1997 Jack Benedick did something he loathed – he went to the doctor. After a battery of tests the results were in – Jack Benedick was diagnosed with Parkinson's disease. While he immediately went on medication, over time the symptoms became worse and worse, and came to include the uncontrollable trembling and balance issues commonly associated with the affliction. Jack had to give up the skiing that he loved so much. As a double amputee the disease affected him more quickly and thoroughly than others, often causing him to stumble or to halt his forward movement. Oftentimes he would control the issues in public by sheer dint of will, but the problems were always evident at home, leaving Jack humiliated and incredibly frustrated.

Neither Jack nor Nancy was going down without a fight. Jack volunteered for an experimental procedure and had two electrodes implanted deep inside his brain designed to stop the tremors. After some adjustment, the treatment worked, and part of the battle was won, but, much to Jack's dismay, the vertigo and balance issues remained, often necessitating use of a wheelchair. Without the circle of military friends provided by his career or that of the disabled athletes who had been his second family, Jack turned more and more to his Charlie Company brothers for support and friendship. Even though it put a strain on the family finances, Jack attended each of Charlie Company's reunions, reveling in the memories of camaraderie and conflict. Nancy, Jack Jr, and Mike all became fixtures at Charlie Company events, patiently aiding boisterous Jack as he played the loving crowd. The reunions were especially important for Jack Jr and Mike. They had grown up idolizing their father, and the reunions gave them needed context regarding his life and why it had unfolded as it had. The VA admitted that Jack's Parkinson's was related to Agent Orange exposure in Vietnam, as was his diabetes. But since

Jack was already on 100 percent disability, there was nothing more they could do but wish him well. For his part Jack never blamed the war for anything. If these difficulties in his life were attributable to his service in Vietnam, so be it. He would deal with it and move on.

Nancy kept on working – Jack would have it no other way. He didn't want to accept his own infirmity, much less have it impact Nancy. Finally, though, Jack Benedick came to accept what was really happening to him; the relentless nature of Parkinson's left him no choice. Moving at all became difficult. Even swallowing his medication and speaking became a considerable chore. For Nancy and the children Jack's slow decline was emotionally devastating. Watching a man who had been the epitome of masculine toughness just wasting away was almost more than they could take. But Nancy and the Benedick children managed the transformation to being Jack's caregivers – doing their best to keep Jack's spirits up even as their own hearts were breaking for him.

Jack Benedick passed away on March 10, 2013, with family and friends gathered around. The family followed Jack's wishes, having his body cremated prior to an interment ceremony at Arlington National Cemetery. Although she had known that the end was coming, it took Nancy a long time to adjust. She really couldn't remember what life had been like without Jack. But, with her children and grandchildren around to help, and her teaching job to keep her busy, Nancy moved on with her life. Motherhood, grandmotherhood, and work would have to take Jack's place. He would have wanted it that way. Nancy still loves to read, and has taken up genealogy as a hobby and enjoys doll collecting. But it is the Benedick family that keeps her the most engaged and involved.

———— † ————

Esther Windmiller

After a comfortable few years raising children in the community of Fort Campbell, Kentucky, it was off to Baumholder, Germany for the Windmillers' next assignment. The Windmiller children were in junior high and grade school, and looked at the family's sojourn to Germany as one big adventure. Esther found the posting to Germany to be enjoyable and fulfilling. Besides the busy workaday life of a mother with four children, Esther got more involved than ever with the lives of the men and families that made up her new military community. Many of the younger soldiers were away from home for the first time and were unable to bring their wives or children with them. So many were lost; so many were lonely. Esther's time in Germany was in many ways like being the leader of a youth ministry. On Monday nights Esther would feed up to 20 enlisted men guests, while Bernie played guitar, and everyone just hung out and talked and enjoyed each other's company.

Bernie's next assignment took the family to Fort Hamilton, in the center of the Bronx in New York. It was a short, educational assignment that lasted nine months, so nobody really had any time to set down roots. Riding the subways and living the big city life was interestingly different, and Esther took the urban opportunity to enroll in nursing refresher courses at Mount Sinai Hospital. After the big city whirl it was off to Fort Sill, Oklahoma. The children were now getting older, with the eldest, Beth, midway through high school and the youngest, Becky, nearing the completion of elementary school. With all of the children at school, Esther went back to work, taking a position at the Lawton Indian Hospital. The transformation was immensely challenging for Esther. Every morning it was getting the children ready for school, and then it was off to a full day of work. The family took the change in life like troopers, with everyone pitching in on extra chores. And Esther knew just what to do with her first paycheck. She went out and bought the family's first automatic dishwasher. No more washing dishes by hand for her.

Next followed three moves in rather rapid succession. First the family moved to a rented house in North Carolina where Bernie worked on an MA in World Religions. Beth was now a senior, with Leslie, Keith, and Becky trailing behind down through middle school. Next it was off to the US Army Chaplains' School at Fort

Wadsworth, New York on Staten Island. Esther got a job working at a local hospital and the children fanned out to their new schools, except Beth, who had gone off to college. Esther's work consisted of the typical, demanding shifts expected of hospital nurses. Times were often hard to predict, and the pressure was through the roof. Patients' lives depended on her.

The pressure also grew at home. The second wave of Windmiller children were deeply involved in high school, and everything that comes with it from learning how to drive, to concerts, to athletic events. As Becky neared her graduation, the last high school graduation in the family, the family moved yet again, this time to Fort Monmouth, New Jersey. It was a move, which, of course, necessitated another new school for Becky, but it wasn't all that far away. Esther figured that she could just keep her old job and commute into the city. She tried it, getting up at 4am for an hour commute to work and then a ten-hour shift before coming home. But it just took too much of her time, and her last child was in her final year of high school. Years like that don't ever come back, and Esther decided that she was just missing too much of it, so she switched jobs to a local public health hospital, and got a schedule that allowed her to spend more quality time with her daughter.

The Windmiller nest was officially empty when Becky graduated high school and went off to Wheaton College in Chicago – the same college that Esther had once attended. Bernie was then assigned to Germany once again for three years, and Esther found her usual place within a group of welcoming wives and got back to helping the enlisted men every way that she could. Next came an assignment as Post Chaplain at Fort Leonard Wood, Missouri. Bernie's final posting was such a great honor – he was named Commandant of the US Army Chaplains' School. Life, though it kept the Windmillers constantly on the move, had developed something of a slow and comfortable pace. The children were now marrying, with Bernie performing the ceremonies. Soon there were visits with grandchildren in tow. Esther no longer felt the pull of nursing, and settled down to work with the many wives' groups on the bases where Bernie served. It was a bit different at the Chaplains' School, in part because Bernie was the top man and everyone was on their best behavior around him. But it didn't take Esther long to break down the barriers of familiarity, and she found a fulfilling role in mentoring the wives of the up and coming young chaplains. She had a wealth of experience to offer, and they had a lot to learn. In many ways the military had become Esther's extended family.

Bernie Windmiller retired from the military at age 62 in 1993. He and Esther then moved to Princeton, Illinois, to be nearer to their children and grandchildren. They remained vital and wanted to play a role in their new world. It had been a long time since Bernie regularly stood behind the pulpit, so he called the local Evangelical Covenant pastor and said that he was open to a small church of his own. The pastor thanked Bernie for his enthusiasm, but informed him that he was too old either to start or pastor his own church. Esther was probably more incensed at the slight than was her husband, but they both decided to bide their time. It was less than a month later when the call came in. The church in Moline, Illinois needed an interim pastor. It was only a couple of hours' drive away; would Bernie be willing to take the job? This is the way that it worked for the Windmillers for the next decade. Bernie bounced from church to church and from congregation to congregation. Bernie was the religious fireman, called to rescue congregations in their time of spiritual need. Somehow the new regimen fit the Windmillers like a glove.

As Bernie moved from church to church, Esther was always at his side, working with wives and families. There was always so much she could do, from food drives for the disadvantaged in the community, to prayer groups, to counseling sessions. Where Bernie had a job, Esther always did too. There were an increasing number of trips to see family, now numbering 12 grandchildren and three great-grandchildren. But Esther also found a new calling. Esther had always had an easy way about her – people just felt comfortable in her presence and valued her input, so she became a guidance writer for the massively popular *Guideposts Magazine*. Subscribers wrote to the magazine outlining their problems and asking for spiritual guidance – and it was Esther who wrote them back in print.

Bernie had suffered from nightmares when he had just gotten back from Vietnam. He had startled at loud noises. But neither he nor Esther had ascribed those incidents to Vietnam. They talked about everything, but Vietnam never came up. Vietnam had been difficult for them both, but life had seemed to wash the war's footprints away like the tide on a beach. It was only as life began to wind down a bit that Vietnam peeped out from the corner of the Windmillers' existence. At reunions Esther heard the stories. Those stories had been covered in Bernie's letters, but it couldn't have been that bad, could it? Her memory had recorded the good and jettisoned the bad or ugly.

> I've never really had a problem with Vietnam. When I first got back to a "normal life" it took some time. I was a little jumpy. To this day the sound of a helicopter brings back Vietnam. The most difficult thing is recalling the loss of so many young lives. Duffy Black, Fred Kenney, John Hoskins. They all meant so much. It still tears at me. It is not like I put Vietnam in a box and shoved it under the bed someplace. It has only been the last couple of years that I was able to talk about my experiences with my children. Like anyone else who has been in war you realize that nobody else can understand what it was like. It is the memory of those guys who didn't make it that hurts the most. I couldn't go to the Vietnam Memorial for many years. I just couldn't make myself go.

> *Bernie Windmiller*

Living with Vietnam was comfortable for the Windmillers. The war and its many memories were not fearsome adversaries, but more like a faded background painting. But Vietnam was there. Vietnam in many ways had transformed the Windmillers and their relationship, as it had with all of the Charlie Company families, for good or ill.

On a brisk day in March 2014 at Arlington National Cemetery, Vietnam was back full force. Nancy Benedick had requested that Bernie preside over the interment of her husband Jack Benedick.

Both Bernie and Esther were touched that Nancy had entrusted Bernie with such a meaningful moment in her life. It had been a while since he had worn them, but Bernie got out his dress blues. They were a bit tight, but they would do. In all of his many duties as a military chaplain, Bernie had never before presided over a formal interment at Arlington, so he was a bit nervous. The procession started at the visitors' center, and all of Bernie's friends from Charlie Company were there. Bernie asked around to see where he should be and at what time. A functionary at the cemetery was a bit unnerved by the whole thing. He asked, "Why are you here again, sir?" Bernie looked a little perplexed and replied that he was there to preside over the interment ceremony for his friend Jack Benedick. The functionary informed Bernie that there had to be some kind of mistake. Arlington had chaplains for such occasions; the ceremony had to be performed by one of their number. Bernie looked at the functionary and pointed to the colonel's eagles on his shoulder and simply said, "Son. I am going to handle this ceremony." As the caisson began its slow procession the functionary whispered to Bernie that it was going to be a long walk from the center to the gravesite, and that there would be nobody there to pick Bernie up if he fell out, exhausted. Bernie just smiled and patted the functionary on the shoulder. He wasn't going to fall out. He had his wife Esther by his side to help him along. She had been helping him along his life journey for more than 60 years, and wouldn't let him fall out now.

CONCLUSION

As with the veterans themselves, there is no single story of how wives and families interact with the brutal, intimate reality of conflict. Perhaps it sounds trite, or so generalized as to have no meaning, but there are as many stories of how combat wives are impacted by war as there are combat wives. So much of who they became began with who they were. The Charlie Company wives were women of the baby boom, influenced by everything from the Beatles to the gender realities of their time. But whether they were from tiny villages or big cities, the wives of Charlie Company universally dreamed dreams of lives that were more varied, meaningful, and free than the norms placed on their generation by magazines, movies, and mores. Whether they were aware of a second wave of feminism was immaterial: they were part of it and embodied it. Marriage was part of all of their plans, and they all married young – some very young. And they all wanted families. But they all also wanted something more; they wanted to matter in a society that was being made anew, a society where more doors were open to women than ever before. The Charlie Company wives wanted everything – husbands, families, and careers.

War had interrupted their planning and dreams of the future, a war that impacted all of the women deeply. Each negotiating their own relationship to war through correspondence with their husbands, the Charlie Company wives found themselves alone in a society that rushed towards an indistinct future while their own lives were on hold. Some cared for families alone while their husbands were at war, while others waited for their marriages to start. Through it all, the Charlie Company wives found something that they weren't expecting – independence. Even if it was obscured by living in their old bedroom with their parents; even if it was obscured by the dizzying pace of life of a now single mother caring for multiple children; even if it was obscured by the grief of a husband's life lost – independence was there and it was real. Many of the wives were still teenagers, but war taught them that they could handle anything, without a man around to help. It wasn't a conscious thing, but gender norms were shattered. The Vietnam War forced the Charlie Company wives to be everything, to take on every role. And that became their new reality.

Most of the wives were able to welcome their Charlie Company husbands home – husbands altered by war that they would have to learn how to live with, and husbands who would have to learn to live with their newly unbound wives. The aftermath of war called upon the wives of Charlie Company to be many things. Most of the wives trended back toward familiarity – toward the cherished marriage ideals of their boomer dreams. But to achieve this normality, the wives universally had to step outside of what many in society had until recently considered normal for women or marriage. Almost all worked outside of the home, in jobs that were often both challenging and fulfilling. Within the home these women maintained their expected duties, from cleaning to child-rearing. Many of the women were also called upon to act as emotional confidants and sometimes even caregivers for husbands who still wrestled with the realities of combat. For most there wasn't even a name for it yet, leaving them to cast about in futile attempts to find answers and solace. Only later, sometimes too late to save marriages, did these wives even hear the term PTSD, with all of its myriad implications. For the wives of Charlie Company, Vietnam remains an organic part of their lives. Whether seen or unseen, Vietnam is always there.

——— † ———

It was brisk and clear that day at Arlington National Cemetery. The flags fluttered and snapped in the glare of bright sunshine as a biting wind cut across from the nearby Potomac. The fresh smell of a spring shower played in the air and at a glance the buds on the trees portended the coming of a new season. A visual river of America's martial past flowed and tumbled past as I slowed my step to try to take in my surroundings. Robert E. Lee's mansion brooded from its hilltop; the Kennedys' eternal flame danced amidst the eddies of the breeze; six Marines were locked in eternal struggle to raise their proud flag atop Mount Suribachi; tombstones of the fallen from America's conflicts old and new marched off into the distance in their sad, regimented splendor. Amid those sights, I watched as the veterans of Charlie Company and their families gathered to attend the funeral for their Lieutenant Jack Benedick.

Following in the wake of the caisson and the honor platoon, the procession wended its mournful way through the waiting sea of white headstones, and reached its destination. Nancy Benedick and the closest members of Jack's family gathered and sat while a military color guard and honor guard stood stock still nearby. The bugler joined in as Taps rolled out across the green hillsides of Arlington. The message, Jack's last goodbye, was delivered as requested by Bernie Windmiller, who had shared many a battlefield with Jack Benedick in 1967. After the ceremony ended, Chaplain Windmiller's words faded, and the folded flag was delivered, there was a deep silence. Members of Charlie Company made their way to the graveside in ones and twos to say their farewells, but the silence remained. Even the breeze seemed to still as the silence continued – a mournful silence. Slowly Nancy and the children rose to their feet, and the procession returned, and only the silence remained.

The members of the Charlie Company family were all staying at a nearby hotel – it was a solemn reunion of sorts. But this time it was a reunion of farewells instead of a reunion of new greetings. Drink flowed to be sure, but some fragment of the Arlington silence had persisted. Nobody seemed sure what to say, or even if they should say anything at all. Nancy and the Benedick children were at the center of the group, receiving solace and well-wishes from true friends who mourned along with them in their loss. After a while the crowd dwindled somewhat, and I got a chance to sit next to Nancy. I had always seen that the Benedick children, Jack and Mike, had a strong resemblance to their father, both physically and in spirit. Now that resemblance was more noticeable than ever. Jack and Mike refused to let their mom get down; they stood as a barrier between her and despair, doing whatever it took to keep her spirits up, whether it was to hug or joke or just to be publicly strong in the face of adversity.

Nancy and I began to talk about Jack and about my work. Nancy had followed my efforts to tell the story of Charlie Company for years. Jack Benedick had been one of my first interviews, and he had helped me to meet and work with the other guys in the unit over the years. Better than anyone else, Nancy knew of Jack's heroism, and she knew that he had a story that was worth telling; a story worthy of honor. She had read the book *The Boys of '67*, and was approving of its treatment of her beloved husband. Nancy was fiercely proud of Jack's accomplishments, and I knew it. As I took a sip of my beer in an effort to play for time to put together something meaningful to say, Nancy turned to me and caught me with her gaze. She said that it was wonderful that I had been able to tell the stories of Jack and the guys. They had been brave. They had done what their nation had asked of them and more. But, she said with her eyes darting around the room indicating wives and family members of the men of Charlie Company, "No one has ever told our story."

Her words hit me like a hammer. How could I have been so blind? Nancy continued to speak, and my mind was racing in a thousand different directions at once. I wondered how many silent struggles were there out there in the room that night? How many sleepless nights wondering whether or not a husband would make it home to see his child for the first time? How many wives in the room had pushed their husbands on to familial and financial success even though Vietnam hung around their necks like an albatross? How many marriages had collapsed under the weight of the war? How many marriages and family lives had been unaffected or made stronger by the experience? It began to dawn on me that in measures great and small the Vietnam War was the unrelenting force that had crafted the landscapes of these women's adult lives. They had not fought in the steaming rice paddies, but they were veterans of the war in their own right.

Our conversation that spring evening in 2014 was short, rushed, and often interrupted. But what Nancy Benedick told me that night about her life both began and concluded this project – the story of *Charlie Company's Journey Home*:

I'm doing good. Really good. The ceremony in Arlington was good and healing; you have to have closure. I feel that for each segment of my life I did pretty much the best that I could. I made the most of it, and I enjoyed it. When the next segment came along, it was like a new adventure. The changes just seemed to flow; this is the next stage so this is what we are going to do. Vietnam absolutely changed my life, because it changed his. And when you are in a marriage, one affects the other. Vietnam freed me to be more myself instead of following the role set out more by society. I discovered that I liked having responsibility. I had matured, life had changed, and I changed along with it. I had been pretty dependent on Jack before Vietnam, but afterward I was much more independent. After he came back from Vietnam I had to move to a different plane. Jack's experiences and injuries opened up a lot of new doors for both of us, even though it was such a tragic thing for him to have to experience. I had to try to keep up with him. I've often said that I wouldn't be the person I am today if I hadn't been married to Jack and he hadn't gone to Vietnam. I think that I'd be very, very different. I don't think that I would have had a good a life as I've had. We had our trials and tribulations, but I feel that the full circle that I've come is the result of an evolution of being with him for all those years. I don't know where we would have been without it, but Vietnam absolutely changed our lives. It was a monumental change.

———— † ————

Perhaps one day you will chance to find yourself in Washington DC, gazing at the Vietnam Veterans Memorial. If so take time to find the names of these young men – the married men of Charlie Company who died in Vietnam. Remember them and those whom they left behind.

Name	Panel	Line
Benito Alaniz	16	109
Charles "Duffy" Black	18	021
Phillip Ferro	23	051
Elmer "Fred" Kenney	23	052
Don Peterson	20	003
Sheldon Schulman	22	019
John Winters	22	022

AFTERWORD

Charlie Company's Journey Home has attempted to shed light on the lives of the nearly 1 million women who were married to US combatant soldiers in the Vietnam War. Attacking such a vast subject, while maintaining a cast of characters that was limited enough that it did not become unwieldy, made for a writing nightmare. The result was a compromise that, while it hopefully led to readability, left the story maddeningly incomplete. While *Charlie Company's Journey Home's* conclusions have drawn on the sum total of 24 extensive interviews, the book focused on the stories of only a representative handful of the Charlie Company wives. But all of their stories are important and deserve to be told. For that reason each of the Charlie Company wives who were not a major focus of the book's story line will have her individual story told here.

——— † ———

Vivian Conroy

As her husband Tom returned from Vietnam, Vivian Conroy could not have imagined how his life had been changed by the loss of Fred Kenney. Understanding that Tom had changed dramatically was something for the future, and Vivian was occupied by the present. Tom got a job in a chicken-rendering plant, and then as a truck driver. Viv kept her job with the home finance firm until she had the couple's first child, Kimberly, in 1969, after which Viv found a new position at Edwards Air Force Base. It was handy living near to her parents; Edwin and Kathleen could look after little Kim while Viv worked. And work she did, earning a shift to a better job with the Federal Aviation Administration. Tom landed a teamster's job moving heavy equipment with a local construction company that left him exhausted at night and only able to grab a few hours of sleep before getting up at 4am to start it all over again. Two more children following in rapid succession, Tom Jr and Chad, meant that Viv had to work harder than ever just to keep up.

As the Conroy children began to graduate high school and set out on their own lives, Vivian was left with more time alone with Tom. And she couldn't help but notice that the changes that she had seen in him after his return from Vietnam had become permanent. Tom was also diagnosed with diabetes, which the couple attributed to his service in Vietnam. The diabetes, combined with years of grueling, physical labor had taken their toll, and Tom took an early retirement package in 2000, with Vivian following suit in 2008.

After so many years of working hard, retirement agreed with the Conroys. There were now grandchildren to enjoy, with Tom especially loving to pitch in by taking the young ones to school in the mornings. The subject of Vietnam had never really come up in all of their years together, but in retirement Tom's issues with anger, now mixed with a general darkness, seemed to intensify. Even Tom's buddies could tell that he was having a difficult time, so one, a fellow veteran, handed Tom a pamphlet on PTSD.

Finally it was becoming clear to Viv why the Tom who had come home from Vietnam had been so different than the young man who had left for war. Tom went to the VA for counseling, and they suggested that he talk to his wife about the war. They also suggested that he reconnect with his old comrades, so the Conroys started attending the Charlie Company reunions. Vivian had long since lost touch with the few wives she had known at Fort Riley, so the reunions gave her a chance to meet other wives like her really for the first time. The wives, who had once felt so alone, began to talk about how their husbands were all so similar – quick to anger, emotionally distant; all the common symptoms of PTSD. Sharing with other wives was wonderful for Viv. She now knew the depth of the connection between the new Tom and Vietnam.

Following his experiences at the Charlie Company reunions, Tom now wants to talk about Vietnam, which he never did before, and Viv understands the therapeutic value of his often one-sided conversations. The best thing she can do is sit back and listen. Each time he talks and each time she listens, Viv cherishes the moment, because it is in those times that a little bit more of Tom Conroy finally makes it home from Vietnam.

Talking with the Charlie Company guys has stirred my memory and my thoughts are flowing out. Fred was in the tree line and he was yelling that he needed help and he had been hit. I remember lying there behind a rice paddy dike, which seemed like an eternity, and being completely helpless to get to Fred. He needed help and we were pinned down – this has haunted me forever since. Finally at nightfall, we scrambled back to the last tree line and spent the night wide awake. It was barely light the next morning when we ventured across the rice paddy and into the tree line to find Fred laying there. The Viet Cong had left the area during the night. As I picked up Fred to carry him to a chopper a stream of his blood came out on me and I cried.

After 40 years I'm finally able to write this. It was seeing Fred dead in my arms that terrible day that caused me to lose almost all of my memory of that war and everything that happened.

Tom Conroy

——— † ———

Norma Crockett

Norma Jean was born to Rosure and Ethel Rains in 1935 in the tiny village of Churntop, outside of Albany, Kentucky. Her parents divorced when she was only three, leaving Norma and her two siblings to be raised alone by Ethel. Ethel worked hard to raise the family on her own, mainly doing odd jobs in the homes of her social superiors. On most days Ethel earned only one dollar, often taking Norma along until she was old enough to go to school. The Rains' household had no indoor bathroom and electricity only came on the scene when Norma was ten, and then only for the first floor of the house. Ethel was strict and very religious, never sparing the rod and making certain that the girls were always dressed properly and well behaved. There were to be no short sleeves, makeup, comic books, or boyfriends for them.

Norma knew that most of the girls in her small town wound up in menial labor like her mom, or got jobs in a nearby factory. But Norma was determined to find another route forward – she never wanted to be reliant on others or beneath them again. She wanted to go to college, and her mom agreed. After high school graduation, Norma went to work in a factory in nearby Byrdstown, and soon she had saved enough money to enroll at Lindsay Wilson College in Columbia, Kentucky, to earn a degree and an elementary school teaching certificate.

After graduating with her associate's degree, Norma went back to live at home and began her career by teaching 1st and 2nd grade at nearby Clearfork school. At 23, an age by which most of the local girls had long since been married, Norma met Lynn Crockett. Lynn was already in the military, so his courtship with Norma was largely by mail. It didn't take long for Norma to realize that Lynn Crockett was the man for her. Tall, handsome, charming, kind. Since it was a long-distance relationship it took a bit longer than many others, but, when Norma was 25, the couple married in Jamestown, Tennessee. Both of Lynn's parents were there, but Ethel still didn't approve of much of anything Norma did, so she stayed away.

After the arrival of their son Gregory in 1962, the couple lived for a while in Germany before the call came for Lynn to report to Fort Riley to join the 9th Infantry Division. Both Lynn and Norma were excited. While Lynn was at war Norma continued her teaching career and was quite busy with Gregory, but there were constant rumors flying around all over town about the horrors and bloodshed of Vietnam. Norma really did wonder whether Lynn would ever come home to her, but it was something she never let on to Gregory. She would only cry after she was sure he was asleep at night.

> May 15 is the day that we lost Don Peterson. I got on the radio and called in a dustoff for the wounded, but there wasn't enough room for Peterson's body, so Peterson stayed with the unit one more night. As they carried Peterson past, many of the guys were crying or standing quiet. Ben Acevedo of 1st Platoon looked at me and said, "First Sergeant, is this all worth it? What the hell are we doing over here?" The men had trained together and had become brothers, which was a great thing. But it also meant that it was a real shock when one of their buddies got killed. I had to calm them down, and let them know that we were here to do a job and that there was nothing that anyone could have done to save Peterson.

Lynn Crockett

When Lynn returned from Vietnam in 1968 there was a joyous reunion at the Louisville airport, but it couldn't last long. The moving van was already on the way to pick them up and take the family to Lynn's next posting at Fort Knox. Norma quickly found a teaching job at the base school, and enrolled Gregory in 2nd grade. As a career non-commissioned officer, though, Lynn was going to have to make a second tour of duty in Vietnam. Gregory didn't think that it was fair at all – his dad needed to be taking him fishing instead of going off to war. And Gregory seemed to have some idea of what war meant. After Lynn's departure he cried for the whole day at school. Norma took him to a friend's house later to play to get his mind off of things, but even that didn't work. Gregory was disconsolate for days, which hurt Norma to the core. There was so little she could do to help him through it. She read him Lynn's letters, but that always set him off to sadness again. That was a difficult year.

When Lynn returned from Vietnam for a second time, he was already complaining of some physical ailments, and military life was losing its luster. The couple bought a 500-acre farm not too distant from Fort Knox, and Lynn retired in 1973, with his full 20 years of service and a nice pension. Norma kept her job teaching on the base at Fort Knox, though, and eventually taught there for a total of 30 years. Although there was the obligatory farm garden, which was quite productive, Lynn spent most of his time and effort with cattle.

Vietnam never really seemed to be an issue; Lynn didn't talk about it, at all. In retrospect Norma rather wishes that he had; perhaps she would have known her husband better and been of greater help to him if he had done so. But Vietnam had a very real impact on his physical life. It started with hearing loss, but went on to become pervasive. Lynn has Agent Orange-related diabetes, which has to be held in check with insulin shots and constant monitoring of his blood sugar. Over one stretch he had ten surgeries in 11 years, including back surgery, colon surgery, kidney surgery, hip surgery, and knee surgery, all related to his extensive military service and especially to the rigors of two wartime tours of duty. Each physical setback necessitated another round of paperwork and arguing with the VA. By the late 1990s, Gregory had married and embarked on his own career as a veterinarian. And when grandchildren began making their appearance, Norma knew that it was time for her to retire.

By the mid-2000s, Lynn's various physical maladies had pushed him to the point where he could no longer work full time on his farm. It was a difficult admission, one that sent him into a quiet form of depression, but it was necessary. The Crocketts leased out most of the farm to others, mainly keeping the house and its immediate land area. Norma pushes Lynn to remain engaged, to head into town to have coffee and tell stories with the guys. He is happiest, though, when he hears from another veteran of Charlie Company. The

Crocketts went to many of the earlier reunions, where he held court with the men who used to serve under him. But now his health is at the point where he can no longer attend, so he relies on phone calls to remind him of that most important part of his past. Norma had always understood Vietnam as a time of worry, a time of absence, and a time in which she had to assert herself amid an adult life alone. But now she understands Vietnam as an event so powerful that, once it was almost forgotten, it was able to reach into Lynn's present and alter his life.

———— † ————

Kaye French

The first child born to Hubert and Lessie Barbour, Kaye was raised in Tampa, Florida, near to MacDill Air Force Base where Hubert worked as a mechanic, and Lessie was a housewife. Dinner was promptly on the table every evening after dad got back from work, the kids lived by strict but fair rules, there were chores to do, and both Kaye and her younger brother Donny were expected to keep up their grades in school or else. Church, of the Southern Baptist variety, was a big part of family life. Kaye lived a young life full of faith, and gravitated toward her friends from the church youth group, especially enjoying the fun and fellowship offered by youth group picnics and outings to the beach.

Kaye met Bob for the first time in the summer of her freshman year, and they were soon dating as much as their parents would allow, but, just as Kaye's senior year began, Hubert announced that he had taken a job at NASA, which meant that the family was going to move to Titusville, near Cape Kennedy. It was a real move up in the world, but for Kaye it meant a new high school for senior year, and it meant moving away from Bob. The distance, though, only served to bring the couple closer together, and soon wedding plans were being made. With the ceremony planned for August 1966, Kaye and Bob went to

Tampa to look for a house. They were walking through a home that Kaye particularly liked when Bob told her that there was something they needed to talk about. He had received his draft notice.

Kaye cried for what seemed like an entire day, but then she got a hold of herself. The wedding was moved up, with engraved invitations being altered by hand, and as soon as the vows were said, Bob and Kaye had to hop in his car for the trip to Fort Riley. The couple found a small, sparsely furnished basement apartment, and then Bob reported for duty. Then it all kind of hit Kaye – she was 20, married, and essentially living alone for the first time. She was immediately both lonely and scared. Kaye sat on the edge of the bed and cried herself to sleep, wondering what she had gotten herself into. As training neared its end, Bob took Kaye back to Florida to be with her parents. There were tears all around as Bob departed, waving and saying that he would write every day. The day that Bob's troopship departed for Vietnam, Kaye discovered that she was pregnant. She was elated but also feared that Bob might never make it home to meet his child. Kaye broke down into tears in her mother's arms.

Kaye lived in constant fear of a casualty team knocking on her front door. The fear intensified in June 1967 when Bob's letters suddenly just stopped coming. And, at the same time, she heard on the news that Charlie Company had been in a major battle and that many soldiers had been killed. Kaye was frantic, but, try as she might, she couldn't find out anything about Bob or Charlie Company. Finally a letter arrived, but it wasn't from Bob, it was from Steve Moede, one of his Charlie Company friends. Bob had been wounded, shot in the waist near his spine, but had been saved by the radio he was wearing. A few days later, Kaye got what she wanted most, a letter from Bob. His handwriting was halting, but there was no doubt it was his. He was going to be in the hospital for a couple of months, and had some interesting staples holding his guts together, but he would be fine.

When the firing began on June 19, everybody knew that we were in deep, deep doo-doo. We knew that we were in for it. We all immediately got down behind the rice paddy dikes. I was carrying the radio for Lieutenant Benedick. I was one of the first ones hit. I remember feeling this awful pain in my back, and that is all I remember. I was out of it until I woke up two days later. I was lying in the mud, and the bullet entered my body about my waist and missed my radio by less than an inch. I came to just for a second after they put me on the helicopter, but it got maybe 2 feet into the air before it was shot down. Then it was back into the rice paddy. The bullet that entered my waist went all the way through my body and the doctors took it out of my shoulder.

Bob French

About the time that Bob was getting well enough to rejoin Charlie Company, Kaye gave birth to the couple's daughter, Charlene, and went home to her parents' house once again. Kaye tried to sleep, with Charlene's crib next to her bed. But all she could do was cry. Hubert asked if there was anything he could do to help, and Kaye replied that she was fine, but with the baby and Bob being wounded and away at war, her life had gone all topsy turvy. When Bob came home from Vietnam, there was some readjustment time, and Bob had a few nightmares and some lingering pain in his back, but the Bob French who returned from war was pretty much the same Bob French whom Kaye had watched depart for Vietnam. He was a little clumsy around Charlene at first, but Bob took to parenting quickly and did everything he could to help out and make up for lost time. His job at the post office was waiting for him, and he took night classes to complete his college degree. He was gone nearly all the time, and studying during what little time he had at home. A second child, Michelle, came along, which kept Kaye increasingly busy.

Bob had gone to the VA a couple of times with his back problems, but the line had always been so long that he had left. But, in 1972, when Bob was 27, he discovered that he couldn't read the mail out of his right eye. Bob had Multiple Sclerosis. Given the uncertain nature of the disease, Kaye went back to work, hired into the dean's office of the College of Education at the University of South Florida. Other than his physical problems related to Vietnam, for which Bob received 60 percent disability from the VA, Bob didn't seem much troubled by his wartime experience. There were a few nightmares, but nothing severe. His most vivid memories, which needed the most working through, concerned the battle of June 19. Bob had been wounded in the opening exchange of fire, and the 2nd Platoon medic, Bill Geier, rushed to his side to stabilize him before moving on to care for the other wounded. Geier was a soft-spoken kid from Chicago, and he was all heart. As Bob watched, Geier moved on to work on the other wounded men. Suddenly Geier's chest exploded as Viet Cong bullets struck home, and Bob could only watch in horror as his friend slowly died. Understandably Bob gets emotional when he talks about Bill Geier and the fighting on June 19, 1967. And he does talk about it, to those who are willing to listen. But those days, as frightening and soul-rending as they were, never seem to have gotten the best of him. Kaye is his grief counselor when he needs it, but he doesn't need it often.

Once Charlie Company began to have reunions, Kaye learned that Bob had been put in for a Bronze Star for his role in the fighting on June 19, 1967. That the award had been lost in the maze of army paperwork so long ago incensed Jack Benedick and Herb Lind, so they started a campaign to make sure that the heroes of June 19 received their due. Bob's local congressman, Gus Bilirakis, wrote a letter of support. After two years of effort, in March 2013, almost 46 years after the battle, police cars pulled up to the French family home in Tampa to escort Bob and Kaye to MacDill Air Force Base for the ceremony to award him the Bronze Star for valor. Major General Karl Horst presided over the ceremony, and Bob spoke of how much he owed to his friends in Charlie Company, especially Bill Geier. As her husband spoke, Kaye wept openly. Bob then motioned into the crowd. He wanted Kaye to pin the medal on, not the general. It was Kaye who had been there through it all, and it was Kaye to whom he owed the most.

——— † ———

Iris Sclimenti

Iris was the middle child of Tom and Ann Boyd, and spent her first years in Culver City, California, near Los Angeles, where Tom worked as an insurance adjustor. Ann had been accepted to Julliard to study opera, but had gotten married and become a housewife instead. Still, music was a mainstay of the Boyd household with Ann constantly singing as she went about her household chores, with Tom sometimes joining in, adding his baritone to Ann's soprano. Money was always tight. One pair of shoes had to last the entire year, and school clothes were handed down and mended until they just couldn't last any longer. From the very beginning, Iris Boyd knew that life wasn't going to give her anything; she had to take it. Iris got a full-time job when she was 15, working at the local Kentucky Fried Chicken and lying about her age. She worked so hard and so well that she was quickly made the first female manager of the KFC.

When Iris started high school, her older brother Steve introduced her around to all of the right kids on the social scene, including John Sclimenti, who was the most popular guy in the entire school. It also didn't hurt that John had the physique of a star gymnast, and was a great dancer. Iris Boyd was smitten with John Sclimenti almost instantly, and he returned her affections.

A few months before Iris's graduation, John received his draft notice. Iris had no doubt in her mind that John would return to her after his service and that they would pick up right where they left off. But she got desperately lonely after he went off to Fort Riley. Sitting there with her family at Christmas 1966, Iris made a snap decision. She was going to Fort Riley to surprise her man. She flew to Kansas City, but that is where her planning fell short. She really didn't know where Fort Riley was, how to get there, or where John was once she got there. By pure luck, while sitting there in the airport wondering what to do next, Iris met a soldier who not only knew how to get to

Fort Riley but also knew John Sclimenti. Catching a ride with the serviceman, Iris found John and the couple spent nearly a week together bunking in with some friends in a nearby apartment.

Before John departed, Iris returned to California, keeping her surreptitious trip hidden from her parents. She scored a good job as an office clerk at a stereo tape manufacturer but soon began to feel sick pretty much every day, having to duck into the bathroom at work to throw up. She was pregnant. Donna went with her to break the news to Tom and Ann, and they took it wonderfully well. John got the news through a sit-down talk with Bernie Windmiller. John seemed surprised, but happy. The only misgiving expressed in his letters was that he wouldn't be there for the child's birth or first few months of life. John got leave to come home in March so that the couple could get married in Las Vegas.

It didn't take long before the folks at work figured out that Iris was pregnant, and, when they did, they fired her. Ann went to the hospital with her in September for the birth of John James, who weighed in at 8½ pounds. After her release from the hospital Iris went to live with her parents in Lancaster. Shortly after John James's birth, Iris made the mistake of reading a letter that John had sent to her brother Steve. In that letter he didn't pull any punches; he described the death and horror of Vietnam in vivid detail. Iris tossed that letter down and had to go and collect herself. She had to put that letter and the risks it implied out of her mind. She was a 19-year-old, unemployed mother. John had never even had the chance to meet John James. She couldn't bear to think of the possibility that he might not return. What would she do then?

> After the battle of June 19, every day you were out there you would think, "Okay; I just have to make it through the day; make it through the day." I remember walking through one area and thinking, "Oh my God. I think I'm going crazy." Your mind would be reeling every minute of the day. Your mind would be thinking, "Am I going to get hit by a sniper here? Is that a booby trap up there? Are the Viet Cong hiding there?" Every minute of the day you were going through that

when you were on operations. We had lost so many people. Half of the unit was gone. Before you didn't have to even say some things because you were so used to each other. But you didn't want to get attached to the new guys; they were just bodies. I tried to leave it all behind me, but there are still things that I have problems with.

John Sclimenti

In January of 1968, John did make it home, but the Sclimentis were not even sure of how to live together – who should do what and when – so everything had to be negotiated and discovered. As she began to build her life together with him, Iris couldn't help but notice that John wasn't the same cool, funny guy who she had known for so long. He was instead nervous and jittery. The jokes and humor were gone, replaced by a simmering anger that seemed to always lurk just below the surface of his personality. John never spoke of Vietnam; that was part of his past. He only spoke of their future. So Iris just figured that John was having trouble adjusting to the startlingly new reality of being a husband and father.

John and Iris moved to Reseda, California, where he found a good job in the post office. Two more children came along in short order, Steve, born in 1969, and Christopher, born in 1972. As the family expanded, Iris returned to work, eventually landing a job with Hydro-Aire, a maker of antiskid technology for aircraft. She wanted a job as a buyer, but was initially laughed off. Women just weren't buyers. Serendipitously, though, two buyers quit simultaneously, leaving Hydro-Aire with little choice. They gambled on hiring Iris as an electronics buyer at just the same time that she really needed a job. Iris quickly proved herself working in a "man's world" and soon received a level of professional respect that she had never even really known existed. But as Iris moved into the professional business world, she and John began to grow apart. There wasn't rancor or drama, it was just a matter of two adults growing and changing. John Sclimenti was Iris's first true love, and that would never change. But, in 1976, they both realized that their marriage wasn't really going anywhere, and the couple decided to divorce.

After the Sclimentis' amicable divorce, Iris's career continued to blossom, and she also lived out dreams in the successful lives of her children. She had long been determined that John James's, Steve's, and Christopher's futures hinged on educational opportunity. All three went to college, with all three even achieving graduate degrees. John James is a curator of mammals at the Los Angeles Zoo, Steven works in business for Wells Fargo Bank, and Christopher works in risk management for a major investment company. Determined to set a good example, Iris also went to college, working through ten years of night school while keeping up her full-time job to receive her Bachelor of Science degree from Pepperdine University. Iris remains close to John Sclimenti and is fiercely devoted to her family, spending as much time as humanly possible with her grandchildren; she has also become heavily involved in church life. The ministries that she works with the most are those dedicated to the care of soldiers and children. She remembers well what it was to be a young mother with a husband off at war, and knows how much young military families need a helping hand, especially if one of the spouses is deployed to a war zone. Iris isn't sure if talking about Vietnam, confronting the war that had changed John's life, would have changed anything. They still don't talk about it much. But she is determined to help young military families; it is almost like therapy, almost like helping her younger self.

—————— † ——————

Jeannie Hartman

Joseph and Irene Sweeney decided to name their second daughter Jeannie. The family, which included older sister Roberta, lived in the tiny town of Busti, New York, about 90 miles south of Buffalo. Joseph, a World War II veteran, ran Bob Sweeney's garage, which was attached to the family home. Irene was a housewife who was always caring, but strict. And Irene made certain that the children knew that education mattered. They needed to do well in school to get ahead in life. Maybe marriage and family would happen, but a girl needed to be able to make her way in the world just as well as any boy.

Jeannie had met Ernie Hartman way back in the 3rd grade at the local roller skating rink. It was only in the 10th grade, though, that Jeannie decided that she liked Ernie. One day Jeannie decided to go to his house to see him; it pretty much took all of her courage. As she sat there in the car in his driveway wondering what to do next, he looked out of the window. Jeannie got so flustered that she tried to back out and leave, only to wind up getting the car stuck in a ditch. After the somewhat rocky start, it was all pretty much a whirlwind. Within a year they were engaged and got married the September following their June 1966 graduation from high school. Ernie got a job working in a nearby factory, and the couple bought a trailer and put it in the Sweeneys' back yard. After getting started and settled, the young couple took a belated honeymoon trip to Florida, but while they were away they got word that Ernie had received his draft notice.

A few weeks later and Ernie was off to Fort Jackson, South Carolina, for his training. On one visit to Fort Jackson the danger of war became clear because the couple had to fill out the life insurance forms that would provide Jeannie with benefits in case of Ernie's death. Jeannie was nearly overwhelmed when Ernie finally left for Vietnam, where he was an early replacement with Charlie Company, and she cried when she moved back in with her parents.

While Ernie was away, Jeannie worked as hard as she could to help make the time pass quickly. Ernie wrote a lot, and his letters got progressively more agitated. Something was going on that bothered him profoundly, but he wouldn't let on what. Once he even asked for a divorce, prompting a buddy to write and tell Jeannie not to listen. He said that Ernie was having a tough time in the wake of a major battle that had taken place in June 1967 and that she should stick with him. It would pass. Suddenly, though, the letters just stopped, leaving Jeannie in a panic. Had her husband spurned her? Was he dead? She had no real way of knowing, until a phone call came in at the beginning of August telling her that Ernie had been wounded. The voice on the other end of the phone wasn't Ernie; it was one of his buddies. Ernie would call just as soon as he was able. Then another two weeks went by, maybe the worst two weeks of Jeannie's life. She didn't have any information other than that her husband had been wounded. Was he dying? She had no way to know or to find out. She had terrible nightmares and moved into her parents' room to sleep on the floor next to their bed. Finally, though, Ernie was able to call. He was badly hurt, but they were going to keep him in Vietnam after his recovery. The good news was, though, that he would not have to go back out into the field for combat duty.

In 1968 Ernie was finally home. Ernie didn't talk about Vietnam, at all. If the subject came up, he would go quiet or walk away. But Jeannie couldn't help but notice how much Ernie had changed. He drank – a lot. To the point where Jeannie wondered if he was already an alcoholic. He had violent nightmares in which he screamed and fired imaginary guns. He hit the floor at loud noises. His sense of humor was almost gone, and what remained was dark. He had a volcanic temper and flew into fits of rage, especially at her. He didn't like crowds at all, and he had quit believing in God. This wasn't her Ernie; it was like someone had ripped out and replaced his personality. Jeannie took her wedding vows seriously, and she deeply and truly loved Ernie Hartman. But there were times in those early years after his return from war that she wondered how long she would be able to take the new Ernie.

On one of my first days with Charlie Company my squad was headed out to a night ambush when we got into a fight with two snipers. We wounded and captured one, but the other got away. The squad leader, John Young, said that we were in too much danger – a squad behind enemy lines and now the enemy knew where we were – to let the prisoner live. He ordered him to be killed, and the machine gunner did it. That machine gunner killed because he liked to kill. I'm a kid from a little town of 600. It all went against my morals. I don't know if I had many, but killing was sure as hell one. He had his hands up in the air, and he shot him. This was July 4, not too long after June 19. Some of the guys had so much hate after that. I was new to the unit. I hadn't been there on June 19. I didn't have that hatred yet. It was after the battle of July 11 that I began to fit in. It was a day of firing, trying to kill not to be killed, and then bagging up bodies. I had only been with Charlie Company a few weeks. Got there right after June 19. Then there were the events of July 4. Then the battle of July 11. And I had only been there such a short period. I now knew that they were trying to kill me, and that I was going to have to kill them.

Ernie Hartman

Ernie got a good job with a tool and die company, and Jeannie took a job working as a teacher in a local elementary school. She worked with children from pre-kindergarten through the 5th grade and loved it. The work made Jeannie feel both vital and needed, and she stuck with it for more than 35 years. Jeannie Hartman had found her place in the world. Ernie was making good money and was rising up the ladder of responsibility at work. With a house and two salaries, the Hartmans began to think about having children, but years of trying netted no results – something the couple put down to Ernie's wounding in Vietnam. With that avenue shut down, the Hartmans decided to adopt, being put on a ten-year waiting list. They wanted a baby, but when the call finally came that there was a two-year-old boy who needed a home the Hartmans jumped at the chance to meet him – a meeting that took place in a local department store. The child's birth parents had lived quite rough, and had badly abused their son, leaving the youngster with behavioral issues. Jeannie, though, was sure that he was the one and that she could have a positive impact on his life. So, one bedroom in the house was quickly converted into a toddler's room and the Hartmans became parents to Corey. With Corey facing both behavioral and developmental issues, life as parents for the Hartmans required dedication and almost constant hard work. Corey eventually married and had a child of his own, Dylan, who now lives with the Hartmans. Both work for

Aspire, which provides learning, fellowship, and employment opportunities for persons with developmental disabilities. Both Corey and Dylan are thriving in their own corners of the world, with Jeannie as their constant companion and helpmeet. And, where Ernie's relationship with Corey was perhaps distant, in part due to the nature of Ernie's work schedule, Dylan and Ernie are nearly inseparable. Ernie is Dylan's hero.

Through the years of raising Corey, booze, anger, and depression remained a part of Ernie's life. Those issues, coupled with the pressures of child-rearing, nearly shattered the Hartmans' marriage on a couple of occasions. Each time Jeannie reminded herself how much she loved Ernie and what a great guy he was. But things worsened dramatically when Ernie lost his job at age 55. Working at the tool and die works had become a huge part of Ernie Hartman; it in some ways defined him. And, just like that, the job was suddenly gone and the company didn't need him. It set Ernie adrift. His drinking got worse than ever, with Ernie disappearing from time to time for days. He totaled the car in a drunken drag race, leaving him hospitalized for weeks and bedridden for nearly two months. His depressions were deep and black, with Ernie hardly speaking and often just sitting there and staring for hours. Intrinsically Jeannie knew that it was all related to Vietnam. That war had been like a dividing line in Ernie's life. After years of cajoling it was a veteran friend who finally convinced Ernie Hartman to go and seek some help from the VA.

Finally Jeannie Hartman had a name to put with her life – PTSD. Ernie's symptoms were classic and severe. Granted VA disability and a level of validation for his pain, Ernie finally spoke of Vietnam with his wife. He told her about the days being covered in leeches; he told her about the day when his squad leader had no choice but to kill a prisoner because there was a battle looming in which the men would be fighting for their lives and would not be able to spare time to look after the young Vietnamese; he told her of the sniper incident in which he had been wounded but the man next to him had his brains blown out. He told her everything he could, and Jeannie began to understand.

Ernie Hartman continues to learn to live with Vietnam through PTSD treatment, and he continues slowly to improve. But Jeannie feels more alone than ever. Ernie has support groups, the VA, his wartime pals. But she has nothing – no counseling and no friends who can relate. There can be little doubt that Jeannie Hartman also has Vietnam-related PTSD – brought on by the considerable aftermath of war. But there are no government programs for her. So Jeannie Hartman prays. And she can't help but look back on how the Vietnam War changed her life. The war changed everything that she had hoped for. In so many ways she loves her life regardless of its many challenges, but Vietnam bequeathed to Jeannie Hartman an unexpected life.

———— † ————

Deana Harvey

The youngest of four surviving children born to Henry and Dorothy Scarborough, Deana was something of a miracle baby. While pregnant, Dorothy had a surgery to remove a tumor the size of a cantaloupe from her abdomen. The doctors gave Deana very little chance of survival after the trauma, but somehow she made it. Henry was very much a jack of all trades, but in the main was a hardware man. Dorothy was beautiful, but tiny and frail. The family moved several times for Dorothy's health, with Henry taking odd jobs and sometimes working in hardware stores. Things got so bad that at one point the whole family lived in a tiny gardener's shack. Bad luck, though, changed everything. One afternoon Henry was crossing the street from work to get his lunch and was struck and nearly killed by a drunk driver. Providentially the accident ended in an insurance settlement large enough for Henry to be able to buy the family a house in Van Nuys, California and to solidify the Scarborough financial future.

Deana went to high school in Van Nuys where she dreamed of getting married, having a family, and being a mom – the same dream that was shared by most of her friends. Deana met Gene Harvey by chance on a double date with Linda Munis, one of her very best friends. Gene was cute, popular, and just a touch cocky, which proved an attractive mix for Deana. The couple started dating almost immediately, but soon Gene was drafted and sent to Fort Riley, and in September 1966 the couple got engaged via a letter and a phone call.

After the wedding, and Gene's departure for war, Deana took a job with Pacific Bell, hoping to use that money and the money that Gene sent home to get a real nest egg saved up before his return. She wrote to Gene faithfully, and sent him care packages every Friday, filled with his favorites – cookies, licorice, and kosher pickles. She tried to keep the harsher possibilities of war at arm's length, but since so many local boys were in the 9th Infantry Division, Charlie Company's parent unit, war coverage was everywhere. She couldn't avoid it. And Gene was so stark in his letters, writing about battles, risk, and death. The pictures he sent usually showed him carrying a machine gun with crossed bandoliers. One picture even showed several body bags. Deana just couldn't take it anymore, and asked that Gene tone down his letters. It's not that she didn't sympathize with him or support him, but the fear for him generated in her by reading his letters was getting debilitating.

> Thinking of Don Peterson and his baby, a sudden fearful realization struck me like lightning. I needed to get back out there to Pete and the others and I needed to go now! I then went up and over the dike, and started my run out. "OK, I'm coming up to one of our guys," I thought, "Gosh he is very still, maybe unconscious. Do I have my wound dressing pack with me? Check my pocket, yes; my training did not let me down. Drop in, check in. Who is it? It's Pete (Don Peterson)." Roll him over; he's heavy. "Pete!", "Pete!", I shout again but louder this time. I roll him back a bit, lean over to see his face, not easy, he's not helping, and God he's heavy. His eyes are closed; I cannot tell if he is breathing. Can't see any blood yet though. Roll him over farther and there they were, three or four holes in Pete's chest right at his heart. I continued to speak out-loud to Pete as though he were still alive even though

I knew the awful truth. When I say that I was speaking out-loud, it was really more of a mutter. While my voice was audible, it was barely audible. My voice didn't have the volume for anyone more than a few inches away to actually hear me. I don't know why I was doing this. I hadn't deceived myself that Pete wasn't dead. Perhaps it was that I thought his spirit was still hanging around and he could still hear me but could simply no longer answer. Perhaps I thought his spirit could still help me in some unknown way. Somehow, it just seemed to be right for the moment. I guess that it seemed, in some way, more respectful too.

Gene Harvey – excerpts from his prose "The Ultimate Game: The Battle of Rice Paddy Angle, May 15th, 1967"

When Gene returned from Vietnam, the couple first moved to follow his next duty assignments in Georgia and then Germany before returning to live in North Hollywood, California. Gene went back to college to complete the degree that had been interrupted by war and worked at night for United Parcel Service (UPS). With the birth of their first child, Eric, in 1969, money was especially tight, so Deana decided to go to work as well, finding employment as a bank teller. Deana had noticed some changes in Gene since his homecoming. He didn't like crowds or unfamiliar things or surroundings – both made him nervous. And he had never been nervous before. Deana figured that she could get used to these changes in Gene's personality; they were small after all. He was the same great guy who had gone to Vietnam, just a bit different. Over time his startle response to loud noises and nervousness faded. Vietnam was consigned to a forgotten corner of the Harveys' lives as the future rushed on.

Soon enough Gene had proven himself invaluable at the local UPS office and was moved to a full-time position in management, while Deana shifted to a new job at Glendale National Bank. The couple welcomed a second son, Jason, in 1979, and through it all Deana managed successfully to balance career with a loving family. She was an incredibly hard worker and always stood out for her efficiency and dedication, which led to a steady stream of promotions and raises. Soon she had moved from bank teller, through note collection, to a home loan processor complete with company car. Next she moved to commercial loans, then she managed the employee loan department, and next she worked as a loan underwriter. With both of their sons safely grown and beginning their own families and lives, after 30 successful years at their respective companies both Gene and Deana retired.

On one hand, retirement meant travel and movies. On the other, it left Gene time to think. It is common that PTSD first shows itself at a time like retirement when the mind can slow and focus on the past. And such was the case for Gene Harvey. Both Gene and Deana attended Charlie Company reunions. All of the guys were swapping stories – some hilariously funny and others deeply tragic. Hearing it all, Deana could hardly believe what they had been through. She had once told Gene not to write about the bad things, but she had no idea that it had been that bad, that difficult. Vietnam came flooding back for Gene as Deana was acquainted with it for the first time. At first Gene would weep openly at some of the memories, and at other times he would sit quietly and just think for hours. As with so much in his life, Gene Harvey decided to tackle the new version of Vietnam head on. He gathered all of the memories and documents he could find and began to write down his Vietnam War experiences in prose.

Gene had never been much of a complainer, so Deana knew that it had to be bad when he told her that he had been urinating blood for a while. Gene was diagnosed with a very aggressive form of prostate cancer, which, on top of a previous diagnosis of diabetes, floored the family. Both, along with Gene's emerging PTSD, were tied to his service in Vietnam. It had bided its time, but Vietnam had come back into the Harveys' lives with a vengeance. There were surgeries and radiation treatments, and Gene received a prognosis of surviving for perhaps another five to eight years. Deana was determined to help Gene fight – doctors' visits, strict diets, and a liberal dose of love. There was still family, fun, and joy. Gene is now well past the doctors' diagnosed survival time. Perhaps it is a miracle.

Regardless, the Harveys are dedicated to the idea of living. They could choose to look back on the Vietnam War as a villain or a culprit, but they don't. In some ways the Vietnam War brought them together, and it made them strong and resilient. The Vietnam War made them into family.

——— † ———

Jennifer Hopper

Jennifer Powell had grown up in the tiny town of Greenfield, Illinois. Jennifer, the youngest, had two older siblings, Joe and Susan. The family patriarch, Joseph, worked selling feed to farmers and had served in the army in World War II. He never did talk much about his wartime service, but Jennifer was able to learn from her mother, Joan, that his time in the military had changed him a great deal. Joseph drank, sometimes managing to stay drunk for days on end. He worked hard, but was emotionally distant from both Joan and the children. The family situation worsened when Joseph suffered a cerebral hemorrhage while Jennifer was in the 4th grade. From that point on, Joseph's health was always an issue as he bounced from job to job, eventually landing in a position working for the state of Illinois. Joan was the stabilizing influence on the family, taking control of the children and working to chart their futures.

Jen had begun to date Steve Hopper in high school, a relationship that survived Steve's eventual drafting and service in Vietnam.

> Looking back on the battle of October 6; it was hard to believe that it had happened. I'd just lost two guys in my squad. When you lose somebody it hurts. And at a point too you know that you are out there and responsible for these guys and their lives. I remember writing home to both Alldridge's and Burkhead's parents, letting them know what had happened that day. I apologized for the fact that we didn't get them home and keep them alive. It is a pretty solemn moment.

You just went through what you went through and now you are a part of death in terms of taking other people's lives. And you are also a part of death in watching some of your own comrades get killed. You become accustomed to death. As you travel to Vietnam and try to figure out what you are made up of, you wonder whether or not you can take another person's life. But that is probably what you are going to end up doing. You quickly come to grips with that, that it is either you or them. And they are thinking the same thing. Someone has to lose, and you just pray to God that it won't be yourself.

Steve Hopper

After Steve's return and the couple's wedding, Steve got a job once again at Caterpillar Equipment (CAT), so the Hoppers moved to Peoria, landing in a one-bedroom apartment. Jen immediately got down to the hard work of making the tiny apartment into a real home, decorating, buying furniture, cooking. Then came twin shocks; Jen found out that she was pregnant, only to miscarry shortly thereafter. The loss tested both Jen and Steve, but they fell back on their considerable Christian faith to buttress their souls in their time of need.

Jen was excited and worried both when she found out that she was pregnant again. But everything turned out well, with Jill being born in April 1970. Since Steve was making decent money, and Jen had been diligent about saving what money the couple had, she was able to quit work and stay home with Jill. Another daughter, Carrie, followed in 1972. After a short stay in the Atlanta area, Steve went back to college at night to work towards a marketing degree. For a few years there it meant very long hours, with Steve working during the day, wolfing down a meal, and then running off to night class. When Carrie entered kindergarten, Jen took a position as a tech at a local pharmacy. Jen was determined that Jill and Carrie understand that their educations would not end with high school graduation. They needed college to stay ahead in life. And they both got the message, graduating high school with good grades, and then both heading off to university.

After the children were grown CAT began to move Steve around with a vengeance, first to Vancouver, then to Nashville, then to DeKalb, Illinois, before an eventual return to Peoria. Through all of the packing, unpacking, and general upheaval, Jen stopped working and got very good at moving house and very much enjoyed the transient life. Finally, things came full circle when the Hoppers moved back to their hometown of Greenfield in 2005 and retired. After having lived in so many big towns, it was a bit of an adjustment moving back to rural America. Greenfield now boasts 1,200 residents, and there are still cornfields as far as the eye can see.

With family all around, and with lots of grandkids living within a short drive, life still somehow managed to remain busy. Steve did his best to stay out of Jen's way, especially in the kitchen, was elected to the city council, and enjoyed tinkering in his wood shop. Jen got increasingly involved in the church and with a host of small-town social activities, especially rival high school football games.

Steve and Jen, sometimes along with both Jill and Carrie, began to attend Charlie Company reunions in the mid-1980s. For Jen it was an education just to see Steve interact with those guys. Even though they hadn't seen each other in 20 years, in many ways Steve was closer to them than he was to his own biological siblings. For Steve the reunions meant camaraderie, not mental anguish. Vietnam took up a larger part of Steve's retired life. He studied it with his buddies, and worked with it for reunions. It never came up in anger, but after so many years together Jen could tell that sometimes Steve would recede into his own world where he quietly dealt with things. Then, in 2016, came a once in a lifetime opportunity. The Greatest Generation Foundation was going to take Steve and other Charlie Company veterans back to Vietnam. The trip was densely emotional. Steve traveled back to Charlie Company battlefields to see where so many of his friends had died. He met Vietnamese soldiers he had once fought against. He got a chance to pay his respects to the fallen, with his best friends by his side. The catharsis was great, leaving Steve with a sense of closure he had never quite realized he needed.

When Steve returned home, the whole town of Greenfield turned out to welcome him – the welcome home that his generation of soldiers had been so long denied. That night, as Jen looked on beaming with pride, Steve talked more about Vietnam than he had in nearly 50 years. It turned out that, even though it had been held well beneath the surface, Vietnam had always been part of the Hoppers' life. Now that Jen thinks back on it, Vietnam had been the foundation of their lives together. There had, of course, been negatives in Steve's Vietnam experience, but the war had set the Hoppers on a path that they would never regret.

——— † ———

Karen Huntsman

When she was seven years old, Karen Wegner was in the kitchen with her father Edwin. He had just come home from a work trip and the two were talking about dinner. In mid-sentence, Edwin clutched his chest, his eyes rolled back, and he fell to the floor dead. For a while after that day Karen's memories aren't very clear, but she does remember becoming closer than ever to her mother Neuta, whom everyone called Val. A devout member of the Church of Jesus Christ of Latter Day Saints, Val doted on Karen. The two talked endlessly about how Karen would grow up, go to beauty school, get married and have four children, and how much Val would enjoy being a grandma. As Karen navigated her way through school, her relationship with her mother was everything. It was near to Karen's 14th birthday when Val came down with the flu and went to the doctor. But it wasn't the flu at all; instead Val was diagnosed with a brain tumor. She went into the hospital and never came out, dying two days later, her entire body wracked with cancer. Karen remembers thinking that her dad could now be happy. He had loved mom so much, and now they would be together forever.

Now alone, Karen was packed off to live with an older half-sister in Las Vegas. Everyone meant well, but Karen found it difficult to concentrate. Her school work and life began to slip. But everything changed when she met Steve Huntsman – a good-looking, older boy. When she was a senior in high school at age 17 the couple wed, and three weeks later Steve's draft notice arrived. Karen followed her new husband to training at Fort Riley, Kansas, where they shared a house with two other Charlie Company couples. It was so much fun being a homemaker for the first time, trying out new dishes, window shopping on the streets, and just learning how to be married. Through it all Karen and Steve became especially close with two of their roommates, Don and Jacque Peterson, with whom they shared everything, both couples learning the ropes of married life together and at the same speed. Everything was made even more exciting by the fact that Jacque was very pregnant and nearing her due date. For Karen it meant helping Jacque shop for baby clothes and conversations about everything from nurseries to nursing. For the guys it meant talk of cigars and whether or not the baby, which they all believed would be a boy, would be a football star like his old man.

While Steve was in Vietnam, Karen lived with his parents and got a job at a local grocery store, trying to save money for his return and the beginning of their life together as a married couple. Karen preferred to learn what she could of Steve's war through letters, but his father kept up with every bit of news he could on television, often weeping as he watched the reports. Sometimes Karen would dream that she was with Steve in Vietnam, helping him bear his burden of war. The battle of May 15 altered everything for Karen and Steve – ending any delusions about the reality of war. Their good friend Don Peterson was killed in battle, and Steve was badly wounded. Today Karen wonders if she was old enough then really to understand the gravity of the situation, but war had entered her life with a vengeance.

Karen was saddened by her friend's loss, and frightened by Steve's wounding. But everything was made right when Steve came home, safe and sound, from Vietnam. There was a short visit to Disneyland, then the couple picked up their married life where it had left off, very near its beginning. When Karen was 20 the couple had their first child, whom they named Vince, and Steve served out his military service and then got a job with a trucking company. Although in a perfect world she would have stayed home as a mom, Karen worked as a secretary for a local attorney in Saint George, Utah and later got a job with SkyWest Airlines. Soon the family came to include three children, but something was wrong and had been wrong since 1968.

> I had my head resting on my arm, and all of a sudden I felt this thing hit me. I felt the burn and the pain. I looked down at my arm, and it was really kind of surreal. I saw the blood; they must have hit an artery. Every time my heart beat, blood would spurt. All I remember thinking was, "Oh my hell; I got hit." That was my only thought. So I took out my bandage and wrapped up my own arm. They pulled the guys who were wounded back to this tree line. I remember getting back there safely. Jarczewski was already there. I remember him not having any shirt on. He was covered with blood from his head to his waist. And he was sucking air; one of the bullets had punctured his lung. I remember him lying there on the ground about 3 or 4 feet from me and every time he would take a breath hearing "gurgle, gurgle, gurgle." Jarczewski and I were pretty good friends. I remember saying to him, "Hang in there, Jarczewski." I never thought I would see him alive again. I just said, "Hang in there, Jar."
>
> My kids didn't even know I had been in Vietnam. I didn't talk to anybody when I got home… nobody. I've asked my sister if I had changed after the war, and she said, "Yeah, you weren't even the same person when you came back." And I didn't see it. I never did see it. She's told me here within the last month that I was not the same person after I got back. Today I don't want to see things that remind me of Vietnam. I just want to be normal.

Steve Huntsman

The Huntsmans had only really been married a short time, with most of their marriage having been consumed by a war. Perhaps they got married so young that they really didn't know each other in the first place. But Steve had come home from Vietnam different. He was quicker to anger, and he drank more than he should. Karen didn't question anything; after all they were still newlyweds. Maybe they were just experiencing the normal bumps in the road that impacted any young marriage? The whole time, though, Karen wondered about Vietnam. Losing Don Peterson had hurt her; it was bound to have hurt Steve even more deeply. But every time she brought up Vietnam he closed down. He didn't want to talk about it. As time went on Karen couldn't ignore the changes. She talked to her doctor, her sister, and her pastor about it, but nobody could help her. And whenever she brought it up with Steve, it ended in a fight. So they quit talking about it at all. What was so frustrating was that Steve was such a good man. So smart and so giving of his time. But within that good man she loved, there was something else. Something darker. After 16 years of trying, Steve and Karen divorced in 1982.

Not long after her divorce Karen went back to work and then remarried a nice man who was strong in the church and seemed like he would make a good father to her children. Soon after their marriage, though, Karen's new husband lost his job, which left the family to get by on the money that she brought in while he worked to raise the children. Household finances were always something of an issue from that point on, but everyone made do, with the kids pitching in with jobs when they were old enough. Karen was very involved with the lives of her children and did her best to make sure that they lacked for nothing, both physically and spiritually.

By 1999 the children were off raising families of their own when Karen's second husband informed her that he didn't love her anymore. The couple divorced, leaving Karen fully on her own for the first time in her life. Karen hopes to retire, to devote her time to her dream of being a grandmother – with a family that now includes 15 grandkids. When not working or with her brood of grandchildren, Karen can be found most often at church. Her Mormon faith was always strong in her life, even though it sometimes had to take a back seat to workaday reality. But now she spends as much time as she can on faith, in part because she realizes that it was faith that saw her through the tough times in her life – especially those related to the Vietnam War. Steve has opened up about the Vietnam War, and has received counseling for PTSD. Karen has also received counseling to help her understand how Vietnam impacted their life together. She even thinks that it would be a good idea for the kids to go to a group meeting about PTSD and Vietnam – that it would help them understand. But this hasn't happened yet.

———— † ————

June Layman

June Gardner was the next to last of seven children from a family from the Cleveland area that was so poor that it once lived out of a car for a short time. Eventually her dad, William, got a better job, good enough to keep a roof over their heads, while her mom, Josephine, worked as a maid. Things picked up when Josephine got a job in a Lawson local convenience store. She was incredibly hard working, and the whole family pitched in to help. It wasn't long before Josephine was managing her own store, with June and the other children all working shifts in what became a real family affair. Day shifts; night shifts; holidays. It was a busy life for a teenager, but June liked being busy and liked helping out. Given her work schedule, June was an average student at school. Her mom had dropped out as a junior in high school, and her father had not even completed the third grade. Her parents approved of Ray Layman, whom she started dating when she was a junior in high school. Ray was patient and caring, working first at a gas station and then at a civil service job; it seemed that he had a pretty good future ahead of him.

When Ray received his draft notice he asked June to marry him, and she agreed. The newlyweds, both 19 years of age, traveled to Fort Riley to begin their lives together as Ray trained to go to Vietnam. By the time he shipped out June was pregnant; something that she would have to go through alone. She almost hadn't had time to adjust to him being gone before she got the news that he had been wounded, shrapnel penetrating his foot and severing nerves before lodging in his butt. The wound was bad, and frightened June terribly, but not bad enough to have Ray sent home. June's pregnancy went well, even if it was lonely, and the couple's son Raymond was born on June 27, 1967. He would be eight months old, however, before he ever met his father.

Ray returned home in early 1968 and got a job working shifts at a local electrical plant shoveling coal into the furnaces and coming home at night with soot covering his face. It was hard work, but good work, and the family prospered. Ray carried physical scars from Vietnam, but if there were mental ones he hid them well. The Laymans lived a wonderful middle-class life, and June was convinced that her dreams had come true. The family, which came to include another child, was prospering and happy. When he was 50, though, Ray complained of having a kidney stone. It was painful, but nothing all that unusual. The doctors treated it and the pain went away. They told him to come back in a month for a checkup just to be sure. That checkup, which was supposed to be so routine, resulted in the discovery of a cancerous tumor that engulfed Ray's entire left kidney.

The doctors removed Ray's kidney, but the cancer had spread, resulting in further operations to remove part of his lung. Treatments were aggressive, including both radiation and chemotherapy, but the situation continued to worsen. Ray was accepted for experimental treatment in Washington DC, which resulted in long drives and lengthy stays. The treatments were excruciating for Ray, but they didn't work. By 2001 the cancer had spread to his spine, resulting in more surgery. For the five years that the disease ran its awful course June gave up everything to be everything to Ray. She was his hands, his spiritual and mental crutch, his coach. She was the one who pushed him to live even when he didn't want to. This was not how she had seen her life unfolding, but it was what she had to do. Her beloved was in pain and need, and only June stood between him and collapse. She kept lonely vigil; the steward of her husband's health and life.

Ray Layman's struggle with cancer was especially difficult for his children Raymond and Joey. It was like the Vietnam War was stealing a part of their lives away. For June, though, the loss was even more devastating. She knew that her remaining time with Ray was very limited and wanted to make the very best of every precious moment. It was during his final fight with cancer that Ray had reconnected with his buddies from Charlie Company. It was his old 2nd Platoon leader, Jack Benedick, who found Ray's name in the phone book. Once Ray's condition had been made clear, Jack responded that he was going to give Ray one final order. He had to attend the company reunion in 2001. June knew what it would mean to her husband to see these guys again. Ray went under one condition; nobody else could know that he was dying. Everyone was so happy to see Ray. When they arrived, one of Ray's 2nd Platoon buddies from Vietnam, Willie McTear, grabbed him in a bear hug and lifted him off of the ground. There were tears, stories, reminiscing. It was like all of the years had just slipped away and they were all young again.

Ray Layman died in 2002, leaving June bereft and alone. It was at the Charlie Company reunion that June first heard about the cause of his cancer. Ray had mentioned Agent Orange, but it had never really registered. But the guys in Charlie Company told her that she ought to contact the Veterans Administration. They had all been around Agent Orange all the time in Vietnam. Ray had been killed by Agent Orange. Ray was a casualty of the Vietnam War. For June Layman it wasn't about money; it was a matter of pride. Ray had served his country with gallantry and had gotten nothing in return but a national cold shoulder. She was determined that Ray should at last get some measure of his due, so she contacted the VA. The man who handled her case was a Vietnam veteran himself. He thought that she had a good case, but warned her that everyone gets turned down for benefits the first time. Don't worry, he said, just keep the case alive and don't give up. As it turned out the government didn't link kidney cancer too closely with Agent Orange. Ray's case was denied, but it did remain in the system.

After Ray passed away, June sold the couple's house and moved into a condo in the Cleveland area. June now spends her time being involved with her grandchildren and loves to travel. There is one particular event that is always marked on June Layman's travel itinerary – the next Charlie Company reunion. As the Laymans made ready to leave Ray's sole reunion in 2001, Jack Benedick – who was one of the few who knew the full gravity of Ray's illness – took June aside and told her that she was one of the family. That in the future she should continue coming to reunions and should bring her family as well. At the reunions June feels at home with her children, Raymond and Joey, accompanying her. Nothing will ever replace Ray Layman in the eyes of his family, but at the Charlie Company reunions they can at least hear the echo of his voice. And each time she arrives Willie McTear walks over and grabs her in a big bear hug, just like he once greeted her husband.

> Charlie Company is still my family. The boys and I still go to every reunion that we can. The guys really love seeing Ray's sons – they love it when the boys come. And the boys are so proud to represent their father. They are so proud of their father and what he did for his country, and they are also there to support me. This all helps to keep Ray's memory alive. I gave my oldest granddaughter, Melissa, a watch that Ray used to wear to work every day. Now she wears it every day. She is a junior in high school and said that someone asked her once why she was wearing that watch. She told me that, "I looked at them and said, 'You wouldn't understand.'"

> *June Layman*

Every year June contacted the VA to see if anything had changed. The answer was always "no," that kidney cancer was not linked to Agent Orange. But in 2013, 11 years after Ray's passing, the VA rating of kidney cancer rose in its linkage to Agent Orange. As we sat chatting at the reunion June told me that the government is presently once again reevaluating the linking of kidney cancer to Agent

Orange. Her fight to get her husband his due continues; a fight born of a war half a century ago that changed her life forever.

—————— † ——————

Kay Lukes

Kay Reinsch was the second of eight children born to Clarence and Bernice Reinsch in the farming community of Geneva, Nebraska. Clarence, a World War II veteran, worked the 120-acre farm, while Bernice and the children took care of an expansive garden and more than 300 chickens. All of the work on the farm left little time to the Reinsch children for social activities. At school Kay focused on courses like bookkeeping and typing that would help get her a job after graduation. Perhaps in the few moments spared for childhood there was time for a weekend movie or a VFW dance, but growing up was pretty much a full-time job.

In the summer between sophomore and junior year in high school, Kay went on a double date with her sister and met Larry Lukes. It wasn't love at first sight or anything like that, but the couple began to date on and off, especially enjoying drive-in movies. By the time they were seniors, Larry gave Kay his class ring on a chain, and they were officially going steady. Kay and Larry were kindred spirits, and long before high school was over they realized that they would be together for many years – but the bond remained unspoken. The couple graduated in 1965, and Kay got a job at the local John Deere dealership as a bookkeeper. She was one of only two women in the office, where she did most of the paperwork. It was a job that she enjoyed thoroughly. It came as a shock when Larry received his draft notice, but he was off to Fort Riley before the couple really had time to think about what being drafted and war really meant. When he was at home on furlough after basic training, when they were both 19, Larry took out a diamond ring and asked for Kay's hand in marriage. It seemed rushed, but right, and both families were very supportive. The couple wed on December 17, 1966, with Larry due to ship out to Vietnam in three weeks. Kay and the couple's parents drove to Fort Riley to say goodbye to Larry on his last day, but there was a miscommunication and they could only wave at the train as it whizzed past without stopping. Nobody was sure whether they saw Larry in the windows of the crowded train or not. The drive back to Nebraska was the worst of Kay's life – knowing what she had missed and wondering if she would ever see Larry again.

While Larry was away at war, Kay lived at home and continued working at her job at John Deere, saving money for Larry's return. She wrote to him every night and sent a care package every week. He wrote to her at least once a week and told her about everything. The big battles, the deaths, the injuries – they were all there in black and white. As the weeks went by, Kay could tell from the tone of the letters that the war was changing Larry. His language continued to darken, and depression seemed to sink in. Kay felt helpless in the face of distant war. She could be impacted by the events that were tearing apart Larry's life, but couldn't impact them in return. All she could do was to keep on living and praying.

Kay was ecstatic when Larry came home. She went to meet his flight in Omaha and jumped into his arms. Larry told her about the protestors in California, and it made her blood boil. How could they say such things to her husband after all he had been through? It didn't take Kay long to realize that the differences she had seen in Larry's letters had made the trip home with him. He was quicker to anger, impatient – different. Kay didn't have a word for what Larry was going through or any real idea about how to deal with it. She had no idea what could help her husband other than patience. Larry still had some time left in the military, so Kay followed him to Colorado Springs and got a job in the local Dairy Queen. The couple then moved back to Nebraska where Kay got a job at a local bank, while Larry worked for a mobile home factory. After a few years, the family moved to Sioux Falls, where Larry got a job working as a long-haul trucker. The solitude and regimen of a truck driver fit his personality well. Even though the job meant that Larry would be gone sometimes for weeks on end, leaving Kay lonely, she knew that it was the best job in the world for the new Larry Lukes.

> After I got home from Vietnam, my dad took me down to the VWF in order to buy me a drink. Over in Vietnam we could not get anything like 7-Up, Squirt, or anything. All we could get was grape and orange soda. So I drank scotch and root beer or scotch and grape soda. I got to the VFW bar and the bartender asked, "What are you going to have soldier?" and I said, "Scotch and root beer." He said, "What, are you sick?!" The guys at the VFW treated me well. Matter of fact a couple of the older guys gave me a lifetime membership to the VFW. They and my family treated me great. But for a good ten years you did not dare put Vietnam on a job application, they would not even hire you or talk to you.

> *Larry Lukes*

The Lukes family came to include two children, Rebecca and Christopher. Kay took what time she could away from her bank job, but the family needed the money, so she embraced the idea of being a working mother. In 1988 the Lukes relocated back to Nebraska but retained the same jobs and routines. Larry was a great father, but was gone so often that Kay was left with most of the child-rearing duties. Both Rebecca and Christopher have prospered, and Rebecca now has three children of her own, who have lived with Larry and Kay for nearly the last ten years bringing a good deal of activity to their lives now that they are both retired.

Larry had long complained of physical ailments after his service in Vietnam, starting with sores on both legs for which he received treatment at the VA. It was in the 2000s, though, that the heart problems began. Larry underwent open heart surgery in 2009, which was followed by the onset of diabetes and Chronic Obstructive Pulmonary Disease. All of Larry's health problems are Vietnam related. Life is still quite happy for the Lukes. They have some land, horses for the grandkids to ride, and their family. Kay's patience has worked.

Larry has found a comfortable place in the world, a place where Vietnam is a memory. They enjoy going to Charlie Company reunions, sometimes with family in tow. There, Vietnam is a positive, not merely a memory. But Larry's physical problems threaten to derail that balance. Now it will take both patience and continued hard work. Vietnam has already stolen a year from the Lukes, and it is trying to invade their present. Kay Lukes refuses to allow that to happen.

———— † ————

Mary Ann Rademacher

Born the eighth of 13 children of Gilbert and Marie Simon, Mary Ann enjoyed life on the 180-acre family farm. Taking classes in typing and accounting in school, Mary Ann hoped to work for the state of Michigan after graduation – a good job that would help anchor a steady family life like that provided by her parents. In the 8th grade Mary Ann had begun to take special notice of a cute guy in her class, Jim Rademacher, who also happened to live just under a mile away from her family's home in their little rural corner of Michigan. Mary Ann and Jim didn't go on their first formal date until freshman year of high school – a double date to a drive-in movie.

Vietnam had interrupted Mary Ann's life plans, forcing her to follow Jim's wounding and recovery through his letters home from the war. Jim Rademacher finally did return home in May 1968, and on the ride home from the airport he pulled an engagement ring from his pocket and made it official. The happy couple wed in a ceremony with 350 guests packed into their local church. Jim was back; both his and Mary Ann's dreams had survived. He was the same Jim Rademacher that she had sent off to Vietnam. Still smiling. Still happy. He was just Jim.

When Jim returned from Vietnam, and their wedding finally took place, there was a short period in which Jim was unable to work due to his extensive injuries. Soon, though, he was back to his old job on construction sites working to frame houses. Construction was booming at the time, and by 1969 the couple had saved enough money to buy a house of their own in Fowler, Michigan. It was something of a fixer-upper, but since Jim was so good with his hands it was a steal. In 1970 the couple had their first child, Sheri, which left Mary Ann torn. She so wanted to be a good mother, but the house also needed so much work that she felt that she had to get a job to help the family have the house they deserved. Mary Ann's sister, Janet, stepped in with a solution. She was raising five children of her own – she could just add Sheri to that considerable mix while Mary Ann was at work. Mary Ann returned to work at her clerical job with the state government and plowed money into the house for two years until she had her second child, Lisa.

Jim's construction work continued to blossom, and he went into business for himself in 1993. With Lisa's arrival, Mary Ann quit work in favor of being a stay-at-home mom, and loved it. Jim was always home on time, and dinner was on the table and ready for family conversation by 5.30pm. Life was very much the way that Mary Ann had once dreamed it would be. After the kids were safely in school, Mary Ann went back to work at a doctor's office where her hours could conform to those of her children. After that she worked with Jim in his construction business. Family life was complete with the eventual arrival of grandchildren.

Through all of those steps of life, the old Jim Rademacher was still there. He was happy, hard working, and dependable. Then, all too suddenly, everything seemed to change. First Jim retired, which left him with a great deal of time on his hands. Then, in late 2006, news came in that a man living nearby had been killed in Iraq, and Jim felt an urgent need to go and pay his respects to this 19-year-old soldier who had died for his country. The sight of the flag-draped casket, though, engulfed Jim in a sea of emotions – 40 years prior, it had very nearly been him in such a casket. He started crying, and it lasted for days. The flashback to Vietnam left Jim confused and depressed to the point where Mary Ann wondered if he was perhaps suicidal. A few weeks later Jim was in the VA for counseling and treatment. It was then that Mary Ann realized that there had been subtle warning signs there for years – startling at loud noises, unexplainable nightmares. Now a new level of stress had brought back the nightmares in full force, and the old Jim Rademacher was gone. His outgoing happiness was gone – replaced by the more somber demeanor of someone who seemed to have something constantly weighing heavily on his heart. At the end of our interview Mary Ann told me, "It made me realize how much he has changed because of the war. It saddens my heart and brings tears to my eyes. I would love to have that old Jim back, but that is not going to happen. He is still a great husband, who is so kind, caring, and loving, but so much of the joy has gone out of his life."

> I remember all the details of that day of June 19. The noise of gunfire can be triggered by the kids popping bubbles with their chewing gum, some fireworks have the sound of artillery and rockets and bombs going off. The sound of helicopters flying overhead will trigger events of that day. The battle scene is very clear. If I was an artist, I could take the scene and paint it on canvas. I could paint the man to my right who was hit in the ankle – the blood streaks on his ankle. I could paint the men in front as they looked at me, the streaks of blood in the water as I lay in it from the wounds in my chest. The very last memory I have until I woke up in the recovery ward is one that defies human reasoning. It is still very clear to me even to this day. I saw what I believe to be an image of a man, Jesus Christ, with a pure, bright light radiating from behind him.

> *Jim Rademacher*

Shortly thereafter Jim started receiving counseling for PTSD, something that he keeps up to this day. Once a week like clockwork Jim is there with his friends, confronting the Vietnam War. Once there was even a counseling session for wives. There were 13 other women there who were going through something similar to what Mary Ann was experiencing. It was wonderful to talk about it. It was wonderful not to feel alone. Jim confronted his past head on, gathering together wartime letters and writing much of his story. His World War II veteran uncle had returned home an alcoholic riven with PTSD and had never talked about it. His story was lost. Jim Rademacher was determined that his story would not be lost and would be passed on to his children so that they could, in part, understand. The family also drew on a considerable wellspring of faith, spending time in worship and Bible study. But most importantly Mary Ann and Jim are now totally open with each other about everything, including Vietnam. They talk. If Mary Ann Rademacher had a chance to talk to any wives of returning veterans that would be her advice – simply to talk.

———— † ————

Sue Reed

The second child of Kay and Marilyn Kaiser, Sue was so close in age to her older sister Linda that the two were the best of friends from the very beginning. Kay worked in construction, while Marilyn was a homemaker. The family lived a middle-class lifestyle near Long Beach in southern California, but neither of the Kaisers took particularly well to parenting. Marilyn was a thoroughgoing alcoholic, starting each day with a vodka and orange juice and going to bed at night with a final shot of bourbon. And, while Kay wasn't a clinical alcoholic, he certainly seemed always to have a beer in his hand. Kay and Marilyn never really could afford a house of their own, so they lived behind the home of Marilyn's parents, who owned and operated their own home-style restaurant. It was at that restaurant and with her maternal grandparents that Sue always had her best of times.

As Sue moved on toward high school she got a job helping out in her grandparents' restaurant. It was at the local pool one day, when Sue was 14, that she met Bill Reed. He was older, at 16, and cute. Sue knew that she couldn't yet date, but she engineered ways to bump into Bill as often as she could. He had a job at the local grocery store and later at the local liquor store, so he wasn't hard to find. Bill and Sue soon started dating, and, even though there was still friction at home, the years of dating Bill were some of the happiest in Sue's young life.

Sue got along well with Bill's parents, with his mom sometimes working in her own grandparents' restaurant. That the families were so close helped a great deal, and soon Bill and Sue were thinking of marriage. Bill graduated high school first and enrolled part time in a local community college. In the spring of 1966, when Bill was 19 and Sue was getting ready to graduate from high school, Bill's draft notice arrived. Marriage, which had been more of a future dream, suddenly became a pressing necessity. Both Bill and Sue wanted the wedding to happen before he shipped out to Vietnam. Sue had long valued her life of faith, attending a local Baptist church – so the wedding was a religious ceremony which was quickly arranged, with the reception held at her grandparents' restaurant. And then, all quite suddenly, Sue Kaiser was Sue Reed and found herself headed to Fort Riley to live as part of a married couple.

The new couple bunked in with Tom and Viv Conroy. The house had roaches and was so small that they could hardly open the front door because one of the lone pieces of furniture, a tattered couch, blocked the way. Although the place was something of a dump, nobody really knew how to cook, certainly nobody knew how to be married, the guys were gone nearly all of the time, and Vietnam hung like a cloud. . . still it was a heady and exciting time. There was just laughing, fellowship, and fun. At Christmas there was a going-away dinner for Bill's last leave, but it wasn't a joyous affair. It was serious, with Bill's deployment imminent.

The couple wrote almost daily while Bill was gone, and the letters were always upbeat. Bill had developed a debilitating back condition in Vietnam that kept him out of combat for much of the first portion of his year-long tour – something that left him feeling guilty but proved of great solace for Sue. Only once did doubt or fear cloud Bill's letters, and that was on the occasion of losing Don Peterson in battle on May 15, 1967. But soon his letters and demeanor were back to normal. Sue meanwhile held down two jobs, one as a legal secretary with a local law firm, hoping to save enough money so that she and Bill could have a place of their own once he got home.

> After three months in country I was sent to Saigon to be evaluated by a US doctor regarding lesions on my back and hip areas that were getting infected. These lesions began during patrols while at Camp Bear Cat. The doctor issued a profile that took me out of field duty. For the next few months all visits to the doctor resulted in the same outcome, "no field duty." At first I was happy to escape the likely death sentence of combat duty. But later I had increasing guilt feelings of not being with the guys in the field. The June 19 battle that killed several guys, including Timmy Johnson and Kenny Frakes, devastated me. I wanted back in the field but had to get around the doctors. I was told in the later part of June that I was being infused to the 2nd Battalion, 60th Infantry within the 9th Infantry Division. When I reported to the first sergeant in my new battalion I did not disclose that I had a profile, and with the way the Army kept records nobody found out. I was then back in combat and I felt that my guilt feelings were gone. After returning home I discovered that I still had the guilt feelings. I went through a couple of years with depression and struggled with how the public portrayed the Vietnam veteran.
>
> *Bill Reed*

When Bill came home in January 1968, Sue couldn't help but notice that Bill seemed somehow changed. Bill Reed was still a wonderful guy, but he was much more quick to anger and had developed a deep streak of jealousy. He didn't want to lose Sue, and it showed. Bill and Sue moved back to southern California where he found a job working for the county, and Sue discovered that she was pregnant. Their son Jeffrey, though, required hospitalization. The stress of very nearly losing a child was compounded by the considerable expense of the necessary treatments, which nearly bankrupted the couple. Combined with a Vietnam-linked depression that had set in on Bill, the burdens were fatal to the Reeds' marriage. After five years of marriage the couple split.

Although her relationship with Bill remained cordial, Sue found herself alone for the first time in her life. It was a frightening time, raising a child on her own and learning to live as an independent adult, both at the same time. Sue had to work to keep her finances afloat, eventually moving into the field of real estate. No matter the difficulties, though, Sue had to keep plugging forward. She worked her way through a college degree and even took flying lessons to get her private pilot's license. Her grandfather had loved to fly, and he had always wanted Sue to get her degree, and she was determined to do both before his death; and she succeeded. Although there were a good many difficult times, Jeffrey made it through high school and is now married and with a family of his own. After so many years of being single that she had nearly forgotten what married life was like, Sue met her second husband, Steve. Through it all, Sue made sure to make regular visits north to spend time with her sister, who now lives in a nursing home still suffering the effects of her childhood bout with encephalitis. Linda is Sue's chief link to her past, and it is a link, love, and relationship that she cherishes.

Now that they are in their 70s, Bill and Sue talk about Vietnam and about the things that tore them apart in their short-lived marriage. Both feel guilt over the collapse of their relationship and wonder how that collapse was impacted by the Vietnam War. Bill felt guilt in Vietnam for not being there with his brothers while they were in battle. He was later moved to another unit where he made certain that he saw combat, but things were never the same. While others in Charlie Company were impacted by violent combat, Bill Reed was perhaps even more deeply impacted by not sharing in that combat. PTSD specialists often term the problem "survivors' guilt." Wrestling with what he did do in Vietnam, as well as what he didn't, Bill is only now coming to grips with the idea that he returned to Sue a changed man. For her part, Sue could tell that there were differences in the man she loved, but never really understood why until a full 50 years later. Bill and Sue continue an amicable relationship, but both are left to wonder at what could have been without the intervention of the Vietnam War.

——— † ———

Noemi Sauceda

In a book that opened with a snapshot from a dramatic moment in the life of Noemi Sauceda, it is only fitting that the book concludes by completing her story.

Noemi Rodriquez was born in Weslaco, a small town just outside of Mercedes, Texas. Her father, Luiz, drove a big truck making deliveries, first for Jax Beer and then for a cookie company; her mother, Viola, worked for the city. Two younger brothers, Mario and Jaime, soon joined the family, and with both parents working hard the Rodriquez enjoyed a solidly middle-class upbringing. Since Luiz was an only child, Noemi was especially close to his doting parents, often spending weekends at their home before going to Spanish Mass on Sundays. As their only granddaughter Noemi always held a special place in the eyes of her grandparents and spent as much time there as she could, soaking in their love and attention.

Excelling in school, Noemi hoped to go to college, and her parents, understanding the reality of hard work, supported Noemi's aspirations. But Noemi kept getting sick with asthma, which greatly limited both her interaction with others and her educational opportunities. Noemi was rarely allowed to play with the other neighborhood children for fear of getting sick, leaving her standing in the doorway watching others run and romp while wondering what it would be like to join them in their revelries.

When she was 15 and a high school sophomore, Noemi met Jose Sauceda in class, and pretty much pegged him right then and there as the boy for her. He was suave and handsome, older, and full of good humor. Jose and Noemi quickly became a couple, but, since

Jose and his family were migrant workers, he was often gone following the ripening crops across the country. Somehow the distance made Noemi love Jose all the more, communicating their deepest thoughts and dreams through a stream of letters and a few rare phone calls.

In the spring of her senior year Noemi's future was jumpstarted when she got the news that she was pregnant just at the same time that Jose received his draft notice prior to leaving for Fort Riley. The twin events shocked the parents on both sides of the family, but they all liked one another and knew that Jose and Noemi belonged together. Since pregnant girls were not allowed in school, Noemi dropped out and in August 1966 the couple married in the local church followed by a large reception and dance. As his training had already begun, Jose couldn't linger for a honeymoon. It was back to Fort Riley for him.

Life had changed radically and suddenly for Noemi Sauceda. Just a few months before she had been a rather carefree high school senior with a great boyfriend – the future was limitless. Now, though, she was married, pregnant, living at home, and with a husband who was headed off to war. It was like someone had drawn a line in Noemi's life. Making matters worse was the fact that Viola had really only been putting on a brave face at the wedding. She was plainly hurt by Noemi's pregnancy, and a gulf grew between the two, leaving Noemi feeling more alone than ever.

Belinda Sauceda was born on February 10, 1967, with Jose receiving the news while on operations near Camp Bear Cat in Vietnam. Two months later Noemi's grandmother died unexpectedly, robbing Noemi of her closest confidant and friend right when she needed her the most. Trying to cover the pain of loss and separation, Noemi threw herself into raising Belinda. It was her daughter's love and need that saw her through, and, in the spring of 1968, just like that, Jose was back. It took Belinda a good bit of time to get used to sharing Noemi with a man, but father and daughter quickly became close.

One evening soon after his return Viola dropped some pots and pans in the kitchen, making a racket. Noemi heard another noise and turned to look and saw that Jose had dove to the floor. He also had terrible nightmares in which he would scream and often lash out at Noemi. He didn't want to talk about Vietnam; he wanted to protect her from what he had seen there. But the couple realized that Vietnam had to be the culprit. Jose borrowed some money and went to the VA in San Antonio to ask for help, but they told him that he was fine and sent him on his way.

> Working at migrant camps in the summers got me ready for Vietnam – all the heat, ants, and mosquitoes. And the farmers worked us like slaves and didn't give a shit about us. On May 15 Jim Cusanelli and I were walking point when we came under heavy fire from in front of us. We dove into a nearby canal that was used for watering the rice paddies. We were returning fire at the Viet Cong positions when one Viet Cong shot a rocket propelled grenade at us. Cusanelli and I were about 5 feet apart and the grenade landed between us. We figured we were dead, but the grenade had hit that brown gravy mud we were in and didn't go off. Talk about luck! When we headed back to the rest of the platoon, Cusanelli and I bumped into some Viet Cong, maybe a hospital, and we opened fire, killing everyone we saw. When we came home from Vietnam, the protestors were out in force calling us baby killers. What a welcome home. You know, it took me 35 years to tell anyone that I was a Vietnam veteran. That is how ashamed I was for anyone to know. I kept it all bottled up inside me. I have a lot of hate in me. I don't know if PTSD is the right word for it.
>
> *Jose Sauceda*

The Saucedas then embarked on something of an odyssey, trying to find their place in the world. The first major move was to Michigan, when Belinda was two years old. Jose got a job in an automobile factory and the family rented a small apartment. A few years later the couple returned to Mercedes, Texas, where Jose went back to college to get his teaching certificate and worked part time in a gas station. A second child, Jose Junior, joined the family in 1970, and Noemi had to go back to work for the local government. Jose kept having his nightmares, and was quicker to anger than ever. After the birth of Omar in 1973 Jose began work with the police department, doing anything he could to help earn the money that his growing family needed to stay afloat. The stress of working so hard while still dealing with the war almost broke the couple on several occasions, and pushed Jose to the point where he leveled a pistol at his beloved wife threatening everything that he held dear. Nobody knew it, because there wasn't a name for it yet, but Jose was haunted by PTSD. Noemi knew that the angry and mercurial Jose was not "her Jose." It was like he was two different people. Most often he was the wonderful Jose with whom she had fallen in love. But on occasion he was a man tortured by the grips of unseen memory.

Seeking a better future, the Saucedas returned to Michigan, living in Kalamazoo where Jose finished his degree and got a job as a schoolteacher. But, with three children, his salary wasn't nearly enough to get by, so Jose got a second job and Noemi worked two jobs of her own. Life seemed to be nearly constant toil for the Saucedas. It was physically draining, but satisfying. Next came a move to Houston. On the journey south Noemi drove the family car, carrying Belinda and Omar. Jose, with Jose Junior at his side, drove the truck that carried the family's belongings. Tragedy struck on the trip. Jose was involved in an accident, and Jose Junior perished. He was nine years old.

The whole family was stunned at the loss. Noemi was devastated and existed in a haze of grief for months. Family members came to help as best they could. Jose got a job working for Lord and Taylor department store, and Noemi took a position as a bank teller. Prayer became an ever closer companion for Noemi as she navigated the most difficult years of her life. Belinda and Omar made their way through their school years, with Belinda heading off to the courthouse to get married the day that she turned 18. Noemi barely even knew the boy, but there was nothing that she could do to change anything. Shortly thereafter Lord and Taylor transferred Jose's job to New Jersey, so the Saucedas moved once again. They lived there for ten years, with Omar finishing school and falling in with something of a rough crowd.

In the 1990s Noemi and Jose returned to Mercedes where they retired. Life had rushed by at such a terrific speed pushed forward by the needs of family and work. Both Noemi and Jose help out at the local church and keep busy around the house in retirement. Belinda and her children live within a few hours' drive, so there is company when they want it. Omar passed away eight years back, adding to the somber undertone of the Saucedas' life. Jose and Belinda have attended a Charlie Company reunion, where they both discovered that they were not alone in how Vietnam impacted their lives. The VA finally recognized what Jose and so many other Vietnam veterans were going through as a real problem, and Jose now undergoes regular counseling for PTSD. It gave Noemi some solace that what had affected Jose so thoroughly now had a name and some treatment, but it didn't change much. Vietnam was still a taboo subject at home. And, though treatment helped, Jose had been left so long alone with the specter of Vietnam that many of his symptoms remained – nightmares, anger, depression. There were so many times where the Saucedas' marriage could have fallen apart. But both Noemi and Jose took their vows seriously, and they both loved each other deeply. Both worked on their marriage tremendously hard in their own respective ways.

The Saucedas' marriage, which began in such haste in 1966, has now lasted for more than half a century. So much has come and gone in their lives together, from endless toil to great personal tragedy. But through it all, Noemi Sauceda is quick to point out where everything really changed. There weren't adequate words for it back then, but Noemi realized instantly that the man she sent to Vietnam was not the same man who returned. She says that it is like Vietnam flipped a switch in their lives. Everything that happened after the war was impacted by the war. As for so many others, for Noemi Sauceda Vietnam, a war in a faraway country that she has never even seen, was the pivotal event of her life.

CAST OF CHARACTERS

Charlie Company Wives

Nancy Benedick: Daughter of Don and Elizabeth Rolle; grew up outside Kansas City. Met Jack Benedick while in college and married during his training at Officer Candidate School. After Jack was badly wounded in 1969, Nancy devoted herself to his care and to the raising of the couple's two children, Jack Junior and Mike. After Jack's recuperation Nancy helped with all of his efforts on behalf of disabled athletes and took on a new career as a teacher. The family now includes five grandchildren, Maura, Michael, Mason, Mikayla, and Devin.

Jacqueline Bradfield: Daughter of Roman and Betty Boyd and raised by her grandmother Vaselee near Cleveland, Ohio. Met John Bradfield when she was 12; the couple married when she was 17 and while John was at training at Fort Riley. The couple had two sons, Barnard and Byron, and Jacqueline worked at an insurance firm. A rift had grown, though, and the couple divorced, with Jacqueline moving to Texas with the children. Jacqueline continued to work before being called to the ministry and now devotes much of her time to her church and her grandchildren, Christopher, Jonathan, Barnard John, Kayla, and Donovan.

Barbara Kenney: Daughter of Marilyn Tobin, Barbara was raised in the San Fernando Valley outside Los Angeles. Married Fred Kenney before he was drafted and sent to Fort Riley. The couple's child, Frederick, was born while Fred was on the troopship to Vietnam. Fred was killed in action on July 11, 1967. Remarried Don Hill after Vietnam and went on to have four more children, Tracey, Terry, Matthew, and Chrissy. The family now includes seven grandchildren, Jonathan, Darian, Cheyne, Taylor, Olivia, Emilee, and Brandon.

Judy Lilley: Grew up in Bakersfield, CA; daughter of Doc and June Wittman. Married Larry Lilley during his Christmas leave from training in Fort Riley. After the war, Judy went to work with Larry in the family's Honda dealership and the couple had two children, Jodi and Keith. Following a divorce, Judy went to work as a bookkeeper and eventually remarried Mark Williams. The Lilleys now have five grandchildren and step-grandchildren, Savannah, Casey, Jenna, Devin, and Alex.

Becky Lind: Daughter of Clyde and Nawdean Barth; born and raised in rural Nebraska. Met Herb Lind near the end of high school and married him after he had been called to military duty. Herb was the commander of Charlie Company. Herb remained in the military after Vietnam until his retirement in 1985. Becky received her MA in Food and Nutrition from Kansas State University and worked at various positions in the profession until she retired to help take care of Herb after his cancer diagnosis. The couple had two children, Mark and Tara, and four grandchildren, Lindsey, Tommy, Theron, and Diana.

Mary Ann Maibach: From a rural area outside of Akron, OH; daughter of Ernest and Louise Graf. Met and married Gary Maibach through their membership in the Apostolic Christian Church. Mary Ann worked as a nurse during Gary's deployment and after his return, until the arrival of the couple's third child. After her retirement she devoted her time to her burgeoning family and to the furthering of Gary's ministry with the church. The family now includes four children, Karen, Mark, David, and James, and several grandchildren and great-grandchildren, Julie, Jana, Jason, Rhett, Trace, Brant, Miranda, Rachel, Luke, Reed, Yikalo, Sintay, Abby, Clint, Cole, and

Quinn.

Jacque Peterson: Daughter of Harriet McMullen and raised with her stepfather Deloy; often moved due to Deloy's career in the US Air Force. Married Don Peterson just after graduation from high school, and found out that she was pregnant the day that Don was drafted. Don was killed in action on May 15, 1967. Jacque remarried Don Bomann and went on to have four children, James, Heather, Chris, and Jessica, and five grandchildren, Brittany, Devon, Ava, Ellie, and Zachary.

Aurora Salazar: Daughter of Paul and Otillia Gonzales, from Johnson City, Texas. Met and married Jimmie Salazar, with the wedding taking place on a break during Jimmie's training at Fort Riley. Became a noted local businesswoman after Jimmie's experience in the Vietnam War. Divorced Jimmie, but the couple remarried shortly thereafter. The couple had three children, Richard, Gary, and Jimmie Junior. The couple also cared for the daughters, Jamie, Annette, and Molly, of Aurora's brother after his death. The Salazars have ten grandchildren.

Esther Windmiller: Daughter of Kenneth and Lydia Avery; raised in the small town of Wellington outside Cleveland, OH. Met Bernie Windmiller while attending Wheaton College. The couple married after Bernie's deployment to Korea. After Bernie's service with Charlie Company as chaplain, he remained in the military until his retirement in 1993. The couple has four children, Beth, Leslie, Keith, and Rebekah, 12 grandchildren, Rachel, Peter, Andrew, Megan, Chelsey, Cameron, Abby, Reid, Tori, David, Max, and Kalliope, and three great-grandchildren, Will, Brady, and Lucas.

—————— † ——————

Esther Bradfield: Daughter of Martha Stone; raised in Cleveland, Ohio, where she wanted to join the Air Force. Took a job in the US Post Office after high school graduation. A single mother to twins, Jason and Kayce. Second wife of John Bradfield, whom she met at work. Retired from the post office when John was diagnosed with colon cancer. She now dedicates much of her life to the church and helps John with his Vietnam-related health issues. Esther has three grandchildren, Brekken, Penn, and Elizabeth.

Norma Crockett: Daughter of Rosure and Ethel Rains; raised in rural Kentucky near Albany. Was a schoolteacher when she met and married Lynn Crockett, who was already in the military and eventually served as First Sergeant of Charlie Company. Norma remained a teacher as Lynn navigated his military career. The couple has one son, Gregory, and two grandchildren, Dean and Sara. After their retirement the Crocketts settled down to a life of farming.

Vivian Conroy: Daughter of Edwin and Kathleen Maxwell; grew up in Palmdale, California. Married Tom Conroy while he was on a break from his training at Fort Riley. Worked with the Federal Aviation Administration after Tom's return from Vietnam. The couple has three children, Kimberly, Tom Junior, and Chad. The family now includes grandchildren Tracy, Tyler, Travis, Jasmine, Caden, and Cooper; step-grandchildren Taylor and Matthew; and great-grandchildren Tanner and Tino.

Kaye French: Daughter of Hubert and Lessie Barbour; lived in Tampa, FL before relocating to Titusville, near Cape Kennedy. Married Bob French shortly before his initial departure for Fort Riley. Gave birth to the couple's first child, Charlene, while Bob was deployed in Vietnam. After the war, Kaye worked in the College of Education at the University of South Florida. Later the family came to include a second child, Michelle. The family has one grandchild, Amber.

Iris Grable [Sclimenti]: Daughter of Tom and Ann Boyd and from Culver City, California. Married John Sclimenti in March of 1967 after she discovered that she was pregnant. The couple had three children, John James, Steve, and Christopher. Iris worked in major sales positions for technology companies before owning her own business for several years. The couple divorced in 1976. The family now includes three grandchildren, Roman, Giavanna, and Chloe.

Jeannie Hartman: Daughter of Joseph and Irene Sweeney and from Busti, New York outside Buffalo. Married Ernie Hartman after high school, before he was drafted and later joined Charlie Company in

Vietnam as one its first replacements. Worked as a schoolteacher after Vietnam. The couple adopted a child, Corey. Jeannie eventually retired to help Ernie with Vietnam-related health issues and to help raise the couple's grandson, Dylan.

Deana Harvey: Daughter of Henry and Dorothy Scarborough and grew up in Van Nuys, California. Married Gene Harvey on a break during his training at Fort Riley. After Vietnam, Deana worked in various positions in banking before her retirement after 30 years. The couple has two children, Eric and Jason, and a stepdaughter, Haleigh.

Jennifer Hopper: Daughter of Joseph and Joan Powell; grew up in rural Greenfield, Illinois. Met and fell in love with Steve Hopper in high school, but put off marriage until his return from the Vietnam War. The family moved often after Vietnam, with Steve working for Caterpillar Equipment. The couple had two daughters, Jill and Carrie, and now lives back in Greenfield. The family now includes several grandchildren, Grace, Chloe, Reid, Drew, Jake, and Brady.

Karen Huntsman: Daughter of Edwin and Neuta Wegner, both of whom died when Karen was young. Sent to live with a sister in Las Vegas, Karen met Steve Huntsman, and the couple wed three weeks before Steve got drafted. Lived with Don and Jacque Peterson during training at Fort Riley. The couple had three children, Vince, Michelle, and Sheri, before getting divorced in 1982. Karen worked at many jobs, including with AT&T, to help make ends meet. Now retired, Karen enjoys the company of a host of grandchildren and step-grandchildren – Riley, Ashton, Chaz, Joshua, Brady, Wyatt, Garret, Ashley, Zachary, Chelsey, McKenna, McKailey, Andrew, Izzy, Emma, and Olivia.

June Layman: From the Cleveland area and daughter of William and June Gardner. She married Ray Layman just after high school graduation and before his training at Fort Riley. The couple had two children after the war, Raymond and Joey, before Ray was first diagnosed with kidney cancer. After that, much of June's life revolved around her children and the care for Ray's Vietnam-related health issues. Ray died in 2002, and the family still struggles with his loss and its relationship to the war. The Layman family now includes four grandchildren, Mitch, Marissa, Isabella, and Carleigh.

Patty Lilley: Daughter of Dominic and Winifred Massimino; grew up in Palmdale, California. Had her first child, Brian, shortly after high school. Later married and had three more children, Bill, Bob, and Brad. The couple divorced after 18 years, and, after a second marriage, Patty met and became the second wife of Larry Lilley. She worked with Larry in his motorcycle shop and later followed him into retirement. The couple now lives in Georgia, and Patty has seven grandchildren, Pierce, Grant, Jordan, Khylee, Taylor, Faith, and Bryce.

Kay Lukes: Daughter of Clarence and Bernice Reinsch, from a farming community in rural Nebraska. Met Larry Lukes before her junior year in high school, and the couple married while he was on Christmas leave from training at Fort Riley. After Vietnam Kay worked often in banking, but devoted most of her time to being a mother. The couple had two children, Rebecca and Christopher, and now has three grandchildren, Robert, Stephen, and Breann. Larry worked as a long-haul trucker, and Kay worked in banking until her recent retirement. Kay now helps Larry with his Vietnam-related health issues and spends much of her time helping to raise her grandchildren.

Mary Ann Rademacher: From rural Michigan, Mary Ann was the daughter of Gilbert and Marie Simon. Her boyfriend, Jim Rademacher, was drafted before the couple could marry, so the wedding was postponed until his return from war. Jim was badly wounded during the fighting on June 19, 1967. The couple married after Jim's homecoming, with Mary Ann working for the state government until the arrival of the couple's children, Sheri and Lisa. After her children both started school, Mary Ann resumed her career, while Jim worked in construction. The family came to include two grandchildren, Ethan and Eric. Jim and Mary Ann have both retired, and the couple now faces having to deal with Vietnam-related PTSD.

Sue Reed: Daughter of Kay and Marilyn Kaiser; raised in Long Beach, California. She met Bill Reed when she was 16, and the couple married after high school graduation and Bill's subsequent drafting. Lived with Viv and Tom Conroy during training at Fort Riley. Bill returned from Vietnam changed, and the couple divorced after five years of marriage and with one child, Jeffrey. Sue worked in real estate for several years, and enjoyed piloting small aircraft.

Noemi Sauceda: Raised outside Mercedes, Texas; daughter of Luiz and Viola Rodriquez. Fell in love with Jose Sauceda at age 16, and was married during his training at Fort Riley. The couple's first child, Belinda, was born while Jose was away at war. After Vietnam both Jose and Noemi often held down multiple jobs to help with finances, as the family grew to include two more children, Omar and Jose Junior, who perished in a car accident at age 9. Jose came to struggle with PTSD, but his dedication to his family, and Noemi's dedication to him, never wavered. The family lost Omar seven years ago. The couple has two grandchildren, Rogelio and Christopher.

The Men of Charlie Company

Ben Acevedo: One of ten children; brought up in the rural Yakima Valley of Washington where his father Benjamin worked as a farm laborer and his mother Berta was a housewife. Served as a team leader in 1st Platoon, where he knew Don Peterson.

Gale Alldridge: Replacement who came to Charlie Company in September, 1967. Member of 3rd Platoon. Killed in action, October 6, 1967.

Jack Benedick: From Omaha, Nebraska; graduate of Officer Candidate School. Married Nancy in 1965 and had a son, Jack Junior, in 1966. Platoon Leader, 2nd Platoon, Charlie Company. Wounded in the fighting on June 19. Returned to Vietnam in 1969 as commander, Charlie Company, 3rd of the 60th Infantry. Wounded by a booby trap in April 1969 and lost both legs below the knee. Continued with military career and became a champion downhill skier.

Duffy Black: From Peoria, Illinois. While at Fort Riley with Charlie Company met and wed Ida, the daughter of the postmaster of the 9th Infantry Division. Served as company executive officer in

Vietnam. Wounded by a booby trap in the Rung Sat Special Zone on April 8, 1967, and died in the hospital three days later. Close friends with Bernie Windmiller.

John Bradfield: From Cleveland and was only eight when his father died in an industrial accident. Member of 3rd Platoon. Wounded by a booby trap in August. Married to Jacqueline Bradfield. Returned home and worked for the Post Office. The couple later divorced and John remarried Esther, his "angel and care giver."

Danny Burkhead: Replacement who came to Charlie Company in September, 1967. Member of 3rd Platoon. Killed in action, October 6, 1967.

Stan Cockerell: From North Hollywood, California. Served in 2nd Platoon. Was part of the group that met with Fred Kenney to tell him about the life of his father.

Tom Conroy: Son of a meat cutter from Lancaster, California. Married Vivian after basic training. Member of 3rd Platoon. Carried Fred Kenney's body from the field on June 11, 1967. Worked several jobs after the war, especially in construction. Tom retired in 1999 and now loves tinkering on cars.

Carl Cortright: From Mission Hills, California. Came to 1st Platoon of Charlie Company as a replacement in April, 1967. Wounded in action and paralyzed on May 15, 1967. Became a champion athlete in the National Veterans Wheelchair Games.

Lynn Crockett: Born into a farming family near Cumberland, Kentucky. Entered the military at age 17. Married to Norma, and served as First Sergeant for Charlie Company. Served a second tour with the 25th Division in 1969–70. Retired from the military in 1973.

Don Deedrick: Member of 1st Platoon. He and his wife Sue lived with Steve and Karen Huntsman and Don and Jacque Peterson while at Fort Riley.

Butch Eakins: From Cape Girardeau, Missouri, and later worked at Caterpillar in Peoria, Illinois. Member of 2nd Platoon. Killed in action on July 11, 1967.

Phil Ferro: From Northridge, California, where he won the Los Angeles city championship in high hurdles during high school.

Member of 2nd Platoon. Killed in action on July 11, 1967.

Kenny Frakes: From Lancaster, California, where he was on the high school track and wrestling teams. Drafted with friends Larry Lilley and Tim Johnson. Member of 4th Platoon. Killed in action on June 19, 1967.

Bob French: From Tampa, Florida, where he had quit college to work in the Post Office, which left him open to the draft. Married Kaye, who accompanied him to Fort Riley. He did not find out that she was pregnant until he was in Vietnam. Wounded in action on June 19, 1967. After the war returned to Tampa and worked in the Post Office for 21 years.

Ernie Hartman: From Sugar Grove, Pennsylvania. After high school took a job as a precision grinder and married his sweetheart, Jeannie. Arrived in Charlie Company as a replacement in 1st Platoon just after the battle of June 19, 1967. Wounded in action on July 29, 1967. Went back to work as a precision grinder for 37 years before the company was sold.

Gene Harvey: From North Hollywood, where his father worked for Lockheed. Married sweetheart Deana before departing for Vietnam. Member of 1st Platoon. In the fighting on May 15, 1967 volunteered to search for the downed squad.

Steve Hopper: From the rural area near Greenfield, Illinois. After high school worked for Caterpillar in Peoria, Illinois. Member of 3rd Platoon. Wounded in action on July 1, 1967 and on October 6, 1967. After the war returned to Greenfield, married his sweetheart Jennifer, and worked for Caterpillar.

John Hoskins: US Military Academy graduate, class of 1966. Platoon leader of 3rd Platoon of Charlie Company. Wounded in action on July 11, 1967. Later served as company commander, Echo Company, 3rd Battalion of the 60th Infantry. Killed in action May 6, 1968.

Henry Hubbard: Replacement to Charlie Company in June 1967. Served in 2nd Platoon. With Frank Schwan, narrowly avoided Viet Cong patrols following the fighting on July 11, 1967.

Steve Huntsman: From Saint George, Utah. Attended Brigham

Young University and married Karen before going to Fort Riley, where the couple lived with Don and Jacque Peterson. Served in 1st Platoon. Wounded in action May 15, 1967. Later reenlisted. After the war worked as a truck driver for 27 years.

Dave Jarczewski: From Depew, New York. After high school worked in the Lackawanna, New York, plant of Bethlehem Steel. Wounded in action May 15, 1967. After returning from Vietnam, went back to work for Bethlehem Steel until it closed and then worked in the US Post Office.

Fred Kenney: From Chatsworth, California. Married Barbara, who gave birth to their son, Freddie, while Kenney was on the troopship to Vietnam. Served in 3rd Platoon. Killed in action July 11, 1967.

Harold Wayne King: From Copper Hill, Virginia. Arrived in Vietnam in February 1967 and became one of the early replacements in Charlie Company. Served in 2nd Platoon. Killed in action on July 11, 1967.

Rollo Larson: From Macon, Georgia. Joined the National Guard in 1952 as an enlisted man. First commander of Charlie Company in Vietnam before his departure in 1967.

Larry Lilley: From Lancaster, California. Champion motorcycle rider in high school. Drafted with his friends Kenney Frakes and Tim Johnson. Married Judy during his Christmas leave from training. Served in 1st Platoon. After Vietnam took over the family group of motorcycle dealerships.

Herb Lind: From St Paul, Nebraska. Got his draft notice as a senior in college in 1961 and went to Officer Candidate School. Married Becky during his initial assignments. Took over command of Charlie Company when Rollo Larson rotated home. Retired from the military in 1985. Settled in Manhattan, Kansas.

Larry Lukes: From Sioux Falls, South Dakota. After high school moved to Fairmont, Nebraska and worked on farms. Married Kay in December 1966. Served in 3rd Platoon. After the war, returned to Nebraska and worked in a factory before taking a position as a truck driver. Now retired and owns nine acres in the country where his grandchildren can come and play.

Gary Maibach: From Sterling, Ohio. Worked for the local family store and was a member of the Apostolic Christian Church. Married Mary and had one child before departing for Vietnam. Was a conscientious objector, and joined 1st Platoon of Charlie Company as a medic. After returning home eventually took over the family business and became a minister in the Apostolic Christian Church of America. Is especially involved in veteran outreach.

Willie McTear: From Newellton, Louisiana. Was drafted out of Las Vegas, while also attending school part-time at Southern University. Served in 2nd Platoon. After Vietnam, returned to Las Vegas, married and had two children. Then spent a few years homeless and addicted to drugs, before getting clean and working in California hospitals aiding those with chemical and alcohol dependencies.

Charlie Nelson: From the Navajo reservation in Arizona and later moved to Los Angeles with his parents. Served in 1st Platoon. Wounded in action on May 15, 1967. After the war, tried living in Los Angeles, but returned to the reservation to deal with issues arising from the war.

Don Peterson: From Arroyo Grande, California. After high school, worked with his father painting houses before marrying Jacque, who followed him to Fort Riley. Son Jimmy was born just before Peterson shipped out to Vietnam. Killed in action on May 15, 1967.

Jim Rademacher: From Fowler, Michigan. Charlie Company replacement, arriving in June 1967. Served in 2nd Platoon. Wounded in action on June 19, 1967. Returned home to marry Mary Ann.

Forrest Ramos: From Wapato, Washington, where he often worked in the fields with his father as a hop thrower. Served in 3rd Platoon. Killed in action on June 19, 1967.

Bill Reynolds: Lived in Texas and Australia before settling in the San Fernando Valley of California. Served as a squad leader in 2nd Platoon. After the war, worked at Lockheed and was instrumental in setting up the website of the 9th Infantry Division; works tirelessly to document the history of Charlie Company.

Dusty Rhodes: US Navy commander who took his monitor gunship up a tiny stream to aid Charlie Company in the battle of June 19, 1967.

Jimmie Salazar: From Austin, Texas. Married Aurora before departing for Vietnam. Served in 2nd Platoon. After the war, returned to Texas, where he worked for the Lower Colorado River Authority. Suffered from PTSD and heart disease, but he and Aurora fought through the hard times and reconnected with Charlie Company.

Sheldon Schulman: Platoon leader of 4th Platoon. Killed in action on June 19, 1967.

Frank Schwan: From a Hungarian neighborhood in Cleveland. Served in 2nd Platoon. Wounded in action on July 11, 1967, with he and Henry Hubbard having to evade Viet Cong patrols at night.

Ron Schworer: From Las Vegas, Nevada. A computer whiz who served in 2nd Platoon and was especially close to Willie McTear. Killed in action on April 8, 1967.

John Sclimenti: From the San Fernando Valley of California. Served in 1st Platoon. Rescued Charlie Nelson from the battlefield on May 15, 1967 after having returned home briefly to marry Iris. Has worked in communications since returning home from Vietnam.

George Smith: Squad leader in 2nd Platoon. Led the squad that first made contact in the battle of July 11, 1967. Killed in action on July 11, 1967.

Don Trcka: From League City, Texas. Served in 3rd Platoon. Wounded in action on May 15, 1967.

Guy Tutwiler: From Birmingham, Alabama. Was a lieutenant colonel and served as commander of the 4th Battalion of the 47th Infantry (the parent unit of Charlie Company) during 1967.

Bernie Windmiller: From Gary, Indiana. Was drafted in 1954 and served his hitch in the military before going to seminary and becoming a minister in the Evangelical Covenant Church of America. Married Esther and served as a chaplain in the 2nd Brigade of the 9th Infantry Division. Rose to the rank of colonel before his retirement from the military in 1992. Worked in various interim positions in the Evangelical Covenant Church and became Executive Director of the Board of the International Association of Evangelical Chaplains, working to train chaplains all over the world.

John Young: From Saint Paul, Minnesota. Served as a squad leader in 1st Platoon. Wounded in action on June 19, 1967.

BIBLIOGRAPHY

Oral Interviews

Extensive oral interviews with wives and veterans of Charlie Company and their families form the bedrock source for this work. The recordings of the interviews are now open to use by researchers and are housed in the Center for Oral History and Cultural Heritage at the University of Southern Mississippi. Written interviews are also open for research purposes and, along with copies of other relevant primary source material, are housed in the McCain Library and Archives at the University of Southern Mississippi.

Interviews

Charlie Company Wives and Family Interviews
Benedick, Nancy; Benedick, James; Bomann, Jacque (Don Peterson's wife); Bradfield, Esther; Bradfield, Jacqueline; Conroy, Vivian; Crockett, Norma; French, Kaye; Grable, Iris (John Sclimenti's wife); Hartman, Jeannie; Harvey, Deana; Hill, Barbara (Fred Kenney's wife); Hopper, Jennifer; Huntsman, Karen; Kenney, Fred; Kenney, Susan; Layman, June; Lilley, Patty; Lind, Becky; Maibach, Mary Ann; Peterson, Jimmy; Peterson, Rich; Rademacher, Mary Ann;

Reed, Sue; Salazar, Aurora; Sauceda, Noemi; Williams, Judy (Larry Lilley's first wife); Windmiller, Esther.

Charlie Company Interviews

Charlie Company Headquarters: Crockett, Company First Sergeant Lynn; Larson, Captain Rollo; Lind, Captain Herb; Lind, Windmiller, Chaplain Bernard.

1st Platoon: Hunt, Lynn (platoon leader); Acevedo, Benjamin; Cortright, Carl; Dennison, James; Eisenbaugh, Bob; Hartman, Ernie; Hartman; Huntsman, Steve; Inada, Ron; Jarczewski, Dave; Lilley, Larry; Maibach, Gary; Nall, James; Nelson, Charlie; Reed, Bill; Renert, Martin; Sclimenti, John; Shires, Clarence; Spain, Kirby; Stancil, Wayne; Stephenson, Jim; Stephens, Jim; Thomas, Ray; Wilson, Doug; Wilson, Ralph; Young, John.

2nd Platoon: Benedick, Jack (platoon leader); Burleson, Henry; Casares, Idoluis; Cockerell, Stan; Cramer, Mike; Ehlert, Bob; French, Robert; Garcia, Theodore; Harvey, Gene; Kerr, Daniel; Lopez, Mario; McTear, Willie; O'Gara, Mike; Rademacher, James; Reynolds, Bill; Reynolds, Ronnie; Radowenchuk, Walter; Salazar, Jimmie; Searcy, Ted; Schwan, Frank; Varskafsky, Frank.

3rd Platoon: Bradfield, John; Caliari, Tony; Conroy, Tom; Fischer, Tim; Hopper, Steve; Howell, John; Johnston, Jace; Lukes, Larry; Marr, Joe; McBride, Terry; Riley, Bill; Rubio, Richard; Sauceda, Jose; Smith, James; Taylor, Elijah; Trcka, Don; Vidovic, Ron.

4th Platoon: Fadden, Paris; Gann, Ronnie; Northcott, Richard; Richards, Alan.

Personal Papers

Several Charlie Company veterans have been kind enough to share their personal papers (including letters, diaries, pictures, notebooks, and writings) with the author, a collection that forms a major source for this work. The papers (some of which are restricted by agreement with the donor) are now housed in the McCain Library and Archives at the University of Southern Mississippi.

Personal Paper Collections

Benedick; James; Conroy, Tom; Dennison, James; Fischer, Tim; Geier, Bob (a collection of his brother Bill Geier's papers); Harvey, Gene; Lind, Becky; Lind, Herb; Maibach, Mary Ann; Nelson, Charlie; Hopper, Steve; Rademacher, James; Reynolds, Bill; Sclimenti, John; Shires, Clarence; Wilson, Doug; Windmiller, Bernard; Young, John.

Other Collections

In the digital age, several important websites have become repositories for documents of all types. Of the most importance to this work was the website founded and administered by Bill Reynolds, one of the Charlie Company originals, located at http://www.9thinfantrydivision.com/default.htm. The site is dedicated to the 4th Battalion, 47th Infantry and contains a myriad of documents ranging from pictures, to personal accounts of battles, to reports from hometown newspapers. The website is a goldmine for researchers. Also of value were the websites of the 9th Infantry Division at http://9thinfdivsociety.org/, an organization for riverine veterans at http://www.rivervet.com/, and the Mobile Riverine Force association at http://www.mrfa.org/.

Primary Source Material

3rd Battalion, 47th Infantry, 2nd Brigade, 9th Infantry Division, After Action Reports, February–December 1967. RG 472, United States Army in Vietnam. National Archives and Record Center, College Park.

4th Battalion, 47th Infantry, 2nd Brigade, 9th Infantry Division, After Action Reports, February–December 1967. RG 472, United States Army in Vietnam. National Archives and Record Center, College Park.

4th Battalion, 47th Infantry, 2nd Brigade, 9th Infantry Division, Operations Orders, February–December 1967. RG 472, United States Army in Vietnam. National Archives and Record Center, College Park.

9th Infantry Division, Asst Chief of Staff G-2, Operations Planning Files, 1967. RG 472, United States Army in Vietnam, Box 1. National Archives and Record Center, College Park.

9th Infantry Division, Asst Chief of Staff S-3, Daily Journal, 1967. RG 472, United States Army in Vietnam, Box 2-6. National Archives and Record Center, College Park.

9th Infantry Division, Asst Chief of Staff S-3, Operations Report, Lessons Learned, 1966-1967. RG 472, United States Army in Vietnam, Box 1. National Archives and Record Center, College Park.

9th Infantry Division, 2nd Brigade, Asst Chief of Staff S-3, Operations Report, Lessons Learned, 1968-1969. RG 472, United States Army in Vietnam, Box 1. National Archives and Record Center, College Park.

9th Infantry Division, 2nd Brigade, Organizational History, 1966-1969, RG 472, United States Army in Vietnam, Box 1. National Archives and Record Center, College Park.

9th Infantry Division, 2nd Brigade, Asst Chief of Staff S-3, After Action Reports, 1967-1968. RG 472, United States Army in Vietnam, Box 1. National Archives and Record Center, College Park.

"Base in the Swamps," 1967, Douglas Pike Collection, Unit 02, Military Operations. The Vietnam Archive, Texas Tech University.

"Benewah Bulletin," Joy Wilkerson Collection. The Vietnam Archive, Texas Tech University.

Charlie Company, 4th Battalion, 47th Infantry, Morning Reports, 1967. Author's Collection.

Clark, Paul W. "Riverine Operations in the Delta." CHECO Report 67, US Air Force, 1968. The Vietnam Archive, Texas Tech University.

Headquarters, United States Army in Vietnam Command Historian, After Action Reports. RG 472, United States Army in Vietnam, Box 23. National Archives and Record Center, College Park.

Ninth Infantry Division. *The Old Reliable*. (Divisional newspaper). Author's Collection.

Octofoil. A quarterly magazine published by the 9th Infantry Division. January-December, 1967. Author's Collection.

Order of Battle Study 66-44, VC Tactical Use of Inland Waterways in South Vietnam, 1965-1966. The Vietnam Archive, Texas Tech University.

Professional Knowledge Gained from Amphibious Experience in South Vietnam, 1968. Arthur Price Collection. The Vietnam Archive, Texas Tech University.

Riverine Warfare – Field Manual, 1971. Glenn Helm Collection. The Vietnam Archive, Texas Tech University.

Rung Sat Special Zone Intelligence Study, 1966. The Vietnam Archive, Texas Tech University.

US Census Bureau. Household Economic Studies. "Number, Timing, and Duration of Marriages and Divorces: 2001." February, 2005.

US Naval Forces in Vietnam, Monthly Historical Summaries, February–December 1967. The Vietnam Archive, Texas Tech University.

Secondary Sources

9th Infantry Division: "Old Reliables" (Paducah, KY: Turner, 2000).

Appy, Christian, *Working-Class War: American Combat Soldiers and Vietnam* (Chapel Hill: University of North Carolina, 1993).

Atkinson, Rick, *The Long Gray Line: The American Journey of West Point's Class of 1966* (Boston: Houghton Mifflin, 1989).

Bailey, Beth, *From the Front Porch to Back Seat: Courtship in Twentieth-Century America* (Baltimore: Johns Hopkins University, 1989).

Christopher, Ralph, *Duty, Honor, Sacrifice: Brown Water Sailors and Army River Raiders* (Bloomington, IN: AuthorHouse, 2007).

Clarke, Jeffrey J., *Advice and Support: The Final Years* (Washington: Center of Military History, 1988).

Cohen, Lizabeth, *A Consumer's Republic: The Politics of Mass Consumption in Postwar America* (New York: Alfred A. Knopf, 2003).

Coontz, Stephanie, *Marriage, a History: How Love Conquered Marriage* (New York: Penguin, 2006).

Croizat, Victor, *The Brown Water Navy: The River and Coastal War in Indo-China and Vietnam, 1948-1972* (Poole, UK: Blandford, 1984).

Cutler, Thomas, *Brown Water, Black Berets: Coastal and Riverine Warfare in Vietnam* (Annapolis: Naval Institute, 1988).

Douglas, Susan J., *Where the Girls Are: Growing Up Female with the Mass Media* (New York: Three Rivers, 1995).

Dunnavent, R. Blake, *Brown Water Warfare: The U.S. Navy in Riverine Warfare and the Emergence of a Tactical Doctrine, 1775-1970* (Gainesville: University Press of Florida, 2003).

Echols, Alice, *Daring to Be Bad: Radical Feminism in America, 1967-1975* (Minneapolis: University of Minnesota, 1989).

Elliott, David, *The Vietnamese War: Revolution and Social Change in the Mekong Delta, 1930–1975* (Armonk, NY: M.E. Sharpe, 2003).

Fitzgerald, Frances, *Fire in the Lake: The Vietnamese and the Americans in Vietnam* (New York: Random House, 1972).

Forbes, John and Robert Williams. *The Illustrated History of the Vietnam War: Riverine Force* (New York: Bantam, 1987).

Fulton, Major General William, *Vietnam Studies: Riverine Operations, 1966-1969* (Washington, DC: Department of the Army, 1985).

Gargan, Edward, *The River's Tale: A Year on the Mekong* (New York: Alfred A. Knopf, 2002).

Gologorsky, Beverly, *The Things We Do To Make It Home* (New York: Random House, 1999).

Gregory, Barry, *Vietnam Coastal and Riverine Forces* (Wellingborough, UK: Patrick Stevens, 1988).

Gruhzit-Hoyt, Olga, *A Time Remembered: American Women in the Vietnam War* (Novato, CA: Presidio, 1999).

Hackworth, Colonel David. *Steel My Soldiers' Hearts.* (New York: Simon and Schuster, 2002).

Hunt, Major General Ira, *The 9th Infantry Division in Vietnam: Unparalleled and Unequaled* (Lexington: University Press of Kentucky, 2010).

Jenkins, E. H., *A History of the French Navy: From its Beginnings to the Present Day* (London: Macdonald and Jane's, 1973).

Junger, Sebastian, *Tribe: On Homecoming and Belonging* (New York: Twelve, 2016).

Karnow, Stanley, *Vietnam: A History* (New York: Viking, 1983).

Kessler-Harris, Alice, *Out to Work: The History of Wage-Earning Women in the United States* (Oxford: Oxford University, 1982).

Kinard, Douglas, *The Certain Trumpet: Maxwell Taylor and the American Experience in Vietnam* (London: Brassey's, 1991).

Koburger, Charles, *The French Navy in Indochina: Riverine and Coastal Forces, 1945-1954* (New York: Praeger, 1991).

Kolko, Gabriel, *Anatomy of a War: Vietnam, the United States, and the Modern Historical Experience* (New York: Pantheon, 1985).

Krepinevich, Andrew, Jr, *The Army in Vietnam* (Baltimore: Johns Hopkins University Press, 1986).

MacGarrigle, George, *Combat Operations. Taking the Offensive: October 1966 to October 1967* (Washington, DC: Center of Military History, 1998).

Maraniss, David, *They Marched Into Sunlight: War and Peace, Vietnam and America, October 1967* (New York: Simon & Schuster, 2003).

Marolda, Edward and Fitzgerald, Oscar, *The United States Navy and the Vietnam Conflict, Vol. 2, From Military Assistance to Combat, 1959-1965* (Washington: Naval Historical Center, 1986).

May, Elaine Tyler, *Homeward Bound: American Families in the Cold War Era* (New York: Basic, 2008).

McAbee, Ronald, *River Rats: Brown Water Navy, U.S. Naval Mobile Riverine Operations, Vietnam* (Honoribus, 2001).

Military History Institute of Vietnam, *Victory in Vietnam: The Official History of the People's Army of Vietnam, 1954–1975*, Translated by Merle L. Pribbenow (Lawrence: University Press of Kansas, 2002).

Mobile Riverine Force. America's Mobile Riverine Force in Vietnam (Paducah, KY: Turner, 2005).

Moore, Harold and Galloway, Joseph, *We Were Soldiers Once ... and Young: Ia Drang, the Battle that Changed the War in Vietnam* (New York: Random House, 1992).

Moreau, Donna, *Waiting Wives* (New York: Atria, 2005).

Moyar, Mark, *Triumph Forsaken: The Vietnam War, 1954-1965* (New York: Cambridge University, 2006).

Nguyen Thi Dieu, *The Mekong River and the Struggle for Indochina: Water, War, and Peace* (Westport, CT: Praeger, 1999).

Prados, John, *Vietnam: The History of an Unwinnable War, 1945-1975* (Lawrence: University Press of Kansas, 2009).

Race, Jeffrey, *War Comes to Long An* (Berkeley: University of California, 1972).

Schreadley, R. L., *From the Rivers to the Sea: The U.S. Navy in Vietnam* (Annapolis: Naval Institute, 1992).

Rosen, Ruth, *The World Split Open: How the Modern Women's Movement Changed America* (New York: Viking, 2000).

Sharp, Admiral U. S. G., *Strategy for Defeat: Vietnam in Retrospect* (Novato, CA: Presidio, 1978).

Sheehan, Neil, *A Bright Shining Lie: John Paul Vann and America in Vietnam* (New York: Random House, 1988).

Sorley, Lewis, *The Vietnam War: An Assessment by South Vietnam's Generals* (Lubbock: Texas Tech University, 2010).

Stanton, Shelby, *The Rise and Fall of an American Army: U.S. Ground Forces in Vietnam, 1965–1973* (Novato, CA: Presidio, 1985).

Stur, Heather, *Beyond Combat: Women and Gender in the Vietnam War Era* (Cambridge: Cambridge University, 2011).

Taylor, Sandra, *Vietnamese Women at War: Fighting for Ho Chi Minh and the Revolution* (Lawrence: University Press of Kansas, 1999).

Uhlig, Frank, ed., *Vietnam: The Naval Story* (Annapolis: Naval Institute, 1986).

Vuic, Kara Dixon, *Officer, Nurse, Woman: The Army Nurse Corps in the Vietnam War* (Baltimore: Johns Hopkins University, 2011).

Westmoreland, William, *A Soldier Reports* (New York: Doubleday, 1976).

Wiest, Andrew, *The Vietnam War, 1956–1975* (Oxford: Osprey, 2002).

Wiest, Andrew, *Vietnam's Forgotten Army: Heroism and Betrayal in the ARVN* (New York: NYU, 2008).

Wiest, Andrew, *Vietnam: A View from the Front Lines* (Oxford: Osprey, 2013).

Zaretsky, Natasha, *No Direction Home: The American Family and the Fear of National Decline, 1968-1980* (Chapel Hill: University of North Carolina, 2007).

Articles

Baker, John and Dickson, Lee C., "Army Forces in Riverine Operations." *Military Review* 47 (August 1967), 64-74.

Dagle, Dan, "The Mobile Riverine Force, Vietnam." *U.S. Naval Institute Proceedings* 95 (January 1969), 126-128.

Dominian, J., "Introduction to Marital Pathology: First Phase of Marriage." *British Medical Journal*, 15 September 1979.

House, Jonathan, "Into Indian Country." *Vietnam* (April, 1990), 39-44.

Naval History Division, "Riverine Warfare: The U.S. Navy's Operations on Inland Waters," Navy Department, 1969.

Lamb, Vanessa Martins, "The 1950s and the 1960's and the American Woman: the Transition from the 'Housewife' to the Feminist." *History*, 2011. <dumas-00680821>

Marriage and Divorce Statistics United States, 1867-1967, U.S. Department of Health, Education, and Welfare, U.S. Census Bureau, Current Population Survey, Annual Social and Economic Supplements, 1947 to 2016.

Smith, Albert C., Jr, "Rung Sat Special Zone, Vietnam's Mekong Delta." *U.S. Naval Institute Proceedings* 94 (April 1968), 116-121.

Unpublished Secondary Sources

Grau, Reagan, "Waging Brown Water Warfare: The Mobile Riverine Force in the Mekong Delta, 1966-1969." Master of Arts Thesis, Texas Tech University.

ACKNOWLEDGMENTS

At its core *Charlie Company's Journey Home* is a story about the interaction between warfare and humanity. It is a story of how young men and women were impacted by violent conflict. As an author I was blessed with the stories and trust of a wonderful group of people – the Charlie Company family. I owe them a profound debt of gratitude. They allowed me into their lives; they gifted me their stories. Special thanks, though, must go to the brave women who shared their stories with me. These women have really never told their stories before, and the whole process of interviewing, writing, and publishing was new to them. This book is theirs.

Four within the Charlie Company family, though, stand out. Bill Reynolds has long served as Charlie Company's historian, reunion planner, communicator, and advocate. Bill's tireless work on behalf of his Charlie Company brothers and sisters was fundamental to the success of my research into and writing on Charlie Company. Bill is the keeper of the Charlie Company flame, and I am forever in his debt. My connection to the families of Charlie Company and the stories of the wives started with Nancy Benedick and Jacque Bomann [Peterson]. They were in many ways the founders of this project, and they are among my greatest heroes. In a VA medical center twenty years ago I met John Young, who first introduced me to the story of Charlie Company. We became fast friends; he was my Vietnam War mentor, he was a tireless advocate of the study of the war, and he was eloquent beyond measure. John was there every step of the writing way for *Boys of '67* and for *Charlie Company's Journey Home* – prodding, helping, being. Sadly John did not live to see the publication of this book. I miss my friend.

During my time working on this project I have been the fortunate recipient of funding from the Dale Center for the Study of War & Society and the University of Southern Mississippi, without which this book would not have been possible. Through the Dale Center I received a Margaret Boone Dale Women and War Fellowship grant, and I received funding from Osprey Publishing that helped to defray the important cost of interview transcriptions, which formed a fundamental building block of this project. I am in debt to Dr Robert Thompson and John Mortimer for undertaking the transcriptions. Southern Miss also granted me a sabbatical, during which much of the writing of this project took place. For this, and many other reasons, I am grateful to the Southern Miss President, Dr Rodney Bennett; Provost, Dr Steven Moser, the Dean of the College of Arts and Letters, Dr Maureen Ryan, and the Chair of the History Department, Dr Kyle Zelner.

The Dale Center and its parent, Southern Miss History Department, form a wonderful and supportive group of colleagues who helped me shepherd this project to completion. The Dale Center counts in its number a stellar group of community supporters, whose efforts have taken the Center to great heights – efforts that make new research possible. I would like to thank Dr Beverly Dale, General (Ret.) Buford Blount, Colonel (Ret.) Wayde Benson, Dr Richard McCarthy, and Dr Craig Howard for everything they have done for us. Among my wonderful group of faculty peers, special thanks are due to Susannah Ural, Allison Abra, and Andrew Hayley for their friendship and support. Kevin Greene, who directs the Southern Miss Center for Oral History and Cultural Heritage, and who plays a mean guitar, gave me valuable professional, friendship, and musician help all through this project. I would also like to thank my brother-in-law Daniel Ortman for reading the book in its manuscript form and for offering valuable comments that bettered this project immeasurably. I also had a job-shadow student, Anna Smith of Oak Grove High School, who sat in my office during our down-time on the day that she was visiting and helped me with editing. I hope that I didn't scare her off from a potential career as a historian. My greatest thanks go to my pal and colleague Heather Stur. A formidable Vietnam War scholar in her own right, Heather read the manuscript and made many valuable comments. She also was my guide through the world of gender historiography during this important period in US history. Finally, I can't say how wonderful it is to have a fellow Vietnam War specialist just two doors away down the work hall – there were so many times I bugged her for information, wandered by to share a research victory, or just enjoyed shooting the Vietnam War historical breeze.

I would like to thank my agent, Tom Wallace, for his friendship and support, and the team assembled by Jody Hotchkiss at Hotchkiss and Associates for everything they have done for me. I have also had the great good fortune of working with Scott Reda and Liz Reph at Lou Reda Productions on several documentaries, including Brothers in War, which tells the story of Charlie Company. Its premier at National Geographic Headquarters coincided with the burial ceremony for Jack Benedick at Arlington, which was the signature moment that gave rise to this project. Finally, I have had the great good fortune of working with wonderful colleagues and friends at Osprey Publishing. Thanks to Marcus Cowper, Laura Callaghan, Margaret Haynes, and especially to Kate Moore for the faith that they have shown in me over the years and for all of their hard work in taking my writing and making it so much better.

Finally, there are colleagues and pals who have been hearing about this project and Charlie Company for years. Their encouragement, kind words, and ideas have always helped me move forward – just a few include Ben Buckle, Ruby Cook Buckle, Sean McKnight, Sue McKnight, Gary Sheffield, Andrew Richardson, John Harris, Bob Pierce, Jay Van Orsdol, Chad Daniels, Miles Doleac, Lindsay Williams, Lori Gibbs, Kevin Gibbs, Casey Greene, Kim Crimmins, Sarah Crimmins, Joey Gagliano, Brian Butler, Jeff Lee, Phyllis Lee, David R. Davies, Jennifer Brannock, David Tisdale, Joe Bishop, Jennifer Bishop, Dave Ware, Amy Ware, Robert Reams, and Aimee Reams.

Dedication

This book is dedicated to my family – to my wife Jill Wiest
and our wonderful children Abigail, Luke, and Wyatt.
Without them, nothing would be possible.

ENDNOTES

1 Alice Rossi, "Family Development in a Changing World," *The American Journal of Psychiatry*, March 1972.

2 US Bureau of the Census, Current Population Reports, Series P-60, No. 68, "Poverty in the United States: 1959–1968," US Government Printing Office, Washington, DC, 1969.

3 Marriage and Divorce Statistics United States, 1867–1967. US Department of Health, Education, and Welfare. US Census Bureau, Current Population Survey, Annual Social and Economic Supplements, 1947 to 2016.

4 While there are many studies of the importance of the earliest phase of marriage, the information in this paragraph is most informed by J. Dominian, "Introduction to Marital Pathology: First Phase of Marriage," *British Medical Journal*, September 15, 1979.

5 From Andrew Wiest, *The Boys of '67* (Oxford: Osprey, 2014), pp. 155–157

6 US Census Bureau, Household Economic Studies, "Number, Timing, and Duration of Marriages and Divorces: 2001," February 2005.

INDEX